D0523890

HAUNTED PLACES *of* SCOTLAND

SECOND EDITION

by

MARTIN
COVENTRY

GOBLINSHEAD

MUSSELBURGH

HAUNTED PLACES OF SCOTLAND
SECOND EDITION
First Edition 1999, reprinted 2000
Second Edition 2009
© Martin Coventry 1999/2009

Published by

GOBLINSHEAD

130B Inveresk Road, Musselburgh EH21 7AY, Scotland
Tel: 0131 665 2894 Email: goblinshead@sol.co.uk

All rights reserved. No part of this book may be reproduced, stored in an information retrieval system, or transmitted in any form or by any means, mechanical or electrical, photocopied or recorded, without the express permission of the publisher and author except for review (but only provided copies of the review can be used by the publisher for promotional purposes without charge) and for educational purposes (educational purposes do not include use of material from this work on any website or other electronic media without the express permission of the author and publisher and without full and proper acknowledgment).

British Library Cataloguing in Publication Data
A catalogue record for this book is available from
the British Library.

ISBN 978 1899874 42 2

Typeset by GOBLINSHEAD
Printed and bound in Scotland by Bell & Bain

Disclaimer:
The factual information contained in this *Haunted Places of Scotland 2 edn* (the "Material") is believed to be accurate at the time of printing, but no representation or warranty is given (express or implied) as to its accuracy, completeness or correctness. The author and publisher do not accept any liability whatsoever for any direct, indirect or consequential loss or damage arising in any way from any use of or reliance on this Material for any purpose. Ghost stories included are simply stories and no claims are being made regarding veracity or factual accuracy by the inclusion of a story in the text.

While every care has been taken to compile and check all the information in this book, in a work of this complexity and size it is possible that mistakes and omissions may have occurred. If you know of any corrections, alterations or improvements, please contact the author or the publishers at the address above.

CONTENTS

ACKNOWLEDGEMENTS

SECOND EDITION
Many thanks to Lindsay Miller for all her hard work in getting this book to press, and as always to Joyce Miller for all her support: emotional and practical. Particular thanks (in no particular order) to the following for permission to use photographs (© copyright remains with the site/individual) in particular order: H Watson at Renfrewshire Leisure; Charlotte Mckay at George Heriot's School; Silke Dallmann at Winnock Hotel, Drymen; Jules/Samantha at Lunan Lodge; Neil Blackburn of Fernie and Lordscairnie at Fernie Castle; James Mitchell at Scotland's Secret Bunker; Christopher Croly at Aberdeen City Council (Aberdeen Tolbooth); Gilliam Simison at East Ayrshire Council (Dean Castle); Kareen McHardy at Thunderton House; Jane Organ at Inverawe House; Jen Gordon at the Scottish Fisheries Museum; Sandra Still at Aberdeen Art Gallery; Kenneth Dunsmuir at Dumfries House; Peter Jones at the Lodge Hotel, Edinbane, Skye; Lauren Taylor at His Majesty's Theatre, Aberdeen; Jeannette Swankie at the Dreel Tavern, Anstruther; Leslye Strang at the Drover's Inn, Inverarnan; Jayne Fortescue at the Edinburgh Filmhouse; Gill Omand at the Bunchrew House Hotel; Cecile at Aberdeen Arts Centre; Louise Turner at Oran Mor, Glasgow; Culloden House; Mr Benjamin White at the Inn at Lathones; Frances Mann at Mercat Tours; Roseanne Sturgeon (Tron Theatre, Glasgow); Graham Coe (Craighouse and Glamis Castle); Doug Houghton (Ruthven Barracks); Ackergill Tower; Airth Castle; Balgonie Castle; Borthwick Castle; Busta House; Coylet Inn; Culcreuch Castle; Dalhousie Castle; Dalmahoy; Delgatie Castle; Duns Castle; Eilean Donan Castle; *Glenlee* (Tall Ship); Kylesku Hotel; Meldrum House; Neidpath Castle; New Lanark; Rammerscales; Rosslyn Chapel; Roxburghe House

FIRST EDITION
Many thanks to Joyce Miller (as ever), Hilary Horrocks at The National Trust for Scotland, Donna Laidlaw at Historic Scotland, Gordon Mason, George Montgomery, Graham Coe, Norman Adams, Duncan Jones, Caroline Boyd, Grace Ellis, Bob Schott, Hamish at Altered Images, Edinburgh, Stephen at Mitchell Graphics, Glasgow, and Charlie at Bath Press, Blantyre. And particular thanks to the following for permission to use photographs or illustrations: Joan Johnston at Delgatie; Jim MacDonald at Neidpath; Clare Simpson at the Royal Lyceum; Peter McKenzie at Dunnottar; Dalkeith House; Tibbie Shiel's Inn, St Mary's Loch and Susan Robinson at The Roxburghe Hotel (formally Sunlaws). Also to Melanie Newman at Dunvegan Castle; Meryl Duncan, Castle of Park, Cornhill; David Littlefair at Culcreuch Castle; Scott Trainer, Fasque; Jessie Fraser at Ferniehirst; Cathy Fyfe at Ravenswood Hotel, Ballater; Gordon Stewart at Mercat Tours; Shirley Young, the original St Andrews Witches Tour, Bon Accord Tours, Aberdeen for their time and help. Many thanks also go to the staff and proprietors of all the many hotels and visitor attractions (see first edition for a full list) who have helped with numerous ghost inquiries. In some cases, information had to be edited because of limited space.

PREFACE

In a book about ghosts it is important to establish the viewpoint of the author: what exactly are my beliefs about ghosts and bogles.

Like much else in life, they are muddled.

I should say at the outset, to be clear, I am not a paranormal investigator and ghost hunter or finder (or a bogle-bagger), and I am not trying to prove the existence (or non-existence) of ghosts. Nor do I wish to spend the night in a haunted room and experience eerie manifestations, real or imagined, at first hand.

What I am interested in is ghost stories themselves, in all their glorious diverse and uniquely similar manifestations, including the background to a haunted place, what reportedly happened to have caused such manifestations there, and what strange activity has been recorded down the years.

There has been a huge increase in interest surrounding the supernatural and paranormal, even since the first edition of this book ten years ago, although (to my mind) much of it is sensationalist, partly fuelled by certain television programmes, and partly by ghost tours vying with each other to be the 'scariest'.

Some claim that ghosts injure people, even perhaps resort to arson, leave scratches, drain electrical equipment and the like. It might be worth pointing out that boglekind (whatever that actually is) and humankind have been coexisting quite amicably for as long as people told tales around the fire – and the darkness beyond the light was the realm of the unknowable. As will be seen from this book, there are hundreds of haunted places just in Scotland, and just a very few mention ghosts being unpleasant. Indeed the violence done to the living by ghosts is not a drop in the ocean as to the violence done by the living to each other.

My own interest in this area stems from a very young age: my favourite story was that of the haunting of Burton Agnes Hall by the unhappy spirit of Anne Griffith, read over and over (along with the nameless horror of Berkley Square) to frighten myself and my wee sister.

The story goes that Anne was murdered by robbers, but before she died she asked that part of her – her severed head, to be specific – was to be kept at Burton Agnes, as she had loved the building. Her family, perhaps not surprisingly, had all her remains buried, but then fearful disturbances plagued the building, until eventually her coffin was opened, her head removed, and it was brought to the hall.

All was peace, but on several occasions her skull was removed, and each time the terrible disturbances also returned.

It was years later that I discovered Burton Agnes Hall was a real place, the events, which date from 1620, do appear to have happened as described, and there was even a portrait of Anne hanging on the wall. And, of course, her skull is said to have been sealed up in the great hall, so that she would finally rest in peace. This is the kind of story I liked, with internal consistency and a historical basis. 'The Canterville Ghost' and the 'Water Ghost of Harrowby Hall' were pale and factually insubstantial phantoms in comparison.

Despite the thrill of a really good ghost story, and visiting a supposedly haunted site, I do retain a scepticism about the whole area of the paranormal. Besides which, hunting bogles is a perilous pastime, mostly from the spooks lurking in the dark recesses of our own imaginations.

I have had some unusual experiences, along with my family, but these do not fall into the area of terrifying, and there may be 'rational' explanations for them all. These are some of them.

When we were children, my three sisters and I remember visiting a house in Newbattle Terrace, Edinburgh, when my parents were looking to purchase a new property. Although my wee sister can only have been six or seven at the time, we all clearly remember that this house, particularly the area around the stairs, had a strong unpleasant – even evil – feel. Apparently a murder had been committed there.

While staying by myself in a modern council house at Greater Sankey, near Warrington, there were a series of unexplained thumps on the ceiling above the lounge coming from one of the bedrooms. This was prolonged, and has no explanation.

My younger sister had a frightening dream about a man dressed in an RAF uniform around the time my grandfather died – he had been in the RAF during the war. This happened before my parents were phoned and told that my grandfather had died – he had not previously been ill.

Joyce and I, on separate occasions, saw a what we thought was a man going up to a terraced house we were renting in Helmsley – but on approaching the door we found there was nobody there. We did not tell each other about our independent sightings until we were on our way home.

A few days before my aunt died after a long illness, I had a dream about my mother coming into my bedroom and telling me that my aunt was dead. I told my parents about the dream and they went to visit my aunt, and a few days later my mother came into my bedroom to tell me my aunt was dead – just as in the dream.

While visiting the toilets at Craignethan Castle I had an urgent feeling that I should leave and was being watched. My guidebook also ended up in the pan; I am not quite sure how but it did not apparently want to stay on the top of the cistern.

I am not prone to these feelings: it was a fantastic summer day and I did not know of the supposed haunting at that time. I have also, with Joyce, visited many castles and sites in the dead and dark of winter, stood in many rooms which were supposedly haunted, just the two of us, and never given it a second thought.

I relate these simply as experiences from my life, and have no idea of their significance or validity as events of a supernatural nature – nor do I care. They are simply events that happened, which cannot easily be explained away, just like the many diverse and similar tales in this book.

And finally, after researching the second edition over the last ten years, 16-hour days for the many weeks, too little sleep but more bogles and spooks than you can shake an ouija board at, two people wanting to take legal action against us for including them in the book (perhaps more to come), endless rounds of proofs and indexes and checking, the office being a horrible mess of books, brochures, wads of paper, maps, disks, photographs, notes, pens, empty glasses, rubbish, I am anticipating spending a few days out in the open air tidying up the boisterous garden, squashing some of the myriad greenfly between my fingers, sending their little aphid souls to whatever fate awaits them.

And, thankfully, I am yet to come across anyone tormented by the restless bogles of greenfly...or by their legal experts.

INTRODUCTION

Do ghosts exist? And if they do, what exactly are they?

Many stories (and I emphasise these are stories: I make no claim as to their accuracy or truth) have been gathered together from many books, guidebooks, newspaper articles, websites and word of mouth to try to gain an understanding of the mysterious phenomena that is known as 'ghosts'. The emphasis has been on the tales which have stood the test of time, and those associated with historic sites. These are, however, only a small proportion of ghostly activity – many disturbances are now said to happen in council houses.

Despite the assertion that this is a sceptical and materialistic age, belief in the supernatural and in ghosts appears to be stronger than ever, perhaps even stoked up by many often overblown and overly embellished television programmes and spooky walking tours. There is also now a plethora of paranormal investigators of one sort or another: some trying to contact spirits, others trying to prove that there are rational explanations for 'unexplained' activity.

It is not clear what those trying to prove the existence of paranormal phenomena would do if they finally got unequivocal proof of the existence of ghosts. The idea of spending an eternity in heaven or hell does not seem all that appealing to a mortal creature such as myself, but the proposal that eternity might be spent earthbound, flicking light switches and clumping about making disembodied footsteps surely has even less attraction.

Many custodians, owners and managers have been delighted to help in providing information, while a few endorse or confirm the ghost stories, perhaps believing a bogle or two can attract visitors and guests. Others, however, are extremely hostile to the whole idea – which is interesting in itself. So far, the two editions of this book have drawn more interest and stirred up more protest – in the form of brusque letters, abrupt phone calls and two threats of legal action – than anything else published by Goblinshead.

Many of the reported ghosts are believed to be those of real people, many of whom died in horrific or tragic circumstances. Yet there is a general mixing up of witchcraft and hauntings (and even fairies, angels and UFOs) into a general brew of the 'supernatural'. Most ghost stories make no reference to sorcery, black witchcraft, or the diabolic arts, and usually the people described are just ordinary folk. While ghosts of the dead may be frightening – and challenge beliefs regarding life and death – it is the living who are far more dangerous. In all the stories collected over the years only a few mention any physical harm to the living, and that in a very minor, usually mischievous, way.

Hauntings themselves are not of one type, and there are several different areas of activity, although no attempt is made at a clear distinction here – apparitions are often accompanied by poltergeist activity, while poltergeists can occasionally be accompanied by apparitions; some harbingers of doom are also ghosts in the true sense, while others appear to be 'real' creatures..

Although these are mostly reported, particularly 'Green Ladies' in Scotland, they are rarely witnessed. Far more common are the sounds of feet or the rustle of clothing, unexplained raps and bangs, the opening and closing of doors, and interference with electrical equipment. All this activity is often associated with a violent event, such as a murder, killing or suicide, and if apparitions are experienced it tends to be in the same place or repeating the same – often mundane – task, such as walking from one area to another and then vanishing. Other causes seem to be when the person has some unfinished business, such as searching for a baby or loved one, repaying a loan, or making sure a hotel is kept in good order. Manifestations are also reported to increase during renovations or building work.

Apparitions – Black Men

Many reported apparitions, or disturbances, are associated with folk simply too wicked to rest or who have dabbled in witchcraft or had dealings with the Devil. Many of these stories originate in the Covenanting times of the late 17th century, although they share details with older tales. These dark characters include Alexander Stewart, the Wolf of Badenoch; Alexander Lindsay, Earl Beardie, the Earl of Crawford; Cardinal David Beaton, Archbishop of St Andrews, a very worldly fellow, but who is said to haunt more places than any other man in Scotland; Tam Dalziel of The Binns, who reputedly played cards with the Devil; John Graham of Claverhouse, known as Bloody Clavers, who was said to be a warlock and could only be killed by silver weapons; Sir Robert Grierson of Lagg, who could allegedly turn wine to blood and whose spit burned holes; the lairds of Pringle and Buckholm, Skene and Kinnaird; the 'Bloody' Bruce of Earlshall. Many of these 'wicked' fellows were summoned off to hell by the means of a black coach and horses, one of the damned (William Douglas, Duke of Queensberry) even finding his way, propelled by a phantom carriage, to the fiery pits through the erupting volcano of Mount Etna.

And there is also Sir George Mackenzie of Rosehaugh, known as both 'Bloody Mackenzie' and as the 'Mackenzie Poltergeist', whose vengeful bogle is said to have caused all sorts of mayhem in and around Greyfriars Kirkyard in Edinburgh and elsewhere. Mackenzie does not need anyone to defend him, yet there seems to be no appreciation of the vilification made of what were (for the time) perfectly decent and honourable men, attacked by their sworn enemies; these claims are repeated parrot-like without taking the trouble to appreciate that there are two sides to every story. While there were undoubtedly excesses by both sides, the Covenanters and the Cameronians could be seen as religious fanatics and zealots. It might well be the case that, given the rational and secular times we now live in, Mackenzie and the rest would be regarded as the moderate and reasonable faction, and the Covenanters (who so effectively demonised him and many of his contemporaries) as the blood-thirsty revolutionary terrorists, who would not respect government authority or the law because of their extreme religious beliefs.

Perhaps there are a few parallels in the 21st century...

Apparitions – Ladies

At least 84 sites in Scotland are said to have 'Green Ladies', the most numerous single type of ghost. Stories are often unclear as to what is meant by a Green Lady: whether it is just an apparition seen wearing a green dress, whether the phantom is bathed in an eerie green light, or whether the ghost is a traditional type of phantom that presents itself in a series of manifestations, most usually footsteps, movement of objects, cold spots, doors opening and closing, electrical equipment being interfered with, and the rest, but also either as a fully formed apparition or a fuzzy area of indistinct vapour (or, some have claimed, orbs).

Green Ladies are associated traditionally with a high-status site or a significant building, such as a castle or a mansion, or even a large hotel. There are no stories of Green Ladies being found primarily in open areas, even although at times they have been known to wander some distance from their home. The presence of the ghost is not connected directly to the family that owns the property, and the ghost will continue to manifest, even when the place has changed hands more than once. In these cases the apparition could originally have been a gruagach (see below), although only some of the traditional aspects have survived the centuries. It also seems quite likely that the 'genesis' story regarding the ghost is often newer than the bogle itself, as the idea of ghosts being the specific spirit of a dead person from Lowland areas pushed out the idea of a guardian spirit.

Many ghosts, indeed, should be thought of as a guardian, concerned with the welfare of the household under their care. Some echo of this lives on in stories where a place has the ghost of a housekeeper or nanny – or a previous owner who so loved a building that they did not want to leave it even after their own death.

White Ladies are not quite so numerous, with some 60 sites said to have this kind of phantom. Although often also associated with castles and mansions, White Ladies are also primarily connected with places in the open air, such as bridges, rivers and even wells. This may be part of a traditional belief system: that these places had supernatural guardians or spirits, and the story of a murder or untimely death may be a later overlay of traditional ghost belief.

There are some 52 places purported to have Grey Ladies, and other colourful ghosts include Pink Ladies, Blue Ladies and Brown Ladies, along with Black Ladies, although this latter description can be from the colour of the skin of the apparition as well as from the colour of the dress.

No other ghost is said to haunt more places in Scotland than Mary, Queen of Scots, and probably in England too. Her ghost is reputed to have been seen in ten or more sites around Scotland, and nearly as many in England (although many of the sightings seem problematic – apparitions of females are mostly reported, and it is not clear how they could identify a ghost with such certainty, especially if the bogle is apparently headless). In one instance Mary has became confused with the equally tragic Lady Jane Grey, although they have little in common except they both lost their heads.

Why Mary would wish to return to places such as Hermitage, Craignethan or Dalkeith – which played such a small part in her life – is not certain.

Crisis Apparitions

The belief is that when a person is facing a great crisis, such as the fear of impending death, their disembodied phantom can be spotted by loved ones or friends, sometimes thousands of miles away. The apparition, however, is not how the person appears at the time – which is probably just as well, if they are suffering a violent death – but a vision of how the person has appeared sometime in the past. Perhaps it is a reflection of how the person saw themselves.

Poltergeist Activity

This involves the movement of objects, often violently, as well as noises, cries, footsteps and the rest without an apparent apparition. This activity is often associated with teenage girls and boys, or old people nearing death, and may have a telepathic rather than ghostly cause. These are sometimes reported after a violent event, sometimes the activity is centred around one individual. Often the haunting stops suddenly, or when the individual leaves the place. Poltergeists have – if anything – become more restrained compared to their ancient counterparts.

Violent poltergeists are relatively rare in ghost stories, except for three stories from the south-west around the turn of the 18th century (Glenluce, Galdenoch and Ring Croft of Stocking), but this all seems to have changed in recent years, along with growth in ghost tours. Some of the claims made about activity in the Covenanter's Prison in Greyfriars Kirkyard are far-fetched to the sceptical mind, as are those made about the tours of the vaults beneath the streets of Edinburgh. No doubt some visitors will be disappointed if they do not get pushed about a bit by invisible hands, receive scratches or get something thrown at them.

Premonition Spirits or Activity

A spectre or corporeal creature exhibits a specific behaviour as a portent of coming disaster or – less often – good fortune. These are quite numerous in Scotland, and a wide range of phenomena and creatures are involved, from robins, red-breasted swans and white deer and even branches of trees falling off to the toll of wraith bells, ghostly drummers, 'Green Ladies' and headless horsemen.

These are not always accurate: the laird of Cameron House was predicted to die when Loch Lomond froze over. While there may be excellent reasons why someone might perish in a year of extreme cold, it has been shown that the freezing over of the Loch had nothing to do with the life expectancy of the laird.

People also fit the facts to suit the witnessing of the phenomena. In the case of the Cortachy drummer, on one occasion he was supposedly heard six months before one of the extended Ogilvie family died – this seems just a little far in advance to be called an accurate prediction in an extended family.

Brownies, Gruagach, Glaistig and Other Guardian Ghosts

There are numerous tales of brownies (more than 20 in this book), household spirits who would carry out repetitive tasks, such as threshing corn, cleaning, clearing stones from roads. Some would need to be rewarded with presents, such as milk, cream, food or other drink, but others preferred to be left alone. If angered, which was usually quite easy to do, the brownie would leave, taking their benison or good luck with them, and calamity would strike the house. These creatures seem to have inhabited a world between the corporeal and the supernatural, and to have much in common with fairies. Descriptions of them vary between small and hairy to golden-haired and green clad (although this latter description is probably more properly a gruagach, which have been confused in a non-Gaelic interpretation of these spirits).

Gruagach, usually described as 'Green Ladies', often the spirits of former mistresses who had died in childbirth or had been enchanted, were said to share in the fortunes of their house, although not necessarily the occupants – they were bound to the site. When they would weep, there was ill news to follow; when they were happy, good tidings were to come. They also reputedly looked after young children and babies, were able to pass on handicraft skills, and could even befuddle enemy forces attacking their castle.

Glaistig, sometimes described as an amphibious sprite, was another supernatural being akin to the brownie, who would tend cattle and the like. They were often rewarded with offerings of milk.

What Are Ghosts?

Many suggestions have been put forward as to the cause of hauntings, but none are especially satisfactory or fit in with details often found in stories.

In a Christian cosmology, apparitions could be explained in terms of the immortal soul, that a part of the person survives after death. This part, the soul, could be 'trapped' on earth, unable to travel on to whatever lies beyond, as a punishment, or desiring to complete business on earth. Stories often relate that manifestations cease when the mortal remains are buried in consecrated ground or when the task is completed, such as the repaying of a loan or a grave being moved because it is waterlogged.

One explanation for crisis apparitions is that they are experienced through telepathy between the person suffering the crisis and the 'viewer', that an enormous amount of stress seems to open a telepathic 'door'.

Another suggests that a psychic record, a 'stone tape', is imprinted on a building or location when a violent act is committed – that the apparition is simply like a video recording of the event and is not the result of a 'sentient' spirit. Corpses exude nucleic acids which remain in the atmosphere. Those sufficiently sensitive to this telepathic message can then pick it up and 'view' it.

Ghosts are also said to exist in a spirit world where the temperature is 3 Kelvin, which is as cold as outer space. This is thought to explain why rooms become cold when ghostly activity is present or imminent, and ghosts are said to have failed to achieve sufficient energy to cross to the other world.

Some believe that ghosts 'fade' over time, that colour slowly drains away – a 'Green Lady' gradually becomes 'White'. Eventually the apparition itself becomes less strong and defined, often described as being like a mist, and finally all that is left is a 'presence', a feeling in an area or that someone is pushing past.

All these theories have deficiencies.

If ghosts are the souls of dead people, but only humans have souls, what are the manifestations of animals or objects? Some ghosts just have no unpleasant reason to haunt an area, and appear to have been happy in life. Indeed ghosts are sometimes believed to 'hang about' because they particularly liked a place. Ghostly activity has also been reported to increase when remains are given a Christian burial.

Activity may not be connected to the committing of a violent crime – indeed apparitions wander about doing the mundane, even when carrying their head under their arm. Ghosts seem interested in modern machinery and activities, suggesting a more 'sentient' spirit, and spend much of their time interfering with electrical apparatus.

Parts of the ghost can be missing, such as their head, hands and whole torso. It must be assumed that the person was dead before being dismembered, and it seems unlikely that the apparition could include information conducted by telepathy when the person was already dead. Whole groups of people are also reported to witness paranormal disturbances at the same time, so other factors must also come into play apart from the sensitivity of a particular individual.

It should be emphasised that the stories in this book are most likely no more than that. Virtually all female ghosts are beautiful – which may be a comfort to ugly folk in that only good-looking people come back as ghosts – but it is more probable that the extra attractiveness of the apparition is a later artistic embellishment. There is also little evidence that ghosts float or glide about, but it sounds more eerie than simply walking.

Paranormal investigations undertaken from Victorian times (and even before) can be especially untrustworthy, and reports have been deliberately misleading: it tends to be believers or those with a preexisting agenda who did (and are doing) the investigations. The Meggernie ghost story, when two friends shared adjoining rooms and were kissed by the resident phantom, sounds fabricated and doubts were raised at the time. Other investigations at Ballechin and Penkaet seem similarly exaggerated. It should be remembered that there was a huge growth of interest in spiritualism from late Victorian times, but virtually all spiritualists were later shown to be frauds, barring one who was not tested.

There are now many groups who undertake paranormal investigations, using a variety of methods, from state-of-the-art electronic equipment to mediums and ouija boards. The reports of many investigations can be found on websites (see the main text and additional information), and many of these investigations make interesting reading, if nothing else. Use has not, however, been made of the results of these investigations in the text of this book.

The lengths some will go to fool or trick others can not be underestimated. The widespread introduction of digital cameras seem to have ushered in a new era of ghost pictures, not seen since photography was in its infancy. Again many of these are intriguing and disconcerting (try googling Blairadam forest ghost photo).

It should also not be dismissed, however, how easy it is for the viewer, particularly the believer, to fool themselves or to ignore inconsistencies or trickery. The falling in temperature during ghostly activity can be due to the adrenaline response, provoked by fear, rather than by bogles. In many instances, however, the witness is unaware – until later – that anything unusual has happened: often apparitions are thought to be real people.

Noises sound much louder at night than during the day – a dripping tap can go ignored during the day but can drive the sleeper demented at night. During sleep paralysis – a period of limbo between sleep and being awake when a person can believe they are awake, but are unable to move – may also be responsible for many stories, such as waking up being strangled or feeling a large weight loaded on their chest or seeing a phantom on the end of the bed. The waker can have auditory and visual hallucinations, such as voices and apparent phantoms, as they believe they are awake. It is also quite usual for people to create faces or the appearance of figures, especially half-seen, from background clutter, such as foliage and shrubs, shadows on windows, and even wallpaper or stone walls.

It is also a myth that all ghostly activity is reported during the night. Incidents are as likely to happen on a beautiful sunny afternoon as in the dead of the night.

Having said all this, there does seem a good case for belief in the phenomena of 'ghosts' – there are simply too many stories reported by sensible people for the whole body of evidence to be dismissed as superstition, fabrication or just plain foolishness. What exactly the explanation for what this activity might be ranges from a series of natural events that the human brain interprets as supernatural activity to the disembodied spirits of wronged or confused or desperate people, doomed to wander the Earth (and to be chased about by paranormal investigators) in perpetuity.

On the pages that follow are more than 720 places with around 1,000 of these ghost stories, some detailed, some fragmentary, some derivative, some unique, some famous, some less well known.

Readers will have to make up their own minds.

LIST OF ILLUSTRATIONS

*© Martin Coventry or from collection of the author.
◊ © see acknowledgements.

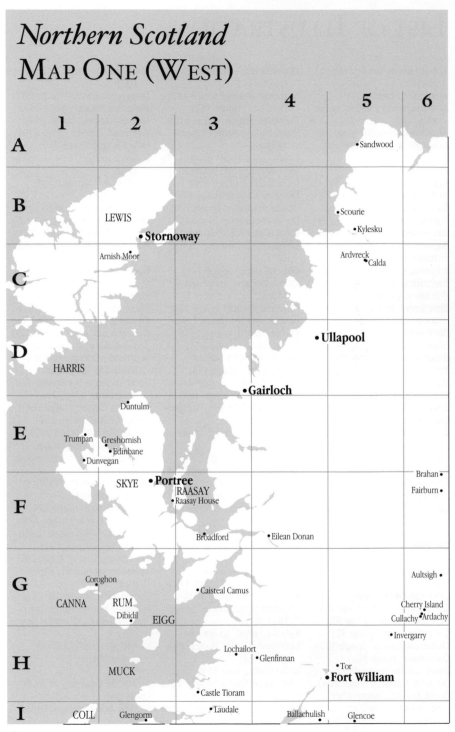

Northern Scotland
MAP ONE (WEST)

4   **5**   **6**

1   **2**   **3**

A   • Sandwood

B
LEWIS
• Scourie
• Kylesku
• **Stornoway**

Arnish Moor
Ardvreck
• Calda

C

D
HARRIS
• **Ullapool**

• **Gairloch**

Duntulm

E
Trumpan   Greshornish
• Edinbane
• Dunvegan

Brahan •
Fairburn •

F
SKYE   • **Portree**
RAASAY
• Raasay House

Broadford   • Eilean Donan

G
Coroghon
• Caisteal Camus

CANNA   RUM
Dibidil
EIGG

Aultsigh •

Cherry Island
Cullachy • Ardachy

• Invergarry

H
MUCK
Lochailort
• Glenfinnan
• Tor
• **Fort William**

• Castle Tioram

I
COLL   Glengorm
• Laudale
Ballachulish •
Glencoe

MAP TWO (EAST)

11   **12**

7   **8**   **9**   **10**

Muness

Brims   Castle of Mey   Windhouse   **A**
•Bighouse   •**Thurso**

Ackergill•   Busta   **B**
•**Wick**   Lerwick

SHETLAND   **C**
Noltland

•Lairg   •Dunrobin   Skaill   **D**
Clumly
Carbisdale   Skibo•   •**Kirkwall**
•   •**Dornoch**   **Stromness**
•Ardgay Tain
Balnagown   ORKNEY

Balconie   Spynie   •Cullen   **Fraserburgh**
Castle   •Thunderton House   Duff House•   Gardenstown Kinnaird Head   **E**
Leod•Tulloch   •**Cromarty**   Kinloss   •   •Inchdrewer   Rathen
•Strathpeffer   •Brodie   **Elgin**   •Castle of Park
Fort George   •Rait   Delgatie   Fedderate
Avoch   •Cawdor   Deer •   •Aden
Ord•Red Castle•Castle Stuart•Achindown   Dunphail
Bunchrew   •Culloden   •Rothiemay
Inverness •Clava Cairns   Wester Elchies   **Huntly** •Frendraught   Slains   **F**
•Castle Spioradain   •Balvenie   Fyvie•   •Methlick
Aldourie   •Ballindalloch   Gight   Haddo
•Castle Grant •Glenlivet   •Leith Hall   Meldrum• •Tolquhon
•Auchnarrow   Pittodrie• •Pitcape   Menie
•Dulnain Bridge   **Inverurie**• •Thainstone

•Breda •Kemnay   **G**
Boat of Garten   Skellater •Colquhonnie   Monymusk •Castle Fraser   Aberdeen
Craigard   •Corgarff   •Craigievar •Skene
•Doune of Rothiemurchus   Gairnshiel •Candacraig   Kingcausie
Kingussie •Balavil   Knock **Ballater**•   •Coull   Loch of Leys •Ardoe
•Ruthven   Braemar Castle   •Tomnaverie   •Maryculter
Inverey   Abergeldie   **Banchory** Crathes• Durris
Morrone   •Kindrochit   •Birkhall   Muchalls•
Braemar   Fetteresso• •**Stonehaven**
•Dunnottar   **H**
•Drumtochty
•Fasque

Killiecrankie   •Hallgreen   **I**
Cortachy   Careston   •Benholm
Vayne•   House of Dun
Pitlochry• •Ashintully   Inverquharity• Finavon• Melgund   •**Montrose**
•Kinnaird

XV

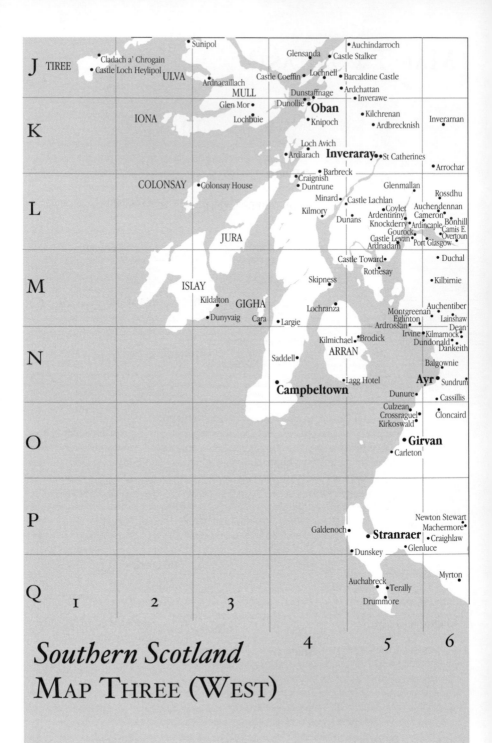

Southern Scotland
MAP THREE (WEST)

xvi

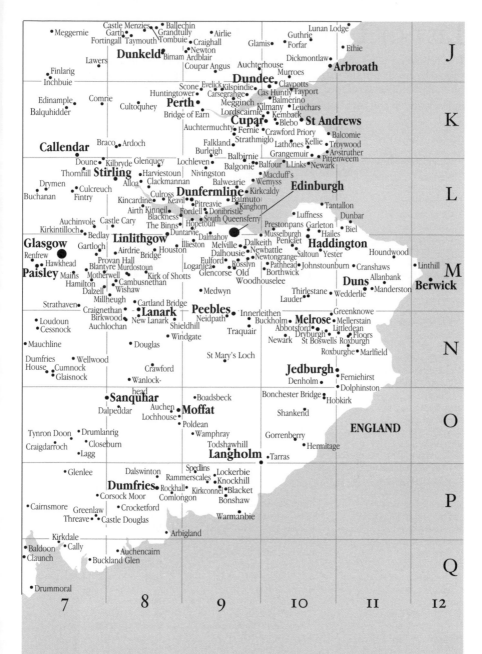

MAP FOUR (EAST)

LIST OF HAUNTED PLACES

The following is an alphabetical list of all the places listed in the main text and should be used with the maps on the previous pages. The map number and reference (in square brackets) refer to the places on the maps. Indented entries are sites covered individually in the text but with the same place on the maps.

Caisteal Camus [Map 1, 3G]
Calda House [Map 1, 5C]
Callander [Map 4, 7K]
    Bridgend House Hotel
    Dreadnought Hotel
    Old Rectory Guest House
Cally House [Map 4, 7Q]
Cambusnethan [Map 4, 8M]
    Castlehill
Cameron House [Map 3, 6L]
Camis Eskan (Camis E.) [Map 3, 6L]
    Camis Eskan
Campbcltown [Map 3, 4N]
    Glen Scotia
Candacraig [Map 2, 9G]
Cara House [Map 3, 3M]
Carbisdale Castle [Map 2, 7D]
Careston Castle [Map 2, 10I]
Carleton Castle [Map 3, 5O]
Carsegrange [Map 4, 9K]
Cartland Bridge Hotel [Map 4, 8M]
Cassillis House [Map 3, 6N]
Castle Cary [Map 4, 8L]
Castle Coeffin [Map 3, 4J]
Castle Douglas [Map 4, 7P]
    Cuckoo Bridge
Castle Fraser [Map 2, 11G]
Castle Grant [Map 2, 8F]
Castle Huntly [Map 4, 9K]
Castle Lachlan [Map 3, 4L]
Castle Leod [Map 2, 7E]
Castle Levan [Map 3, 5L]
Castle Loch Heylipol [Map 3, 1J]
Castle Menzies [Map 4, 8J]
Castle Spioradain [Map 2, 7F]
Castle Stalker [Map 3, 4J]
Castle Stuart [Map 2, 7E]
Castle Tioram [Map 1,3H]
Castle Toward [Map 3, 5M]
Castle of Mey [Map 2, 9A]
Castle of Park [Map 2, 10E]
Cawdor Castle [Map 2, 8E]
Cessnock Castle [Map 4, 7N]
Cherry Island [Map 1, 6G]
Clackmannan Tower [Map 4, 8L]
Cladach a' Chrogain, Tiree [Map 3, 1J]
Claunch [Map 4, 7Q]
Clava Cairns [Map 2, 7F]
Claypotts Castle [Map 4, 10K]
Cloncaird Castle [Map 3, 6O]
Closeburn Castle [Map 4, 7O]
Clumly Farm [Map 2, 9D]
Colonsay House [Map 3, 3L]
Colquhonnie Castle [Map 2, 9G]
Comlongon Castle [Map 4, 8P]
Comrie [Map 4, 7K]
    Royal Hotel
Corgarff Castle [Map 2, 9G]

Cornaig Bay, Vatersay
Coroghon Castle, Canna [Map 1, 1G]
Corsock Moor [Map 4, 7P]
Cortachy Castle [Map 2, 9I]
Coull Castle [Map 2, 10G]
Coupar Angus [Map 4, 9J]
    Royal Hotel
Coylet Inn [Map 3, 5L]
Craigard House Hotel [Map 2, 8G]
Craigdarroch House [Map 4, 7O]
Craighall [Map 4, 9J]
Craighlaw Castle [Map 3, 6P]
Craigievar Castle [Map 2, 10G]
Craignethan Castle [Map 4, 8M]
Craignish Castle [Map 3, 4L]
Cranshaws Castle [Map 4, 11M]
Crathes Castle [Map 2, 11G]
Crawford [Map 4, 8N]
    Old Post Horn Inn
Crawford Priory [Map 4, 10K]
Crocketford [Map 4, 8P]
    Galloway Arms Hotel
Cromarty Castle [Map 2, 7E]
Crossraguel Abbey [Map 3, 5O]
Culcreuch Castle [Map 4, 7L]
Cullachy House [Map 1, 6G]
Cullen House [Map 2, 10E]
Culloden [Map 2, 7F]
    Culloden House
    Culloden Moor
Culross [Map 4, 8L]
    Culross Abbey
    Culross Palace
Cultoquhey [Map 4, 8K]
Culzean Castle [Map 3, 5O]
Cumnock [Map 4, 7N]
    Craighead Inn
Cupar [Map 4, 10K]
    Royal Hotel
Dalhousie Castle [Map 4, 9M]
Dalkeith [Map 4, 9M]
    Bridgend
    Dalkeith House
    Melville Grange
Dalmahoy [Map 4, 9L]
Dalpeddar [Map 4, 8O]
Dalswinton Castle [Map 4, 8P]
Dalzell House [Map 4, 7M]
Dankeith House [Map 3, 6N]
Dean Castle [Map 3, 6N]
Deer Abbey [Map 2, 11E]
Delgatie Castle [Map 2, 11E]
Denholm [Map 4, 10N]
    Cross Keys Inn
Dibidil Bothy, Rum [Map 1, 2G]
Dickmontlaw Farm [Map 4, 10J]
Dolphinston Tower [Map 4, 11N]
Donibristle Castle [Map 4, 9L]

Dornoch [Map 2, 7D]
    Dornoch Castle Hotel
    Witch's Stone
Douglas Castle [Map 4, 8N]
Doune [Map 4, 7L]
    Doune Castle
    Doune Highland Hotel
Doune of Rothiemurchus [Map 2, 8G]
Drumlanrig Castle [Map 4, 7O]
Drummoral [Map 4, 7Q]
Drummore Castle [Map 3, 5Q]
Drumtochty Castle [Map 2, 11H]
Dryburgh [Map 4, 10N]
    Dryburgh Abbey
    Dryburgh Abbey Hotel
Drymen [Map 4, 7L]
    Winnock Hotel
Duchal Castle [Map 3, 6M]
Duff House [Map 2, 11E]
Dulnain Bridge [Map 2, 8F]
    Tigh na Sgiath Country House
    Hotel
Dumfries [Map 4, 8P]
    County Hotel
    Dumfries Priory
    Globe Inn
    Greyfriars
    King's Arms Hotel
Dumfries House [Map 4, 7N]
Dunans Castle [Map 3, 5L]
Dunbar Castle [Map 4, 11L]
Dundee [Map 4, 10K]
    Bell Street Car Park
    Coffin Works
    Discovery Point
    H M Frigate Unicorn
    Logie House
    Mains Castle
    Starz & Deacon Brodie's Bars
    Tay Bridge
    Wellgate Centre
Dundonald [Map 3, 6N]
    Dundonald Castle
    Old Castle Inn
Dunfermline [Map 4, 9L]
    Abbot House
    Alhambra Theatre
    Creepy Wee Pub
    Dunfermline Palace
Dunkeld [Map 4, 8J]
    Atholl Arms Hotel
Dunnottar Castle [Map 2, 11H]
Dunollie Castle [Map 3, 4K]
Dunphail Castle [Map 2, 8E]
Dunrobin Castle [Map 2, 8D]
Duns Castle [Map 4, 11M]
Dunskey Castle [Map 3, 5P]
Dunstaffnage Castle [Map 3, 4J]

> **Many of the places listed are private homes or businesses and the privacy of the owners should always be respected.**

How to Use the Book

The main part of this book is arranged alphabetically. Entries consist of the name of the site and whether there is a photo (to the right) along with the page on which the photo appears. What follows is a brief description and history of the place, along with any ghost stories. Additional information provided is the location along with map number and reference (for use with the maps on pages xiv-xvii), whether the site is open, and contact details for the place.

Please note that these details should only be used for general enquiries: please do not burden staff with requests for more details about any paranormal activity. The stories in this book are not always confirmed by the places mentioned. Many managers and owners are happy to discuss hauntings, while others are not and some may even be hostile and threaten legal action. Many places are private homes or businesses and the privacy of the owners should always be respected.

Opening and access information is believed to be correct at time of going to press, but it is for basic guidance only and should be checked if any visit is planned as details do change and mistakes are made.

Maps on pages xiv-xvii locate all the sites mentioned with the map divided into a grid with references of the form letter then number (eg M9 or H2).

A list of all the places located on the map follows from page xviii: many places, such as Edinburgh, Glasgow and Aberdeen, have multiple sites. This includes the map number and map reference using the grids of the maps.

Some further reading appears on page 300, a list of some ghost tours appears on page 302, and a selection of paranormal investigators and information is on page 304.

There are indexes by ghost type (page 308) and by site type (page 314), while the main index follows on page 319. Please note that this lists places with ghost stories and associated material, but only such individuals, places and events that are mentioned in the text in direct relation to the ghost stories.

Many sites are in the care of the following organisations:

The National Trust for Scotland
Wemyss House, 28 Charlotte Square, Edinburgh EH2 4ET
Tel: 0131 243 9300 Web: www.nts.org.uk

Historic Scotland
Longmore House, Salisbury Place, Edinburgh EH9 1SH
Tel: 0131 668 8800 Web: www.historic-scotland.gov.uk

Abbot House, Dunfermline (page 1)

Abbotsford (page 1)

Aberdeen Arts Centre (page 2)

Aberdeen Tolbooth (page 2)

Ackergill Tower (page 3)

ABBEY INN, KINLOSS

The Abbey Inn, parts of which date from the 16th century, was established as a public house in the 1950s, and before that had been used as cottages as well as a bakery. It is now a welcoming hostelry with open fires in the winter. The name comes from Kinloss Abbey, which was founded by David I in 1150, the scant ruins of which are located nearby in an old burial ground.

The inn is said to be haunted. Manifestations are said to include the sighting of indistinct apparitions and unexplained intense chills.

Map 2, 8E (Kinloss). On B9011, 2.5 miles NE of Forres, Findhorn Road, Kinloss, Moray. Inn. (01309 690475)

A paranormal investigation was undertaken in February 2006 by Ghost Finders (www.ghostfinders.co.uk/abbey_inn.html)

ABBOT HOUSE, DUNFERMLINE   ILLUS PAGE XXIV

Standing in an attractive location near the ancient abbey, Abbot House is a fine pink-washed town house, dating from the 16th-century (or earlier) and used by the commendators of Dunfermline Abbey. The property of the Abbey was acquired by Robert Pitcairn after the Reformation, but soon went to Alexander Seton, first Earl of Dunfermline (see Fyvie Castle), and then to others. The house is now a heritage centre, and has displays about the building and the town, including on Robert the Bruce, whose body (apart from his heart) is buried in the nearby church.

Abbot House is said to be haunted by the ghost of a monk, footsteps and the rustle of a robe reputedly having been heard on the main staircase. Other spooky manifestations are reportedly sudden drops in temperature on the landing, and folk feeling as if they are being pushed from behind.

Map 4, 9L (Dunfermline). Off A994, just N of Dunfermline Abbey, Maygate, Dunfermline, Fife. **Open all year, daily (except 25/26 Dec and 1 Jan). (01383 733266 / www.abbothouse.co.uk)**

ABBOTSFORD   ILLUS PAGE XXIV

Nestling in fine grounds by the River Tweed, Abbotsford is an attractive baronial mansion with turrets, battlements and corbiestepped gables. The house dates from the first quarter of the 19th century, and was built by, and was home to, Sir Walter Scott. Scott wrote *Ivanhoe*, the *Lay of the Last Minstrel* and many other popular novels, and he was also a distinguished historian and collector of artefacts: there is an impressive collection of armour and weapons at the house, including Rob Roy MacGregor's gun and the Marquis of Montrose's sword.

Sir Walter's ghost is said to haunt the dining room, where he died in 1832 after exhausting himself trying to pay off huge debts, and sightings of his apparition have been reported in recent times.

Another ghost, said to have been witnessed here, is the spirit of George Bullock, who died in 1818 and was in charge of the rebuilding of Abbotsford. The sounds of furniture being dragged across the floor have reportedly been heard.

Map 4, 10N (Abbotsford). On B6360, 2 miles W of Melrose, Abbotsford, Borders. **Open mid Mar-Oct, daily; other dates (Mon-Fri) by appt for parties of more than 10. (01896 752043 / www.scottsabbotsford.co.uk)**

ABERDEEN ARTS CENTRE   ILLUS PAGE XXIV

The arts centre is a venue for theatre, exhibitions and meetings, along with a cafe bar, and is housed in the former North Church, a fine neo-Greek style building, dating from 1829, with a portico of columns and a tall distinctive tower.

The building is said to be haunted by the ghost of a maid, reported to be witnessed on the upper floor and in corridors.

There are also stories of a disembodied face having been witnessed in the Green Room. The centre has been the subject of at least one paranormal investigation.

Map 2, 12G (Aberdeen). On A9013, 33 King Street, Aberdeen.
Arts centre (theatre, gallery, cafe/bar & meeting rooms). (01224 635208 / www.digifresh.co.uk)

ABERDEEN CENTRAL LIBRARY

The central library, located in an attractive and a romantic building dating from the end of the 19th century, is said to be haunted.

Manifestations reputedly include unexplained footsteps from unoccupied areas, disembodied whispering, and the sound of a bell tolling.

Map 2, 12G (Aberdeen). Off B983, Rosemount Viaduct, Aberdeen.
Library. (01224 652500 / www.aberdeencity.gov.uk/libraries/)

A paranormal investigation was undertaken in June 2008 by East of Scotland Paranormal (esparanormal.org.uk/reports/centrallibre.html) and in March 2008 (esparanormal.org.uk/reports/Library28052008.html)

ABERDEEN TOLBOOTH   ILLUS PAGE XXIV

The tolbooth, which is one of the best preserved of Scotland's jails, is home to Aberdeen's museum of civic history. The building dates from 1616 and has a large squat battlemented tower at its core, much of which is hidden by later additions, crowned by a spire.

The museum charts the history of local government and crime and punishment, and the old cells can be visited (Quakers were held here, as were Jacobite prisoners in 1746).

An apparition, which has been reported more than once, is said to be the spectre of a man wearing a trilby hat and dressed as if from the 1920s. The ghost is reputed to be that of a very short fellow, perhaps only four-foot tall, although the height of the floor has been raised since the 1920s, so it is possible that the lower part of the bogle is hidden.

Other manifestations which have been reported are unexplained footsteps, as well as the rattling of a chain.

Map 2, 12G (Aberdeen). Off A956, Castle Street (continuation of Union Street), Aberdeen.
Open Apr-Sep, daily. (01224 621167 / www.aagm.co.uk)

A paranormal investigation was undertaken in February 2006 by Paranormal Investigation Scotland (www.paranormalinvestigationscotland.co.uk) and by in August 2008 by East of Scotland Paranormal (esparanormal.org.uk/reports/tolboothjoint.html)

ABERGELDIE CASTLE

Abergeldie Castle, a simple rectangular tower house, has been a property of the Gordons from 1482. During a feud with the Forbes family, the seven sons of Alexander Gordon of Knock (see Knock Castle) were murdered by Alexander Forbes of Strathgirnock. They had been cutting peats on disputed land, and their severed heads were spiked on their spades. Forbes was tracked down and executed by Alexander Gordon of Abergeldie. The castle was burnt in 1592, and saw action in the Jacobite Rising of 1689-90. The castle was leased to Queen Victoria from 1848, but is again occupied by the Gordons.

The castle is reputedly haunted by the bogle of Catherine Frankie, also known as 'Kittie Frankie', a French servant. The story is that the unfortunate Kittie was asked by the wife of the laird why her husband was delayed from returning home. When Catherine, who had a reputation for magical powers, told the wife that the laird was dallying with other women, the wife had Catherine imprisoned in the castle dungeon and then accused of witchcraft (a similar fate befell the Brahan Seer, who was burnt to death on Chanonry Point). Kittie was found guilty and burned to death.

Her ghost reputedly then began to haunt the castle, most often being spotted in the tall clock tower. Other spooky goings-on are said to include mysterious noises, and the ringing of a bell when misfortune or death is about to strike the family.

There is no record of a Kitty Rankie or a Catherine Frankie being accused of, or executed for, witchcraft in the records of trials etc.

The records could have been lost, of course...

Map 2, 9G (Abergeldie). Off B976, 5 miles W of Ballater, Kincardineshire.

ACHINDOWN

Part of the Cawdor estate and set in fine gardens, Achindown, a square mansion of about 1700, was occupied by Hamish Munroe in 1746. He gave shelter to Jacobites fleeing from the slaughter at the Battle of Culloden, and hid them in the basement. A band of Hanoverian troops, under the orders of Butcher Cumberland, searched the house and found the fugitives. They were taken from the house and then shot, along with Munroe himself. The shot marks can still be seen in a garden wall.

The house is allegedly haunted. The apparition of a girl, thought to be Elspeth, daughter of Hamish Munroe, is said to have been seen, collecting flowers. Her apparition is reported as wearing a blue dress and having brown hair. Elspeth is said to have eloped with a shepherd, although to what end is not recorded.

There are also stories of more unpleasant and frightening manifestations, including a misty apparition, accompanied by a sudden drop in temperature, telling the then occupant of the drawing room to 'get out'.

Map 2, 8E (Achindown). Off B9090, 1 mile S of Cawdor, Achindown, Highland.

ACKERGILL TOWER   ILLUS PAGE XXIV

Set on the rugged coast of Caithness, Ackergill Tower is an imposing tower house with later extensions, formerly defended by a 12-foot-wide moat, and rising to five storeys and an attic. The castle was remodelled by the well-known Scottish architect David Bryce in 1851, and was restored in 1987.

This part of Caithness was a property of the Cheynes, but passed by marriage to the Keith Earls Marischal in about 1350, and they built the present castle. Ackergill passed to the Dunbars of Hemprigg in 1699, whose descendants owned it until the 1980s. The castle is now used as a conference and hospitality centre.

The Keiths of Ackergill had a long and bitter feud with a local clan, the Gunns, who had their own castle at Clyth. The Gunns were defeated at battles at Tannach Moor in 1438 and again at Dirlot in 1464. The chief of the Gunns and four of his sons were slain. Another Gunn chief was 'basely murdered' by the Keiths in 1478, although Keith of Ackergill and his son were then slain in revenge.

The feud was apparently triggered by Helen Gunn, the 'Beauty of Braemore'. She was betrothed to a man she loved. But Dugald Keith of Ackergill desired her for himself. Keith attacked her father's house at Braemore, killed many of her family, and seized poor Helen. She was imprisoned in an upstairs chamber at Ackergill Castle but, rather than submit to Dugald, threw herself from the battlements and was dashed on the ground below. Her ghost, a 'Green Lady', is said to have been seen in the castle and a rowan tree, 'Fair Ellen's Tree', to still grow at Braemore.

Map 2, 9B (Ackergill). Off A9, 2.5 miles N of Wick, Ackergill, Caithness.
Conference and hospitality centre. (01955 603556 / www.ackergill-tower.co.uk)

ADEN HOUSE

Aden House, a mansion of 1832, replaced at least two earlier houses, although this building is itself now a gutted shell. The lands were a property of the Keiths in 1324, but passed to the Russells of Montcoffer in 1758, who held them until 1937. The ruin now stands in Aden Country Park, and there are over 230 acres of woodland and farmland.

The later mansion was said to be haunted be one of the daughters of the house, who is thought to have run off with a servant. Her father had forbidden her from seeing her lowborn lover and took to locking his daughter in (what became) the haunted room. Her lover had the sense to get a ladder and the couple ran off.

Her ghost, however, was reputedly often witnessed in this bedroom during the first quarter of the 19th century, although what circumstances would have caused this are not known. The disturbances are believed to have been so troublesome, at one time, that the 'haunted' portion of the chamber was reportedly walled off.

Map 2, 12E (Aden). Off A950, 1 mile W of Mintlaw, Aden Country Park, Aberdeenshire.
Aden Country Park, open all year. (01771 622807 / www.aberdeenshire.gov.uk)

AIRLIE CASTLE

Standing on a commanding position between two rivers, Airlie Castle was built in 1432 by the Ogilvies, later Earls of Airlie, and was once a place of great strength. The family were much involved in the troubles of the 17th and 18th centuries. James Ogilvie, 1st Earl of Airlie, escaped from Scotland rather than sign the National Covenant, and in 1640 the castle was sacked by the Earl of Argyll. Ogilvie joined the Marquis of Montrose, but in 1645 was captured after defeat at the Battle of Philiphaugh; fortunately for him he managed to escape execution by swapping clothes with his sister. David, the 4th Earl, fought in the Jacobite Rising of 1745-46, but had to flee the country, although he was later pardoned. The castle was re-placed by a mansion in 1793, which is still occupied by the Ogilvies.

A ram, the 'Doom of Airlie Castle', is said to circle the castle when one of the family is near death or bad fortune is about to strike.

Map 4, 9J (Airlie). Off A926, 4 miles NE of Alyth, Airlie, Angus.

AIRTH CASTLE

ILLUS PAGE 7

In acres of woodland, Airth Castle is a large and splendid mansion, and incorporates much old work, including Wallace's Tower, a squat keep dating from the 14th century. William Wallace rescued his uncle, the Priest of Dunipace, from here during the Wars of Independence. Around 1470 Airth passed to the Bruces, and in 1488 the castle was attacked and burned by James III. In 1642 the property went by marriage to the Elphinstones, and in the 18th century was acquired by the Grahams, whose descendants owned it until 1920. Since 1971 Airth has been used as a hotel and a country club.

One room of the castle is said to be haunted by the ghost of a 17th-century housekeeper. The story goes that she neglected two children in her care, and still searches the building for them after they were killed in a fire: her presence is reputed to be felt most in three of the rooms. The unexplained sounds of children playing in corridors of the building have also been reputedly heard.

The hotel is also said to have much other ghostly activity, which has been witnessed by both guests and staff.

Map 4, 8L (Airth). Off A905, 4 miles N of Falkirk, Airth.
Hotel. (01324 831411 / www.airthcastlehotel.com)

A paranormal investigation was undertaken in July 2005 by Ghost Finders (www.ghostfinders.co.uk/airth.html)

ALBION BAR, STIRLING

In the heart of Stirling, the Albion Bar is a popular local bar and was established in 1864 (it is called after the local football team, Stirling Albion).

The bar is said to be haunted.

Map 4, 8L (Stirling). Off B8052, Barnton Street, Stirling.
Public House. (01786 461252/469533 / www.albionbar.com)

A paranormal investigation was undertaken in April 2006 by Paranormal Investigation Scotland (www.paranormalinvestigationscotland.co.uk/albionreport.htm)

ALDOURIE CASTLE

Aldourie Castle, an impressive Gothic turreted mansion of 1853 which was restored about 1900, incorporates a simple fortified house with a round tower and parapet of 1623. Aldourie was a property of the Frasers, then of the Grants, but passed to the Mackintoshes in the 18th century and then to the Camerons. It was sold in 2003; the asking price was offers of more than £1.2 million, and the house and estate are to be redeveloped as an exclusive leisure complex.

A 'Grey Lady' is said to haunt Aldourie Castle, and her apparition reputedly walks from a bedroom in the ancient part of the castle to the old hall.

Map 2, 7F (Aldourie). Off B862, 8 miles SW of Inverness, Aldourie, Highland.

ALHAMBRA THEATRE, DUNFERMLINE

The Alhambra Theatre was opened as a variety theatre in 1922, and was then used as a cinema and then a bingo hall, and is now a venue for bands, music and comedy. The theatre is housed in an impressive brick building, and there are stories that it is haunted by as many as three ghosts.

One ghost is said to haunt the actors' box, the bogle of an actress from Italy, believed to be a principal singer with the operatic O'Mara Theatre Company, who played at the theatre in the 1920s. The actress was one corner of a menage a trois and, when her husband found out that she had been having an affair, she fled and shut herself in the box. Her husband broke his way in, but in doing so knocked her over and the poor woman broke her neck. Her ghost is said to have haunted the box from that day on.

An apparition clad in black, with a hood or cowl, has been witnessed in the aisle, and it has been suggested that it is the same ghost but dressed in costume, although another explanation is that it is the spectre of a monk.

A third ghost is said to be felt at the back of the balcony, rather than being seen or heard.

Map 4, 9L (Dunfermline). Off A823, 33 Canmore Street, Dunfermline, Fife. **Entertainment venue. (01383 740384 / www.alhambradunfermline.com)**

A paranormal investigation was undertaken in August 2008 by the Ghost Club (www.ghostclub.org.uk/alhambra.htm)

ALLANBANK HOUSE

Allanbank House, a small mansion designed by David Bryce in 1848, was demolished in 1969. The mansion replaced an earlier house, dating from the 17th century, which was a property of the Stewart family.

Robert Stewart of Allanbank, made a baronet of Nova Scotia in 1687, met a pretty and very young (perhaps only 15 years old – and reputedly a nun) Italian or French girl, called Jeanne de la Salle, in Paris and they became lovers. Stewart, however, seems to have tired of her, or his parents disapproved: whatever, he planned to return to Allanbank. On the day of his departure from Paris, Jean tried to stop him leaving, but was thrown under Stewart's carriage and was trampled to death under the horses' hooves.

Her ghost, called 'Pearlin Jean' because of the lace she wore, is said to have followed Stewart back to Allanbank and began to haunt the grounds and house (despite this, Stewart went on to marry). Jean's apparition was seen, doors would open and close by themselves, and ghostly feet and the rustling of her gown were heard round the passages. The room in which the ghost was most often witnessed was abandoned. The old house was demolished in 1849, and a new mansion built, but the disturbances appear to have continued, occurrences being reported as late as the turn of the century. So are the stories.

The only thing that is said to have placated the ghost, at least partially, was when Jean's portrait was placed between that of her lover and his wife.

Map 4, 11M (Allanbank). Off B6437, 4.5 miles east of Duns, Tofthill, Allanbank, Borders.

ALLOA TOWER   ILLUS PAGE 7

Alloa Tower is a lofty rectangular tower with very thick walls, dating from the 14th century, and it stands in a public park in the town. The top floor has a fine and rare medieval timber roof, and the medieval dungeon also survives. The property was given to Sir Robert Erskine, Great Chamberlain of Scotland, in 1360, and has re-mained with his descendants, the Earls of Mar, since. Mary, Queen of Scots, was reconciled with Henry Stewart, Lord Darnley, here in 1565 and James VI also visited the castle. One of the family was 'Bobbing John', the 11th (or 6th) Earl of Mar, and

Airth Castle (page 5)

Alloa Tower (page 6)

Arbroath Abbey (page 10)

Ardchattan Priory (page 12)

the leader of the Jacobites in the unsuccessful 1715 Jacobite Rising.

A large mansion adjoining the castle was destroyed by a fire in 1800, and a portrait of Mary, Queen of Scots, as well as many other treasures, were burned. It was this event that was apparently the origin of one of the ghost stories: it is said that, on the anniversary of the event, smoke can be smelt throughout the tower.

Other ghostly activity is said to include the sightings of an apparition on the first floor and on the turnpike stair, while both staff and visitors have apparently reported feeling as if they had been touched or were being watched.

A further mysterious occurrence is the painting of the 'Lady in Black', which is said to mist over without explanation.

Map 4, 8L (Alloa). Off A907, 7 miles E of Stirling, Alloa, Clackmannan.
NTS: Open Apr- Oct, daily. (01259 211701 / www.nts.org.uk)

A paranormal investigation was undertaken in November 2007 by the Ghost Club (www.ghostclub.org.uk)

AMATOLA HOTEL, ABERDEEN

The Amatola Hotel was a large hotel, but the building has been demolished and the site is occupied by housing.

The hotel was reputedly haunted. A lady, garbed as if in 19th-century dress, reportedly appeared on the landing of the old part of the building. It is believed that she was the great-great-grandmother of the then house owners, as she was dressed in a similar way to that seen in a portrait which used to hang in the hotel.

There do not appear to be any recent stories of her haunting the site.

Map 2, 12G (Aberdeen). Off A93, 448 Great Western Road, Aberdeen.

ANN STREET, EDINBURGH

A house here is said to be haunted by the ghost of Mr Swan, a former occupant. Although he died abroad, his apparition – a small man dressed in black – was reportedly then seen in the house. An exorcism was performed but, when the house changed hands in 1936, the apparition apparently reappeared, and was witnessed most often in one of the bedrooms. The ghost seems to have been friendly and to have said goodnight to children sleeping in the room.

Map 4, 9L (Edinburgh). Off A90, 0.5 miles NW of Edinburgh Castle, Edinburgh.

ANNFIELD HOUSE, GLASGOW

Annfield House, which was built in 1770 but was demolished almost exactly 100 years later, was said to have been haunted by a 'White Lady'.

Map 4, 7M (Glasgow). Off A8 or A89, Belgrove, Glasgow.

APPLEBANK INN, MILLHEUGH

The Applebank Inn, which is thought to date from 1711, stands to the west of Larkhall, not far from the site of the mansion of Broomhill.

The inn is said to be haunted, and items are reported to have been mysteriously moved around the inn, both in the kitchen and in the bar, while others have been hidden. One paranormal investigation was undertaken at the inn in 2004, suggesting that the activity was linked to a lintel brought here from Broomhill.

The manifestations are reputedly linked to the 'Black Lady', the same ghost which haunted the now demolished Broomhill (also see that entry). The story goes that the Black Lady is the bogle of a beautiful Indian woman, who disappeared in about 1900. The poor lady may have been murdered, and she is said, in life, to have been the mistress of Captain Henry McNeil-Hamilton, who owned the house; he died in 1924.

Map 4, 8M (Millheugh). Off B7078, 0.5 miles W of Larkhall, Millheugh, Lanarkshire.
Public house. (01698 884667)

A paranormal investigation was undertaken in August 2004 by the Ghost Club (www.ghost club.org.uk) and in October 2006 by Spiritfinders Scotland (www.spiritfindersscotland.com)

ARBIGLAND HOUSE

Arbigland House is a fine classical mansion, with a main block and pavilions, and was built by William Craik in 1755 to replace an older house. The property was held in turn by the MacCullochs, by the Murrays, and by the Carnegie Earls of Southesk, but was sold to the Craik family in 1679, then to the Blacketts in 1852, who still own the house. John Paul Jones, father of the American Navy, was born at nearby Kirkbean and worked on the estate of Arbigland as a gardener.

The grounds around the house are reputedly haunted by the daughter of one of the Craik lairds, the phantom being known as the 'Ghost of the Three Crossroads'. This daughter is said to have fallen in love with a groom called Dunn, but her parents forbad them to marry or to even see each other. Dunn then mysteriously disappeared – the rumour was that he was murdered by the girl's brothers – so the daughter fled the house and she was never seen again. Whatever end she came to, her apparition is said to have been seen in the grounds and also occasionally in the house.

Dunn's ghost, on a phantom horse, has also been reported near the main gates of Arbigland.

Map 4, 8P (Arbigland). Off A710, 2 miles E of Kirkbean, Arbigland, Dumfries and Galloway.

ARBROATH ABBEY
ILLUS PAGE 8

Arbroath Abbey is (now) the substantial ruin of a Tironsenian establishment, which was founded in 1178 by William the Lyon, King of Scots, in memory of Thomas a' Becket. Some of the church survives, including the fine west end, as well as the gatehouse, sacristy and the Abbot's House, which has a museum. The Declaration of Arbroath was signed at the abbey in 1320, a document which asserted Scottish independence over English aggression; Mary, Queen of Scots, visited the abbey in 1562. The Stone of Destiny was set before the high altar after being taken from Westminster Abbey in 1951 – the stone is now on display at Edinburgh Castle.

There are stories that the abbey buildings are haunted, and that unexplained manifestations have been witnessed in the Abbot's House, such as knocks and thumps coming from unoccupied areas. The sacristy, which was later used as a place of imprisonment, is also said to be haunted.

Map 4, 10J (Arbroath). Off A92, Arbroath, Angus.
His Scot: Open all year, daily; closed 25/26; check opening for New Year. (01241 878756 / www.historic-scotland.gov.uk)

A paranormal investigation was undertaken by Paranormal Encounters Group (www.p-e-g.co.uk)

ARDACHY

Ardachy, a modern mansion, stood on lands which were held by the Frasers of Lovat from the 15th century. The property was sold to the MacEwans in 1952, and is said to have been haunted by the apparition of a previous owner, a Mrs Brewin. The house was later sold, and is said to have been demolished.

Map 1, 6G (Ardachy). Off A82, 1 mile S of Fort Augustus, Ardachy, Highland.

ARDBLAIR CASTLE

Ardblair Castle is a fine 16th-century tower house, designed on the L-plan, with later wings and a wall enclosing a courtyard. The lands were held by the Blairs of Balthayock from 1399, but unfortunately the family feuded with the Drummonds of nearby Newton Castle (also see that entry, as Jean is also said to haunt that building). In 1554 Patrick Blair of Ardblair was beheaded after being found guilty of the murder of George Drummond.

More trouble was to come when Lady Jean Drummond, of nearby Newton, fell in love with one of the Blairs of Ardblair. Her love was doomed, and she appears to have died of a broken heart, drowning herself in a local marsh. Her ghost, a 'Green Lady', dressed in green silk, is said to have been witnessed at Ardblair. She is reportedly seen in the late afternoon and early evening on sunny afternoons, sitting in the gallery staring out of a window, or searching for her love through the chambers of the castle.

Ardblair passed by marriage to the Oliphants of Gask in 1792, and the Blair Oliphant family now own the castle. Laurence Oliphant was an aide-de-camp to Bonnie Prince Charlie, and Caroline Oliphant, using the pen-name Mrs Bogan of Bogan, wrote many ballads, including 'Charlie is my Darling' and 'Will ye no come back again?'

Map 4, 9J (Ardblair). Off A923, 0.75 miles W of Blairgowrie, Ardblair, Perthshire.
Open by appointment only; holiday cottages available. (01250 873155)

ARDBRECKNISH HOUSE

Standing in a picturesque spot on the banks of Loch Awe in 10 acres of woodland gardens (which have red squirrels), Ardbrecknish House is a grand baronial mansion with corbiestepped gables. The house incorporates an old tower house or keep in the West Tower.

The lands were held by the MacDougalls, but were given to the MacArthurs in the 14th century as reward for supporting Robert the Bruce. The MacArthurs got into trouble with the acquisitive Campbells and some of the MacArthurs were drowned during a confrontation in 1567; they managed to hold on to their lands here until 1751. The house became a hotel in the 1930s.

The house is said to be haunted.

One story is that there are two phantom bloodhounds, known as 'the MacDougall's Hounds', which appear from the hearth, stretch, and then disappear through a closed window. Another tale is that the spectre of an old housekeeper, with a candle, has been spotted in the dead of night. All activity is said to be friendly rather than frightening.

One recent tale is that a party of builders were renovating part of the house when they heard a call of 'tea-up'. Being a dedicated lot, they hurried off without delay in search of refreshments, only to find nobody had made the call. In the meantime, the internal wall on which they had been working suddenly collapsed.

Map 3, 5K (Ardbrecknish). Off B840, 7.5 miles N of Inveraray, 2 miles W of Cladich, Ardbrecknish, Argyll.
Hotel. (01866 833223 / www.loch-awe.co.uk)

ARDCHATTAN PRIORY   ILLUS PAGE 8

Standing in a scenic location on the north side of Loch Etive, the surviving buildings of Ardchattan Priory are mostly ruinous or fragmentary, although some parts were built into the adjacent Ardchattan House.

This priory was founded in 1231 by Duncan MacDougall, and Robert the Bruce is said to have held a parliament here in 1309. The property passed to the Campbells of Cawdor early in the 17th century, but Ardchattan was burned in 1644 and then again in 1654. Colin Campbell of Glenure, murdered in 1752, is buried here; the events surrounding his death feature in the novel *Kidnapped* by Robert Louis Stevenson.

The ruins are said to be haunted by the ghost of a young nun, and unexplained moaning and whispering have been reported, as well as the sighting of an apparition. The ghost is believed, in life, to have been the lover of one of the priory monks. The couple had arranged a refuge should they be in danger of being found together, a pit in the floor where the nun could hide. The prior, however, knew of the affair and tried to surprise the lovers. The girl had time to secrete herself in the pit, but the prior already knew of it and had her trapped inside, effectively burying her alive and leaving her to suffocate or to die of thirst.

The ruins of the priory are in the care of Historic Scotland, and there are 16th-century carved grave slabs, a fine carved sarcophagus, and an early Christian carved wheel cross. The four acres of gardens around the house, in private ownership, are also regularly open to the public.

Map 3, 4J (Ardchattan). Off A828, 6.5 miles NE of Oban, Argyll.
His Scot: Ruins of priory (Historic Scotland; www.historic-scotland.gov.uk) open at reasonable times. Garden also open. (01796 481355 / www.gardens-of-argyll.co.uk/gardens/ardchattan-priory-garden.html)

ARDENTINNY HOTEL

Ardentinny Hotel, which stands in a fine spot on the west side of Loch Long, is an old inn which dates from the eighteenth century. There may have been an older building here as Mary, Queen of Scots, stayed at Ardentinny in 1563; the lands around here were long held by the Campbells. Sir Harry Lauder, who for some years had a country house nearby at Glenbranter, was a regular visitor.

One of the bedrooms is said to be haunted by the ghosts of children.

Map 3, 5L (Ardentinny). On A880, Ardentinny, west side of Loch Long, Cowal, Argyll.
Hotel. (01369 810100 / www.ardentinny-hotel.co.uk)

ARDGAY

An old house in Ardgay was thought to be haunted at one time. Reported disturbances included items being thrown about and footsteps being heard coming from unoccupied areas. The occupant called in the local priest, and he stayed in the bedroom where the activity was centred. Here, he is said to have witnessed the apparition of a woman clothed in black, and to have exorcised the ghost.

The origin of the haunting was believed to be that a serving girl had become pregnant and had suffocated her newborn baby. The poor girl had then hidden the small body in a chest of drawers in the haunted room.

Map 2, 7D (Ardgay). Off A9, in Ardgay, 1 mile SW of Bonar Bridge, Highland.

ARDINCAPLE CASTLE

Ardincaple Castle, formerly a large castellated mansion, incorporated part of a castle of the MacAulays, perhaps dating from as early as the 12th century. The castle had a moat, traces of which were still visible in the 1930s. The castle was, however, a roofless ruin when it was sold to the Campbells in 1767, and it was then rebuilt and remodelled. The building was demolished in 1957, except for a square tower of four storeys, for the construction of a naval housing estate.

The old castle is said to have had a brownie, probably a gruagach or 'Green Lady'.

Map 3, 6L (Ardincaple). Off A814, W of Helensburgh, Ardincaple, Dunbartonshire.

ARDLARACH

The present house, with later additions, was built by the MacDougalls in 1787, although the property was held by them from the beginning of the 17th century.

Ardlarach is said to be haunted by the ghost of the wife of one of the MacDougall owners. Her son was slain at the Battle of Talaveera in 1809, and unexplained noises were reported on the night he died, although it is her ghost which is now said to have been witnessed here at times.

Map 3, 4K (Ardlarach). Off minor road, 0.5 miles W of Toberonochy, W side of Isle of Luing, Argyll.

ARDNACAILLACH

The island of Ulva, which nestles in the arms of Mull, was a property of the Mac-Quarries from 1473 (or earlier) until the 18th century. The clan's war cry was 'the Red Tartan Army', and they fought at Bannockburn in 1314, at Inverkeithing in 1651, when the chief and many of the clan were slain, and at Culloden in 1746, when many of the clan were also killed – a stone at the battlefield marks their burial place. The chiefs had an old house or castle at Ardnacaillach, near the present Ulva House, the site of which is now occupied by a farm steading.

Reputedly it was this building that had a 'Green Lady' or glaistig.

There is a museum and tearoom on Ulva, along with many other attractions, and the island is reached by a regular (and quick) ferry service from Ulva Ferry on Mull.

Map 3, 3J (Ardnacaillach). Off track, near Ulva House, Ardnacaillach, Isle of Ulva, Argyll.

ARDNADAM

A house at Ardnadam was allegedly haunted by the apparition of an old man, dressed in white trousers and shirt, and a red turban. There were also reports of the sounds of heavy objects being pulled over the floor of the attic when it was empty.

The story goes that the house had been occupied by an old soldier, who served for many years in India and who often wore a turban. He is said to have shot himself in the attic, after piling up furniture against the door.

Map 3, 5L (Ardnadam). On A815, 1.5 miles N of Dunoon, Argyll.

ARDOCH ROMAN FORT

Ardoch Roman Fort is one of the largest Roman stations in Britain, and there are a series of substantial and impressive earthworks and ditches, which date from the 2nd century. This was one of a series of defences, roads and watchtowers built by the Romans in what is now Perthshire, but the legions were eventually withdrawn back to the frontier of Hadrian's Wall.

The site is said to be haunted, and there are reports of unexplained footsteps and other noises, as well as a foreboding atmosphere after dark and sightings of apparitions of Roman legionnaires.

Map 4, 8K (Ardoch). Off A822, 14 miles S of Crieff, NE of Braco, Ardoch, Perthshire.
Access at all reasonable times.

ARDOE HOUSE HOTEL

Commanding a magnificent view of the River Dee and in 30 acres of open country, Ardoe House Hotel is an impressive castellated mansion dating from 1879, which is now used as a luxury hotel.

Ardoe is reputedly haunted by a 'White Lady', said to be the apparition of Katherine Ogston. She was the wife of Alexander Milne Ogston: he bought the property in 1839 and was involved in the manufacture of soap. A portrait of Katherine hangs above the main stair of the building, and it was here that, in 1990, the apparition was reported before vanishing at the main entrance.

An alternative version of the story is that the ghost is that of a daughter of a previous owner, who in the late 19th century was raped and became pregnant. She despaired of life and killed her child and then herself.

Map 2, 11G (Ardoe). Off B9077, Banchory Devenick, Ardoe, Aberdeenshire.
Hotel. (01224 860600 / www.mercure-uk.com)

ARDROSSAN CASTLE

Standing on a ridge overlooking the sea and the harbour, Ardrossan Castle is a ruinous but ancient stronghold. William Wallace captured the castle from the English during the Wars of Independence, slew the garrison, and piled their bodies into the basement: the episode became known as 'Wallace's Larder'.

Wallace's ghost is still reputedly seen here on stormy nights.

The castle was acquired then rebuilt by Sir John Montgomery, who fought at the battle of Otterburn in 1388, capturing Harry 'Hotspur' Percy. The family later became Earls of Eglinton, and sheltered here in 1528 when their castle at Eglinton was torched by the Cunninghams.

One story is that the castle was the abode of the 'Deil of Ardrossan', a fearsome sorcerer, early in its history.

Map 3, 5M (Ardrossan). Off A78, in Ardrossan, Ayrshire.
Access at all reasonable times - view from exterior.

ARDVRECK CASTLE

In a lonely and picturesque place, Ardvreck Castle consists of a ruined square keep, with a distinctive round stair-turret which is corbelled out to square at the top. The lands were a property of the MacLeods of Assynt from the 13th century, and they built the present castle about 1490. It was here that in 1650 the Marquis of Montrose took refuge, but he was turned over to the Covenanters, and executed in Edinburgh. The castle was sacked in 1672, and replaced by nearby Calda House (also see that entry), itself burnt out in 1760 and never restored.

Ardvreck is reputed to be haunted by the daughter of a MacLeod chief, who threw herself out of one of the windows. The story goes that the chief wanted a grander castle than he could afford, and the Devil offered to build him one, but the price was his soul. MacLeod offered the hand of his daughter in marriage instead, which the Devil accepted, and the wedding took place. When the poor girl found out who her bridegroom was, she climbed to the top of the castle and in despair threw herself to her death. Her weeping apparition has reportedly been witnessed.

Another ghost is said to be a tall grey-clothed man, who is thought to be friendly but only speaks Gaelic.

Map 1, 5C (Ardvreck). Off A837, 1.5 miles NW of Inchnadamph, Ardvreck, Highland.
Access at all reasonable times – view from exterior.

ARNISH MOOR, LEWIS

The main road between Stornoway and Harris, where it crossed bleak moorland at Arnish, was long believed to be haunted. The apparition of a man, wearing a coat and woollen stockings in the manner of the 18th century, was reputedly often seen on the road, even as late as the 1960s. It was thought that a young man had been murdered here by a friend sometime in the 18th century, and his body buried on the moor to conceal the crime. The remains of a man were found in 1964, near where the hauntings took place, dressed in a similar fashion to the reported apparition.

Map 1, 2C (Arnish Moor). Off A859, 2.5 miles SE of Stornoway, Arnish Moor, Lewis.

ART HOUSE HOTEL, GLASGOW

Located in a fine building dating from 1912, this house in Bath Street was used as offices for the local education board until the end of the 1990s. The house still retains an impressive sweeping stair, and was converted into the Art House, a fashionable urban hotel. In 2005 this was itself refurbished and transformed into the Abode Hotel, featuring 60 luxury rooms.

During the time it was the Art House Hotel, one of the chambers on the top floor was said to have been plagued by poltergeist activity.

Map 4, 7M (Glasgow). Off A8, 129 Bath Street, Glasgow
Luxury hotel. (0141 572 6000 / www.abodehotels.co.uk)

ASHINTULLY CASTLE

In an attractive wooded setting, Ashintully Castle, built by the Spalding family in the 16th century, is a tall L-plan tower house, which was later greatly extended by a long wing.

During the ownership of the Spaldings, the property is said to have been held by

Jean, a daughter of the house, in her own right. Her ruthless uncle, however, wanted Ashintully for himself. He visited Jean, and in one of the castle chambers slew her by slitting her throat; he also murdered her servant, whose body he hid up the large chimney. Jean's ghost, dressed in a green gown, then began to haunt the castle. The bogle is said to have been seen at the family burial ground, beside her memorial, and disembodied footsteps have also been reported in the castle.

Two other ghosts are recorded as haunting the vicinity. One was Crooked Davie, a messenger killed when it was thought he had not delivered a message – which in fact he had; the other a tinker, hanged for trespassing, who cursed the family.

The property passed to the Rutherfords in 1750, and the castle is still occupied.

Map 2, 8I (Ashintully). Off B950, 2 miles NE of Kirkmichael, Ashintully, Perthshire. **Holiday accommodation available. (01250 881237 / www.ashintully.com)**

ATHOLL ARMS HOTEL, DUNKELD

At the north end of the picturesque and historic village of Dunkeld is the Atholl Arms Hotel, a grand and imposing establishment, which was visited by Queen Victoria in 1844.

The hotel is said to be haunted by the apparition of a maid, known as 'Chrissie' and who is believed to have died in the building; the bogle is said to have been seen in the corridors of the hotel.

Map 4, 8J (Dunkeld). Off B8079, by station, Dunkeld, Perthshire. **Hotel. (01796 481205 / www.athollarmshotel.co.uk)**

ATHOLL PALACE HOTEL, PITLOCHRY

Standing in 48 acres of wooded parkland with magnificent views over the Perthshire countryside, the Atholl Palace is a magnificent sprawling castellated hotel, built in 1875 as a hydropathic establishment.

It is said to be haunted by a 'Green Lady', and her apparition has – reputedly – often been seen by staff and guests in one of the rooms.

Map 2, 8I (Pitlochry). Off A924, SE of Pitlochry, Perthshire. **Hotel. (01796 472400 / www.athollpalace.com)**

AUCHABRECK

A farm house here is said to have been haunted, although the building was apparently at a different site than the present house.

A daughter of the house fell in love with a young man, but the fellow was poor so he went to sea to make his fortune. Doing well, the young man sent fine clothing and money back to his love, but these were intercepted by the girl's brother, who kept the presents for himself. Getting no reply from his love, the fellow wrote again and again, but each time the letters were seized by the brother, so that the girl believed that he had lost interest in her. The young man died untimely, and his angry ghost is said to have returned to Auchabreck, causing all sorts of commotion and banging, no matter what was done to prevent it.

Another version is that it was a ghost of a brother of the lady in question, who had fallen from his horse and been killed. His apparition was reputedly witnessed, on a grey horse.

Another story relates that one room was haunted by the sound of scratching, as if a pen was being drawn across parchment. This noise was so persistent and loud that eventually nobody would sleep in the haunted room. The owner asked the local schoolmaster to stay in the room and see if he could find the source. The story then goes that the man fled the house come the morning, and immediately emigrated to America without saying what he had experienced, but the sound of scratching is also said to have ceased.

Map 3, 5Q (Auchabreck). On B7065, 1 mile N of Port Logan, Auchabreck, Rhins of Galloway, Dumfries and Galloway.

AUCHEN CASTLE

Built to replace the ancient Auchen Castle, a new mansion, also called Auchen Castle and described as 'a structure of considerable extent', was built about 0.5 miles to the north by General Johnstone in 1849. The property passed by marriage to the Youngers, who were made baronets in 1911, and the mansion is now a hotel.

Auchen Castle is said to be haunted by the ghost of a child. The ghost is said to have been seen on the main stairs and in corridors, and an apparition has also been witnessed in the formal garden.

Map 4, 8O (Auchen). Off M74, 1.5 miles W of Moffat, Auchen Castle, Dumfries and Galloway. **Hotel. (01683 300407 / www.auchencastle.com)**

AUCHENDENNAN CASTLE

Set in wooded parkland in a lovely spot, Auchendennan Castle is a grand baronial mansion, and dates from the middle of the 19th century when it was owned by the Chrystal family. The castle is now used as the Loch Lomond Youth Hostel.

The building is reputedly haunted by the ghost of a young girl, known as 'Veronica', witnessed in one of the rooms. One story is that she was a daughter of the family and fell in love with an unsuitable fellow. She was locked in one of the chambers on the upper floor, but then tried to escape and fell to her death. Her bogle is then said to have begun to haunt that chamber (reputed to be Room 27).

Map 3, 6L (Auchendennan). Off A82, 2 miles NW of Balloch, Auchendennan, Loch Lomond, Dunbartonshire. **Youth hostel. (0870 0041136 / www.syha.org.uk)**

AUCHENTIBER

The area around Auchentiber is said to be haunted, according to an old story from the 1820s called the 'Lady o' Clumbeith'. A girl from Clonbeith Farm was going to Blair Tavern in Auchentiber to meet an admirer, but she and her horse fell down a mine shaft and were killed; an alternative version is that her admirer murdered her, disposed of her body, and then in remorse leapt to his death after her.

Map 3, 6M (Auchentiber). Off A736 or B778, 4 miles NE of Kilwinning, Auchentiber, Ayrshire.

AUCHINDARROCH

Auchindarroch, a rambling building of two storeys, was built by the Stewarts of Appin and dates from the 18th century. There was probably an older dwelling here.

The house is said to be haunted by the 'Maid of Glen Duror', the ghost of a woman called MacColl, thought to have been killed with the cattle she was tending in a flood that swept her out into Loch Linnhe. The apparition is said to be a 'Grey Lady', and has reportedly been seen in the house, particularly in the Haunted Room, adjoining the dining room, and in the neighbouring countryside. Other manifestations are alleged to include the opening of doors and windows, thumps and bangs, and the moving of objects: all said to have been witnessed in recent times. Other apparitions are recorded as being that of an old woman and that of a hooded figure, seen both in the dining room and at the foot of the staircase.

Map 3, 5J (Auchindarroch). Off A828, 4 miles S and W of Ballachulish, Duror, Auchindarroch, Argyll.

AUCHINVOLE HOUSE

Auchinvole House mostly dated from Victorian times but the building incorporated an old L-plan tower house of the 16th century. The whole house has been demolished, except for a doocot. Auchinvole was long associated with the Stark family.

The castle was reported to be haunted by the ghost of a lady. The story is that her apparition was repeatedly seen, sitting at a window, looking out to where her treacherously murdered lover was buried. After his death, she had pined away by the window, and her spirit returned to do the same.

Map 4, 7L (Auchinvole). Off B802 or B8023, 0.5 miles S of Kilsyth, Auchinvole, Lanarkshire.

AUCHLOCHAN HOUSE

Records of the Auchlochan estate go back to about 1200, and the lands were the property of the Browns of Auchlochan from 1575, or earlier, until into the 20th century. There was a castle on the site but this was replaced by a fine mansion, Auchlochan House, in the early 19th century. The house had become derelict when it was restored in the 1970s, and it is now part of a residential development for elderly people.

The house is said to be haunted by a 'Black Lady', the beautiful black wife of one of the Browns.

Map 4, 8N (Auchlochan). Off B7078, 1.5 miles S of Lesmahagow, Auchlochan, Lanarkshire. **Old people's residences. Cafe. (01555 893592/892221 / www.auchlochan.com)**

AUCHNARROW

The farm reportedly had a brownie called Maggie Moloch or 'Hairy Meg'.

Map 2, 9F (Auchnarrow). Off B9008, 2 miles S of Tomnavoulin, Auchnarrow, Moray.

AUCHTERHOUSE

The mansion, a large whitewashed building with dormer windows, incorporates part of the ancient castle of Auchterhouse. The lands were held by the Ramsays in the 13th century, but by 1497 had gone to the Stewarts, and then went to other families. The building was latterly used as a hotel (known as the Old Mansion House), but this appears to have closed.

William Wallace is said to have visited the castle.

There are accounts of a ghost haunting the building, but the spirit is said to be friendly.

Map 4, 9J (Auchterhouse). Off B954, 7 miles N of Dundee, Auchterhouse, Angus.

AUCTIONEERS, GLASGOW

The pub, housed in a building dating from the 19th century which was formerly used as an auctioneers, is reputed to be haunted. Manifestations are said to include the sighting of the apparition of a young girl, perhaps 13 or 14 years old. The phantom is reported to be dressed as if from Victorian times, in a long grey dress with a white overall, and to have shoulder-length hair. On one occasion the ghost was apparently wearing clogs, which were heard as well as seen; and it is reported that the bogle goes from the office area along a corridor.

Other strange occurrences are footsteps being heard coming from unoccupied areas, and uncomfortable feelings in parts of the building, including in the toilet area.

Map 4, 7M (Glasgow). Off M8 or A89, 6 North Court, Glasgow.

AULD HOOSE, TAYPORT

Standing in the Whitenhill area of the old part of Tayport, the Auld Hoose is a public house and dates from the early 19th century; the building is located beside the graveyard of the old kirk.

There are reports of spooky happenings in the Auld Hoose, including glasses falling off the bar for no reason, doors opening by themselves, the feeling as if somebody was rushing past, the sound of pool balls clacking together when nobody was playing, and other mysterious noises.

A misty apparition has also reputedly been seen in the lounge area.

Map 4, 10K (Tayport). Off B945 or B946, 1-3 Whitenhill, Tayport, Fife.
Public house. (01382 552359)

A paranormal investigation was undertaken in August 2007 by Paranormal Discovery (www.paranormaldiscovery.co.uk/theauldhoose.htm)

AULTSIGH

Standing on a picturesque spot on the shore of Loch Ness, the former Aultsigh Hotel, now the Loch Ness Youth Hostel, is reputedly haunted.

It is recorded that two brothers, Malcolm and Alasdair Macdonnell, desired the same attractive lass, Annie Fraser. Annie and Alasdair were together on the hill behind the building when they were surprised by Malcolm, who was furious about the couple's meeting. He attacked and killed his brother, then strangled or stabbed the unfortunate Annie and hid her body under the floor in a then abandoned room of what is now the youth hostel. He gathered together his belongings and fled, but drowned crossing the loch.

The room in which Annie's remains were thought to be hidden is reputedly plagued by ghostly footsteps, crossing and recrossing the floor (although the present building was only completed in 1930). Her apparition has also reportedly been witnessed, both at the hostel and in the neighbouring countryside.

Map 1, 6G (Aultsigh). On A82, Loch Ness, 10 miles NW of Fort Augustus, Aultsigh, Highland.
Youth Hostel. (0870 0041138 / www.syha.org.uk)

AVOCH

The phantom of a young boy was reported in an old house in the village of Avoch. The apparition was allegedly witnessed in one of the bedrooms, and toys and other items were moved around when nobody had been present in the room. The ghost is said to be the son of a previous owner, the tale being that the young boy had fallen to his death from the bedroom window while sleepwalking.

Map 2, 7E (Avoch). On A832, Avoch, Highland.

BALAVIL HOUSE

Surrounded by a 7,500-acre estate in a beautiful part of the country, Balavil House is a grand and impressive mansion, dating from 1790, with sumptuous interiors. The present house replaced an old castle of 1576 or earlier. The property was held by the Macphersons, and was home of James Macpherson, who became famous for the translation of the ancient poems of Ossian from Gaelic into English, although he was subsequently accused of inventing much of the work. Balavil is now held by the Macpherson-Fletchers.

The house is said to be haunted by a friendly ghost. The story, from the 1860s, is that the bogle is the spirit of a young maid, who (in life) became besotted with the butler. Such a match was totally unsuitable because of their respective positions, and the young woman despaired and cast herself off a nearby bridge and was killed.

The ghost was reputedly often witnessed in the 1940s but activity apparently lessened after a renovation. Further building work appears to have increased manifestations, which are said to include interference with electrical equipment, the switching on of lights, of a kettle and of radiators, as well as the turning on of water taps.

Map 2, 7G (Balavil). Off A9, 3 miles E of Kingussie, N of River Spey, Balavil, Highland. **Serviced accommodation available and venue for weddings and events; sporting estate. (01540 662020 / www.balavil-estate.com)**

A paranormal investigation was undertaken in September 2005 by Paranormal Investigation Scotland (www.paranormalinvestigationscotland.co.uk/balavilhousetwo.htm)

BALBIRNIE HOUSE

Nestling in 416 acres of country park and gardens, Balbirnie House is a fine classical mansion with Greek influences, which dates from 1777, although it was extended in 1815-19 and later. The present house replaced an ancient castle, and may incorporate some older work in the current fabric. The lands were a property of the Balfours from 1642 until the 20th century, and since 1989 Balbirnie House has been used as a hotel.

There are stories that the building is haunted by a 'White Lady', and it is said that a servant or maid was murdered in the courtyard. There are also reports of much other activity in chambers, corridors and stairs, including apparitions being seen, the unexplained sounds of feet and of voices, and people feeling as if they have been pushed.

Map 4, 9L (Balbirnie). Off A92 or B9130, 2 miles NE of Glenrothes, Balbirnie, Fife. **Hotel and country park. (01592 610066 / www.balbirnie.co.uk)**

A paranormal investigation was undertaken in May 2005 by Scottish Paranormal Investigations (www.scottishparanormalinvestigations.co.uk)

BALCOMIE CASTLE

The spirit of a young man is said to haunt Balcomie Castle, an L-plan tower house of the 16th century, which rises to five storeys and an attic and which is now a farmhouse.

Manifestations reportedly mostly consist of the sound of unearthly whistling, apparently coming from a tin whistle (or piping, according to another version). The story goes that the ghost is that of a cheery young lad, who spent much of his time playing the tin whistle, as he went about his business. This began to irritate the then laird, but the lad would not stop, despite being repeatedly warned. The laird locked the lad in a chamber to teach him a lesson, but then forgot what he had done, was called away, and the lad starved to death.

Other activity apart from the whistling is said to have included furniture being moved about by itself, candles burning with an eerie blue light, and even one individual claiming to have spotted an apparition of the lad, with an old rusty whistle, seen on the roof of the castle.

Map 4, 10K (Balcomie). Off A917, 1.5 miles NE of Crail, Balcomie, Fife.

BALCONIE

Balconie House, built in the 19th century, incorporated part of an ancient castle, but the whole building has been demolished. The castle was held by the Earls of Ross and saw action in the Wars of Independence.

One story associated with Balconie is that the then lady of the house was seized by a sinister man, clad all in green, and she vanished from the area. Years later, it is said, she was finally found, but the poor woman was chained in a deep cavern from which she could not be rescued.

The house was said to have been haunted, a party of fishermen fleeing from the building after witnessing a ghost.

Map 2, 7E (Balconie). Off A9, 3.5 miles SW of Alness, Balconie, Ross and Cromarty, Highland.

BALDOON CASTLE

Little remains of Baldoon Castle, a stronghold of the Dunbars, but the ruins are said to be haunted by the apparition of a woman in a blood-stained wedding dress. The origins of the ghost are said to date from events in 1669.

Janet Dalrymple of Carscreugh was in love with Archibald Rutherford, son of Lord Rutherford, but he was rather without prospects and Janet's parents were against their marriage. Instead, they chose Sir David Dunbar, heir to the lands of Baldoon, and persuaded the reluctant Janet to marry him at the church at Old Luce. Trouble followed, although there are at least three versions of which happened next. Janet may have been murdered on her wedding night, may have committed suicide after having tried to murder her new husband, or may have died insane soon after the wedding.

Her sorrowing bogle is said to be seen here on 12 September, the date of her death (although at other times, it is claimed, the phantom can also be spotted). Sir Walter Scott's *Bride of Lammermuir* (and then Gaetano Donizetti's opera *Lucia di Lammermoor*) are based on (or inspired by, anyway) the events here.

Dunbar recovered sufficiently to marry a daughter of the Montgomery Earl of

Eglinton, while Janet's lover, Archibald Rutherford, remained a bachelor until his death in 1685.

Map 4, 7Q (Baldoon). Off A746, 1.5 miles SE of Wigtown, Baldoon Mains, Dumfries and Galloway.

Balfour House

Virtually nothing except a mound of rubble remains of Balfour House, once a large castellated mansion. The building mostly dated from the 19th century, but it also incorporated the vaulted basement of a strong 16th-century L-plan tower house. Carved wooden panels, originally from Arbroath Abbey, were saved from the house before it was demolished and are now located in Dean Castle, near Kilmarnock.

The lands were owned by the Balfours, but in 1360 passed by marriage to the Bethunes or Beatons, who held the property at least until the end of the 19th century. Mary, Queen of Scots, is said to have visited, along with her husband, Henry Stewart, Lord Darnley.

One of the family was Cardinal David Beaton, Archbishop of St Andrews, who is said to have been born at Balfour and who was murdered at St Andrews (also see that entry) in 1546. This is another of the places where he is said to haunt.

Map 4, 9L (Balfour). Off A911, 4 miles E of Glenrothes, Balfour, Milton of Balgonie, Fife.

Balgonie Castle   ILLUS PAGE 25

Balgonie Castle is a grand building consisting of a strong keep within a courtyard enclosing ranges of buildings, some of which are ruinous. The barrel-vaulted Great Hall and the chapel are fine chambers, and the castle is undergoing a long-term programme of restoration.

The original castle was probably built by Sir Thomas Sibbald in about 1360, but it passed to the Lundies, then to the Leslies; and famous visitors include James IV in 1496, Mary Queen of Scots in 1565 and Rob Roy MacGregor, who garrisoned the castle against Hanoverian forces in 1716.

One owner was Alexander Leslie, who died here in 1661. Leslie was captured at Alyth in Angus after the Battle of Dunbar in 1650, while on the losing side against Cromwell, and was imprisoned in the Tower of London – only the intervention of the Queen of Sweden saved his life. An apparition said to have been seen here has been identified as his ghost.

The most haunted part of the castle is reputed to be the Great Hall, where ghostly voices and apparitions have apparently been witnessed, and sometimes also the smell of pipe smoke. A skeleton was found buried under the floor in 1912.

A 'Green Lady', Green Jeanie, thought to be the spirit of one of the Lundies, has reportedly been seen in recent times, and was recorded in 1842 as being a 'well-known ghost'. She is described as being pea-green in colour, and wearing a long full-skirted dress and a hood, which hides her face. The apparition was reputedly often spotted in the ruinous 18th-century wing, but has apparently not been witnessed since 1994.

The apparition of a 17th-century soldier is also said to have been witnessed in the courtyard, with one arm outstretched as if opening a door. An outhouse once stood on the spot where this ghost appears. This apparition is also recorded as being seen walking through the gateway of the castle.

The sounds of a spectral dog have also been reported, as well as other phantoms, including a hooded figure and a medieval apparition.

Map 4, 9L (Balgonie). Off A911, 6.5 miles NE of Kirkcaldy, Balgonie, Fife.
Open all year, daily (tel in advance), unless hired for a private function. (01592 750119 / www.balgonie-castle.com)

A paranormal investigation was undertaken in February 2005 by the Ghost Club (www.ghostclub.org.uk) and in March 2003 by Scottish Paranormal Investigations (www.scottishparanormalinvestigations.co.uk)

BALGOWNIE

A house at Balgownie is said to have been haunted by the bogle of a man, his apparition witnessed climbing a stair and entering one of the bedrooms. The story goes that the poor fellow had committed suicide in that room.

Map 3, 6N (Balgownie). Off A79, Balgownie, Prestwick, Ayrshire.

BALGRAY TOWER, GLASGOW

Also known as 'Breeze's Tower' after Captain Breeze, the tea and rum merchant who built it, Balgray Tower dates from the first quarter of the 19th century. The house stands in a prominent position, once in open countryside but now somewhat overtaken by urban sprawl, and has an octagonal tower rising to 60 foot with a 50-step turnpike stair.

The tower is said to be haunted by a 'Green Lady'.

Map 4, 7M (Glasgow). Off A803, 50 Broomfield Road, Springburn, Glasgow.

BALLACHULISH HOUSE

Ballachulish House, dating from the 18th century, replaced an earlier house which burnt down in 1746. The lands were a property of the Stewarts of Appin, and it was from the earlier house that in 1692 Campbell of Glenorchy ordered the start of the Massacre of Glencoe. The village was a centre of slate mining in the 19th century, which employed over 600 men at one time. Ballachulish House is still occupied, was used as a country house hotel, but is now a private residence again.

The house is said to be haunted by several ghosts.

One is reputedly the apparition of a Stewart of Appin, who is spotted riding up to the door and there vanishes; the sounds of a horse have also reportedly been heard on the drive up to the house.

Other ghosts are said to be that of a tinker, and an apparition which walked through a wall.

A further eerie event is said to have been when the apparition of an old woman was spotted in the house, believed to be the ghost of Sophia Boulton, who died in 1900. What is unusual in this story, however, is that the apparition was seen some time before Sophia Boulton died. The then occupier had observed the phantom, but then later met Sophia when she visited the house, so confirming it was, indeed, her ghost...

Map 1, 4I (Ballachulish). Off A82, Ballachulish, Highlands.

BALLECHIN

Ballechin, a mansion of 1806, was partly demolished because of dry rot in 1963. Much is now ruinous, although a wing survives and is still occupied. Ballechin was a property of the Stewarts until sold to the Honeyman family in 1932.

The reports of a ghost here caused much controversy.

The mansion was said to be haunted by the spirit of Major Robert Stewart, who died in 1876. After his death, inexplicable sounds were reputedly heard: mysterious voices, footsteps, banging, rapping, groans and shrieks, and other noises, and the disturbances are said to have continued for decades. In the 1890s one family renting the house for a year reputedly left early because of the hauntings, as had a governess. The house was investigated by paranormal researchers a few years later, when noises and apparitions were recorded. This investigation caused a furore, as the then owner had not been told, and the reports of activity were hotly refuted. Later episodes of unexplained noises were reported, however.

There are also reports of a 'Grey Lady', the apparition of a nun, which has reputedly been seen on the drive near the mansion, as well as in a nearby cottage.

Map 4, 8J (Ballechin). Off A827, 4 miles E of Aberfeldy, Ballechin, Perthshire.

BALLINDALLOCH CASTLE   ILLUS PAGE 25

Set in fine gardens and grounds, Ballindalloch Castle is an impressive 16th-century Z-plan tower house, which was altered and extended in later centuries to form the present handsome sprawling mansion. Ballindalloch had passed to the Grants by 1499, with whose descendants it remains, and the castle was looted and burned by the Marquis of Montrose in 1645 after the Battle of Inverlochy.

Several ghosts have been recorded in the castle and in its vicinity.

A 'Green Lady' has reputedly been seen in the dining room, and sightings of a 'Pink Lady' are also recorded. Another ghost is said to be that of General James Grant, who died in 1806. Grant was very proud of the improvements he had made to the estate, and his phantom is said to ride around the estate every night to survey his achievement. He is then said to go into the wine cellar for a drink.

Another ghost, reportedly seen at the nearby Bridge of Avon, is a that of a girl believed to have been unlucky in love.

Map 2, 9F (Ballindalloch). On A95, 7.5 miles SW of Aberlour, Ballindalloch, Moray.
Open Good Fri-Sep, closed Sat. (01807 500205 / www.ballindallochcastle.co.uk)

BALMERINO ABBEY   ILLUS PAGE 25

Near the banks of the Tay are the fragmentary but picturesque remains of Balmerino Abbey, a 13th-century Cistercian monastery. Balmerino was founded by Ermengarde, widow of William the Lyon, and their son, Alexander II, in the 1220s. Ermengarde herself died in 1233 and she was buried in front of the high altar (the site of which is marked by a wooden cross). Her tomb was ransacked in the 1830s and her bones were removed and are said to have been sold or given away as curiosities. Her coffin of white stone was smashed up and then used to sand a kitchen floor. A ghost, said to be a 'Green Lady', has reputedly been seen in the abbey precincts, and is thought by some to be the angry bogle of Ermengarde.

The abbey was torched by the English in 1547, and was ransacked by a Reforming mob in 1559, and only the basement of the chapter house and adjoining buildings

Balgonie Castle (page 22)

Ballindalloch Castle (page 24)

Balmerino Abbey (page 24)

Balnain House, Inverness (page 28)

Balvenie Castle (page 28)

survive, while the church is very ruinous. Mary, Queen of Scots, had dinner at the abbey in 1565, and the property passed to Sir James Elphinstone, Lord Balmerino, in 1603. There is an old chestnut tree, said to have been planted by the monks.

A spot near the abbey is said to be haunted by the ghost of a robed and hooded man, perhaps a monk, seen pushing a wheelbarrow.

Map 4, 10K (Balmerino. Off A914, 4.5 miles SW of Newport on Tay, Balmerino, Fife.
NTS: Access at all reasonable times. (0131 243 9300 / www.nts.org.uk)

BALMUTO TOWER

Balmuto Tower, although altered in later centuries, incorporates a strong 15th-century keep. The lands were a property of the Glens, but passed to the Boswells and Sir Alexander Boswell of Balmuto was killed at the Battle of Flodden in 1513. The castle was slighted in the 1560s or '70s, although it was later restored and it is still occupied.

The castle is said to be haunted by the spirit of (a later) Sir Alexander Boswell: this Boswell was killed in a duel at Balmuto on 26 March 1822 by James Stewart of Dunearn, after Boswell had caricatured and insulted Stewart.

Map 4, 9L (Balmuto). Off B9157, 2.5 miles N of Burntisland, N of Meadowfield, Balmuto, Fife.

BALNAGOWN CASTLE

Balnagown Castle, an impressive Gothic mansion with towers and turrets, incorporates a much-altered tower house and dates from the 14th century. Balnagown was long a property of the Ross family and branches of them owned it until 1978. The Rosses were an unruly lot in medieval times.

Alexander Ross, 8th laird, terrorized the neighbouring properties until imprisonment in Tantallon Castle curtailed his activities. George, his son, was accused of murder and with helping Francis Stewart, 5th Earl of Bothwell, who – among other things – was accused of trying to sink James VI's ship by witchcraft. George's sister, Katherine – wife of Robert Munro of Foulis – was actually tried for witchcraft, incantation, sorcery and poisoning. Some of her friends were found guilty and executed, but at her own trial she packed the jury with her own people, the accusations were judged unproven, and she was freed.

It is not, however, one of the Ross family who supposedly haunts Balnagown. 'Black' Andrew Munro was a man believed guilty of many dastardly deeds. He was finally brought to account in 1522, and hanged from one of the windows off the Red Corridor of the castle. His ghost is said to haunt Balnagown, and to manifest itself to women, who he had liked to abuse in life: his female servants were made to thresh corn naked. Sounds of footsteps from unoccupied areas have also been recorded.

The castle is also thought to be haunted by a 'Grey Lady', the ghost of a young woman, clad in a grey dress with auburn hair and green eyes: a murdered 'Scottish princess'. Her apparition is said to have appeared in the dining room, then walked to the drawing room, and there vanished.

Both ghosts are recorded as having been witnessed in the 20th century.

Map 2, 7D (Balnagown). Off A9, 8 miles NE of Alness, Balnagown, Highland.
Cottages available to rent on the estate. (01862 843601 / www.balnagown.co.uk)

BALNAIN HOUSE, INVERNESS

ILLUS PAGE 26

Standing on the banks of the River Ness, Balnain House was built in 1722 for the Duff family, and was used as a field hospital by Hanoverian troops after the Battle of Culloden in 1746. The house was restored to accommodate a museum about Scotland's musical heritage, but this closed within a few years and the building is now home to the regional office of The National Trust for Scotland.

The building is said to have had a 'Green Lady', one story being that the ghost is the spirit of a girl who lost her husband or lover at Culloden. There was apparently a sighting of the bogle in 2000, when one of the staff saw a woman behind her when looking in a mirror in the ladies' toilets in the cellar bar. The apparition was described as being small and was dressed in an old-fashioned manner. The witness said the ghost appeared as if it was in black and white.

Map 2, 7F (Inverness). Off A82, 40 Huntly Street, Inverness, Highland.

BALVENIE CASTLE

ILLUS PAGE 26

In a pleasant and peaceful location, Balvenie Castle is a large ruinous courtyard castle, dating from the 13th to 17th centuries. The Comyns had a stronghold here, which was taken by the forces of Robert the Bruce in 1308. Balvenie was later held by the Douglases, by the Stewarts, by the Innes family, then by the Duffs. Mary, Queen of Scots, visited in 1562. The castle was garrisoned during Covenanting times and the Jacobite Risings.

There is more than one account of ghosts. The apparition of a woman, a 'White Lady', has reportedly been seen here. The phantom of a red-haired groom and two horses, with other disturbances, was apparently witnessed by a visitor in 1994. The horses were led across the courtyard but then disappeared, although sounds of them moving could still be heard. Other reported manifestations include a disembodied voice and the sounds of a flute playing when nobody is present.

Map 2, 9F (Balvenie). Off A941, N of Dufftown, Balvenie, Moray.
His Scot: Open Apr-Oct, daily. (01340 820121 / www.historic-scotland.gov.uk)

BALWEARIE CASTLE

Balwearie Castle is a ruinous old stronghold, dating from the 15th century, which may stand on the site of an earlier castle. It was a property of the Scotts until the 1690s, and may have been home to the infamous Sir Michael Scott. Scott is said to have been born at Aikwood in the Borders and to have studied at Oxford, Toledo and Padua, after which he became known as 'the Wizard' because of his alleged supernatural powers. He died in about 1250.

The ghost story relates to a later owner. Thomas Scott of Balwearie, Justice Clerk, died in 1539, and on the night of his death his apparition – with a company of devils – is said to have appeared to James V in his bed chamber at Linlithgow Palace. Scott apparently told the king that he was damned to everlasting hell for serving him.

Balwearie has been suggested as the site of the bloody events described in the old ballad 'Lamkin'. The mason who built the castle was not paid the agreed fee and took his revenge by murdering the son and wife of the house. The mason and a nurse, his accomplice, were executed on a gallows tree near Balwearie.

Map 4, 9L (Balwearie). Off B925, 2.5 miles SW of Kirkcaldy, Balwearie, Fife.

BANCHORY

The old part of the town is believed by some to be haunted by the apparition of a monk, which is said to have been seen in recent times. The spectre may be associated with the old monastery founded by St Ternan about 430. The town had long associations with the saint – he is reputedly buried at Banchory – and his head, bound books of gospels, and 'Ronnecht', a bell gifted by the Pope, were preserved here for many centuries until the Reformation, although they have now been lost.

Map 2, 11G (Banchory). Off A93, Banchory, Aberdeenshire.

BARBRECK HOUSE

Located in a prominent and picturesque spot, Barbreck House is an impressive classical mansion, dating from 1790, which is still occupied by the Campbells. Barbreck's Bone, a piece of elephant ivory which is now in the Museum of Scotland, was believed to be able to cure madness and was thought to have fallen from the skies.

A place near the house is said to be haunted by the apparition of a young woman, observed dressed and hooded in plaid and tartan sitting on a rock. The apparition is said to fade away should anyone approach too closely.

Map 3, 4K (Barbreck). Off A816, 4 miles N of Kilmartin, Argyll.

BARCALDINE CASTLE   ILLUS PAGE 35

Set in a fine location, Barcaldine Castle is a restored L-plan tower house which dates from the end of 16th century. The castle was built by Sir Duncan Campbell of Glenorchy, also known as 'Duncan of the Castles' and 'Black Duncan'. He held lands from Barcaldine to Taymouth in Perthshire, and built strongholds to secure his wide possessions. Barcaldine is still a property of the Campbells and, although the building was ruinous at one time, it was completely restored in 1896.

Harriet Campbell was the spinster sister of Sir Duncan Campbell third baronet, and a great lover of music. She died in the castle around the turn of the last century, and her ghost, a 'Blue Lady' has reputedly been seen in what was her room. It is also said that piano music can be heard on some windy nights.

Map 3, 4J (Barcaldine Castle). Off A828, 8 miles N of Oban, 4 miles N of Connel, Barcaldine, Argyll.
B&B accommodation available. (01631 720598 / www.barcaldinecastle.co.uk)

BARLINNIE PRISON, GLASGOW

There were once eight prisons in and around Glasgow, but all but two of these had closed by 1840. A new jail at Barlinnie was established, on what had been a farm, in 1882, and the original bell, which started and ended work on the farm, has been preserved. The prison was developed down the years, and takes prisoners from the west of Scotland who are on remand or who are serving sentences of less than four years, as well as longer-term prisoners before they are sent to other prisons.

There are stories that an apparition of a woman, dressed as if from Victorian times and carrying a lantern, has been seen outside the surgery wing and at a bricked-up entrance to the former execution block.

Map 4, 7M (Glasgow). Off A8 or A80, 81 Lee Avenue, Riddrie, Glasgow.
Prison. (0141 770 2000 / www.sps.gov.uk)

BARNBOUGLE CASTLE

Standing in the picturesque grounds of Dalmeny House, Barnbougle Castle dates from the 16th and 17th centuries, although there was an older stronghold on the site before the present building.

Barnbougle was held by the Mowbrays from the 12th century until 1615, and the story dates from their ownership. A ghostly hound is said to haunt the grounds of Barnbougle, and appears howling shortly before the laird of Barnbougle is to die. The story dates from the time of the Crusades and Sir Roger Mowbray, and this tale is reputedly the origin of 'Hound Point', just to the north-west of Barnbougle, and now a tanker berth. Sir Roger's favourite dog was not to accompany him on Crusade, but it was so distressed because its master was leaving without it that Sir Roger relented and took the faithful hound with him. Some months later the fearful howling of a dog was heard – and it was later found that this had happened at the same time that Sir Roger had died. From then on, the howling of a dog, and sometimes its phantom, was witnessed as a herald of a death in the family.

In 1662 Barnbougle was acquired by the Primrose family, and in 1815 they built the far more comfortable and impressive Dalmeny House. Barnbougle was allowed to fall into ruin, but was restored around 1880 by Archibald Philip Primrose, 5th Earl of Rosebery, who was Prime Minister from 1894-95.

Map 4, 9L (South Queensferry). Off B924, 2.5 miles E of South Queensferry, Edinburgh.

BEDLAY CASTLE

Bedlay Castle is said to be haunted by the ghost of John Cameron, Bishop of Glasgow, who (according to many accounts) died in suspicious circumstances about 1350. There was, however, no bishop of this name at that time: the story may refer to John Cameron who was bishop in 1426-46. An alternative identity has been suggested as John Campbell, one of the lairds, who died in the 1700s.

Hauntings in the house, including an apparition of a large bearded man, dressed in clerical robes, were recorded in the 1970s, and other manifestations are said to include heavy footsteps being heard coming from unoccupied areas, either going down corridors or pacing to and fro, and people being repeatedly touched by invisible hands.

In the 1880s a priest had been called in to exorcise the ghost, during a period of increased supernatural activity, but his attempts do not appear to have been successful.

The castle, an L-plan tower house, was built by the Boyds of Kilmarnock in the 16th century on the site of an older stronghold which had been held by the Bishops of Glasgow. The property later passed to the Campbells, and they built a mausoleum in the garden. Subsequently there were reports of apparitions around the castle and, when the mausoleum was relocated to Lambhill, the ghosts are said to have followed. Bedlay Castle, and six acres of grounds, were put up for sale in 2006 for offers of more than £750,000.

A further haunting is said to be the sounds of a spectral coach, heard approaching the back entrance of the castle. Reputedly the apparition of a girl then appears, which is followed by an eerie scream, and then the phantom fades away and the noises cease.

Map 4, 7L (Bedlay). Off A80, 3 miles SE of Kirkintilloch, Bedlay, Lanarkshire.

BELL STREET CAR PARK, DUNDEE

The car park was built in the 1960s on what had been a large burial ground. This had been opened in 1836 and which was in use for nearly 50 years – there is thought to have been some 10,000 people laid to rest here. When the burial ground was cleared, Bell Street and the surrounding area was inundated with hundreds of rats. Only one small part of the graveyard survives with a few original grave stones erected against the west wall.

The car park is reputed to be the scene of unexplained sounds, including half-heard sobs, wailing and cries.

Map 4, 10K (Dundee). Off A923 or A991, Bell Street, Dundee.
Car park.

BELL'S WYND, EDINBURGH

Bell's Wynd, one of the many closes to run off the Royal Mile, is named after John Bell, who was a brewer and owned property here; the Wynd later went to the Bishops of Dunkeld.

One of the dwellings on the first floor is said to be haunted, as is the close itself, reportedly by the phantom of a woman clad in white. The story goes that in the 18th century a woman living in the house was having an affair and, when her husband found out, he brutally murdered her. He then locked up the house and fled Edinburgh.

More than 20 years later, the house was broken into by a locksmith, who occupied the property above and wondered why this dwelling remained unoccupied. The poor locksmith was no doubt perturbed to see the apparition of a woman passing him in the hallway, and was even more so to then find the mortal remains, now a shrunken skeleton, of the woman in a bedroom. Another version of the story relates that it was both the woman and her lover who were murdered by her husband.

Map 4, 9L (Edinburgh). Off A1, Bell's Wynd, High Street, Edinburgh.

BEN MACDUI

The mountain and the surrounding area are reputedly haunted by the 'Grey Man of Ben MacDui'. The mountain, one of the highest in Britain, is situated in the Cairngorms and rises to a height of well over 4000 feet (1309 metres). There are many reports of unexplained footsteps following climbers when the hill is swathed in mist. Other stories are of a huge grey apparition, said to be ten foot in height. Reports of both footsteps and the apparition have often been recorded from 1890 until recent times.

Map 2, 8G (Ben Macdui). Off A9, 10 miles SE of Aviemore, Cairngorm Mountains, Highland.
Accessible weather permitting – long walk!

BENHOLM CASTLE

Standing above a deep ravine, Benholm Castle consists of a ruinous tower, dating from the 15th century, as well as a later mansion. The castle was built by the Lundies but later passed to the Ogilvies, then to the Keiths and to the Scotts.

The castle is believed to be haunted.

Map 2, 11H (Benholm). Off A92, 2 miles SW of Inchbervie, Aberdeenshire.

BERWICK CASTLE

Although now in England, Berwick was an important Scottish burgh by 1120, and had its own strong fortress. In 1296, at the onset of the Wars of Independence, it was seized by Edward I – and 16,000 men, women and children were slaughtered by the English. The 'Ragman Roll' was signed here that same year: the list of the many Scots, nobles and churchmen who paid homage to Edward; the streets were apparently still full of rotting corpses. Isabella Duff, Countess of Buchan, who had crowned Robert the Bruce (despite being married to a Comyn), was imprisoned for four years in a cage hung from the castle walls of Berwick.

One story tells that the ruins are haunted by the ghost of Edward I.

The Scots recaptured the burgh and castle in 1318, and it was fought over for many years until in 1482 when taken by the English for the last time. Much of the old castle was destroyed when the railway was built, and the station stands on the site of the great hall.

Map 4, 12M (Berwick). Off A1, Berwick-upon-Tweed, England.

BIEL

The ancient estate of Biel was a property of the Hamiltons, who were made Lords Belhaven in 1647, and the property was held by the family until 1958. John Hamilton, 2nd Lord Belhaven, was imprisoned for opposing the succession of James VII, and strongly opposed the Union of Parliaments. He died in 1708. There is a plaque on the outside of the house with the inscription in Latin: 'The first year of the betrayal of Scotland'. The house is still occupied, and dates mostly from the 19th century, although the building incorporates the basement of a 13th-century castle.

The grounds, and especially 'The Lady's Walk', are said to be haunted by Anne Bruce of Earlshall, the 'White Lady of Biel'. She was the wife of John Hamilton, 3rd Lord Belhaven. He was made Governor of Barbados, but he was drowned after his ship sank in 1721.

Anne is said to have been a great beauty and to have had very pale and translucent skin. The story goes that she became disenchanted with her husband after he was unfaithful to her, and took to walking the grounds of Biel by herself, even after the death of her husband.

Map 4, 11L (Biel). Off B6370, 3.5 miles W of Dunbar, East Biel, Lothian.
Groups (20-25) by appt only. (01620 860355)

BIGHOUSE

The large and imposing symmetrical mansion dates from 1765, and there is a walled garden, more than an acre in extent. This was a property of the Mackays of Bighouse, who held the lands from 1597, but the building is now used as an exclusive hotel and restaurant.

Bighouse is said in some stories to be haunted by a 'Green Lady', the spirit of a woman who hanged herself in one of the bedrooms at the end of the 19th century. The apparition is reputedly seen mostly in one room, and is said to have been observed walking through walls.

Map 2, 8A (Bighouse). Off A836, 14 miles W of Thurso, Bighouse, Sutherland.
Exclusive hotel and restaurant: accommodation available all year. (01641 531207 / www.bighouseestate.com)

BIRKHALL

The present small mansion of Birkhall dates from 1715, although there are later extensions, and it replaced an older residence or castle. The lands were originally known as Sterin, and were held by the Gordons. The property was sold to Prince Albert, consort of Queen Victoria, in 1848 – he also purchased nearby Balmoral. Birkhall was used by Elizabeth Bowes Lyon, the Queen Mother, until her death in 2002.

The grounds around Birkhall are reputed to be haunted by the 'White Lady of Sterin', a ghost which heralded deaths in the Gordons (or the resident family). A sighting was reported in 1901 before Queen Victoria died (although doubt was cast on the account); while another report in 1926 has the phantom going through the grounds before vanishing with a shriek into the River Muick.

Map 2, 9G (Birkhall). Off B976, 2 miles S and W of Ballater, on W side of the River Muick, Deeside, Aberdeenshire.

BIRKWOOD HOUSE

The former hospital incorporated Birkwood House, a large old Gothic mansion of five storeys. The house was probably built by the Tod family, who owned the property in the 19th century, but was then inhabited by the McKirdy family. From 1923 Birkwood was used as a psychiatric hospital, then known as the 'Institution for Mental Defectives', but this was recently closed. There are plans afoot to convert the mansion into a hotel and leisure facility, and build houses in the wooded grounds.

The building was said to be haunted. Activity is reported to have included footsteps being heard repeatedly coming from unoccupied areas, lights turning themselves off and on, and locked doors unlocking themselves. The smell of cigar smoke was apparently often witnessed near the Blue Staircase when nobody was smoking.

Map 4, 8N (Birkwood). Off B7078, to SW of Lesmahagow, Birkwood, Lanarkshire.

BIRNAM HOUSE HOTEL

In the picturesque village of Birnam, the hotel is an impressive castellated mansion with a large Baronial Hall and a tower with an unusual pagoda roof. The mansion was built around 1850 for Sir William Stewart, and the interior had to be restored after a fire of 1912. The building is now used as a hotel, although this may have closed recently.

The hotel is said by some to be haunted.

Map 4, 8J (Birnam). Off A9, Birnham, Dunkeld, Perthshire.

BISHOP'S PALACE, KIRKWALL

In the attractive burgh of Kirkwall and just across the road from the fine medieval cathedral, the ruinous Bishop's Palace consists of a rectangular block and impressive round tower. The building dates from the 12th century and a courtyard wall probably joined it to the nearby Renaissance Earl's Palace. The Bishop's Palace was the residence of the Bishops of Orkney from the 12th century, when the islands were held by the Norsemen. King Haakon Haakonson died here in 1263 after his defeat by the Scots at the Battle of Largs.

There are stories of an underground tunnel connecting the Bishop's Palace to the cathedral. This tunnel is said to be haunted by a ghostly piper, an unfortunate fellow sent to explore the subterranean passageway. He reputedly never returned, but at times phantom pipes are reputedly heard, skirling up from beneath the ground.

Map 2, 10D (Kirkwall). On A960, W of Kirkwall, Orkney.
His Scot: Open Apr-Oct, daily. (01856 871918 / www.historic-scotland.gov.uk)

BLACK BULL INN, KIRKINTILLOCH

On the High Street, the Black Bull Inn used to occupy the site of what is now the Tantra Nightclub. Some of the inn building, perhaps dating from 1731, is said to survive in the fabric of the nightclub, which was originally built as a cinema and then was used as a bingo hall.

A misty presence has reportedly been spotted more than once at the foot of stairs leading down to the fire exit at the rear of the building, and there are also accounts of a sinister black apparition, witnessed overlooking the dance floor and stage. Unexplained crashes and disembodied groans have also reputedly been heard in the building.

The story goes that a man who worked in the cinema in the 1920s or 1930s hanged himself in the upper part of the building, and it is his ghost who haunts the night-club.

Map 4, 7L (Kirkintilloch). Off A803, 17 High Street, Kirkintilloch, East Dunbartonshire.
Night club.

BLACKET HOUSE

Blacket House is a ruined L-plan tower house, dating from the 16th century, and this was a property of the unruly Bell family. The Bells of Blacket were chiefs, and they were warned about their unruly conduct in a royal letter of 1517, while the tower was sacked by the English in 1547. One of the family was the rejected suitor and the murderer of 'Fair Helen of Kirkconnel Lee' as related in the old ballad. He tried to shoot Helen's lover, Adam Fleming, but she took the bullet and was slain instead.

The building was said to be haunted by a ghost, known as the 'Bogle of Blacket House', also called 'Old Red-cap' or 'Bloody Bell'.

Map 4, 9P (Blacket). Off B722, 3 miles E of Ecclefechan, Blacket, Dumfries and Galloway.

BLACKNESS CASTLE   ILLUS PAGE 35

Standing on an outcrop of rock on a promontory in the Firth of Forth, Blackness is a grim and impressive courtyard castle, which was used as the state prison and has a long and eventful history, being besieged and sacked several times. The castle was built in the 15th century by the Crichton family, but was much modified in later centuries for artillery. In 1912 the castle was handed over to the care of the State, and a major programme of restoration and repair was carried out between 1926 and 1935. It is now in the care of Historic Scotland.

Some stories tell of unexplained banging or other sounds (such as furniture being dragged across the floor) coming from areas of the building which are unoccupied,

Barcaldine Castle (page 29)

Blackness Castle (page 34)

Blair Street Vaults (page 37)

Blair Street Vaults (page 37)

and there is an account of a visitor fleeing after being chased by the apparition of an angry 'knight'.

Map 4, 8L (Blackness). Off B903 or B9109, 4 miles NE of Linlithgow, 4 miles E of Bo'ness, Blackness, Falkirk.
His Scot: Open all year: Apr-Oct, daily; Nov-Mar, Sat-Wed, closed Thu & Fri; closed 25/26 Dec and 1/2 Jan. (01506 834807 / www.historic-scotland.gov.uk)

BLAIR STREET VAULTS, EDINBURGH   ILLUS PAGE 36

Described by some as the 'Most Haunted' place in Scotland, the vaults are con-tained within the foundations of the 19 stone arches of South Bridge, which span the dip over the Cowgate and was built in 1788. Tenements were built on each side of the bridge, rising many storeys, and the vaults were put to a variety of purposes, including workshops, storage, and dwellings places, but were eventually abandoned, except for use as air raid shelters during World War II. In the 1990s the vaults were cleared out and opened up for visitors, and there are many reports of bogles and supernatural activity.

The vaults are said to be haunted by at least nine ghosts. One is known as 'Mr Boots', and is described as being clad in a long blue frock coat with leather boots. This phantom is reputed to be an unpleasant spirit, resentful of intruders, and to have often been spotted or witnessed by many visitors, including by a party of 14 people and their guide, at the same time. This ghost is also accused of breathing whisky vapour on people, whispering obscenities, and blocking doorways or pushing past folk. A second bogle is alleged to be that of a boy, called Jack, who pulls on visitors' clothing, while a third is that of a cobbler, said to be a happy spirit, that watches visitors. There are also tales of a 'Lady in Black', a more sinister entity, that is said to focus on pregnant women, as well as a ghostly hound, a man garbed in a cloak and top hat, an old lady, and the apparition of a crouching naked man, observed floating just under the roof (it is thought that there was once a floor at that height).

Other manifestations are claimed to include blowing on the necks of folk and breathing sounds, disembodied footsteps, voices, growling and the sounds of an object been dragged along the floor, mysterious smells, stones being thrown at and scratches inflicted on visitors, people being pushed or jostled, sudden drops in temperature, and torches and lights stopping work without apparent cause. A heavy wooden church pew is also reported to have been smashed by ghostly means, and candles to have been thrown about.

Map 4, 9L (Edinburgh). Off A7, Blair Street, Edinburgh.
Ghost and paranormal tours. (0131 225 5445 / www.mercattours.com)

Paranormal investigations have been undertaken by Ghost Finders
(www.ghostfinders.co.uk) and in 2003/2004 by the Ghost Club (www.ghostclub.org.uk),
and in June 2003 and in October 2003 by Scottish Paranormal Investigations
(www.scottishparanormalinvestigations.co.uk)

Featured in Living TV's Most Haunted, series three (2003).
Featured in Living TV's Most Haunted Live (2006).
Featured in Living TV's Most Haunted, series eleven (2008).

BLANTYRE PRIORY

Perched on a steep bank of the Clyde opposite Bothwell Castle, little remains of the Augustinian priory, founded around 1240 by Patrick, Earl of Dunbar. The property passed to Walter Stewart of Minto in 1599 after the Reformation, and the Stewarts were made Lords Blantyre in 1606.

The Stewarts lived in the priory, but by 1606 Lady Blantyre fled with her daughters, leaving Lord Blantyre in the building. The reason given was the ghostly activities and unexplained noises that plagued the household at night.

Map 4, 7M (Blantyre). Off B758, 1.5 miles N of Blantyre, Lanarkshire.

BLEBO HOUSE

Blebo was long a property of the Trail family, and one of the family was Walter Trail, Bishop of St Andrews in 1385 and ambassador to France. The lands were sold to the Beatons in 1649, and in the 18th century they moved their seat to Blebo House, which stands in fine wooded policies and is still occupied.

A spectral coach being furiously driven by a headless coachman has reputedly been seen along the back drive of Blebo House, and some have suggested that this is another apparition associated with Cardinal David Beaton (although the Beatons did not hold the property until 100 years after his death).

Map 4, 10K (Blebo). Off B939, 3.5 miles E of Cupar, S of Kemback, Blebo, Fife.

BOADSBECK CASTLE

Nothing remains of an old tower house which stood here, a property of the Moffat family. The Moffats got into a long and costly feud with the powerful and warlike Johnstones, which led to the murder of the Moffat chief in 1557, and to the Moffats losing their lands in the first part of the 17th century.

Boadsbeck is said to have had a brownie, which came here after deserting the Johnstones of Wamphray (their tower was also known as Leithenhall). Some versions have the brownie going in the other direction, leaving Boadsbeck after being given inappropriate food, crying:

Ca', brownie, ca'! A' the luck o' Bodbeck's, Awa' to Leithenha'!

This may be a reference to the bitter feud with the Johnstones of Wamphray (also see that entry), although the Johnstones managed to lose Wamphray after they got involved in the Jacobite Rising of 1745-46.

Map 4, 9O (Boadsbeck). Off A708, 5 miles NE of Moffat, to S of Moffat Water, Bodesbeck, Dumfries and Galloway.

BOAT HOTEL, BOAT OF GARTEN

Set in a lovely spot near to the River Spey (and overlooking the Strathspey steam railway), the Boat Hotel is a comfortable and welcoming establishment.

The hotel is said by some to be haunted. The story goes that a man intervened when one of his companions was attacked and was himself killed, and that his ghost has been witnessed in the building.

Map 2, 8G (Boat of Garten). Between A95 and B970, 6 miles NE of Aviemore, Boat of Garten, Highland.
Hotel. (01479 831258 / www.boathotel.co.uk)

BOGLE STONE, PORT GLASGOW

Standing by the road between Port Glasgow and Kilmacolm, the Bogle Stone is a large shattered block of rock, which was formerly much larger than it is today, rising to some eight or nine foot high and being large enough to seat a large company. The stone was associated with a bogle, in this case an unpleasant spirit, which was often seen lurking by the stone and frightening anyone approaching the stone. Despite this, the stone became a place of picnics and trysts. Whether because of this supernatural association or more prosaically to furnish stone to build dykes, the Bogle Stone was blown up by a minister, greatly reducing it, although it was later somewhat rebuilt.

Map 3, 6L (Port Glasgow). Off A761, to N of Port Glasgow, Renfrewshire.
Access at all reasonable times.

BONCHESTER BRIDGE

The road here, the A6088, runs north-west from the English border on towards Hawick, crossing the Rule Water at Bonchester Bridge. The hamlet is overlooked by Bonchester Hill, on the summit of which is a large hill fort.

There are stories that ghostly Roman soldiers have been seen approaching Bonchester Bridge, marching west along the road.

Map 4, 10O (Bonchester Bridge). On A6088, 6 miles E of Hawick, Bonchester Bridge, Borders.

BONSHAW TOWER

Bonshaw is a striking tower house of three storeys with a parapet, which dates from the 16th century. There is a Georgian mansion house adjacent to the tower.

Bonshaw is the seat of the Irvine or Irving family. William de Irvine was armour bearer to Robert the Bruce, and he was granted Drum in Aberdeenshire as reward for long service. Bonshaw was sacked in 1544 by the English, but twice successfully withstood sieges by Lord Maxwell in 1585. James VI was entertained here three years later.

The old tower is said to be haunted by a daughter of the house, who reputedly was thrown from the top of the tower to her death. The lovestruck lass had wanted to marry one of the Maxwells, but such a marriage was, of course, out of the question as the two families feuded. Her ghost has not apparently been seen for many years, but there are reports of some mysterious episodes in the master bedroom, such as the door handle turning by itself and a dog apparently transfixed by something moving when there was nothing there.

Map 4, 9P (Bonshaw). Off M74, 5 miles NE of Annan, Bonshaw, Dumfries and Galloway.

BORTHWICK CASTLE   ILLUS PAGE 41

One of the most impressive castles in Scotland, Borthwick Castle is a massive looming U-plan tower house, rising to 110 foot high with walls up to 14 foot thick in places. The Great Hall is one of the finest in the country and has a massive canopied fireplace. The castle, now a hotel, was apparently recently put up for sale for offers of more than £3 million.

The castle was built by Sir William Borthwick in 1430. The tomb of Borthwick is in nearby Borthwick Church which is open to the public - and there are two stone effigies, thought to be the best preserved in Scotland, and to be of Sir William and of his wife, Beatrix Sinclair, daughter of the Earl of Orkney. The effigies were painted and gilded when first carved.

Mary, Queen of Scots, and James Hepburn, Earl of Bothwell, stayed at the castle in 1567. Bothwell was Mary's third husband, but Mary had to flee, disguised as a pageboy, as her enemies attempted to besiege her here. It is recorded that her apparition, garbed as a man, has been seen at Borthwick.

A second, nastier tale concerns a local girl, called Ann Grant, who was apparently made pregnant by one of the Borthwick lords. The poor young woman, heavy with child, was seized, slashed across the abdomen with a sword, and then left to die in her own blood, in what is now the Red Room. A modern visitor to the castle reported how he had seen a vision of the murder, as did a previous owner.

Manifestations in the Red Room are said to include the temperature suddenly dropping, unexplained scratchings being heard on the inside of the door, as well as disembodied footsteps on the turnpike stair from the room. There is also an account of a heavy fire door opening by itself one night and, during a business conference, weeping and wailing was apparently heard coming from an empty part of the castle. It is believed that one of the previous owners had the Red Room exorcised, but apparently to no effect.

A third ghost is said to be that of a 'chancellor' of the castle who was executed by being burnt to death after having being caught embezzling money from the Borthwicks.

Map 4, 10M (Borthwick). Off A7, 2 miles SE of Gorebridge, Borthwick, Midlothian.
Hotel. (01875 820514 / www.borthwickcastlehotel.co.uk)

A paranormal investigation was undertaken in January 2007 by Ghost Finders (www.ghostfinders.co.uk/borthwick_castle.html) and in February 2008 by Scottish Society of Paranormal Investigation and Analysis (www.sspia.co.uk)

BRACO CASTLE

Braco Castle is a plain tower house of the 16th century, to which has been added extensions and additions, now making the building U-plan. Braco was a property of the Graham Earls of Montrose, one of whom was created a baronet of Braco in 1625. The last of the Grahams to live here died in 1790, and the property later passed to the Smythes. There are fine policies around the castle, as well as woodland and a partly walled garden.

The old part of Braco Castle is said to be haunted, and doors are reputed to open by themselves. Dogs are said to become unusually fearful on the staircase.

Map 4, 8K (Braco). Off A822, 6 miles N of Dunblane, Braco, Perthshire.
Gardens open Feb-Oct. (www.gardensofscotland.org)

BRAEMAR CASTLE   ILLUS PAGE 42

Located in a rugged, mountainous area of Scotland, Braemar Castle is an impressive L-plan tower house, that stands in a strategic position. The castle was built by the Erskine Earls of Mar in 1628, and has a massive iron yett (gate) and an unlit and unventilated pit prison, which measures just 12 by 6 foot. The property later passed to the Farquharsons, when the Erskines were forfeited following the 1715 Jacobite Rising, with whose descendants it remains.

Borthwick Castle (page 39)

Borthwick Castle (page 39)

Braemar Castle (page 40)

*Brodick
Castle
(page 45)*

*Brodie Castle
(page 46)*

42

The castle was captured and burnt out by John Farquharson of Inverey (see that entry), the 'Black Colonel'. His bogle is said to haunt Braemar Castle, leaving a lighted candle, perhaps as a reminder of his torching of the place.

One story is that Braemar is visited by the ghost of a young, blonde-haired woman. A couple on their honeymoon were staying in the castle, during the second half of the 19th century. Early in the morning the husband left to go hunting, but his wife woke later, and (not knowing about the hunting) believed she has been abandoned: the silly lass was rather innocent and thought that she had so displeased her new husband that he had spurned her. In despair, the poor woman threw herself from the battlements. Her ghost is said to haunt the castle, searching for her husband. The apparition reputedly was sighted in 1987, and it is thought that she only appears to those who have recently been married. Ghostly footsteps, the light tread of a woman, have also been reported.

Map 2, 8G (Braemar). On A93, 0.5 miles NE of Braemar, Kincardine and Deeside.
Open May-Oct, Sat & Sun. (01339 741600 / www.braemarscotland.co.uk/ visiting_braemar/Braemar%20castle.htm)

BRAHAN CASTLE

Once a splendid building, Brahan Castle was the seat of the Mackenzies of Brahan, Earls of Seaforth, but was demolished in the 1950s

The Mackenzies lost everything as foretold by the Brahan Seer, Kenneth Mackenzie (so called because the Mackenzies of Brahan were his patrons).

The episode dates back to about 1670. Isabella, 3rd Countess of Seaforth, wanted to know why her husband remained in Paris, and consulted Kenneth. She was furious when she was told that her husband had been dallying with a French woman, accused Kenneth of witchcraft, and ordered him to be burnt in a barrel of tar on Chanonry Point. A similarly ungrateful response to unwelcome news was suffered by Kitty Rankie at Abergeldie (also see that entry).

Before he died, presumably in some discomfort, Kenneth prophesied that the last MacKenzie chief would follow his sons to the grave, deaf and dumb, and that one of his daughters would kill the other. This all seems to have come true: the last chief did become deaf through illness and was finally too weak to speak after seeing his four sons predecease him. His eldest daughter succeeded him, but a carriage she was driving, near Brahan, overturned and killed her sister.

A ford of the Conon River was reputedly frequented by a kelpie or water sprite, who tried to drown the unwary.

Map 1, 6F (Brahan). Off A835, 3.5 miles SW of Dingwall, Brahan, Highland.

BREDA

The present mansion of Breda (pronounced 'Brid-da', with the emphasis on the second syllable) is a baronial pile, dating from the end of the 19th century. It has been refurbished as part of a development, and houses have been built in the grounds. The adjoining Broadhaugh House, which dated from the 17th century, was demolished in 1963. The lands were held by the Forbeses, but they were sold to the MacLeans in 1892, and they built the present mansion.

Breda was reputedly haunted, although the activity appears to have taken place in the now gone Broadhaugh House.

Map 2, 10G (Breda). Off A980, 1.5 miles W and N of Alford, Breda, Aberdeenshire.

BRIDGE CASTLE

Standing on a rocky outcrop, Bridge Castle consists of a substantial tower of three storeys and an attic, with later additions and extensions. The property was owned by the Stewarts at one time, but was sold to William, Lord Livingstone, in the 1580s. The Livingstone family became Earls of Linlithgow, but were forfeited for their part in the Jacobite Rising of 1715, and the property passed to the Hopes. The castle was remodelled and enlarged in 1871, was used as a hotel for some years, but has since been divided into separate residences.

The building is said to be haunted by a 'Grey Lady'.

Map 4, 8M (Bridge). Off B8084, 1.5 miles N of Armadale, Bridge Castle, West Lothian.

BRIDGEND HOUSE HOTEL, CALLANDER

Bridgend House Hotel, a long mock-Tudor timbered building, is located in Bridgend, the oldest part of the holiday-town of Callander. There was once a ferry here over the River Teith, but a bridge was built after the Jacobite Rising of 1745-46. The house may date from as early as the 17th century, although it had to be rebuilt after being damaged when a Spitfire crashed into it during World War II.

The hotel is said to be haunted. The story goes that the building was constructed over what had been a public path to The Meadows, and the ghostly apparitions of people who had used the route can be still be seen, although now wandering through the hotel's chambers, corridors and walls.

Map 4, 7K (Callander). By A81 near junction with A84, Bridgend, Callander, Stirling. **Hotel. (01877 330130)**

BRIDGEND, DALKEITH

Bridgend, to the south of Dalkeith, is the scene of a poisoning and a ghost story, a murky plot worthy of Agatha Christie's great Belgian sleuth.

Charles B. Hutchinson owned a house at Bridgend, and on 3 February 1911 he celebrated his silver wedding anniversary with a group of friends. The party was going well until the coffee was served, at which point most of the guests, and the hosts, fell violently ill. That night Hutchinson died and one of his guests, Alexander Clapperton, a grocer and wine merchant from Musselburgh, perished soon afterwards, while others were made seriously ill.

Suspicion soon fell on John Hutchinson, Charles's son, as he was a chemist and he had served the coffee. It was found that the party had been poisoned using prussic acid but, before John could be taken into custody, he poisoned himself at a hotel in Guernsey (in the presence of the police) and died in a few moments.

The motive for the poisoning appears to be that John was a rival in the affections for a local girl with Clapperton.

John's ghost is then said to have begun haunting the house at Bridgend.

Map 4, 9M (Dalkeith). On B703, to S of Dalkeith, by River South Esk, Bridgend, Midlothian.

BRIMS CASTLE

Brims Castle is a ruinous L-plan tower house of three storeys and a garret, which has a walled courtyard with a moulded gateway enclosing ranges of later buildings. The lands were a property of the Sinclairs of Dunbeath and, although the castle was occupied into the 20th century, it is now derelict and roofless.

Brims is said to have a 'White Lady', the ghost of the daughter of James Sinclair of Uttersquoy. The attractive young woman was the lover of Patrick Sinclair of Brims, but the story goes that he tired of her, murdered her, and then hid her body.

Map 2, 8A (Brims). Off A836, 5 miles W and N of Thurso, Caithness, Brims, Highland.

BROADFORD HOTEL

The hotel, which was established in 1611 and is in a fine building in the village overlooking Broadford Bay, is said to be haunted by the apparition of a house-keeper; in some of the rooms a 'presence' has been reported. The apparition is recorded as being shadowy and ill-defined, like a mist, and the bogle is reputed to be looking for its favourite chair. The same ghost, or perhaps another, is also re-ported to have been spotted on the stair. Other manifestations include the moving of objects, such as ladders, chairs and lamps.

After the Battle of Culloden in 1746, Bonnie Prince Charlie was a fugitive from the forces of Butcher Cumberland for some months. He was sheltered on Skye, after being helped by Flora MacDonald, and was then aided by the chief of the MacKin-nons. As a reward, Charlie gave the chief of that clan the recipe for Drambuie, a whisky liqueur, although the original recipe apparently should have been for cognac instead of whisky. This event is believed to have taken place at the hotel.

Map 1, 3F (Broadford). On A850, Broadford, Skye.
Hotel. (01471 822204 / www.broadfordhotel.co.uk)

BRODICK CASTLE   ILLUS PAGE 42

Standing on a magnificent spot overlooking Brodick Bay and the Firth of Clyde, Brodick Castle, an ancient stronghold but much extended and remodelled in later centuries, was a property of the Hamiltons for many centuries. The castle has a long and turbulent history, being sacked on several occasions, and it was occupied by Cromwell's troops in the 1650s. In more peaceful times, extensive additions were made in 1844 by the architect James Gillespie Graham, when the 11th Duke married Princess Marie of Baden. In 1958 Brodick passed to the NTS.

A 'Grey Lady', clad in grey with a large white collar, is said to haunt the older part of the castle, her spirit possibly that of one of three women starved to death in the dungeons around 1700 because they had the plague. Another version is that a serv-ant lass committed suicide at the Old Quay, below the castle, after becoming preg-nant by one of the Cromwellian garrison. Whatever the story, her apparition is said to have been seen many times.

The spectre of a man dressed in a green velvet coat and light-coloured breeches has allegedly been witnessed in the 17th-century library.

A white stag is said to be seen when members of the resident family are near death, and this event has supposedly been recorded several times.

Map 3, 5N (Brodick). Off A841, 1.5 miles N of Brodick, Cladach, Brodick Castle, Isle of Arran, Ayrshire.
NTS: Castle open Apr-Oct, Sun-Thu (closed Mon-Wed); country park open all year.
(01770 302202 / www.nts.org.uk)

A paranormal investigation was undertaken in July 2003 and in February 2005 by Scottish Paranormal Investigations (www.scottishparanormalinvestigations.co.uk)

BRODIE CASTLE

ILLUS PAGE 42

Brodie Castle, on land held by the Brodie family from 1160, consists of a large 16th-century Z-plan tower house, with extensive additions. The castle was renovated in 1980 after passing to The National Trust for Scotland, and the garden has a fine daffodil collection.

The castle also has a ghost story, possibly regarding Lady Margaret Duff, who was the wife of James Brodie, the then chief. In 1786 she fell asleep in front of the fire, her clothes were set alight, and she burned to death. An apparition of a woman was reported in the nursery room in 1992.

Disturbances, including footsteps and other noises coming from a locked study, were also reported on the night that Hugh, 23rd Brodie of Brodie, died in 1889, but nothing has been recorded since then.

The skeleton of a small child was found when a turnpike stair, from one of the corner turrets, was being renovated. The bones are kept in a glass-fronted cabinet in the Charter Room.

Map 2, 8E (Brodie). Off A96, 4.5 miles W of Forres, Brodie, Moray.
NTS: Open Apr, daily; May-Jun, Sun-Thu; Jul-Aug, daily; Sep-Oct, Sun-Thu (closed Mon-Wed); grounds open all year, daily. (01309 641371 / www.nts.org.uk)

BRODIE'S CLOSE, EDINBURGH

Brodie's Close, which dates from the 17th century and is on Castle Hill (the Royal Mile), is reputedly haunted by the bogle of Deacon William Brodie, whose apparition is said to have been sighted in the close, with a lantern in one hand, a bunch of keys in the other.

Brodie became infamous in Edinburgh as (by day) he was a respectable and respected cabinet maker, city councillor and deacon (president) of the Incorporation of Wrights and Masons, while (by night) he was a burglar and thief with two mistresses, five children and a gambling habit to maintain. He was exposed after a botched job when one of his accomplices was captured and turned against him. Brodie fled to Holland, but he was captured and was returned to Edinburgh where he was executed at the tolbooth in 1788. Brodies's double life is believed to have inspired Robert Louis Stevenson to write *The Strange Case of Dr Jekyll and Mr Hyde*; Stevenson's father had furniture that had been made by Brodie.

Map 4, 9L (Edinburgh). Off A1, Brodie's Close, Lawnmarket (Royal Mile), Edinburgh.

BROOMHILL

Nothing remains of the mansion of Broomhill, a property of the Hamiltons from 1473. The house later passed to the McNeil-Hamiltons of Raploch, but it was demolished after a fire in 1943.

Broomhill was reputedly haunted by a 'Black Lady', seen in both the house and in the policies. The story goes that a beautiful Indian woman, either a servant or a princess, disappeared about 1900, and it is believed that she may have been murdered. She was believed to be the mistress of Captain Henry McNeil-Hamilton, who himself died in 1924.

The house was featured in a television programme *Tonight*, with Fyfe Robertson, in the 1960s, when an exorcism was performed. Her ghost, however, is also said to have been witnessed in nearby Applebank Inn (see that entry).

Other ghosts in the area include a phantom coach and horses, and the apparition of a young lad, seen apparently fishing.

Map 4, 8M (Millheugh). Off B7078, 0.5 miles W of Larkhall, Broomhill, Lanarkshire.

BROOMHILL HOSPITAL, KIRKINTILLOCH

The original house was built as a mansion in the 19th century, but the building was converted into a hospital in 1875 through the generosity of Beatrice Clugston and other philanthropists. Beatrice was the daughter of a wealthy Glasgow industrialist, and she founded the Dorcas Society, which helped poor people who had become ill. She died in 1888, and a memorial to her was built in the grounds. The hospital was closed in the 1990s, and the buildings became derelict: there are plans to build some 200 houses in the grounds and renovate the house as luxury apartments.

The hospital is reported to be haunted by a 'Grey Lady', said by some to be the phantom of Beatrice Clugston, stories dating from as early as the 1920s. The bogle is said to have been witnessed on the stairs and in long corridors, and to have been concerned with the welfare of the hospital. Manifestations are said to have intensified when a portrait of Beatrice was stolen from the house in 1994; this was eventually recovered and is now located in the Auld Kirk Museum in Kirkintilloch.

An alternative identity for the bogle has been given as that of a nurse, who died of typhoid in 1912.

Other manifestations were recorded, including footsteps coming from an area where nobody was present, doors closing by themselves, and disembodied voices and unexplained sounds.

Map 4, 7L (Kirkintilloch). Off A803, to N of Kirkintilloch, Broomhill, Lanarkshire.

BRUNTSFIELD HOUSE

Now part of James Gillespie's School and surrounded by later buildings, Bruntsfield House is a grand Z-plan tower house, dating from the 16th century or earlier. Bruntsfield was held by the Lauders and Sir Alexander Lauder, Provost of Edinburgh, was killed at the Battle of Flodden in 1513. The property was later sold to the Fairlies, and then went to the Warrenders. In 1880 the house was surrounded by 75 acres of parkland, but in 1935 the property was sold to the city of Edinburgh and was used as the school. James Gillespie's had been located from around 1800 at nearby Wrychtishousis (see separate entry) in what is now Gillespie's Crescent.

Bruntsfield House, especially the upper storeys, are said to be haunted by a 'Green Lady'. The tale goes that the remains of a murdered woman (and sometimes her child) were found in a secret room which had been sealed up, the room only being discovered when the number of windows on the outside of the building did not match that on the outside. It is said the floor was blood stained, ashes were in the grate, and a skeleton was later discovered, concealed beneath the floor by the window.

The details have some similarities to that of the ghost story at Wrychtishousis, and the bogle tale may have come, along with the school, to Bruntsfield. 'Green Ladies', however, are not uncommon.

Map 4, 9L (Edinburgh). Off A702, Bruntsfield, Edinburgh.
School. (0131 447 1900 / www.jghs.edin.sch.uk)

BUCCLEUCH ARMS HOTEL, ST BOSWELLS

Standing beside the green in the pleasant village of St Boswells, the Buccleuch Arms Hotel was built by the 5th Duke of Buccleuch to accommodate his friends and guests when he was hunting in the Borders (and hence the name of the hotel). The Buccleuch Arms is now a fine and welcoming establishment.

The building is said to be haunted by a ghost, known as 'Peter', believed to be the last man hanged in Jedburgh, sometime in the 1950s, although the bogle is said to be mischievous rather than frightening. His apparition has been reportedly been seen on several occasions, including at Hogmanay 2005, and other activity is reputedly the hiding and moving of objects.

Map 4, 10N (St Boswells). On A68, 3 miles SE of Melrose, The Green, St Boswells, Borders. **Hotel. (01835 822243 / www.buccleucharmshotel.co.uk)**

A paranormal investigation was undertaken in February 2008 by the Borders Paranormal Group (www.bordersparanormal.co.uk).

BUCHANAN CASTLE

Buchanan Castle, a huge impressive castellated ruin dating from the 1850s, incorporates an old castle. As the name suggests, it was held by the Buchanans, but the property passed to the Grahams of Montrose in 1682. The property was finally sold in 1925 and the building was used as a hotel and than as a military hospital during World War II. Rudolf Hess, Hitler's deputy, was treated here after flying to Scotland in 1941. The building was unroofed in the 1950s (to avoid paying taxes) and is a consolidated ruin; a golf course occupies much of the formerly landscaped grounds (which had been remodelled by Capability Brown).

Buchanan is reputed to be haunted. Manifestations are said to consist of an unexplained gasping sound, heard during summer nights.

Map 4, 7L (Buchanan). Off B807, 0.5 miles W of Drymen, Buchanan, Stirlingshire.

BUCKHOLM TOWER

Buckholm, a ruinous tower house built by the Pringles in the 16th century, has a gruesome story associated with it.

During the Covenanting troubles of the late 17th century, the laird of the time was a cruel man and spent his time persecuting those attending illegal conventicles – the open-air services of Covenanters. Pringle captured several Covenanters, took them back to the dungeon at Buckholm, and there impaled them on hooks hanging from the ceiling (the hooks are still said to ooze ghostly blood and to move by themselves).

Pringle, however, was cursed by the wife of one of his victims, and afterwards lived in great terror, as if pursued by ghostly hounds. Pringle's ghost has reputedly been seen, running from a pack of dogs on the anniversary of his death, and screams and cries are supposedly heard, coming from the dungeon of the tower, on occasion.

Map 4, 10N (Buckholm). Off A7, 1 mile NW of Galashiels, Buckholm, Borders.

Paranormal investigations were undertaken by Spectre (www.freewebs.com/ukspectre)

BUCKLAND GLEN

The glen is said to be haunted by a headless 'White Lady', witnessed near a bridge over the Buckland Burn. The story goes that the woman was murdered by robbers in the glen, and that her ghost then returned, possibly to sometimes help those travelling in the area avoid a similar fate to her own.

Map 4, 7Q (Buckland Glen). Off B727, 1 mile SE of Kirkcudbright, Buckland Glen, Dumfries and Galloway.

BUCK'S HEAD HOTEL, STRATHAVEN

Buck's Head Hotel is said to be haunted by the bogle of a girl, witnessed in different areas of the hotel, and said to appear be about 16 years of age. One sighting was apparently made at the foot of the stairs, when the ghost was described as being clad in a white blouse, long dark skirt and a large hat. There is more than one version of the story behind the haunting. One goes that the poor girl found herself pregnant and hanged herself in one of the rooms, another that again she got pregnant but her lover put a rope around her neck, put her on the back of a horse, and then caused the horse to gallop off, throttling the girl.

The second phantom is said to be that of a very young girl, perhaps 3 or 4, who is reputedly still searching for her one-eyed cat.

A third ghost is reputed to be that of a former owner.

Other manifestations are said to include a television switching itself on and off, a jukebox playing by itself, unexplained footsteps, shadowy apparitions witnessed in the bar area, and a female member of staff being slapped by an invisible hand, leaving a print on her face.

Map 4, 7M (Strathaven). Off A71, 16 Townhead Street, Strathaven, Lanarkshire. **Hotel. (01357 520184)**

A paranormal investigation was undertaken in March 2008 by West of Scotland Paranormal Research (www.wospr.com/buckshead.htm)

BUNCHREW HOUSE   ILLUS PAGE 51

Standing in 20 acres of landscaped grounds on the banks of the Beauly Firth, Bunchrew House is a fine partly-pinkwashed baronial mansion, dating from the 17th century and later, although incorporating an earlier castle or dwelling of 1505.

Bunchrew was a property of the Frasers of Lovat, but was sold to the Forbeses of Culloden in 1622, one of whom, Duncan Forbes, was Lord President of the Court of Session and died in 1747. The property was bought back by the Frasers in 1842, and the house has been used as a hotel since 1986.

The house is said to be haunted by the ghost of Isobel, wife of Kenneth Mackenzie, 12th chief of Mackenzie, although the ghost is reputed to be a gentle spirit. A portrait of Isobel hangs in the hotel.

Map 2, 7F (Bunchrew). Off A862, 3 miles W of Inverness, S shore of Beauly Firth, Highland. **Hotel. (01463 234917 / www.bunchrew-inverness.co.uk)**

BURLEIGH CASTLE

Although once a large and imposing castle, Burleigh Castle now consists of a ruined four-storey tower joined by a surviving section of courtyard wall, with a gate, to a corner tower. Burleigh was a property of the Balfours of Burleigh from 1446. In 1707

49

Robert Balfour, Master of Burleigh, fell in love with a young servant girl and was sent abroad to forget her. On leaving, he swore if she married, he would return and kill her husband. She married Henry Stenhouse, the schoolmaster of Inverkeithing, and Balfour duly returned and then shot and killed the poor man. Burleigh fled, but was captured, tried and sentenced to death by the axe. He managed to escape, however, by changing clothes with his sister, and he fled to the continent. He fought for the Jacobites in the 1715 Rising, after which the family were forfeited. Burleigh died unmarried in 1757.

The castle is said to be haunted by a 'Grey Lady', known as 'Grey Mary' or 'Grey Maggie', said to be the ghost of Lady Margaret Balfour.

Map 4, 9K (Burleigh). On A911, 1.5 miles N of Kinross, Burleigh, Perthshire.
His Scot: Access from Apr-Sep: keys available locally. (www.historic-scotland.gov.uk)

BURNETT ARMS HOTEL, KEMNAY

The Burnett Arms, built in the late 19th century and formerly the station hotel (although the railway is long gone), is an atmospheric and comfortable hotel.

The building is said to be haunted by the phantom of a woman wearing a pink wedding dress, spotted most often in the lounge bar, and believed to be the ghost of a former landlady, Maggie Duffton, who died in 1934. The story circulated that Maggie was buried in a walled-up vault in the basement of the hotel, and that in a second coffin was all her accumulated money. In 2008, however, the vault was broken into, and nothing was found.

The apparition, however, is reported to have been seen on several occasions, including when a member of staff was cleaning at night and saw a phantom appearing through a locked door.

Map 2, 11G (Kemnay). Off B993, 3 miles W of Kintore, Bridge Road, Kemnay, Aberdeenshire.
Hotel. (01467 642208 / www.burnett-arms.co.uk)

BUSTA HOUSE   ILLUS PAGE 51

Located on Muckle Roe to the north of the mainland of Shetland, Busta (pronounced 'Boosta') House is a tall, harled and white-washed mansion, set in a picturesque, tranquil location with its own harbour and extensive policies. The house is believed to date from 1588, but was remodelled and added to in 1714, and then again in 1984. It is now a comfortable and widely acclaimed hotel.

Busta was a property of the Giffords of Busta, who held much property on Shetland. They were descended from a Scots minister, and made their fortune as merchants and fish exporters. In 1714 Thomas Gifford married Elizabeth Mitchell, and they extended the house at this time. Gifford was wealthy and prominent in Shetland, and was made Steward Depute as well as Chamberlain. But tragedy was to follow.

Gifford had four sons, but on 14 May 1748 they were all tragically drowned in a boating accident on Busta Voe. This left Gifford without a male heir, until Barbara Pitcairn, a pretty maid (or guest, depending on the version), said that she had been secretly married to John, the oldest son, and was pregnant by him. She had papers to prove the marriage took place, and when she had a son, Gideon, he was adopted as Gifford's heir. Barbara was shunned, however, by Gifford and his wife, and she was forced to leave Busta. She died at just 36 in the house of a poor relation in Lerwick. It is said that her sad ghost haunts the building, searching for her son.

Bunchrew House (page 49)

Busta House (page 50)

Caisteal Camus (page 54)

Cara (page 57)

Castle Coeffin (page 60)

Gideon himself had no direct heirs, and the resulting lawsuits about who should inherit the property left the estate impoverished.

There have also apparently been several sightings of an apparition in the Linga room. The ghost is said to be a grey-haired woman, in a brown dress and lace cap. It does not appear to be Barbara (as she was young when she died) and it may be the bogle of Elizabeth Mitchell, wife of Thomas Gifford.

Other manifestations are reported to include the sound of heavy footsteps coming from the Foula Room when unoccupied, reported by a guest in the room below. Lights and other electrical equipment have also turned themselves off and on. Disturbances are said to be more prevalent in May, around the anniversary of the death of the Gifford brothers.

Map 2, 11B (Busta). Off A970, 10 miles NW of Lerwick, Busta, Brae, Muckle Roe, Shetland. **Hotel. (01806 522506 / www.bustahouse.com)**

BYRE THEATRE, ST ANDREWS

The theatre was converted from a byre in 1933, but this was demolished in 1970 and a new venue was found for the theatre. This building was itself closed in 1996 for a major renovation to provide increased facilities, and the refurbished theatre hosts music, drama, dance and comedy.

The theatre was said to be haunted by a ghost known as 'Charlie'. Manifestations consisted of cold feelings on the stairs leading to the Green Room, and the impression that a person was pushing past when nobody was apparently present.

Map 4, 10K (St Andrews). Off A917, Abbey Street, St Andrews, Fife. **Theatre with bar and bistro. (01334 475000 / www.byretheatre.com)**

CAIRNEYFLAPPET CASTLE, STRATHMIGLO

Nothing remains of Cairneyflappet Castle, which stood to the east of Strathmiglo and had a large moat. A possession of the Scott family, the castle is believed to have been quickly and poorly built, earning it the nickname 'Cairneyflappet' after a visit by James V. The castle was demolished in 1734, and the town hall steeple was built from its remains.

Cairneyflappet Castle is said to have had a brownie, which is reputed to have stolen food from the stores.

Map 4, 9K (Strathmiglo). Off A912, 1.5 miles SW of Auchtermuchty, E of Strathmiglo, Fife.

CAIRNSMORE

Cairnsmore is an attractive symmetrical mansion, rising to three storeys, the main entrance reached by a flight of stairs. The house dates from the 1740s and was held by the Stewarts of Cairnsmore in 1814.

The story goes that at one time the building was haunted by the apparition of a woman in a long grey dress.

Map 4, 7P (Cairnsmore). Off A75, 3.5 miles E of Newton Stewart, Cairnsmore, Dumfries and Galloway.

CAISTEAL CAMUS

ILLUS PAGE 52

Standing in a picturesque location on a steep headland of the Sound of Sleat, Caisteal Camus is a very ruinous stronghold of the MacLeods, and then of the MacDonalds. The castle was still occupied in 1632, but by 1689 had been abandoned and was decaying, much of the stone being used for the nearby farm. The castle has apparently recently been put up for sale.

Caisteal Camus is said to have had a 'Green Lady', a gruagach, a spirit who was associated with the fortunes of the families who owned the site. If good news was to come the gruagach would appear happy, but if there was bad news she would weep and look sad. The place is also said to have had a glaistig, who was particularly concerned with looking after cattle.

Map 1, 3G (Caisteal Camus). Off A851, 3.5 miles N of Armadale, Isle of Skye, Highland.

CAISTEAL NA NIGHINN RUAIDHE, LOCH AVICH

On an island in Loch Avich, not much remains of an old stronghold called in Gaelic, Caisteal na Nighinn Ruaidhe ('castle of the red-haired girl'), which dates from the 13th century and was held by the Campbells.

The story goes that, when the castle had just been completed, a red-haired serving girl found out about a plan to kill the mason who had constructed the building (thereby saving the owner the money spent in its construction). To keep the girl from betraying the plot, she was thrown from the top of the building and was killed. Her angry ghost is said to have then begun to haunt the castle.

Map 3, 4K (Loch Avich). Off A816 at Kilmelford, 15 miles SE of Oban, on small island at W end of Loch Avich, Argyll.

CALDA HOUSE

Calda House is a large and substantial ruinous mansion, and was built to replace nearby Ardvreck Castle (also see that entry). The lands were a property of the MacLeods of Assynt, but passed to the Mackenzies, who built the house in about 1660. The family were said to have held riotous parties, and soon became short of money, and the house was plundered and torched in 1737. The Mackenzies were forfeited after supporting the Jacobites, and the house was sold to the Earl of Sutherland. Calda was burnt out by the MacRaes in 1760, and the old house was never restored.

The ruins are said to be haunted, after one of the Mackenzies' wild parties continued from the Saturday well into the morning of the Sabbath. The building is said to have been engulfed in flames, perhaps after being struck by lightning, roasting nearly all those inside, divine punishment, it was said, for desecrating the Sabbath. Only one man was saved, a piper who refused to play into Sunday morning.

The ruins are said to be haunted by the apparition of a woman. There are also reports of eerie lights seen around Calda, in the middle of the night, making motorists think that cars are approaching, although they then do not encounter any other vehicles.

Map 1, 5C (Calda). Off A837, 1.5 miles N and W of Inchnadamph, N side of Loch Assynt, Sutherland, Highland.

CALLY HOUSE

Cally House, a grand symmetrical mansion with a porticoed porch, replaced the ancient Cally Castle in 1763. The mansion was built for the Murrays of Cally, and was then held by the Murray-Stewarts of Broughton. The building was extended in 1835 and later, and is now a splendid hotel called the Cally Palace Hotel.

The building is said to have a 'Green Lady', the phantom of a servant or nanny who was murdered by being thrown out of one of the upstairs windows.

Map 4, 7Q (Cally). Off A75, 0.5 miles S of Gatehouse of Fleet, to W of Cally Loch, Dumfries and Galloway.
Hotel. (01557 814341 / www.callypalace.co.uk)

CAMERA OBSCURA, EDINBURGH

The Camera Obscura is housed in the outlook tower of 1853, originally Short's Observatory, while the bottom storeys date from the 17th century. The camera obscura gives a brilliant moving image of the surrounding city, and the scene changes as a guide operates the camera's system of revolving lenses and mirrors. There is also the roof-top terrace, and exhibitions on international holography, on pinhole photography, and on Victorian Edinburgh.

The building is said to be haunted, and the phantom of a man in a long grey coat and hat, dressed as if from the 1930s, is reported to have been observed in the upper chamber, while the bogle of a lady in a brown dress has been spotted on the second floor. Visitors have also reported an oppressive and foreboding atmosphere in these areas. The sounds of children whispering and laughing are said to have been heard coming from the third floor, and disembodied footsteps have also been reported emanating from a stair used as a fire escape although it is unoccupied.

Map 4, 9L (Edinburgh). Off A1, Castlehill (Royal Mill), Edinburgh.
Open all year. (0131 226 3709 / www.camera-obscura.co.uk)

A paranormal investigation was undertaken by in June 2007 Ghost Finders (www.ghostfinders.co.uk/camera_obscura.html) and in February, in May and in July 2008 by Scottish Society of Paranormal Investigation and Analysis (www.sspia.co.uk)

CAMERON HOUSE

Set in a picturesque position on the banks of Loch Lomond, Cameron House is a castellated mansion, dating mostly from 1830 and, following a fire, was remodelled in 1865. The mansion may incorporate an earlier house. The lands were held by several families before they were sold to the Smolletts in 1763. Dr Johnson and Boswell visited in 1772, and Tobias Smollett, the well-known author, came from the family. The Smolletts sold the property in 1986, and the house is now a luxury hotel and leisure centre.

One of the rooms of the house is said to be haunted, with objects appearing which in reality do not exist.

The freezing of Loch Lomond was once reputed to herald a death in the resident family of Cameron House, but over the years this was shown not to be true.

Map 3, 6L (Cameron). Off A82, 2 miles NW of Alexandria, Dunbartonshire.
Hotel & leisure centre – open all year. (01389 755565 / www.cameronhouse.co.uk)

CAMERON'S INN, ABERDEEN

Believed to be the longest established pub in Aberdeen, Cameron's Inn, or Ma Cameron's, is an old coaching inn and public house of some character. The building dates from the end of the 18th century, and was once known as the Sow Croft Inn; the pub is named after Amelia, wife to the then owner, John Cameron.

The pub is said to be haunted. Manifestations are reported to include unexplained noises such as tapping from unoccupied rooms, a noticeable drop in temperature, uncomfortable feelings as if being watched, lights switching themselves on and off, and a beer tap turning on by itself. A dark apparition has also been reported, spotted in the area between the toilets and the snug part of the bar. One incident is reputedly when a painter working on the premises heard tapping noises; he found when he tapped back using his paint brush, the same number of taps then responded.

Map 2, 12G (Aberdeen). Off A9103, Little Belmont Street, off Union Street, Aberdeen.
Public House – closed Sun. (01224 644487)

CAMIS ESKAN

Camis Eskan is an imposing house, dating from 1648 but then remodelled and extended in 1840 and 1915. The lands were a property of the Dennistouns of Colgrain from the 14th century, and the present building replaced an ancient castle. The property was acquired by the Campbells in 1836 and held by them until 1946, when it was bought by the local council. The house had been used to treat Polish soldiers, then as a TB hospital during World War II, but in 1979 was divided into luxury flats.

The building is reported to be haunted.

Map 3, 6L (Camis Eskan (Camis E.)). Off A914, 3 miles NW of Cardross, outskirts of Helensburgh, Camis Eskan, Dunbartonshire.

CANDACRAIG

Candacraig House, an attractive baronial mansion perhaps incorporating part of an older building, mostly dates from 1835, although it was later altered and extended. The lands were once held by the Andersons but were sold to the Forbeses in 1867, then later went to the Wallaces before being bought by the comedian and actor Billy Connolly and his wife Pamela Stephenson.

The building suffered a fire in 1955, and it is from this incident that the ghost story is said to originate: the house is reputed to be haunted by the ghost of a dog killed in the blaze.

Map 2, 9G (Candacraig). On A944, 10 miles N of Ballater, Candacraig, Kincardine & Deeside.

CANONGATE, EDINBURGH

The Canongate, part of the Royal Mile, leads down from the High Street to Holyrood Palace. There are many other points of interest, not least the Scottish Parliament building, Queensberry House (also see that entry), Huntly House (home to the Museum of Edinburgh), the Canongate tolbooth and the Canongate Kirk, in the cemetery of which are buried many eminent Scots (and one Italian, David Rizzio).

The street is reportedly haunted by the phantom of a girl, seen with her clothes and hair ablaze. The story goes that the poor girl was the daughter of a well-to-do family but found herself pregnant by a lowly servant. Her family were furious and punished the poor girl by burning her alive.

Map 4, 9L (Edinburgh). Off A1, Canongate, Edinburgh.

CARA HOUSE

ILLUS PAGE 52

Cara House, now derelict, dates from the 18th century, although it may stand on the site of an older fortified dwelling. The small island was a property of the Mac-Donalds of Largie.

The house and island are said to have had a brownie, although the origins suggest more of a ghost, as the brownie was said to be the spirit of a MacDonald murdered by the Campbells (and hence also had an extreme dislike of members of that clan). The brownie was described in one account of 1909 as a 'neat little man, dressed in brown, with a pointed beard'. Like many brownies, this one was concerned with the welfare of his households, and did all manner of chores: tidying, bringing in the harvest, washing and cleaning, and even chiding or slapping lazy servants.

The ghost is also said to have frequented the MacDonalds' main castle at Largie.

Map 3, 3M (Cara). Off W coast of Kintyre, 4 miles W and S of Tayinloan, N end of island of Cara, S of island of Gigha.

CARBISDALE CASTLE

Carbisdale Castle, a fantastic castellated mansion dating mostly from 1910-11, was built on the site of Culrain Lodge for Duchess Blair, second wife of the 3rd Duke of Sutherland. The Duchess, Mary Caroline Blair (nee Mitchell), married the Duke only a few months after her previous husband died: he had been accidentally shot in a hunting accident. The manner of their marriage caused a scandal and, when the Duke died, Caroline secured a massive settlement. The Duchess and her deceased husband's family did not get on, and she had to build the castle outwith the new Duke of Sutherland's domain (although only just). Carbisdale is an especially noticeable and impressive building, and was no doubt built by Caroline to irritate her husband's family. The building is now a youth hostel, surely one of the most sumptuous such establishments in the world.

The castle is said to be haunted by a 'White Lady', which has been witnessed in many parts of the building, although the manifestation is not recorded as being especially frightening. The ghost has been identified as the Duchess.

Some tales also have the building haunted by a ghostly piper, as well as by a bogle of one of the castle's gardeners, said to have been spotted clad in black with a hood that hides most of his face. The apparition has reputedly been seen in the grounds, searching for his teenage daughter; it is thought this is why the ghost has been seen most often by girls around the same age as his girl.

Map 2, 7D (Carbisdale). Off A9, 3.5 miles NW of Bonar Bridge, N of Culrain, Sutherland, Highland.
Youth Hostel. (0870 0041109 / www.syha.org.uk)

CARESTON CASTLE

Careston Castle is a fine old Z-plan tower house of four storeys, which incorporates older work, but is now part of a large and imposing castellated mansion.

The Dempsters owned the property. One of the family fought with the Bishop of

Brechin over land, and stole cattle and horses and was involved in the kidnapping of monks. The property passed to the Lindsay Earls of Crawford, then later to the Adamsons of Careston in the 19th century – and Careston is still occupied by that family.

The castle is said to be haunted by a 'White Lady', which is reported to wander from chamber to chamber. The spirit of Jock Barefoot, slain for not delivering a message, is also said to haunt the building (as well as Finavon – also see that entry).

Map 2, 10I (Careston). Off A94, 4.5 miles W of Brechin, Careston, Angus.

CARLETON CASTLE

In a atmospheric spot are the ruins of Carleton Castle, the remains of 15th-century stronghold of the Cathcart family.

One tale is that this was the home of Sir John Cathcart, reputedly a serial marryer and murderer. He was wed seven times, but each new wife quickly died or disappeared: he, of course, got to keep their dowries and property.

His final wife turned out to be May Kennedy of Culzean. After their wedding, they were out walking on a cliff top path at Games Loup, some miles from Carleton. Cathcart turned on May, intending to push her to her death, and ordered her to strip, so that he could keep her jewels and fine clothes (and perhaps so it would have been more difficult to identify the body should it have been washed up). May feigned modesty and asked him to turn his back. Cathcart did as requested, and May shoved him from the cliffs, so that he was dashed on the rocks below.

Ghostly screams have been reported from the vicinity of the old castle, although it is not clear whether they are believed to come from Cathcart's victims or from Cathcart's ghost itself.

Map 3, 5O (Carleton). Off A77, 6 miles S of Girvan, Lendalfoot, Carleton, Ayrshire.
Access at all reasonable times – care should be taken.

CARMELITE STREET, ABERDEEN

Carmelite Street runs along side the site of a Carmelite friary, founded about 1273 and dissolved in 1560 after being sacked by a mob. There are no remains, and only the street name survives. The site was excavated before redevelopment, and human bones were found, said to date back 600 years.

The publican of a nearby hostelry, the Old King's Halfway Pub, reported experiencing a 'strange presence' in his pub during the excavations. The apparition of a friar, an old man clad in a dark brown and hooded robe, was also reported in the adjoining shop by two witnesses.

Map 2, 12G (Aberdeen). Off A956, Carmelite Street, Aberdeen.

CAROLINE PARK HOUSE, EDINBURGH

Caroline Park, although much modified and extended in later centuries, incorporates a tower house built by Andrew Logan in 1585, although the building was extended and altered down the centuries. The property was originally known as Royston, but passed to the Mackenzies, then to the Campbell Duke of Argyll, then through Campbell's daughter – Caroline, hence the name of the property – to the Scott Dukes of Buccleuch.

A 'Green Lady', the apparition of Lady Royston, reputed to be the wife of Sir James Mackenzie, younger son of Lord Tarbat, is said to haunt the house. On certain days, her phantom is reported to appear at midnight from an old well, and go to the entrance of the house, where she vanishes. She is said to then reappear in the small courtyard and ring an old bell. One witness reported how, late at night, she often heard the bell tolling, even when there was no wind and everybody else was asleep. The apparition is reputed to be seen dressed in an emerald-green frock, adorned with mystical devices.

A ghostly cannon ball is also said to have been witnessed several times smashing through the window of the Aurora Room. This is recorded as being a relatively common occurrence in the 1850s. One occasion was reportedly late at night and the witness told how the cannon ball smashed the window and then bounced three times before coming to rest against a fire screen. The witness called for help but when she looked again the ball had gone and the window was undamaged. The same strange event happened to a governess in 1879, and the room was thereafter closed up, although servants still reported several unexplained crashing noises coming from the locked chamber. It is said, however, that occupants of the house learned to ignore the uncanny sounds.

Map 4, 9L (Edinburgh). Off A901, 3 miles N of Edinburgh Castle, Granton, Edinburgh.

CARSEGRANGE

There was a monastic grange here, a property of Coupar Angus Abbey from the 12th or 13th century, although nothing remains. After the Reformation, the lands went to the Ogilvies, who had a castle or residence. An old orchard does survive, believed to be the site of a chapel and burial ground, and also said to be haunted by the ghosts of monks.

Map 4, 9K (Carsegrange). Off A85, 9 miles W of Dundee, 2.5 miles S of Inchture, Perth and Kinross.

CARTLAND BRIDGE HOTEL

Originally the private home of Captain James Farie of Farme, 'Baronald House' was converted into a hotel in 1962, renamed the Cartland Bridge Hotel, and is set in 19 acres of woodland. The Farie family, who owned the house, had a seven-year-old daughter named Annie, who died in a riding accident in the grounds of the house. Her ghost has reputedly been witnessed at the hotel, and she is said to be particularly fond of the room which was once her 'Dolls' Room'. Annie is buried in a private graveyard within the policies, overlooking the River Mouse, and a large oil painting of her hangs in the Portrait Room Restaurant.

Another account of the 1970s reports that of a different apparition, the phantom of an old woman seen coming down the stair, clad in a pale blue dress and with a veil obscuring her face – the ghost was described as being solid to look at and not transparent. Three witnesses are said to have to spotted the ghost on that occasion. A few weeks later the same apparition was apparently witnessed by several guests in the lounge.

Map 4, 8M (Cartland Bridge). Off A73, Glasgow Road, 1 mile NW of Lanark, Lanarkshire.
Hotel. (01555 664426 / www.bw-cartlandbridgehotel.co.uk)

CASSILLIS HOUSE

Cassillis House is a romantic old house and castle, first built in the 14th century with walls up to 16 foot thick, but altered down the centuries into a comfortable residence. The property was held by the Kennedys from 1373, and David, 3rd Lord Kennedy, was made Earl of Cassillis in 1509, although he died at the Battle of Flodden four years later. The 4th Earl, Gilbert, had the Commendator of Crossraguel Abbey, Allan Stewart, roasted in sop at Dunure Castle (see that entry) to persuade Stewart to sign over the lands of the abbey. Archibald, 12th Earl, was made 1st Marquis of Ailsa in 1831. Culzean Castle (also see that entry) was the family seat from the 1770s until the 1940s, when the Kennedys returned to Cassillis, and they still live here.

One story is that the house is haunted by the ghost of Lady Jean Hamilton, wife of John, 6th Earl. It is said that her apparition has been seen at a window, peering out. The tale behind the haunting (which does not appear to have any historical basis, as letters between the couple seem to be very cordial) is that Lady Jean was in love with Johnie Faa, the gypsy laddie of the old ballad. They ran off together, but the Earl was having none of it, pursued and caught them, and then hanged Johnie from a tree, making his wife watch the execution.

Map 3, 6N (Cassillis). Off B742, 3 miles NE of Maybole, 1.5 miles SW of Dalrymple, Cassillis, Ayrshire.

CASTLE CARY

Castle Cary, an attractive and atmospheric building, consists of a 15th-century keep and a 17th-century wing, although it is partly built with Roman masonry from sites along the Antonine Wall. The property was held by the Baillies from the 17th century until 1730, when it went to the Dunbars, and the castle is still a private residence.

Castle Cary is said to have two ghosts. One is reputedly the Covenanter, General William Baillie, who was defeated in 1645 by the Marquis of Montrose at Kilsyth. Baillie sheltered at the castle, but it was then torched by Montrose's men after he had left. His ghost is said to haunt the castle, and manifestations include unexplained noises and an apparition, sometimes seen at one of the upper windows from the garden.

Lizzie or Elizabeth Baillie, daughter of one of the lairds, also reputedly haunts the building. She absconded with a poor Highlander, a suitor of whom her father disapproved. Her father had her imprisoned in an upstairs chamber, but with her lover's help she managed to escape and fled the castle. This was not without cost, however, and her father had a stroke and died and, when she found out, Lizzie herself could no longer be happy and she herself died young. Her apparition, a 'White Lady', reputedly searches the castle chambers for her father, and has been often witnessed on the main stair.

Map 4, 8L (Castle Cary). Off A80, 2 miles NE of Cumbernauld, Castle Cary, Falkirk.

CASTLE COEFFIN   ILLUS PAGE 52

Perched on an outcrop of rock on the island of Lismore, Castle Coeffin is a ruinous, overgrown and romantic castle of the MacDougalls of Lorn. It is said to be named after one of its ancient owners, Caifen, the son of a Norse king. An old story tells that Beothail, his sister, died heartbroken after the man she loved was slain fighting in Scandinavia. Beothail was buried on Lismore, but her ghost returned to haunt the castle. She did not rest until her bones were taken to Norway and buried beside her cherished love.

Map 3, 4J (Castle Coeffin). Off B8045, 1.5 miles N of Achnacroish, Isle of Lismore, Argyll.

CASTLE FRASER
ILLUS PAGE 67

Impressive and well preserved, Castle Fraser is a tall and massive Z-plan tower house, dating mostly from between 1575 and 1636, and was long a property of the Fraser family. In 1976 the castle was donated to The National Trust for Scotland, and there is a colourful walled garden.

One story associated with the castle is that a young woman or princess was murdered in the Green Room of the castle's Round Tower – either in the 19th century or the distant past, depending on the version of the tale – and that her body was dragged down stairs before being buried. It was said that blood from her corpse, which stained the stairs and the hearth of the chamber, could not be washed off, and the stairs were eventually boarded over to hide the stains. The stairs, on the other hand, may have been boarded over simply to provide greater comfort.

Other unexplained events include the sound of piano music and voices coming from the apparently empty hall; and the apparition of a woman in a long black gown, said to be Lady Blanche Drummond, wife of Colonel Frederick Mackenzie, who died in 1874, and seen in the upper chambers of the castle. Spooky manifestations are also reputed to have been witnessed in the dining room and east wing. These have been associated the ghost of Mrs Theodora Mackenzie Fraser, the second wife of Colonel Mackenzie, as she apparently spent much of her time in these areas.

Map 2, 11G (Castle Fraser). Off B993 or B977, 6.5 miles SW of Inverurie, Aberdeenshire.
NTS: Open April-Jun & Sep-Oct, Thu-Sun (closed Mon-Wed) & open Bank Hol Mons; open Jul-Aug, daily. (01330 833463 / www.nts.org.uk)

CASTLE GRANT
ILLUS PAGE 67

Castle Grant is an impressive Z-plan tower house, incorporating work from the 15th century, with lower wings enclosing a paved courtyard. This was chief seat of the Grants, and they were Hanoverians, and fought against the Jacobites in both the 1715 and 1745-46 Risings, although the castle was occupied by Jacobites.

Castle Grant is reputedly haunted by the ghost of Lady Barbara Grant, daughter of a 16th-century laird. She was imprisoned in a dark closet, off an upper bedroom in the old part of the castle, known as 'Barbie's Tower'. She had fallen in love with a man of low station, a suitor considered unsuitable by her father, who chose another husband for her. Barbara died of a broken heart and ill treatment after the captivity lengthened, choosing death rather than marriage to a man she did not love.

Her small ghost is said to appear from behind tapestries concealing the closet, and cross the bedroom, stopping to wash her hands, then disappearing through the doorway leading to the turnpike stair. During recent renovation, work men are said to have heard unexplained footsteps, cries and disembodied voices, and the sound of a door opening and closing. They are reputed to have been so scared that they fled the building.

Map 2, 8F (Castle Grant). Off A939, 1.5 miles north of Grantown-on-Spey, Castle Grant, Moray.

CASTLE HOTEL, HUNTLY

The Castle Hotel, a large and stark mansion of three storeys dating from the middle of the 18th century, was partly built using materials from the nearby medieval Huntly Castle. The mansion was extended in 1832, and became the seat of the Duke of Gordon's eldest son. It is now a hotel, and there are red squirrels in the wooded grounds.

The building is said to have a 'Green Lady', the ghost of a girl who found herself with a child but no husband and committed suicide.

Map 2, 10F (Huntly). Off A920, N of Huntly, Aberdeenshire.
Hotel. (01466 792696 / www.castlehotel.uk.com)

CASTLE HUNTLY

Built on a steep rock surrounded by flat land, Castle Huntly is a large, tall and impressive building, enlarged and altered down the years. The Gray family built the tower in 1452 and held the property until 1641 when it went to the Lyons of Glamis (there is said to be a tunnel from here to Glamis) and then to the Pattersons in 1777. They owned the castle into the 20th century, but it is now used as an open prison, although rather too open for some.

The castle is reputedly haunted by a 'White Lady', the ghost of one of the daughters of the house when the Lyons were in possession. The story goes that the poor girl became pregnant by one of the castle servants, and was imprisoned in one of the upstairs chambers, later known as the Waterloo Room. The girl tried to escape out of the window but fell to her death; alternatively, she was pushed from the window. Either way, her ghost is then said to have haunted the Waterloo Room, as well as the grounds, especially around the Bogle Bridge in the castle policies. It is recorded that the apparition has often been seen down the centuries, terrifying servants and people spending the night in the haunted chamber.

A second ghost is claimed to be that of a young boy, seen dressed in a double-breasted sailing jacket. He has reputedly been seen in the Waterloo Room, and the story is that (in life) the boy was Richard, son of Colonel Adrian Gordon Patterson. Richard drowned in a boating accident on the Tay in 1939.

Map 4, 9K (Castle Huntly). Off A85, 1 mile W of Longforgan, Castle Huntly, Perth and Kinross.
Open prison. (www.sps.gov.uk)

CASTLE LACHLAN

In a pleasant location by the sea, Castle Lachlan is an ancient ruinous stronghold of the MacLachlans and is set in 1500 acres of estate. The clan were Jacobites and fought at Killiecrankie in 1689, and also took part in the 1715 and 1745 Risings: their chief was killed at Culloden. The castle became ruinous after the building of a new house nearby, a large and impressive castellated mansion, which is also called Castle Lachlan.

The old castle was said to have had a brownie (possibly a 'Green Lady' or 'grua-gach').

Map 3, 4L (Castle Lachlan). Off B8000, 7 miles SW of Strachur, Cairndow, Argyll.
Holiday accommodation available in castle; venue for weddings. (01369 860669 / www.castlelachlan.com)

CASTLE LEOD

A fine and stately building, Castle Leod consists of an altered L-plan tower house of five storeys and a later higher wing. The castle was built by Sir Roderick Mackenzie of Coigach about 1610. His grandson was made Viscount Tarbat, and then Earl of Cromartie in 1703, but the 3rd Earl was forfeited for his part in the Jacobite Rising of 1745-46. The Earl was imprisoned in the Tower of London and was sentenced to death, but he got remission three years after the end of the rebellion; the property and the titles were eventually recovered.

The drawing room of the castle is said to be haunted, although it is reputed to be by a benign bogle.

Map 2, 7E (Castle Leod). Off A834, 4 miles W of Dingwall, 1 mile N of Strathpeffer, Castle Leod, Ross and Cromarty, Highland.

CASTLE LEVAN

Standing by the edge of a ravine, Castle Levan is a strong castle that was built by the Mortons in the 14th century, but passed to the Semples in 1547. The building was then extended and altered in later centuries and, although it became ruinous, the castle has been restored and reoccupied.

The building is reputed to be haunted by a 'White Lady', the ghost of Marion Montgomery, who was married to the Semple laird of the castle. The story goes that she persecuted, and even tortured, her tenants while her husband was away, and was sentenced to death by Mary of Guise, acting for the infant Mary, Queen of Scots. Marion was not executed, however, although her fate was little better: her husband had her imprisoned in the castle and she starved to death. Her ghost is then said to have haunted the castle, and reports of the bogle date from the 17th century. It has been suggested that the owner of the time, wishing a better house in which to reside, concocted or exaggerated the story so that his father would allow him to build a new house.

Map 3, 5L (Castle Levan). Off A770, 1.5 miles SW of Gourock, Castle Levan, Renfrewshire. **B&B accommodation available. (01475 659154 / www.castle-levan.com)**

CASTLE LOCH HEYLIPOL

On a former island in the loch is the site of a strong castle of the MacDonalds, little or nothing of which remains, formerly square and turreted with a drawbridge. The castle dated from the 14th century or earlier, and was later held by the MacLeans, then by the Campbell Earls and Dukes of Argyll. They had a causeway and factor's house, known as Island House, built on the site in 1748, which was then altered and extended in the 19th century. The castle had been besieged by the Campbells in 1678-9, and was ruinous shortly afterwards.

The factor, called MacLaren, who had the house built is said to have died before he could enter it. His ghost reputedly haunts the house, as does a 'Green Lady', which is said to be responsible for unexplained noises in the 1970s. Lights are also said to be seen in the windows of the house when it is unoccupied.

Island House, renovated in 2005, can be rented as holiday accommodation.

Map 3, 1J (Castle Loch Heylipol). Off B8065, 3 miles W of Scarinish, Loch Heylipol, Tiree. **Island House: holiday accommodation available. (www.inveraray-castle.com/pages/ content.asp?PageID=146)**

CASTLE MENZIES

A grand and substantial building in a picturesque location, Castle Menzies is an extended 16th-century tower house, built in the Z-plan with turrets crowning the corners of the building. As the name suggests, this was long the seat of the Menzies clan. Bonnie Prince Charlie stayed here for two nights in 1746, although four days later the family were thrown out and the castle was taken by Hanoverian forces, led by the Duke of Cumberland. The chief did not support the Rising, but many of the clan, including their leader Menzies of Shian, were killed at the Battle of Culloden in 1746. The last of the Menzies line died in 1918, and during World War II the castle was used as a Polish Army medical supplies depot. The castle became derelict, but is being restored by a trust established by the Clan Menzies Society, who acquired the building in 1957.

Castle Menzies is said to be haunted, and to have a 'Grey Lady', and there are many reports of unexplained activity from recent times. Manifestations are said to include footsteps coming from an unoccupied chamber, shutters closing by themselves (as well as a door), and disembodied voices and laughter being heard, sounding as if they came from children. Strange smells have also apparently been noticed: the fragrance of perfume coming from one chamber on more than one occasion, and an unpleasant smell experienced on the ground floor. Many visitors have reported unpleasant feelings and have decided not to enter the castle, while one account relates how a young girl saw something terrifying in one of the rooms and immediately had to be taken out of the building.

Map 4, 8J (Castle Menzies). Off B846, 1.5 miles NW of Aberfeldy, Castle Menzies, Perthshire.
Open Apr or Easter-Oct. (01887 820982 / www.menzies.org/castle/index.htm)

A paranormal investigation was undertaken by in June 2006 Paranormal Investigation Scotland (www.paranormalinvestigationscotland.co.uk)

CASTLE OF MEY

Castle of Mey is an extended and altered 16th-century Z-plan tower house, which was the Queen Mother's favourite residence before her death in 2002. The lands originally belonged to the Bishops of Caithness, but in 1566 were acquired by the Sinclair Earls of Caithness, who built the castle. Macleod of Assynt, who betrayed the Marquis of Montrose, was imprisoned here.

The castle is said to be haunted by the ghost of Fanny, a daughter of George Sinclair, 5th Earl, who died in 1643. She fell in love with a ploughman, and the Earl, who disapproved, had her imprisoned in one of the attic rooms, 'Lady Fanny's Room'. Here she pined away, but got some comfort from seeing her lover from the window; her father, however, then had that window blocked. Despairing, the poor lass threw herself from one of the still open windows, and she was killed on the courtyard below. Her sad spectre, a 'Green Lady', reportedly haunts the castle.

Her ghost is said to have been witnessed during the renovations of 1953.

Map 2, 9A (Castle of Mey). Off A836, 7 miles N of Castletown, Castle of Mey, Caithness, Highland.
Open to the public in the summer: check with castle or on website. (01847 851473 / www.castleofmey.org.uk)

CASTLE OF PARK

Set in extensive grounds, Park is a large mansion and castle, which may date from 1292, but was built (or rebuilt) into a Z-plan tower house in 1563. The building was extended down the centuries, and is a private residence again. Park was a property of the Gordons and then of the Gordon-Duffs until the 1970s. Sir William Gordon of Park was a Jacobite during the 1745-46 Rising, and had to hide around the grounds before escaping to France, where died in 1751.

Park is said to be haunted by a 'Green Lady'. The story goes that a young servant girl became pregnant and was dismissed from service. She committed suicide by hanging herself, and her ghost is said to have been seen in the grounds, as well as in the house and looking from the window of a second-floor chamber. The apparition of a cloaked and hooded woman was also witnessed on one occasion.

Other apparitions and spooky occurrences include the phantom of a monk, who was walled up in one of the castle chambers on the ground floor, and the sounds of a disembodied child's voice and a music box, only heard in the upper quarters. Quick changes in temperature have also been reported, as well as vague shapes moving across rooms. Items are also reputedly frequently moved or disappear only to reappear later.

Map 2, 10E (Castle of Park). Off A9023, 4 miles NW of Aberchirder, Banff and Buchan, Aberdeenshire.

CASTLE SPIORADAIN

The castle, a property of the MacLeans, was said to be haunted, and its name Castle Spioradain means 'fortress of ghosts'. In the 15th century there was a long-running feud between the MacLeans and the Camerons of Lochiel. The fighting resulted in several Camerons being executed and their dead bodies hung from the battlements, but then many MacLeans were slain in reprisal. Their ghosts, united in death by revenge, haunted the castle and terrorized the neighbourhood. Or so it is said.

The old castle was demolished at the beginning of the 19th century, with the construction of the Caledonian Canal, and human bones were found here.

Map 2, 7F (Castle Spioradain). Off B862, 6 miles SW of Inverness, near Bona Ferry, Highland.

CASTLE STALKER

Dramatically sited on a small island at the mouth of Loch Laich, Castle Stalker (meaning 'hunter' or 'falconer') is a tall, massive and simple tower. The tower was built by Duncan Stewart of Appin, who was made Chamberlain of the Isles for his part in helping James IV destroy the MacDonald Lord of the Isles. In 1620 the castle had been sold to the Campbells, but the Stewarts retrieved it after a long siege in 1685, although the Stewart garrison surrendered to government forces only five years later. The chief sold the lands in 1765, and the castle was soon abandoned. Although roofless in 1831, the building was restored from ruin in the 1960s.

One story about Castle Stalker is that a ball of shining light was seen above the old stronghold as a herald of death in the Stewart clan.

Map 3, 4J (Castle Stalker). Off A828, 20 miles N of Oban, Portnacroish, Argyll.
**Open for some days in the summer. (01631 740315/01631 730354 /
www.castlestalker.com)**

CASTLE STUART

ILLUS PAGE 67

Overlooking the Moray Firth and the mountains beyond, Castle Stuart is a tall imposing tower house with a warren of stairways, passageways and hidden doorways. The property was held by the Mackintoshes, but was given by Mary, Queen of Scots to James Stewart, Earl of Moray. Moray was made Regent for the young James VI but was assassinated at Linlithgow, and the second Earl was also murdered, this time at Donibristle (see that entry). The castle was finished by James, 3rd Earl, about 1625, although it was seized by the Mackintoshes over a dispute about ownership and compensation; the Mackintoshes were bought off and Castle Stuart returned to the Stewarts.

The Three Turret chamber is said to be haunted by some frightful bogle. The story goes that the then Earl offered a reward to anyone who would spend a night in the haunted room. A local man called Big Angus agreed to do so, but the next morning he was found dead in the courtyard, having apparently fallen from the turret, a look of terror on his face.

Map 2, 7E (Castle Stuart). Off B9039, 6 miles NE of Inverness, Castle Stuart, Highlands. **Overnight accommodation by reservation. (01463 790745 / www.castlestuart.com (also www.brigadoon.co.uk))**

CASTLE TIORAM

A picturesque ruin in a wild and unspoilt location, Castle Tioram dates from the 14th century, and was the main seat of the MacDonalds of Clan Ranald. The building was modified by the heiress Amy MacRuari, wife of John, Lord of the Isles, who was divorced by her husband so he could marry Margaret, daughter of Robert II. The Clanranald branch of the MacDonalds came through her. During the Jacobite Rising of 1715, the castle was torched so that Hanoverian forces could not use it, and the chief of Clan Ranald was killed at the Battle of Sheriffmuir. The castle was never reoccupied. Castle Tioram must have been in a fair state of repair, however, as Lady Grange was imprisoned here for a few weeks in 1732 before being taken to the outer isles.

Clan Ranald had a set of magic bagpipes which, when played, is thought to have ensured victory in battle. The clan is also said to have had a familiar spirit, a frog, which had the power to create storm or calm at sea.

Map 1, 3H (Castle Tioram). Off A861, 3 miles N of Acharcle, Moidart, Highland. **Care needs to be taken with tides.**

CASTLE TOWARD

In a scenic location with fine views over the Firth of Clyde, Toward (usually spelt 'Towart' in old documents) Castle is an ancient ruinous stronghold, one wall standing to the height of the parapet, with the remains of a courtyard, which has a decorated arched gateway. The Lamonts held the castle, but in 1646, after the Lamonts had raided Campbell lands, the Campbells bombarded the building with cannon, and then captured, looted and burnt Toward. Although the Campbells had promised that the Lamonts could go free, they massacred and mistreated any Lamonts they found, including old folk, women and children. They took many of the captives back to Dunoon where they hanged 36 from one tree, while others were buried alive in pits. Many Lamonts changed their name to Black after the slaughter.

Castle Fraser (page 61)

Castle Grant (page 61)

Castle Stuart (page 66)

Cawdor Castle (page 70)

Clava Cairns (page 73)

A hoard of more than 200 silver coins was found here in 1821. The old castle was excavated and consolidated in 1970, and is in the care of the Clan Lamont Society.

Castle Toward, a baronial mansion not far from the old stronghold, was built in 1820 for Kirkman Finlay, Lord Provost of Glasgow, and then went to the Coats family of Paisley. The property was purchased by Glasgow Corporation in the 1940s, and the house was used as a boys' residential school and then as an outdoor centre. The BBC TV children's series *Raven* is filmed here.

Toward Castle has a number of ghost stories, including tales that one of the upstairs rooms was haunted by a ghost that would wake sleepers by stroking their hair.

Map 3, 5M (Castle Toward). Off A815, 7 miles SW of Dunoon, S tip of Cowal, Castle Toward, Argyll.
Outdoor centre; ruin accessible with care. (01369 870249 / www.actualrealitycentres.com)

CASTLE VENLAW HOTEL, PEEBLES
Built in a prominent spot with a fine outlook, Venlaw Castle, dating from around 1782, is a large castellated mansion with towers and turrets, and lies in 12 acres of grounds. The mansion replaced the ancient castle of Smithfield, which was held by the Hays in the 16th and 17th centuries, and then by the Dicksons. The present mansion was built by Alexander Stevenson, Sheriff Deputy of Peeblesshire, but later passed to the Erskines, then to other families. Venlaw Castle has been a hotel since 1949, now known as the Castle Venlaw Hotel.

The mansion is reputedly haunted. The story goes that a guest committed suicide by jumping out of one of the upstairs windows. Unexplained sighing and heavy breathing have apparently been heard coming from one of the rooms.

Map 4, 9N (Peebles). Off A703, Edinburgh Road, to N of Peebles, to NW of Ven Law, Borders.
Boutique country hotel. (01721 730384 / www.venlaw.co.uk)

CASTLEHILL, CAMBUSNETHAN
Castlehill is the site of a tower house, little of which survives except a vault. The lands were owned by the Bairds, by the Stewarts, by the Somervilles and then by the Lockharts, later Sinclair-Lockharts of Castlehill, who still held the property in the 20th century.

The site is said to be haunted by a headless horseman.

Map 4, 8M (Cambusnethan). Off B754, 1 mile S of Wishaw, Gowkthrapple Road, Castlehill Farm, Lanarkshire.

CASTLEMILK
Little remains of Castlemilk, a once grand mansion and castle of the Stewarts. Mary, Queen of Scots, may have lodged here rather than Craignethan the night before the Battle of Langside in 1568, when she lost and fled to England. Bought by Glasgow Corporation in 1938, the mansion was occupied as a children's home until 1969. It was then mostly demolished.

The house and grounds were reputedly haunted, and there are stories of a 'White Lady' near a bridge over the burn, a 'Green Lady', and an ancient Scottish soldier that (allegedly) fired a 'real' arrow into the back of the head of a local, who then needed stitches.

There was also the 'Mad Major', an apparition who was said to gallop up to the house by moonlight. This was believed to be the return of Captain William Stirling Stuart from Waterloo.

Map 4, 7M (Glasgow). Off A749, 1.5 miles SE of Rutherglen, Castlemilk, Glasgow.

CATHEDRAL HOUSE, GLASGOW

Cathedral House, which lies close to the medieval cathedral in the old part of the city, dates from the 1870s and was used for some years to rehabilitate female prisoners from a nearby prison. The building is now used as a hotel, bar and bistro.

Cathedral House is said to be haunted. The sounds of children have been reported from the top floor despite none being present, as has an invisible presence pushing past people on the stair.

Map 4, 7M (Glasgow). Off M8, 28-32 Cathedral Square, Glasgow.
Hotel. (0141 552 3519)

A paranormal investigation was undertaken in October 2005 by Ghost Finders (www.ghostfinders.co.uk/cathedralhotel.html)

CAWDOR CASTLE   ILLUS PAGE 68

A magnificent and well-preserved stronghold in fine policies, Cawdor Castle incorporates a tall 14th-century keep with later ranges around a courtyard. There are many fine furnished rooms, as well as a magnificent garden. The method of choosing the site for present castle was quite unusual: a donkey was used and the castle was built where the beast finally stopped and rested by a holly tree. Cawdor was built over the tree, the remains of which are in the basement.

The title 'Thane of Cawdor' is associated with Shakespeare's *Macbeth*, but King Duncan was not murdered here – the castle is not nearly old enough – and history records that he was killed in battle near Spynie. Donald, first Thane of Cawdor, took the name of Calder when he was granted the lands in 1236. William, 3rd Thane, was murdered by Sir Alexander Rait of nearby Rait Castle (also see that entry). The Campbells managed to acquire Cawdor by abducting the child heiress Muriel Calder in 1511 and marrying her to Sir John Campbell, son of the Earl of Argyll. The six sons of Campbell of Inverliver were slain during her abduction, but the Campbells of Cawdor still own the castle.

An apparition of a lady in a blue velvet dress has reputedly been seen here, as has allegedly a phantom of John Campbell, 1st Lord Cawdor.

Map 2, 8E (Cawdor). On B9090, off A96, 5 miles SW of Nairn, Cawdor, Highlands.
Open May-early Oct. (01667 404401 / www.cawdorcastle.com)

CENTRAL HOTEL, GLASGOW

Located in the very heart of Glasgow, the Central Hotel (now Quality Hotel Glasgow) is one of the oldest hotels in the city and is located by Central Railway Station, having been built by the Caledonian Railway Company in 1884. The hotel is a large and impressive building, perhaps the most notable part being the monumental clock tower. The hotel has had many famous visitors down the years, including Laurel and Hardy, Roy Rodgers and his horse Trigger, Danny Kaye, John F. Kennedy, Frank Sinatra, Cary Grant, and even the Queen and Prince Philip. John Logie Baird used the hotel to transmit the first long-distance television pictures.

There are stories that the building is haunted by the bogle of a young maid, who is said to have become pregnant and then committed suicide, as well as by the spirit of a chef who fell from one of the upper windows, seven storeys, to his death.

Map 4, 7M (Glasgow). Off M8, 99 Gordon Street, Glasgow.
Hotel. (0141 221 9680 / www.QualityHotelGlasgow.co.uk)

CESSNOCK CASTLE

Standing above a ravine, Cessnock Castle is a massive rectangular tower house, dating from the 15th century, to which was added a fine mansion.

Cessnock was a property of the Campbells. Mary, Queen of Scots, came to Cessnock after her defeat at Langside, when one of her ladies died here, and her bogle is said to haunt the castle. The reformers George Wishart and John Knox also visited, as did Robert Burns. The property passed through the families of Dick, Wallace, and Scott, to the De Fresnes in 1946. The ground floor was sold off as a self-contained flat in 1981.

The bogle of John Knox, Mary's unstinting opponent and critic, is also said to haunt the castle, quoting scriptures. Hopefully, over the centuries, he and Mary's lady-in-waiting have managed to get along.

Map 4, 7N (Cessnock). Off B7037, 1 mile SE of Galston, Cessnock, Ayrshire.

CHARLOTTE SQUARE, EDINBURGH

Standing in the elegant New Town of Edinburgh, Charlotte Square dates from between 1792 and 1820, and was designed by William Adam. The square is said to be haunted by several ghosts, including by the insubstantial and shifting figure of a monk, by a woman in 18th-century garb, by an old man, and by a phantom coach.

Map 4, 9L (Edinburgh). Off A1, Charlotte Square, Edinburgh.
Accessible at all times.

CHERRY ISLAND

There was an old castle on Cherry Island (also known as Eilean Muireach and Inchnacardoch), which is said to have been used as a hunting seat, and to have been a property of the Frasers at one time. The island was formerly larger than it is now, as the waters of Loch Ness were raised with the building of the Caledonian Canal.

The island is reputed to have had a brownie (possibly a 'Green Lady'/gruagach').

Map 1, 6G (Cherry Island). Off A82, 0.5 miles N and E of Fort Augustus, small island at SW end of Loch Ness, Cherry Island, Highland.

CHESSEL'S COURT, EDINBURGH

Chessel's Court, a courtyard in the Old Town of Edinburgh surrounded by fine restored tenements, dates from about 1745.

In the 1850s one of the upper flats was said to be haunted by the ghost of a woman, who had hanged herself there. Breathing and other sounds were reportedly heard, and also apparently spotted was the apparition of a tall woman, clad in a black silk dress and with a black veil hiding its face.

Map 4, 9L (Edinburgh). Off A1, top of Canongate on Royal Mile, Edinburgh.

CITIZENS' THEATRE, GLASGOW

The theatre, which was built in 1878, became the Citizens' Theatre in 1945 and is one of Britain's leading repertory theatres and is renowned for its innovative productions. The theatre occupies the site of the house of George Elphinstone, who acquired the property in 1579, and a church, and was formerly known as Her Majesty's Theatre and then the Royal Princess's Theatre.

The Citizens' is reputedly haunted by a 'Green Lady' (or a 'Grey Lady', depending on the account), the apparition of a woman, believed to have been that of a former front of house manager, who committed suicide by jumping from the upper circle. Her apparition has been reputedly been repeatedly witnessed here.

There are also stories of another phantom, dark and hooded, being spotted in the circle studio, and reports of several apparitions elsewhere in the building. Other manifestations are reputed to be unexplained noises.

Map 4, 7M (Glasgow). Off M74, 119 Gorbals Street, Glasgow.
Theatre. (0141 429 0022 (Box office) / www.citz.co.uk)

A paranormal investigation was undertaken in April 2004 by Scottish Paranormal Investigations (www.scottishparanormalinvestigations.co.uk)

CLACKMANNAN TOWER

Standing prominently on the summit of King's Seat Hill, Clackmannan Tower is an impressive 14th-century keep of three storeys, which in the 15th century was heightened and then extended to L-plan. Clackmannan was a property of the Bruces from 1359 until 1796, having been given to them by David II. Henry Bruce of Clackmannan fought for the Jacobites in the 1745 Rising, and in August 1787 his widow, Catherine, 'knighted' Robert Burns with the sword of Robert the Bruce. The tower was abandoned only four years later; an adjoining mansion has been demolished.

There have apparently been several strange happenings in the tower, leading some to believe that the building is haunted. A paranormal investigation is apparently planned for the tower.

Map 4, 8L (Clackmannan). Off B910, 7 miles E of Stirling, W outskirts of Clackmannan.
His Scot: Access at all reasonable times: view from exterior only.
(www.clackmannantower.co.uk/www.historic-scotland.gov.uk)

CLADACH A' CHROGAIN, TIREE

Cladach a' Chrogain, a beach on the north coast of Tiree, is said to be where a terrifying supernatural dog has been witnessed, either seen or heard. This is said to be a 'Cu Sith' (pronounced 'coo-shee'), a fairy dog, shaggy and with huge paws, perhaps as large as a bullock, dark green in colour (although another account has the dog being black). Although there are many legends associated with the Cu Sith, the beast is said to be a harbinger of doom, especially when it was heard to bark three times in a row. Accounts have the dog following travellers and then disappearing.

One legend is that the fearsome dogs would hunt down pregnant women and drive them to fairy mounds where the women were forced to produce milk for fairy children. The Cu Sith would also attack men and other dogs.

Map 3, 1J (Cladach a' Chrogain). Off B8068, Cladach a' Chrogain, N coast of Isle of Tiree, Argyll.

CLAUNCH

A spectral carriage drawn by a pair of horses is said to have been seen near Claunch farm.

Map 4, 7Q (Claunch). Off B7052, 4 miles S of Wigtown, Claunch, Dumfries and Galloway.

CLAVA CAIRNS
ILLUS PAGE 68

A very atmospheric site in a wooded location, there are the remains of three large chambered burial cairns along with their associated stone circles, dating from about 1600 BC. Both cremations and inhumations have been recovered during excavations of similar cairns, and these appear to have been the burial places of a few individuals rather than collective tombs for whole communities.

There are stories of people experiencing spooky feelings here, and being frightened by what is a very impressive place. Reports suggest that eerie music has been heard here, said by some to sound like faint fiddling, the story going that the music comes from fairies hidden within the stones. It is believed to be bad luck to remove any rocks or materials from the cairns.

Map 2, 7F (Clava Cairns). Off B9006 or B851, 6 miles E of Inverness, Highlands.
His Scot: Access at all reasonable times. (01667 460232 / www.historic-scotland.gov.uk)

CLAYMORE HOTEL, ARROCHAR

The Claymore Hotel stands on the site of Arrochar House, a residence or castle of the MacFarlanes. Arrochar was the clan seat in 1697, and the hotel incorporates foundations from this building. The MacFarlanes fought for Robert the Bruce at the Battle of Bannockburn in 1314, although the then chief was slain at Flodden in 1513, and another at Pinkie in 1547. The lands were sold in 1767, and went to the Colquhouns of Luss, the MacFarlanes' former bitter enemies.

The present building is said to be haunted. The young daughter of one of the chiefs reputedly fell in love with one of the Colquhouns of Luss. Her father heard about their affair, and forbad her to continue to see her lover. She ignored his warnings, and he decided to make an example of her, locking her in one of the chambers of Arrochar House with no food or water. The poor girl died, and it is said that her apparition, a 'Green Lady', wanders the present building.

A different version of the story is that the chief came home one day, unexpectedly early, and found his wife in a close and compromising clinch with one of his neighbours. The chief was furious and first slew his neighbour and then mortally wounded his terrified wife. Bleeding from her wounds, she dragged herself into the corridor and died in one of the chambers. When the chief realised what he had done he hanged himself.

The apparition of his wife then began to haunt the house, whose sighting was reputed to herald a death or misfortune in the clan.

There are also apparently stories of a black dog haunting the premises.

Map 3, 6K (Arrochar). Off A83, Arrochar, Dunbartonshire.
Hotel. (01301 702238)

CLAYPOTTS CASTLE

An unusual and impressive building, Claypotts Castle is a Z-plan tower house with a rectangular main block and two large round towers at opposite corners. The castle is associated with John Graham of Claverhouse, Viscount Dundee, who was known as 'Bloody Clavers' for his prosecution of Covenanters and 'Bonnie Dundee' after his death in 1689 at Killiecrankie. There are stories that it was at Claypotts that Claverhouse sold his soul to the Devil, as well as him cavorting with witches and demons, making him impossible to kill with lead musket balls and other normal weapons. The tale goes that the shot that killed him at Killiecrankie was made of silver (or, alternatively, that the mortal shot hit a silver button on his clothing and that it is this that killed him).

One ghost story dates from 150 years before his death. The building is said to be haunted by a 'White Lady', reputedly the ghost of Marion Ogilvie, mistress (and wife) of Cardinal David Beaton. Her apparition is reputed to have been seen at a castle window on the 29 May each year: the date of Beaton's murder at St Andrews Castle (also see that entry) in 1546. It seems more likely, however, that she lived at Melgund Castle (also see that entry), as there was apparently no castle here in 1546. There have, however, been many reports of sightings of the ghost.

Claypotts is also said to have had a brownie, which left when one of the servants refused to allow it to help.

Every Halloween it is said that the castle glows with strange lights, while sounds of a demonic orgy taking place can be heard emanating from the castle.

Map 4, 10K (Claypotts). Off A92, 3.5 miles E of Dundee, Angus.
His Scot: View from exterior or tel to check. (01786 431324 / www.historic-scotland.gov.uk)

CLONCAIRD CASTLE

Standing by steep rising ground above a burn, Cloncaird Castle is a square 16th-century tower house of four storeys and an attic, the third storey projecting on corbelling. The castle was much extended and remodelled in the Gothic style in 1841, and stands in a 140 acre estate.

The Mures held the property, and Patrick Mure of Cloncaird was killed at the Battle of Flodden in 1513. The castle passed to other families, including to the Wallaces, and was remodelled, with the addition of the large mansion, in 1841. For a while the castle was used as a convalescent home, but it is now a private residence again.

A ghost of a man is said to have been seen often on the stairs, including in recent times.

Map 3, 6O (Cloncaird). Off B7045, 4 miles E of Maybole, Cloncaird, Ayrshire.
Available for wedding parties and private functions; holiday cottage. (01655 750345 / www.cloncairdcastle.co.uk)

CLOSEBURN CASTLE

One of the oldest continuously inhabited houses in Scotland, Closeburn Castle consists of a large rectangular 14th-century keep and a 19th-century mansion. The castle was held by the Kirkpatricks from 1232 until 1783, and the story of a harbinger of doom dates from their ownership.

A pair of swans, which nested by the nearby lake, returned year after year until the son of the house shot one with a bow and arrow. From then on only one swan returned, with red breast feathers, as a herald of death in the family. The swan has apparently not been seen since the family left Closeburn.

Map 4, 7O (Closeburn). Off A702, 3 miles SE of Thornhill, Dumfries and Galloway.

CLUMLY FARM

The area around the farm is said to be haunted by a phantom horseman. The story relates that two brothers desired the same woman, and they argued and then fought. One killed the other by striking him with a flail, then disposed of his rival's body by dumping it over cliffs into the sea. As the man rode back, he was chased by the dead brother's ghost – or perhaps by his own conscience. During his mad ride home, his horse dislodged stones from a wall, which afterwards could not be repaired, no matter what was tried.

The apparition of a rider is said to have been witnessed several times.

Map 2, 9D (Clumly). On A967, 4 miles N of Stromness, Clumly, Orkney.

CLYDESDALE HOTEL, HAMILTON

The Clydesdale Hotel is reputed to be haunted, and it is claimed that the cellars may belong to a much older building. Manifestations are said to include strange occurrences in one of the bedrooms, and things falling from the back of the bar without apparent cause.

Map 4, 7M (Hamilton). Off A724 or A72, Clydesdale Street, Hamilton, Lanarkshire.
Hotel with accommodation and restaurant. (01698 891897 / www.clydesdalehotel.com)

A paranormal investigation was undertaken in March 2005 by Spectre (www.freewebs.com/ukspectre/clydesdalehotel.htm)

CLYDESDALE INN, LANARK

The Clydesdale Hotel, formerly known as the New Inn (and now the Clydesdale Inn), was a coaching inn built in 1792 on the site of the Franciscan friary of Lanark. The friary was founded around 1326 by Robert I, but was dissolved before 1566, and the property passed to the Lockharts of the Lee. The inn had many notable guests, including William and Dorothy Wordsworth and Charles Dickens. The building is now used as a public house.

The basement is said to incorporate part of the friary buildings, the dormitory. It is here that the apparition of a monk is reputed to have been seen, but the ghost – the 'Grey Friar' – is said to be friendly and concerned with the welfare of the building. Other manifestations include the sound of slamming doors and rattling glasses, as well as the feeling of someone pushing past folk in the cellar.

When it was a hotel, the disembodied weeping of a child was reported, coming from the upper floor of the building, when no children were staying here. A young child is said to have been burned to death in the attic in the 1800s.

Map 4, 8M (Lanark). Off A73, 15 Bloomgate, Lanark, Lanarkshire.
Public house. (01555 678740 / www.jdwetherspoon.co.uk)

COCKET HAT PUB, ABERDEEN

The Cocket Hat Pub is said to be haunted by the bogle of a former landlord, John Walker, who died in the late 1950s. The story goes that his apparition was spotted by a member of staff as she was locking up in 1973. The phantom was described as being that of a man dressed in a long coat and a hat with an upturned brim. The staff member had seen the man, but when she went to serve him he disappeared; her description was identified as the previous landlord by the then manager.

Manifestations are also said to include a half-seen apparition caught out the corner of the eye, an uncomfortable presence in the lounge bar, and on one occasion a glass of whisky moving by itself across a table.

Map 2, 12G (Aberdeen). On A90, North Anderson Drive, Aberdeen.
Public House. (01224 695684)

COFFIN WORKS, DUNDEE

The Coffin Mill, part of the larger 19th-century Logie Works, was once the largest linen/jute mill in Dundee, and it remains a very impressive and striking building. The two blocks of the works are joined by an attractive cast- and wrought-iron footbridge at second-floor level. The mill was closed many years ago, and the building has been redeveloped for residential use.

There is more than one suggestion as to the name: one is that it comes from the coffin-shaped site, another that it refers to an incident when men were killed building the chimney, and the third about the appalling story of a girl who got her hair caught in machinery and was killed, horribly.

The iron bridge linking the two blocks is said to be haunted by the ghost of a girl, which is reputed to be seen crossing the bridge every night. One story is that she was killed by mill machinery (as above), but another is that she was cast from the bridge after finding herself pregnant.

Map 4, 10K (Dundee). Off A923 or A991, Brook Street, Dundee.

COLONSAY HOUSE

Colonsay House, an attractive whitewashed edifice, dates from 1722, although it was extended in the 19th century. The island was held by the MacDuffies, but passed to the MacDonalds and then later to the Campbells and then to the Mac-Neills. The house is how home to Lord Strathcona, the first of whom was Sir Donald Alexander Smith, High Commissioner for Canada in 1896. The fine grounds by the house include some twenty acres of both woodland and more formal gardens.

The 'big house' on Colonsay is said to have had a brownie (probably a 'gruagach' or 'glaistig'), that also acted as a herdsman.

Map 3, 3L (Colonsay House). Off A871, 2 miles N of Scalasaig, Kiloran, Isle of Colonsay, Argyll.
Private gardens open Apr-Sep, Wed & Fri; woodland gardens open daily throughout the year. (01951 200211 / www.colonsay.org.uk)

COLQUHONNIE CASTLE

Overlooking the Don valley, not much survives of Colquhonnie Castle, a ruined 16th-century L-plan tower house of Forbes of Towie, except some of the vaulted basement. The castle was apparently never completed as three of the lairds were killed while overseeing its building.

The ruins are said to be haunted by a phantom piper, one of the Forbeses, who fell from the top of the old tower in the 1600s.

Map 2, 9G (Colquhonnie). On A964, 10.5 miles N of Ballater, Kincardine & Deeside.

COMLONGON CASTLE   ILLUS PAGE 79

Standing in 120 acres of secluded woodland and gardens, Comlongon Castle consists of a massive keep, with walls 14 foot thick in places, to which a mansion was added in the 19th century. The grand hall has a massive fireplace, and there are steps down to the guard chamber and the dark pit prison. Comlongon was held by the Murray family from 1331 after Sir Thomas Randolph had given the lands to his nephew Sir William Murray, and their descendants held it until 1984. The family became Earls of Annandale, and later of Mansfield. The mansion is now used as a popular hotel.

The castle is said to be haunted by a 'Green Lady', the spirit of Marion Carruthers of Mouswald. She was the joint heiress, along with her elder sister Janet, to her father's considerable lands and property after he was slain in a raid in 1548. The poor girl was forced into a betrothal of marriage with John MacMath of Dalpeddar, nephew of Sir James Douglas of Drumlanrig (Douglas was also her guardian), a man she did not love, although the motive appears to have been her property, rather than amorous desire. As Douglas was her guardian he had virtually absolute control of Marion, who nevertheless seems to have been a strong and independent young lady. And the wrangle was to last for years. Even the Privy Council seemed to be against her and in 1563 Marion was ordered into the wardenship of Borthwick Castle.

Marion sought refuge in Comlongon, however, the castle of her uncle, Sir William Murray. She was apparently so distressed from the long dispute that she eventually committed suicide by jumping from the lookout tower. An alternative, and perhaps more likely, version is that she was murdered by the Douglases who gained access to her room and threw her from the roof. Because she was thought to have committed suicide, she was not given a Christian burial, and it is said no grass will grow on the spot where the poor girl died. This happened on 25 September 1570, when she would have been about 29 years of age. Douglas did well from her demise and went on to obtain her share of her father's lands.

Her apparition is said to have been witnessed, both in the grounds and in the castle, the phantom of a forlorn sobbing girl. The sounds of her weeping have also been reported, as well as a ghostly presence which pushes past people. There have been recent reports of activity, including a photograph purporting to show the ghost.

Map 4, 8P (Comlongon). Off B724, 8 miles SE of Dumfries, Comlongon, Dumfries and Galloway. **Hotel. (01387 870283 / www.comlongoncastle.co.uk)**

CORGARFF CASTLE   ILLUS PAGE 79

Corgarff Castle is a plain 16th-century tower house, altered in later centuries and surrounded by pavilions and star-shaped outworks. The old castle stands in one of the most stunning and beautiful parts of Scotland. Corgarff saw much action in Covenanting times and the Jacobite Risings. It was burnt by Jacobites in 1689, and then in 1716 by Hanoverians. In 1748 it was altered into a barracks, and later used as a base to help prevent illicit whisky distilling.

The castle was leased to the Forbes family. The Forbeses feuded with the Gordons, and this came to a head when Adam Gordon of Auchindoun and a force of his family ravaged through Forbes lands and besieged the castle. Corgarff was held by Margaret Campbell, wife of Forbes of Towie, and 26 others of her household, women, children and servants; the menfolk were away. Margaret, however, would not surrender the castle. Gordon of Auchindoun lost patience after one of his men had been wounded, had wood and kindling set against the building, and torched the place. The building went up in flames, killing all those inside, including Margaret and her children. The story is recounted in the ballad 'Edom o' Gordon', although Towie Castle is given as another possible site of the massacre.

Ghostly screams have reportedly been heard in the castle, and the barrack room is supposed to be particularly haunted.

Map 2, 9G (Corgarff). Off A939, 10 miles NW of Ballater, Corgarff, Aberdeenshire.
His Scot: Open Apr-Oct, daily; open Nov-Mar, wknds only; closed 25/26 Dec & 1/2 Jan. (01975 651460 / www.historic-scotland.gov.uk)

CORN EXCHANGE, EDINBURGH (LEITH)

The Corn Exchange (built as a selling hall for the grain trade with offices) in Leith dates from 1860, and is a fine building with a distinctive domed corner. The building was later the headquarters of the Northern Lighthouse Board, then as offices for a scaffolding business, and was then used as a public house. After periods of disuse, the Corn Exchange was recently renovated as offices and a studio/gallery.

The Corn Exchange was reputed to be haunted by two ghosts when it was still in use as a public house.

One is said to be the bogle of a landlord, who was proprietor in the 19th century. The story goes that the man hanged himself, after going bankrupt, because his establishment was boycotted as many locals accused him of torturing children. His phantom is reported to have been caught on camera during the filming of *Understanding the Paranormal*, a US TV series

Other manifestations are said to have been lights going on and off by themselves (which was observed in the former lounge area), unexplained cold blasts of air, and people feeling as if they were being pushed by an unseen presence when entering an upstairs room.

A second ghost is believed to be that of a young child, perhaps one of the landlord's victims, who, the story goes, was locked in a cupboard. The sounds of weeping and other mysterious noises are reported to have been repeatedly heard, coming from the upstairs of the building.

Map 4, 9L (Edinburgh). Off A199, Corn Exchange, 9 Baltic Street, Leith, Edinburgh.
Office and studio/gallery. (0131 561 7300 / www.cornexchangegallery.com)

CORNAIG BAY, VATERSAY

Cornaig Bay is reputedly the site of the murder of the sons of the 29th Chief of MacNeil, who had their stronghold at Castlebay on Barra. MacNeill was widowed and his new wife, known as 'Marion of the Heads', had the sons beheaded so that her own boy would be heir and inherit MacNeil's property. Ghostly screams are reputed to have been heard coming from the spot where the sons were slain.

Marion, at least according to the stories, was a particularly unpleasant woman, and islanders too old or ill to work are said to have been drowned in the sea on her

Comlongon Castle (page 77)

Corgarff Castle (page 77)

Coylet Inn (page 84)

Craighouse, Edinburgh (page 86)

Craignethan Castle (page 87)

orders. Marion, herself, is said to be buried on Uinessan, by the chapel known as Cille Bhrianan or Caibeal Moire nan Ceann (the Gaelic for 'chapel of Marion of the Heads').

Off minor road, 2 miles SW of Castlebay, Cornaig Bay, Isle of Vatersay, Western Isles.

COROGHON CASTLE, CANNA

Not much remains of Coroghon (which means 'fetters') Castle on the summit of a steep rock, except part of a gatehouse or forework, which is in a dangerous condition. The island was a property of the Clan Ranald branch of the MacDonalds, and the surviving ruin may date from as late as the 17th century, although it is probably considerably older.

The site is said to be haunted by the ghost of a woman imprisoned here by one of the MacDonald Lord of the Isles, possibly even his lovely wife, who had fallen in love with one of those dratted MacLeans.

Map 1, 1G (Coroghon). On NE of island of Isle of Canna, on N side of Harbour, Highland.
Ruin may be in a dangerous condition – view from exterior.

CORSOCK MOOR

The moor is said to be haunted by the bogle of a headless piper. The story goes that he was foully murdered and decapitated while crossing the moor.

The sounds of unearthly piping have reputedly been heard on the moor, along with the sighting of a headless man. One sighting of the apparition records that the phantom was hazy and see-through, and bathed in an eerie blue light.

Map 4, 7P (Corsock Moor). Off A712, 7 miles N of Castle Douglas, Corsock Moor, Dumfries and Galloway.

CORSTORPHINE CASTLE, EDINBURGH

The grounds around the site of the castle are said to be haunted by the ghost of Christian Hamilton, wife of Andrew, Nimmo, who was executed in 1679. She was in love with James Forrester of Corstorphine, 2nd Lord Forrester, despite being his niece, and had a child by him. They used to meet under an old tree, supposedly planted in 1429 and which (until 1998) still grew at one end of Dovecote Road. During an argument about the pair getting married, Christian stabbed and killed Forrester with his own sword, and she was quickly arrested, tried and sentenced to death, although she had pled self defence. Christian managed to escape from prison dressed as a man, but she was recaptured at Fala Moor and brought back to Edinburgh where she was executed by beheading. She is said to have been clad in a white dress, and to have conducted herself very bravely.

Her apparition, a 'White Lady', has reputedly been seen around the site of the tree.

Nothing remains of the ancient castle of the Forresters, except for the 16th-century doocot. This has reputedly got supernatural protection: it is said anyone demolishing the building will die within a short time. Also nearby is Corstorphine Old Parish Church, dating from around 1426, which contains tombs with stone effigies of the Forresters.

Map 4, 9L (Edinburgh). Off A8, 3 miles W of Edinburgh Castle, Dovecote Road, Corstorphine, Edinburgh.

CORTACHY CASTLE

Cortachy, an impressive courtyard castle dating from the 15th century, has long been the property of the Ogilvie Earls of Airlie. Charles II spent a night here in 1650 in the 'King's Room', and the building was sacked by Cromwell in revenge.

The castle reputedly has a harbinger of death, a phantom drummer heard to be playing, along with other eerie music, when one of the family is about to die.

The phantom drummer is said to be the bogle of a man who either had an affair with the laird's wife or did not raise the alarm when the castle was about to be attacked – depending on the version. The drummer was killed by dumping him into his drum and throwing him from the battlements of the castle. Before he died he cursed the family, saying that his drums would be heard whenever one of the family neared death. A third version is that the man was burned to death in 1645 after being taken as a hostage.

It is said that the drums were heard several times in the 19th century, and heralded deaths in the family, including two of the Earls, their wives and their relations. The drummer also appears to have been witnessed at Achnacarry, near Fort William, and also abroad, and was not bound to Cortachy.

There are no accounts of the drums having been heard recently, and it might be pointed out that the time between the drums being heard and the death happening was up to six months...

Map 2, 9I (Cortachy). Off B955, 3.5 miles N of Kirriemuir, Cortachy, Angus.
Gardens occasionally open under Scotland's Gardens Scheme. (01575 570108 / www.airlieestates.com/www.gardensofscotland.org)

COULL CASTLE

Coull Castle was held by the Durwards in the 13th century, hereditary 'door wards' to the kings of Scots. The stronghold saw action in the Wars of Independence, but may have been abandoned as early as the 14th century and it is very ruinous.

When one of the Durward family was near death, the bell of the church at Coull is said to have tolled by itself.

Map 2, 10G (Coull). Off B9094, 2.5 miles N of Aboyne, Aberdeenshire.

COUNTY BUILDINGS, AYR

The County Buildings were erected in 1818-22, and then extended in 1931. The site covers the former jail (which has been demolished), and the buildings include the striking classical courthouse, housing the Sheriff Court.

The site is reputedly haunted by a headless apparition of a man, thought to have been one of the prisoners executed here.

Map 3, 6N (Ayr). Off A719, Wellington Square, Ayr.
South Ayrshire Council headquarters. (www.south-ayrshire.gov.uk)

COUNTY BUILDINGS, LANARK

The former county buildings, with an imposing classical edifice, are said to by haunted by the phantom of a nun, and there have reputedly been several sightings, usually in the evening. The building was used as a hospital until the 1960s.

Map 4, 8M (Lanark). Off A73, 22-26 Hope Street, Lanark, Lanarkshire.

COUNTY HOTEL, DUMFRIES

Standing at the end of the High Street, the building dated from the 18th century but was closed in the 1980s. It was here that Bonnie Prince Charlie and his army stopped in 1745 on their way north after withdrawing from England. The Prince held court and slept in the inn, and in 1936 a guest claimed they saw the apparition of a man, dressed in tartan, entering by a disused door, and then returning the same way. The adjoining room is said to have been Bonnie Prince Charlie's bedroom.

The hotel has been demolished and the site is occupied by shops.

Map 4, 8P (Dumfries). Off A75, Dumfries, Dumfries and Galloway.

COUNTY HOTEL, PEEBLES

The hotel buildings incorporate a vaulted cellar, which probably dates from the 16th century. This may be part of one of the six bastle houses which survived in the town as late as 1870.

The County Hotel is said to be haunted by the ghost of a young woman killed in a tunnel behind the dining room, sometime in the early 1900s. Her indistinct apparition has reputedly been seen, objects have mysteriously disappeared or been moved, and ghostly whispers have been reported.

Map 4, 9N (Peebles). Off A72, High Street, Peebles, Borders.
Hotel. (01721 720595)

COURTALDS, WISHAW

The works here, latterly owned by Courtalds, produced lingerie for retailers such as Marks and Spencers, but the plant is apparently to close or has closed, according to recent reports in the media.

The plant is said to be haunted by the spirit of Willie Primrose. The story goes back to the 1930s when reportedly Primrose worked as a labourer in the works, but had the misfortune to be accidentally locked in the boiler room over a weekend and was found dead on the Monday.

Various manifestations were then attributed to Primrose's bogle, including making lifts go up and down by themselves, switching lights on and off, and making machinery operate even though the power had been switched off.

It is said that since the death of the man who locked Primrose in the boiler room the haunting ceased.

Map 4, 8M (Wishaw). Off B754, Netherhall Road, Excelsior Park, Wishaw, Lanarkshire.

COVENANTER HOTEL, FALKLAND

The former Covenanter Hotel, located in the centre of the historic village famous for its royal palace, and now called Luigino's, dates from 1771 but stands on the site of an earlier dwelling. The building is now used as an Italian restaurant, delicatessen and offers accommodation.

During its time as the Covenanter Hotel, the place was said to be haunted by the apparition of a woman, which was identified as Mary, Queen of Scots, although it is far from clear why she should haunt here. One account has the ghost being spotted in one of the bedrooms, where it was reputedly seen to fly across the chamber. Other reported manifestations included the odour of lavender being smelt in one

room, mysterious noises such as footsteps from unoccupied areas, and several instances of unexplained sharp drops in temperature, experienced by guests and staff.

Map 4, 9K (Falkland). Off A912, 3 miles N of Glenrothes, High Street, Falkland, Fife.
**Restaurant, delicatessen and offers accommodation. (01337 857224 /
www.luiginos.co.uk)**

*A paranormal investigation was undertaken in October 2006 by Scottish Paranormal
Investigations (www.scottishparanormalinvestigations.co.uk)*

COYLET INN
ILLUS PAGE 79

Standing on the banks of Loch Eck, the Coylet Inn (originally known as the 'Loch Eck
Inn') is a small family-run country hotel, and dates back to 1650 when it was a
coaching inn on the Glasgow-Dunoon road. The inn is set in a picturesque area,
surrounded by the Argyll Forest Park.

The building is believed to be haunted by a 'Blue Boy', the apparition of a young
lad who returns to find his mother, claimed to have been seen in Room 4. Objects
are said to have mysteriously disappeared from one area, only to reappear in another. Staff have also reported wet footprints when nobody has been present to
make them, and the sound of disembodied footsteps.

The story goes that a young lad staying at Coylet on occasion walked in his sleep.
One night in a dream he left the hotel, crossed the road, and wandered down into
Loch Eck. He was drowned in the cold water, leaving his body chill and blue. It is
thought to be his ghost which causes the disturbances, and the story was incorporated into a film in 1994.

Map 3, 5L (Coylet). On A815, Loch Eck, 8 miles N of Dunoon, Argyll.
Hotel. (01369 840426 / www.coyletinn.co.uk)

*A paranormal investigation was undertaken in November 2005 by Ghost Finders
(www.ghostfinders.co.uk/coylet_inn.html)*

CRAIGARD HOUSE HOTEL

The Craigard House Hotel was built in about 1800 as a shooting lodge, but latterly
was used as a hotel before this was closed and the building converted to residential
use.

The hotel was said to be haunted, the story being that a servant girl threw herself
from one of the tower windows in the 1920s, and that her bogle then returned to
haunt the building. Her ghost was reputedly often witnessed.

Map 2, 8G (Craigard). Off A95 or B970, Kinchurdy Road, S of Boat of Garten, Strathspey, Highland.

CRAIGCROOK CASTLE, EDINBURGH

Nestling beneath Corstorphine hill, Craigcrook is a large castellated mansion which
incorporates an old tower house. The tower was probably built by the Adamson
family in the 16th century, and Craigcrook has been owned by many families down
the centuries, including by Archibald Constable, who started the publishing firm,
and by Lord Francis Jeffrey, the well-known judge, who died in 1850. It is his ghost
that is said to haunt the building.

Many disturbances have been reported in recent times, including unexplained
footsteps and noises, things being moved around and thrown, and the doorbell

ringing when nobody is apparently present. The library is also reputed to be unnaturally cold at times.

Map 4, 9L (Edinburgh). Off A90, 2.5 miles W of Edinburgh Castle, Edinburgh.
Scottish Field. (0131 312 4550 / www.scottishfield.co.uk)

CRAIGDARROCH HOUSE

Craigdarroch House is an elegant classical mansion, built by the famous architect William Adam in 1720 for the Fergussons, although the mansion incorporates an older dwelling or castle. Damaged by fire in 1984, Craigdarroch was restored and is still occupied.

The lands were held by the Fergussons and they opposed the Jacobites, and fled from the house in 1745 when Bonnie Prince Charlie arrived here on the long road back from England looking for lodgings. The house was left in a terrible state, although it was restored and the Fergussons held Craigdarroch until 1962.

Craigdarroch is the scene of an eerie tale regarding a haunted saddle. John Fergusson was a Colonel in the army, and was killed at Killiecrankie in 1689. His servant returned to Craigdarroch with his gear, including his horse and his saddle. The story goes that Elizabeth, his wife, was stunned when she heard the news, would not accept that her husband was dead, and soon ailed and died young. Her ghost then reputedly began to haunt the building, and it is reported that activity was centred around the saddle, which was kept here until 1918. The bogle is said to have been exorcised by a priest in 1920, since which ghostly activity has not been reported.

Elizabeth was, however, married twice following the death of her husband, so an alternative identity has been suggested: the ghost may have been a spirit of John's mother, Elizabeth Maxwell.

It is also said that the ringing of all the bells at the same time in the house would sometimes be heard, heralding the death of one of the family.

Map 4, 7O (Craigdarroch). Off B729, 2 miles W of Moniaive, Craigdarroch, Dumfries and Galloway.

CRAIGHALL

Standing on a steep hill above a river, Craighall (or Craighall-Rattray), a grand 19th-century baronial mansion, incorporates part of an old castle. The property passed to the Rattray family at the beginning of the 16th century (or from earlier). Patrick Rattray of Craighall was driven from his original stronghold of Rattray in 1516 by the Earl of Atholl, who also kidnapped his nieces and then had Patrick murdered in his own chapel. The family supported Charles I, and as a result the castle was besieged around 1650.

The castle is reputedly haunted, the story going back to this siege. The family were in hiding and a young servant girl would not reveal their whereabouts. Although interrogated, the poor girl would not betray the family and she was then thrown from one of the upstairs windows to her death. Tapping sounds are said to come from the window of the chamber from where she was pushed, and unexplained footsteps heard around the building, as well as mysterious knocking and banging.

There is also a tale of a 'Grey Lady', but it is not clear if this is the same ghost.

Map 4, 9J (Craighall). Off A93, 2 miles N of Blairgowrie, Craighall-Rattray, Perthshire.
Accommodation available. (01250 874749 / www.craighall.co.uk)

CRAIGHEAD INN, CUMNOCK

The Craighead Inn dates from 1722 or earlier, and the building is reported to have a ghost in the attic.

Map 4, 7N (Cumnock). Off A76, Glaisnock Street, Cumnock, Ayrshire.
Public house. (01290 424367)

CRAIGHLAW CASTLE

Craighlaw incorporates a square 16th-century tower house of three storeys and an attic, and was originally a property of the Mures. Craighlaw was sold to the Gordons of Kenmure in 1513, and passed to the Hamiltons in 1741 and remains with them. The house was enlarged and altered in 1870, although much of this was demolished in the 1950s, and it is still occupied.

The castle was said at one time to be haunted, when an apparition terrified a cook. The then owner of Craighlaw got his gun and shot at the ghost, but it had no affect. The bogle was apparently exorcised and has not been witnessed since.

Map 3, 6P (Craighlaw). Off B733, 7 miles E and N of Glenluce, 1.5 miles W of Kirkcowan, Craighlaw, Dumfries and Galloway.

CRAIGHOUSE SQUARE, KILBIRNIE

The square is reputed to be haunted by two ghosts, both of them thought to be of people who killed themselves. One bogle is said to be that of an Italian who jumped from a window, while the other is reputedly that of an ice-cream seller, who murdered his family.

Map 3, 6M (Kilbirnie). Off A760, Craighouse Square, Kilbirnie, Ayrshire.

CRAIGHOUSE, EDINBURGH   ILLUS PAGE 80

Craighouse is a much-altered 16th-century tower house, which is dated 1565 and 1746. The castle was built by the Symsons, but passed to Lord Provost Sir William Dick, and then to the Elphinstones. Used for a time as part of a psychiatric hospital, Craighouse is now in the campus of Napier University and is occupied as offices.

In 1712 it was a property of Sir Thomas Elphinstone, who was married to the much younger Elizabeth Pittendale. Elizabeth is said to have fallen in love with Elphinstone's son John, and Sir Thomas caught them together, although there was nothing apparently improper in their conduct. Nevertheless, Sir Thomas got in a terrible rage and stabbed Elizabeth to death; John managed to escape. When Sir Thomas came to himself again, he was aghast and committed suicide. John Elphinstone then inherited the property, and let the house, but a 'Green Lady', the spirit of Elizabeth, began to haunt the building. The hauntings only ceased when Elizabeth's remains were removed from the burial vault of her husband. When John died, he is said to have been buried beside her.

The story does not appear to have any historical basis...

Another ghost said to haunt here is that of a Jacky Gordon.

Map 4, 9L (Edinburgh). Off A702, 2 miles SW of Edinburgh Castle, Craighouse, Napier University, Edinburgh.
Part of Napier University; weddings can be held here. (www.napier.ac.uk)

CRAIGIEVAR CASTLE

A romantic castle in rolling parkland, Craigievar is a tall and massive L-plan tower house, which was completed in 1626. The property belonged to the Mortimer family but passed in 1610 to the Forbeses when the Mortimers ran out of money. The Forbeses held the building until 1953 when it went to The National Trust for Scotland.

The building is reputedly haunted by a member of the Gordon family. The man was murdered by being pushed from a window of the Blue Room by the 'Red' Sir John Forbes, 3rd Laird. It has been pointed out, however, that the bars which formerly secured the window would have made this impossible. Heavy footfalls are said, however, to have been heard to ascend the stair when there is nobody about.

Another ghost is said to be that of a fiddler, drowned in a well in the kitchen, who only appears to those of the Forbes family. There are also stories of other apparitions, which appeared in the Great Hall when the Forbeses were in trouble.

Map 2, 10G (Craigievar). Off A980, 4.5 miles S of Alford, Aberdeenshire.
NTS: Closed in 2009 for conservation work; ground open all year, daily. (01339 883635 / www.nts.org.uk)

Featured in Living TV's Most Haunted, *series six (2005).*

CRAIGMILLAR CASTLE, EDINBURGH

With fabulous views over the south and east side of Edinburgh, Craigmillar is a prominent and imposing ruin of a once strong and stately fortress. Dominating the buildings is a 14th-century L-plan keep, which is surrounded by a later curtain wall with round towers, along with an additional walled courtyard. The Prestons held the property from 1374. James III imprisoned his brother John, Earl of Mar, in one of the cellars here, where he died, and Mary, Queen of Scots, escaped to here in 1566 after the murder of her secretary, David Rizzio. In 1660 Sir John Gilmour bought Craigmillar and had the castle altered into a comfortable residence.

A walled-up skeleton was found in one of the vaults in 1813.

It is said that there is often an unexplained but strong smell of lavender in the great hall, which has been attributed to ghostly shenanigans.

Map 4, 9L (Edinburgh). Off A68, 3 miles SE of Edinburgh Castle, Craigmillar, Edinburgh.
His Scot: Open all year: Apr-Oct, daily; Nov-Mar, Sat-Wed, closed Thu & Fri; closed 25/26 Dec and 1/2 Jan. (0131 661 4445 / www.historic-scotland.gov.uk)

A paranormal investigation was undertaken in August 2005 by Spectre (www.freewebs.com/ukspectre/craigmillarcastle.htm)

CRAIGNETHAN CASTLE   ILLUS PAGE 80

Craignethan is a grand and imposing ruin, set on top of a wooded ravine. It was built to withstand artillery and is arranged around a squat tower house, formerly with a massively thick bastion, curtain walls and corner towers. There is a caponier, a small vaulted building used to defend the bottom of the ditch. Craignethan was built by Sir James Hamilton of Finnart in 1532, but he was beheaded for treason only eight years later.

James Hamilton, 2nd Earl of Arran, was a very powerful man, and acquired the castle. In 1568, Mary, Queen of Scots, may have spent one or more nights here before the Battle of Langside; one of the chambers in the castle was known as the

Queen's Room. A headless ghost, dressed in white, has been reported here, identi-fied by some as the phantom of Mary, although if she is headless (and not handily carrying her head) it is not easy to see how the identification could be made.

Other ghosts are said to have been witnessed in this later house in the courtyard, where the unexplained voices of women have been reputedly heard, and a vague shifting apparition spotted, as well as items being mysteriously moved, pans falling off the cooker and pictures being moved around the walls.

Other unexplained manifestations include mysterious pipe music, and the appari-tion of a woman wearing Stewart-period dress, which was witnessed in the court-yard. Two visitors followed the phantom, thinking it was a historical re-enactment, before the ghost faded away.

Map 4, 8M (Craignethan). Off A72, 4.5 miles W of Lanark, Craignethan, Lanarkshire.
His Scot: Open Apr-Oct, daily; Nov-Mar, Sat-Sun, closed Mon-Fri. (01555 860364 / www.historic-scotland.gov.uk)

CRAIGNISH CASTLE

Set in a fine location by the sea on the Ardfern peninsula, Craignish Castle dates from the 16th century, although it has been altered down the years into a comfort-able residence; a dungeon is carved out of the rock in the vaulted basement.

Craignish was (and is) a property of the Campbells, and withstood a six-week siege by Alaisdair Colkitto MacDonald in the 1640s. Near the castle is the ruinous but scenic old parish church and burial ground, which has many interesting memo-rials.

There are stories of a 'Green Lady' haunting the castle, seen walking from the building – as she had done, in life, to watch helplessly the drowning of her lover, a young French officer from Montrose's army.

Map 3, 4L (Craignish). Off B8002, 4 miles W and N of Kilmartin (further by road), W of Loch Craignish, Argyll.

CRAMOND TOWER, EDINBURGH

Although part of a larger castle at one time, Cramond Tower is a tall and narrow tower house, with a vaulted basement. The tower has been suggested as the model for the 'House of Shaws' in Robert Louis Stevenson's *Kidnapped*. Among the owners were the Bishops of Dunkeld, two of whom died here, but in 1622 the property went to John Inglis, an English merchant. His grandson abandoned the tower for Cramond House in 1680. The tower became ruinous, but was restored and reoccupied in 1983.

There is a story of a 'Green Lady' haunting the tower.

Cramond is also the site of a Roman fort and nearby is Cramond Kirk, an interest-ing building, dating in part from the 15th century.

Map 4, 9L (Edinburgh). Off A90, in Cramond to W of Edinburgh.

CRANSHAWS CASTLE

Standing in a remote and picturesque part of Berwickshire in the Lammermuir Hills, Cranshaws is a stark and solid rectangular tower house of four storeys, dating partly from the 15th century. Cranshaws was a property of the Swintons from 1400 to 1702, but then passed to the Douglases.

The castle is reputed to have had a brownie, a supernatural being, which did all manner of chores. For many years the brownie gathered and threshed the corn without reward or comment, but then one of the servants ungratefully moaned that the corn was not neatly gathered together.

The next day the corn was found two miles away at Raven's Crag in the Whiteadder Water, and the brownie left, vowing never to return, saying:

It's no weel mowed! It's no weel mowed!
Then it's ne'er to be moved by me again!
I'll scatter it ower the Raven Stane,
And they'll hae some wark ere it's mowed again!

Map 4, 11M (Cranshaws). Off B6355, 0.5 miles W of Cranshaws, Borders.

CRATHES CASTLE
ILLUS PAGE 91

Crathes Castle is an imposing and massive tower house, the lower part of which is plain, while the upper storeys have a flourish of corbelling, turrets, and stone decoration. The castle has many fine furnished apartments, some with magnificent original painted ceilings, including the Green Lady's Room.

There is a colourful walled garden, covering nearly four acres.

The lands were a property of the Burnetts of Leys from the 14th century, and they built the castle around 1553. They held it for 400 years until 1952 when it was given into the care of The National Trust for Scotland. The 'Horn of Leys', made of ivory and encrusted with jewels, was given to the family by Robert the Bruce in 1323 and is preserved in the High Hall.

The Green Lady's room, a chamber on the third floor of the tower, was originally a bedroom, and is believed to be haunted by a 'Green Lady' (so much so that it is so named). There are, however, several versions of the story accompanying the ghost. The apparition, in a green dress, reportedly first appeared in the 18th century, and is seen crossing the chamber, with a baby in its arms.

The young woman seems to have been a daughter of the then laird or (in the story in the guide book) a lass in his protection. She had been frolicking with a servant, or was cruelly used by a retainer of the laird. Where versions do agree, however, is that the poor girl was made pregnant and had the child, although it appears that the baby at least was then murdered. A skeleton of an infant was found by workmen in a small recess under the hearthstone during renovations in the 19th century.

Various other details are also added: one being that the ghost appears when a death is to occur in the Burnett family (not unusual in stories of this kind), another that the apparition, with baby, was seen by Queen Victoria.

Whatever the facts, the phantom is said to have been spotted often, even in recent times, wearing a green robe and with a baby in its arms. Some visitors apparently refuse to enter the room without knowing the story, while a guide felt something brush past her when there was nothing – apparently – there.

Map 2, 11G (Crathes). Off A93, 3 miles E of Banchory, Kincardine & Deeside.
NTS: Castle part Apr daily, then wknds to early May, then May-Jun & Sep-Oct, open Sat-Thu (closed Fri); Jul-Aug, daily; grounds and garden open all year, daily. (01330 844525 / www.nts.org.uk)

CRAWFORD PRIORY

Crawford Priory is an impressive gothic mansion, begun in 1809 and added to a few years later, but the building is now a derelict and a deteriorating shell. The present mansion replaced an earlier building on the site, which dated from the mid 18th century or earlier.

Crawford Priory was built for the unwed Lady Mary Crawford, who in 1808 succeeded to the Lindsay-Crawford property and lands on the death of her brother, the 22nd Earl of Crawford. Mary never married but she did have a large menagerie of animals, both pets and wild, in and around the mansion. After her death in 1833 (and a splendid funeral), Crawford Priory was left unused and became derelict (although she did leave provision in her will for her animals). The mansion was then restored in the 1870s after passing to Lady Gertrude Boyle, daughter of the 6th Earl of Glasgow, and her husband, Thomas Cochrane, but it is now very dilapidated again.

It is said that the grounds are haunted by the bogle of Lady Mary, and her apparition has reportedly been seen on more than one occasion.

Map 4, 10K (Crawford Priory). Off A92, 2 mile SW of Cupar, 0.5 miles S of Springfield, Pitlessie, Fife.

CREEPY WEE PUB, DUNFERMLINE

The public house, which is a small and cosy establishment, stands on Kirkgate not far from Abbot House. The pub is said to be haunted by a mischievous bogle, which is reported to have touched (with icy fingers) workers in the bar and also to have murmured in their ears, especially enjoying tormenting new members of staff.

Map 4, 9L (Dunfermline). Off A994, 17 Kirkgate, Dunfermline, Fife.
Public house. (01383 724184)

CRICHTON CASTLE   ILLUS PAGE 91

Standing above the River Tyne in an open and rugged location, Crichton Castle is a fabulous ruinous castle, dating from the 14th century, but much altered and extended in later centuries. Of special note is the diamond-studded facade of one of the ranges.

The castle was held by the Crichtons. Sir William Crichton, Chancellor of Scotland, entertained the young Earl of Douglas and his brother before having them murdered at the 'Black Dinner' in Edinburgh Castle in 1440. Outside the castle are the roofless stables, which are said to be haunted by Crichton. On the anniversary of his death, the story goes, he leaves the stables and enters the castle tower.

The Crichtons were forfeited for treason in 1488, and the property later passed to the Hepburns, one of whom was James Hepburn, 4th Earl, third husband of Mary, Queen of Scots. Mary was present at a wedding here in 1562.

Crichton is also said to be haunted by a horseman, who enters the castle by the original gate, which is now walled up. Some have suggested that this is the same bogle as that which haunts the stables.

Map 4, 10M (Pathhead). Off B6367, 2 miles E of Gorebridge, Crichton, Midlothian.
His Scot: Open Apr-Oct, daily. (01875 320017 / www.historic-scotland.gov.uk)

Crathes Castle (page 89)

Crichton Castle (page 90)

Chinese Bird Room, Culcreuch Castle (page 94)

Culloden House (page 95)

Culloden Moor (page 96)

CROMARTY CASTLE

Nothing remains of Cromarty Castle, a once strong castle, which may have dated from as early as the 12th century. The property was held by the Urquhart family, who were hereditary Sheriffs of Cromarty, and they defended the castle against the English in around 1300. Thomas Urquhart was a prodigious fellow, and is said to have fathered twenty-five sons here, although seven of them are believed to have been killed at the Battle of Pinkie in 1547. The Urquharts, however, lost everything as predicted by the Brahan Seer, and the property was sold in 1763 to the Murrays, and then to the Ross family. They soon demolished the ancient castle (during which – it is said – a large quantity of human bones were recovered, including some headless skeletons) and built Cromarty House, an imposing classical mansion

The old castle was said to be haunted by manifestations such as groans, cries and moans, and sightings of apparitions are also recorded.

Map 2, 7E (Cromarty). Off A832, 0.5 miles SE of Cromarty, Highland.

CROSS KEYS HOTEL, PEEBLES

The Cross Keys Hotel, which was established in 1693, was the townhouse of the Williamsons of Cardrona (the house was built in 1654). One of the innkeepers Marion Ritchie, who died in 1822, was used by Sir Walter Scott as Meg Dods in the novel *St Ronan's Well*. Marion is said to have run an excellent establishment but with a rod of iron.

Marion's ghost is thought to haunt the building. Disturbances have been reported, including items being moved about without being touched, electrical equipment being switched on and off, glasses broken, unexplained bangs and noises heard. Her apparition is also said to have been seen in the hotel, and bedroom five, where she died, is said to be the centre of activity.

Map 4, 9N (Peebles). Off A72, 24 Northgate, Peebles, Borders.
Hotel. (01721 724222 / www.crosskeyspeebles.co.uk)

CROSS KEYS INN, DENHOLM

Standing in the pleasant village of Denholm by the River Teviot, the attractive white-washed building was first built in 1800 as a bakehouse, but was later converted to a coaching inn. The Cross Keys is now a fine hotel and bar, called the Auld Cross Keys Inn.

The cellars are said to be a haunted by a ghost, known as 'Harry'.

Map 4, 10N (Denholm). Off A698, 5 miles E of Hawick, The Green, Denholm, Borders.
Hotel. (01450 870305 / www.crosskeysdenholm.co.uk)

CROSS KIRK, PEEBLES

Impressive ruins remain of the Cross Kirk, a Trinitarian friary (Red Friars), which was founded about 1474, and the place was named following the discovery of a large cross and inscribed stone on the site in 1261. The friary was dedicated to St Nicholas, and was a place of pilgrimage, but was burned by the English in the 1540s.

The church was taken over by the parish in 1561, and used until 1784, after which the buildings became ruinous. Much of the late 13th-century church survives, however, consisting of the tower, nave, chancel and sacristy, with later burial aisles.

It is said that the burial ground is haunted by the ghost of a lady. The story is that she fell from the tower of the church, from a door far up in the building.

Map 4, 9N (Peebles). On A703, Cross Road, N of Peebles, Borders.
His Scot: Access at all reasonable times. (0131 668 8800 / www.historic-scotland.gov.uk)

CROSSRAGUEL ABBEY

Crossraguel Abbey was founded in the 13th century by Duncan, Earl of Carrick, and is now a large and impressive ruin, with substantial remains of the church, cloister, chapter house, gate house, abbot's tower and some of the domestic buildings. The abbey was dissolved at the Reformation, and the property was disposed of to Allan Stewart, commendator of the abbey, in 1570. This did not impress Gilbert Kennedy, 4th Earl of Cassillis, whose family had, down the centuries, done much to endow the abbey with lands and property. Kennedy had Stewart roasted 'in sop' at Dunure Castle (see that entry) until Stewart signed over the lands of the dissolved abbey to the Kennedys.

The ruins of Crossraguel Abbey are said to be haunted by ghostly monks.

Map 3, 5O (Crossraguel). Off A77, 2 miles SW of Maybole, Crossraguel, Ayrshire.
His Scot: Open Apr-Oct, daily. (01655 883113 / www.historic-scotland.gov.uk)

CUCKOO BRIDGE, CASTLE DOUGLAS

It is thought that the body of a murdered baby was buried in the vicinity of the Cuckoo Bridge or was cast into the stream over which it passes. Wailing and weeping are said to be heard by people crossing the bridge, and occasionally an indistinct apparition, white and shapeless, has also been spotted.

Map 4, 7P (Castle Douglas). Off B736, 1.5 miles S of Castle Douglas, Kelton road, Dumfries and Galloway.

CULCREUCH CASTLE   ILLUS PAGE 92

Set in 1600 acres of park land below the Fintry Hills, Culcreuch Castle consists of a 15th-century keep with later additions. The castle was built by the Galbraiths, whose chiefs lived here for 300 years. The Galbraiths were a lawless lot in medieval times, and were noted for their thievery, pillage, burnings and rapine. Robert, 17th chief, had to sell the property in 1630 because of debt. The fine building is now a hotel, and has the largest colony of bats in the UK living in the roof area above the dining room. The Chinese Bird Room, within the old part of the building, has hand-painted Chinese wallpaper dating from 1723, believed to be the only surviving example of this period in Scotland.

The castle is reputed to have several ghosts. The Phantom Harper of Culcreuch relates to events believed to have taken place in 1582. One of the Buchanan family was mortally wounded by Robert Galbraith, later 17th Chief. The dying man was taken to what is now the Chinese Bird Room, accompanied by his mistress. When he died, to comfort herself she began to play a wire-strung harp, known as a clarsach in Gaelic – and it is said that her soft music has often been heard since, particularly in the dead of night. The music has been reported from this and its adjoining room and also in the Laird's Hall. There have also apparently been sightings of the phantom of an old woman in the Chinese Bird Room.

The apparition of a severed animal head has also reputedly been spotted, which apparently flies around the battlements. Another manifestation is supposedly that of a cold grey mass, about the height and proportions of a human. This has been reported in all areas of the old castle.

The lower bar area is also said to be the site of spooky incidents, including people feeling as if they have been touched, gloomy atmospheres, and customers refusing to sit in the end chamber of the bar.

Map 4, 7L (Culcreuch). Off B822, 11 miles W of Stirling, 0.5 miles N of Fintry, Culcreuch, Stirlingshire.
Hotel. (01360 860555 / www.culcreuch-castle-hotel.com)

A paranormal investigation was undertaken in May 2005 by Spectre (www.freewebs.com/ ukspectre/culcreuchcastle.htm) and in December 2004 by Ghost Finders (www.ghostfinders.co.uk/culcreuch.html) and in January 2005 by the Ghost Club (www.ghostclub.org.uk) and in November 2006 by Paranormal Investigation Scotland (www.paranormalinvestigationscotland.co.uk)

CULLACHY HOUSE
Cullachy House is a fine mansion, rising to three storeys and an attic, pink washed, and with corbiestepped gables. The mansion stands in a picturesque spot at the beginning of the old military way that went from Fort Augustus south and east over the foreboding Corrieyarack Pass.

The lands were held by the MacDonnells and by the Mackintoshes, and then later by the Frasers.

The house is said to have had a brownie (perhaps a 'Green Lady' or gruagach).

Map 1, 6G (Cullachy). Off A82, 2 miles S of Fort Augustus, Cullachy, Great Glen, Highland.

CULLEN HOUSE
Said to have had 386 rooms, Cullen House is a large sprawling mansion which incorporates an old castle. This was long a property of the Ogilvie Earls of Findlater, but has since been divided into flats.

The ghost of James Ogilvie, 3rd Earl of Seafield and 6th of Findlater, is said to haunt the building. Although well most of the time, the story is that he suffered from uncontrollable rages, and in November 1770 apparently murdered his factor in the library during a frenzied episode. In remorse, the Earl committed suicide, reputedly by cutting his own throat in one of the attic rooms. His ghost is said to have been seen, such as in 1943, and footsteps from unoccupied areas, including the stairs, have often been reported, including by journalists in 1964. Manifestations are said to take place mostly in the library, and in the Pulpit and Church Rooms.

Map 2, 10E (Cullen). Off A98, 0.5 miles SW of Cullen, Aberdeenshire.

CULLODEN HOUSE   ILLUS PAGE 92
Culloden House, dating mostly from 1772-83, incorporates the cellars of a 17th-century tower house, and is set in 40 acres of parkland. It was a property of the Forbes family. Duncan Forbes of Culloden was a Hanoverian, who fought with Butcher Cumberland at the Battle of Culloden Moor (also see that entry). Many wounded Jacobites were brought here after the battle – against Forbes's wishes but his protests were ignored – and here shot: those who were not killed outright had their

skulls bashed in with musket butts. The house is now used as a hotel.

The house is reputedly haunted by the ghost of Bonnie Prince Charlie, although this is disputed. The apparition of a man, dressed in tartan, is said to have been witnessed on several occasions in the passages, bedrooms and lounge.

Map 2, 7F (Culloden). Off A96, 3.5 miles E of Inverness, Culloden, Highland.
Hotel. (01463 790461 / www.cullodenhouse.co.uk)

CULLODEN MOOR
ILLUS PAGE 92

It was here on the bleak and windswept moor of Drumossie that on 16 April 1746 the Jacobite army of Bonnie Prince Charlie was crushed by Hanoverian forces led by the Duke of Cumberland – the last major battle to be fought on British soil. The Jacobites were tired and hungry, and the Hanoverians had a better equipped and larger army: the battle turned into a rout and many Jacobites were slaughtered. Sites of interest include Old Leanach Cottage, Graves of the Clans, Well of the Dead, Memorial Cairn, Cumberland Stone, and Field of the English. The visitor centre has a Jacobite and historical exhibition and an interesting audiovisual programme.

It is said that many have witnessed visions of the battle or apparitions, especially from by the Well of the Dead and the clan memorials. The descendants of those killed here are supposedly particularly sensitive to such visions.

The car park at the battlefield was voted the most haunted car park in a survey in 2005 by AA Insurance.

Map 2, 7F (Culloden). On B9006, 5 miles E of Inverness, Culloden, Highland.
NTS: Site open all year, daily; visitor centre open all year, daily except 24-26 Dec and 1-2 Jan. (01463 790607 / www.nts.org.uk)

CULROSS ABBEY

Situated in the pretty town of Culross, the Cistercian Abbey was dedicated to St Serf and St Mary, and was founded in 1217 by Malcolm, Earl of Fife. The abbey was dissolved at the Reformation and most of the buildings are ruinous, except the monks' choir, which has been used as the parish church since 1633. The remains of the domestic buildings are open to the public.

A piper is said to have been sent to explore a tunnel, the entrance to which was at the abbey – and which reputedly led to piles of gold and silver. The piper and his dog set off from a vault at the head of Newgate, followed above ground by the locals, but when they reached West Kirk, some distance away, the pipes suddenly stopped. The piper was never seen again, although it is said that the faint sound of pipes can be heard at times.

Map 4, 8L (Culross). Off B9037, 6.5 miles W of Dunfermline, Kirk Street, Culross, Fife.
His Scot: Open all year at reasonable times; parish church, open all year. (0131 668 8800 / www.historic-scotland.gov.uk)

CULROSS PALACE

Also in the village of Culross, is Culross Palace, a fine sprawling building dating from between 1597 and 1611. The complex consists of ranges of gabled yellow-washed buildings, with old decorative paint work and original interiors, as well as an unusual steeply terraced garden. The palace was built for Sir George Bruce of Carnock, who made a fortune from coal mining, but about 1700 it passed to the Erskines. The building has been restored by The National Trust for Scotland.

Some stories have parts of the palace being haunted, and manifestations are said to include people feeling as if they have been pushed, and unpleasant and foreboding feelings in the building.

Map 4, 8L (Culross). Off B9037, 6.5 miles W of Dunfermline, Culross, Fife.
NTS: Open early Apr-May, Sun-Thu (closed Mon-Wed); Jun-Aug, daily; Sep-Oct, Sun-Thu (closed Mon-Wed). (01383 880359 / www.nts.org.uk)

A paranormal investigation was undertaken in July 2003 by the Ghost Club (www.ghostclub.org.uk)

CULTOQUHEY

The picturesque baronial mansion of Cultoquhey, standing in a fine position overlooking the Ochil Hills, dates from 1820, and replaced an earlier house and a castle. The lands were held by the Maxtone family from 1410 or earlier, and Robert Maxtone of Cultoquhey was killed at the Battle of Flodden in 1513. The family, later Maxtone Graham, held the property until 1955 when it was sold. The building is now used as a guest house.

Kate McNiven, who was burnt after being accused of witchcraft, reportedly made a prophecy about the Maxtones: when a 'gleg-eyed' (sharp- or eagle-eyed) laird was born, a treasure would be found at Cultoquhey.

The house is said to be haunted by the bogle of a woman clad in an old-fashioned frock, and reportedly spotted entering one chamber, where she disappears.

Map 4, 8K (Cultoquhey). Off A85, 2 miles NE of Crieff, Cultoquhey, Perthshire.
Guest House. (01764 653253)

CULZEAN CASTLE

One of the foremost attractions in Scotland (and pronounced 'Cul-lane'), Culzean Castle is a magnificent sprawling castellated mansion of the Kennedy Earls of Cassillis. It was built between 1777 and 1792 by the architect Robert Adam, and is now in the care of The National Trust for Scotland. There are caves in the cliffs below the castle.

A ghostly piper is said to herald a Kennedy marriage, and to play on stormy nights. His apparition has reportedly been seen in the grounds, particularly on a drive known as 'Piper's Brae' and near the ruinous Collegiate church. The piper is said to have been exploring caves beneath the castle when he disappeared.

Two other ghosts supposedly haunt the castle: one a young woman dressed in a ball gown. Sightings of an indistinct apparition in one of the passages were reported in 1972 by three independent witnesses, servants who were working in the castle at the time. Another apparition has reportedly been seen several times on the main stair, one incident being in 1976 when two visitors saw a 'peculiar misty shape'. There are tales of a 'White Lady', said to be the spirit of a mistreated servant.

Map 3, 5O (Culzean). Off A77, 4.5 miles W of Maybole, Culzean, Ayrshire.
NTS: Castle open Apr-Nov, daily; country park and walled garden open all year, daily. (01655 884455 / www.culzeancastle.net)

A paranormal investigation was undertaken in February 2005 by Ghost Finders (www.ghostfinders.co.uk/culzean.html)

Featured in Living TV's Most Haunted, series one (2002).

DALHOUSIE CASTLE
ILLUS PAGE 103

Dalhousie Castle, which is situated in many acres of parkland, woods and river pasture, is an imposing castle and mansion with battlements and turrets. The building incorporates an ancient stronghold which was built by the Ramsays. Sir Alexander Ramsay was active in the Wars of Independence, and captured Roxburgh Castle from the English. In 1342 he was starved to death in Hermitage Castle (also see that entry). Dalhousie withstood a siege by the English in 1400, which lasted six months, and the family were later made Earls of Dalhousie. The Ramsays lived at the castle until about 1900, when they moved to Brechin Castle, and in 1925 the castle became a private boys' school. This was closed in 1950, and the castle is now a prestigious hotel.

Dalhousie is said to be haunted by a 'Grey Lady', the ghost of a Lady Catherine. She was the mistress of a Ramsay laird, possibly around the turn of the 16th century. Ramsay's wife had Catherine imprisoned in one of the turrets, where she perished from starvation. Her apparition has allegedly been seen on the stairs, in the dungeons, and along the 'Black' corridor. Other reported manifestations include the rustling of her gown, and scratching or light tapping at doors. There was a sighting of the ghost in 2000, during building work.

Another ghost is said to be that of one of the pupils from when the castle was a school. The story goes that a boy leapt from the top of the building and was killed.

A third spirit is that of a dog, which died in the 1980s after also falling from the castle. Its apparition has allegedly been seen running on the stairs and along the passageways.

Other reported manifestations include a member of staff having her hair pulled when nobody else was present, and a guest being tapped on each shoulder several times by invisible hands.

There is also a legend that when a branch falls from an old oak tree near Dalhousie then someone is about to die at the castle.

Map 4, 9M (Dalhousie). Off B704, 3 miles S of Dalkeith, Dalhousie, Bonnyrigg, Midlothian. **Hotel. (01875 820153 / www.dalhousiecastle.co.uk)**

DALKEITH HOUSE

Standing in acres of parkland, Dalkeith House is a striking classical mansion, which incorporates some of an ancient castle. The property was held by the Douglases from about 1350. Sir James Douglas, first Earl of Morton and his wife Joanna, daughter of James I, are buried in the ruinous chancel of the nearby St Nicholas Buccleuch Parish Church, their tomb marked by weathered stone effigies. The church can be visited (www.stnicholasbuccleuch.org.uk). In 1642 the lands were sold to the Scott Earls – and later Dukes – of Buccleuch, and it remains with their descendants. The house is now used for students from Wisconsin.

Dalkeith House is reputed to be haunted by the ghost of a woman, a 'Green Lady' or 'Grey Lady', which is said to have been witnessed often in recent times. Activity such as unexplained footsteps (especially on the main staircase), mysterious noises, voices, music and laughter, doors opening by themselves, a wardrobe shaking and disgorging hangers, and other manifestations, have also been reported, including sightings of moving balls of light.

One story is that the ghost (or another bogle) is the spirit of a girl around eight-years old, called Anna, who fell out of one of the upstairs windows; another tale that the place is also haunted by her careless nursemaid.

There is also an account of a student waking up to find a headless apparition sitting on the end of her bed, with its head under its arm. The bogle apparently told the sleeper to get out of the room, and was identified (tentatively, presumably) as the ghost of Mary, Queen of Scots.

Map 4, 9M (Dalkeith). Off A6094, 0.5 miles NW of Dalkeith, Midlothian.
Country park, open Easter-Oct. House not open. (0131 654 1666/0131 663 5684 / www.dalkeithcountrypark.com)

DALMAHOY

ILLUS PAGE 103
Commanding extensive views of the surrounding countryside, Dalmahoy is a fine Georgian mansion, designed in 1720 by the architect William Adam. The property was held from 1296 by the Dalmahoys, but was sold to the Dalrymples in about 1650, then went to the Douglas Earls of Morton in the middle of the 18th century. They held it for 200 years as their main seat. The mansion is now part of a hotel complex which features two golf courses and many other leisure facilities.

Dalmahoy is said to be haunted by a 'White Lady'. Sightings of the apparition have been reported in both the corridors and in the bedrooms of the old part of the building. This is said to be a friendly ghost, and is thought to be the bogle of Lady Mary Douglas (daughter of the Earl of Morton who bought the property in 1760). Her portrait hangs in the hotel.

Map 4, 9L (Dalmahoy). Off A71, 7 miles W of Edinburgh, Kirknewton, Edinburgh.
Hotel - open all year. (0131 333 1845 / www.marriott.com/edigs)

DALMARNOCK ROAD BRIDGE, GLASGOW

Dalmarnock Road Bridge, a five-span structure built in the 1890s, is one of eight bridges which crosses the Clyde as the river runs through Glasgow, and the bridge carries the A749 into Rutherglen.

The bridge is said to be haunted by the ghost of a fellow who committed suicide here. The apparition is described as that of a man in his thirties, with cropped hair, and dressed in black trousers and a dark three-quarter length coat. The ghost is said to have been witnessed many times, passers-by believing that the phantom is a real person about to jump from the bridge.

It is said, however, that if the figure is closely approached it then fades away.

Map 4, 7M (Glasgow). On A749, Dalmarnock Road, Dalmarnock, Glasgow.

DALPEDDAR

Nothing remains of a tower house at Dalpeddar, a property of the MacMath family.

John, son of James MacMath of Dalpeddar, was the intended husband for Marion Carruthers of Mouswald, although Marion refused him. The poor girl ended up dead, having fallen (or having been pushed) from one of the turrets of Comlongon Castle (see that entry).

The area near Dalpeddar is said to be haunted by the apparition of a tall woman, sometimes accompanied by that of a young boy, dressed in white, and their figures have been recorded appearing by the roadside.

They are said to be the ghosts of 'Lady Hebron' and her son: Hebron is a family name with origins from near Morpeth in Northumberland in England. The story goes that Lady Hebron was heiress to the small estate of Dalpeddar some time during the 16th century (perhaps 1580). She was married in due course and had a son, but her husband died and she was left a widow. Their uncle, however, wanted the property, and Lady Hebron and her son disappeared. Much later the bones of a woman and child were found, buried near the road: the lady had had her skull split.

A Marion of Dalpeddar is said to have been murdered by one of the Crichton lairds and to haunt Sanquhar Castle (see that entry), and the stories are obviously linked.

Another ghost story involving Dalpeddar has Abraham Crichton of Carco, an unpopular and ruthless landowner, dragged along the ground all the way to Dalpeddar. His ghost is then said to have haunted Sanquhar Kirkyard (see that entry),

Map 4, 80 (Dalpeddar). Off A76, 3 miles SE of Sanquhar, Dalpeddar, Dumfries and Galloway.

DALRY HOUSE, EDINBURGH

Dalry House is a fine white-washed mansion with two hexagonal stair towers and dates from 1661. There is original plasterwork in one of the rooms. Dalry House was the country house of the Chiesly family, and was built by Walter Chiesly, a magistrate and merchant in Edinburgh. It was sold to the Walker family in 1812 and they held the property until 1870 when they gifted it to the Episcopal Church for use as a teacher-training college. The building was renovated in the 1960s and was used as an old person's day centre until 2002, but it has since been divided into several apartments.

The house and area were said to be haunted by a ghost, 'Johnny One Arm'. John Chiesly was executed in 1689 for shooting and killing Sir George Lockhart of Carnwath, after Lockhart, Lord President of the Court of Session, found against Chiesly in a divorce settlement (there were eleven children to support...). Chiesly was tortured to reveal any accomplices and was mutilated by having his pistol arm severed, before being hanged, but his dead body was removed from the gallows before it could be buried.

His one-armed apparition is then said to have been witnessed often, and heard crying and screaming. In 1965 the remains of a one-armed man are said to have been found under a hearth (or in a nearby cottage), and his ghost has reputedly not been seen since his remains were buried.

Chiesly's daughter, Rachel, who was said to be a great beauty, was married to James Erskine. Erskine was Lord Justice Clerk as Lord Grange and Lord of Justiciary; he was also the brother of John, sixth Earl of Mar, leader of the 1715 Jacobite Rising. Rachel (Lady Grange) and Erskine had several children, but it is believed that she flew into rages and they seem to have fallen out. When she discovered his Jacobite plotting in 1732, James had Rachel imprisoned, first in central Scotland and then in the Western Isles by Jacobite friends. After years of poor treatment, Rachel is thought to have died on Skye in 1745 and to be buried at Trumpan (also see that entry).

Map 4, 9L (Edinburgh). Off A70, 1 mile W of Edinburgh Castle, Orwell Place, Edinburgh. **View from exterior. (www.dalryhouse.co.uk)**

DALSWINTON CASTLE

Little remains of Dalswinton Castle, once a strong and fine fortress, except some of the basement and the remains of a round tower. The lands belonged to the Comyns and then to the Stewarts, and the castle changed hands between the Scots and the

English. The lands later passed to the Maxwells, and the old stronghold was replaced by the nearby elegant mansion of Dalswinton House, which dates from 1785 and was built for the Miller family. The house is still occupied, and the gardens are occasionally open to the public.

Dalswinton, when it was held by the Maxwells, was said to have had a brownie, who could perform the work of ten men and would often keep servants awake at night because of his exertions. This brownie also helped in finding the daughter of the house a suitable husband, and was described as a wrinkled, ancient old man. An over zealous Presbyterian minister, however, decided to convert the brownie from (what he presumed) were its heathen ways, and in doing so poured baptismal water over the brownie's head. The story goes that the brownie gave out a huge cry and left Dalswinton forever.

Map 4, 8P (Dalswinton). Off A76, 6 miles N of Dumfries, 1 mile SE of Dalswinton village, Dumfries and Galloway.
Gardens occasionally open as part of Scotland's Garden Scheme. (01387 740220 / www.gardensofscotland.org)

DALZELL HOUSE

Standing on the edge of a rocky ravine, Dalzell House – other spellings can be Dalyell or Dalziel – incorporates an old castle in the large rambling mansion. The property belonged to the Dalziel Earls of Carnforth from the 13th century, but was sold to the Hamiltons of Boggs in 1649. Covenanters were sheltered in the grounds, and held illegal conventicles under a huge oak tree, now known as the 'Covenanter's Oak'. The north wing of the house was used as a hospital during World War I.

The house is said to be haunted by four ghosts: 'Green', 'White', 'Grey' and 'Brown' Ladies.

Sightings of the 'Green Lady' have been reported in the Piper's Gallery, and other manifestations include unexplained flashing lights, footsteps and other noises. The strong smell of exotic perfume has also been recorded, and this is said to presage a appearance of this ghost.

The 'White Lady' is thought to be the ghost of a young female servant. Although unmarried, she became pregnant and in despair threw herself to her death from the battlements. Her ghost is reputed to be seen at the spot from where she jumped.

The 'Grey Lady' was said to haunt the north wing, and to originate from when the house was used as a hospital. Her apparition is believed to be seen wearing a grey nurse's uniform.

The 'Brown Lady' is claimed to have been spotted in the former nursery.

Map 4, 7M (Dalzell). Off A721, 1.5 miles SE of Motherwell, Dalzell, Lanarkshire.
Dalzell Park open, daily dawn-dusk. Dalzell House not open. (0141 304 1907 / www.northlan.gov.uk)

DANKEITH HOUSE

Dankeith House, dating from the 19th century, is a large imposing edifice, although it is not in a good state of repair; the present building replaced an earlier house or castle. The property was held by the Archibalds, and then by the Kelso family from 1693 until 1865. Dankeith was completely rebuilt after a fire, and was later used as the headquarters for the RAF, a borstal, a seminary, and then as a girls' school. There is a static caravan park in the grounds.

The building is said to be haunted, and there have reputedly recently been several sightings of unexplained manifestations, some of which have been captured on camera.

Map 3, 6N (Dankeith). Off B730, 3.5 miles SW of Kilmarnock, Ayrshire.
Caravan park. (01563 830254)

A paranormal investigation was undertaken in September 2005 by Alba Paranormal Investigations (www.albaparanormal.com/dankeithhouseayrshire.htm)

DAVID LIVINGSTONE CENTRE, BLANTYRE

Set in 20 acres of parkland and woodland garden, the David Livingstone Centre is located in the tenement where Livingstone was born, and there are displays on Scotland's greatest missionary-explorer.

The centre is said to be haunted, the bogle identified (by some) as that of Livingstone and known as 'Old Davy', although no apparition has apparently been spotted. Activity is reputed to include objects disappearing and then reappearing a long time later in the place from which they had originally vanished.

Map 4, 7M (Blantyre). Off M74, 2 miles NW of Hamilton, 165 Station Road, Blantyre, Glasgow.
NTS: Open Apr-24 Dec, daily: tel to check. (01698 823140/0844 493 2100 / www.nts.org.uk)

DEAN CASTLE   ILLUS PAGE 103

Standing in acres of parkland, Dean Castle dates from the 14th-century or earlier, and was long a property of the Boyd Earls of Kilmarnock. Robert Boyd was Guardian of James III, and for a time very powerful in Scotland. He fell from favour and had to flee abroad, while his brother was executed. William Boyd, 4th Earl, was Privy Councillor to Bonnie Prince Charlie during the Jacobite Rising of 1745-46, and the ghost story relates to him. Well before the Rising, servants were terrified by an apparition of Boyd's severed head rolling about the floor at Dean. When Boyd joined the Jacobite Rising, he told the Earl of Galloway about the haunting. Boyd was a Colonel in the Prince's guard, but was captured after the Battle of Culloden in 1746 and – as predicted by the apparition – executed by beheading.

Boyd's wife, Anne Livingstone, died the following year and is said to haunt Howard Park further south in Kilmarnock, at the site of the demolished Kilmarnock House (see that entry).

Map 3, 6N (Dean). Off B7038, 1 mile NE of Kilmarnock, Dean, Ayrshire.
Open all year, Apr-Sep daily; Nov to end Mar Wed-Sun; park open all year. (01563 522702 / www.deancastle.com)

DEAN'S COURT, ST ANDREWS

Standing opposite the western end of the ruinous cathedral, Dean's Court is a large building of three storeys with a courtyard and well, and dates from the 16th or earlier (perhaps the 12th century), making it one of the oldest houses in St Andrews. After the Reformation, Dean's Court was held by Sir George Douglas, who was one of those who helped Mary, Queen of Scots, escape from Loch Leven Castle (see that entry) in 1568. In the 17th century the building was owned by Sir James Gregory, an eminent astronomer and mathematician, and Professor of Mathematics from 1668-74. In 1930 Dean's Court passed to the University of St Andrews, and it has been

Dalhousie Castle (page 98)

Dalmahoy (page 99)

Dean Castle (page 102)

Delgatie Castle (page 105)

Delgatie Castle (page 105)

used as a hall of residence for postgraduates since 1952.

Dean's Court is said to be haunted by at least two ghosts: one, a 'White Lady', is believed to be the same ghost that haunts the cathedral and other parts of St Andrews (also see St Andrews Cathedral and Castle). The other is the spirit is that of a black three-legged dog, which is also reputed to have been spotted in the graveyard of the cathedral.

Map 4, 10K (St Andrews). Off A91 or A917, North Street, opposite cathedral, St Andrews, Fife. **Part of St Andrews University: some tours take in Dean's Court.**

Deer Abbey

Deer Abbey, a Cistercian house, was founded in 1219 by William Comyn, Earl of Buchan, and dedicated to the Blessed Virgin Mary. The lands passed in 1587 to Robert Keith, Lord Altrie, and not much of the church remains except foundations, although the infirmary, Abbot's House and the southern cloister range are better preserved.

The University Library at Cambridge now houses the beautifully illustrated *Book of Deer*.

The spectre of a monk has reputedly been seen on the main road that runs past the abbey, the apparition dressed in a dark robe and hood but with a blur for a face.

Map 2, 11E (Deer). Off A950, 9 miles W of Peterhead, 2 miles W of Mintlaw, Aberdeenshire. **His Scot: Access at all reasonable times. (01667 460232 / www.historic-scotland.gov.uk)**

Delgatie Castle ILLUS PAGE 104

Set in a fine location, Delgatie Castle is an ancient and interesting pile with walls up to 14 foot thick in places. The main tower rises to more than 60 foot, and there a fine original painted ceilings of the 16th century and a massive turnpike stair.

The lands were given to the Hays by Robert the Bruce in the 14th century, and they held them for some 350 years. The Hays were made Earls of Errol in 1452, and Francis, the 9th Earl, was accused of treason in 1594, and part of the west wall was demolished by James VI's forces. The castle had to be sold in 1762, and was occupied by the army during World War II. It was then left uninhabited until bought back by the Hays who began the task of restoration.

It is said that Delgatie is haunted by the ghost of a spirited young woman, known as Rohaise. She is thought to have defended the castle from an attack, and reputedly haunts the bedroom off the main stair, which now bears her name. It is said she likes to visit men who stay in the chamber. The ghost could be quite frightening it appears, at least in the imagination.

Troops stationed here during the War twice fled outdoors following unexplained disturbances, although a search of the building found nothing untoward.

Map 2, 11E (Delgatie). Off A947, 2 miles E of Turriff, Banff and Buchan, Aberdeenshire. **Open all year, daily; closed 21 Dec-6 Jan. (01888 563479 / www.delgatiecastle.com)**

Devanha House, Aberdeen

Named after a Roman camp believed to be at the mouth of the Denburn, Devanha is a small mansion of two storeys, built in 1813 for William Black, but later remodelled. Black was a brewer and became famous for his Devanha Porter. The once extensive grounds were broken up in the late 19th century, and the house has been divided into separate apartments.

The house is said to be haunted by the apparition of a woman, although only the upper half of her body is reputedly seen. This may be because of a change in floor levels rather than because of dismemberment.

Map 2, 12G (Aberdeen). Off A956, off Holbourn Street, Ferryhill, Aberdeen.

DIBIDIL BOTHY, RUM

Although not one of the largest of the Western Isles, Rum is one of the most impressive with rugged mountains rising to more than 2500 foot. Once home to more than 400 people, there are now only some 25 residents. On the island is the impressive but slightly incongruous Kinloch Castle, a large Edwardian mansion, which was built by the Bullough family after they had purchased the island in the 1880s.

On the south-east side of Rum, at Dibidil and reached along a rough track, is a bothy. This is said to be haunted by the bogle of a fisherman, who wakes sleepers by sitting on their legs and preventing them from moving, before it disappears through a walled-up doorway.

Map 1, 2G (Dibidil). On track, 4 miles S of Kinloch (further by foot), Dibidil, SE side of Isle of Rum, Highland.

DICKMONTLAW FARM

The sound of pipe music is reputedly to be heard at times, coming from the hearth at Dickmontlaw Farm. The story goes that a piper called Tam Tyrie, his wife and his dog took refuge in a cave by the sea (more than a mile and half away from the farm). Tam found an opening in the back of the cave, and they went to investigate, but got lost in the dark and his spirit is said to still be trying to find a way out, playing the pipes as it wanders the subterranean passageways.

It has been suggested that this was a story put about to dissuade people from frequenting the caves, which are believed to have been used for smuggling at one time.

Map 4, 10J (Dickmontlaw). Off A92, 1 mile N of Arbroath, Dickmontlaw Farm, Angus.

DISCOVERY POINT, DUNDEE

Discovery Point is the home of RRS *Discovery*, Captain Scott's Antarctic ship. Within the complex are eight exhibition areas, using lighting, graphics and special effects to recreate key moments in the *Discovery's* history. The ship has been extensively restored below deck.

Discovery is said to be haunted, by unexplained footsteps on deck and other disturbances. Suggested identities for the ghost include Ernest Shackleton, or Charles Bonner, one of the crew, who fell from the craw's nest to his death in 1901.

Map 4, 10K (Dundee). Off A92, Discovery Quay, Dundee.
Open all year, daily; closed 25-26 Dec & 1-2 Jan. (01382 309060 / www.rrsdiscovery.com)

Featured in Living TV's Most Haunted, *series eight (2006).*

DOLPHINSTON TOWER

There was a once strong castle here, but nothing remains and the site is occupied by Dolphinston Farm. The lands were a property of Dolphin, son of Cospatrick, in the 11th century, hence the name. Dolphinston was held by the Ainslie family from the 13th century or earlier, but passed by marriage to the Kerrs about 300 years later.

The tower is said to have had a brownie at one time, but the easily offended drudge left, after being given a garment which it disliked, reputedly crying:

Since ye've gien me a harden ramp,
Nae mair o' your corn I will tramp.

Map 4, 11N (Dolphinston). Off A68, 4 miles SE of Jedburgh, Dolphinston, Borders.

DONIBRISTLE CASTLE

Once a fine castle and mansion, nothing now survives of Donibristle House except two service wings after the building was accidentally burned down in 1858. The lands were a property of the Abbey of Inchcolm, but passed to the Stewart Earls of Moray; in recent times the housing estates of Dalgety Bay were built on the lands.

It was at the shore here in 1592 that James Stewart, the 'Bonnie Earl of Moray', was murdered by the Gordon Earl of Huntly, as recounted in the old ballad. Huntly had been given a commission to capture Moray, as the 'Bonnie Earl' was suspected of being involved in a plot against James VI (and it has also been suggested that Moray was showing an undue interest in Anne of Denmark, James's wife). The Gordons besieged Donibristle and set it alight, and Moray had no choice but to flee across the beach as the flames took hold, but he was then cornered.

Moray reportedly stuttered, as he was dying after Gordon of Gight had slashed him across the face with his sword: 'You have spoilt a better face than your own.' Moray's mother had a painting made of Moray's hewn body, which is now kept at Darnaway Castle.

Some tales have an apparition of Moray being seen on the beach, hair ablaze, at the spot where he was slain.

Map 4, 9L (Donibristle). Off A921, 1.5 miles E of Inverkeithing, W of Dalgety Bay, Fife.

DORNOCH CASTLE HOTEL

Standing near the fine restored cathedral in the pleasant 'city', Dornoch Palace (or Castle) is a tall and impressive tower and courtyard, dating from the 13th or 14th century, with later additions. The palace was built by the Bishops of Caithness, but passed to the Earls of Sutherland after the Reformation. In 1567 George Sinclair, 4th Earl of Caithness, had Dornoch torched and the castle besieged to secure possession of the young Earl of Sutherland in an attempt to seize that earldom and add it to his own of Caithness. The palace held out for a month, but eventually surrendered and hostages given by the garrison were murdered. The building was then torched, and left a ruin until restored in the 19th century as a courthouse and jail. Latterly the building has been used as a fine hotel.

Dornoch Castle is reputedly haunted by the ghost of Andrew McCornish, who was imprisoned here after being charged with stealing sheep. Sightings of his phantom were reported at the end of the 19th century, and there have also apparently been recent manifestations in the oldest part of the building, such as shaking walls and unexplained noises, as if furniture was being dragged over the floor. There are also stories of phantoms and half-seen apparitions being spotted.

An underground passageway reputedly links the palace to the nearby cathedral, and it was into this tunnel that all the last bishop's wealth was reputedly placed during the Reformation. Should the treasure ever be found, the story goes that this will herald the end of the Earls and Dukes of Sutherland.

Dornoch is also believed to be the last place to witness the execution of a woman accused of witchcraft, Janet Horne, in 1722 or 1727 (see Witch's Stone, Dornoch).

Map 2, 7D (Dornoch). Off A949, near cathedral, Dornoch, Sutherland, Highland.
Hotel. (01862 810216 / www.dornochcastlehotel.com)

A paranormal investigation was undertaken by Ghost Finders in February 2006 (www.ghostfinders.co.uk/dornoch_castle.html)

DOUGLAS CASTLE

Little remains of Douglas Castle, a 13th-century stronghold, which was once a fortress of some renown. The castle was built by the Douglases, and was held by the English in 1307, during the Wars of Independence. Sir James Douglas trapped the English garrison while they were at worship in the chapel, and recaptured the castle for the Scots. He had the garrison slaughtered and dumped in the cellar, before torching the castle, in what became known as 'Douglas's Larder'. The old castle was eventually replaced by a splendid new mansion with round towers and turrets, but this was demolished because of subsidence due to mining. Plans have been put forward to turn the site into a historical theme park.

The castle is believed to be haunted by a phantom black dog.

Map 4, 8N (Douglas). Off A70, 0.75 miles N of Douglas, Lanarkshire.

DOUNE CASTLE

Standing on a strong site in a lovely location above the River Teith, Doune Castle has two strong and lofty towers linked by a lower range. These buildings form two sides of a courtyard, the other sides enclosed by a high curtain wall. The castle was built by Robert Stewart, Duke of Albany, who virtually ruled Scotland during the reign of Robert III and the imprisonment in England of the young James I. When Albany died in 1420, his son, Murdoch, succeeded him as Regent and as Duke, but when James I was freed in 1424 he had Murdoch executed. Doune was kept as a royal hunting lodge, prison, and dower house. The castle was occasionally used by Mary, Queen of Scots, her suite of rooms being in the kitchen tower, and this is another place where a ghostly apparition of Mary has reputedly been spotted.

The property passed to the Earls of Moray. The ballad 'The Bonnie Earl o' Murray' tells the tale of the murder of the Earl of Moray, at Donibristle (see that entry), by the Gordon Earl of Huntly, and has the last verse:

O lang will his Lady.
Look owre the Castle Doune.
Ere she see the Earl o' Moray
Come sounding through the toun.

Map 4, 7L (Doune). Off A820, 7 miles NW of Stirling, SE of Doune, Stirlingshire.
His Scot: Open all year: Apr-Oct, daily; Nov-Mar, Sat-Wed, closed Thu & Fri; closed 25/26 Dec and 1/2 Jan. (01786 841742 / www.historic-scotland.gov.uk)

DOUNE HIGHLAND HOTEL

Located in the quiet village, the Doune Highland Hotel is a small and welcoming family-run hotel.

The hotel is said to be haunted by at least three ghosts. There are stories of an apparition being spotted on the stair, the phantom of a woman with dark hair. Another phantom, of a man dressed in blue overalls, is reported to have been seen going through the restaurant and the toilet before vanishing. There are also accounts of the ghost of a large dog, witnessed in one of the rooms.

Other manifestations are reported, such as unexplained footsteps and voices, the smell of tobacco smoke coming from an area where no smokers were present, and objects being moved or disappearing in the kitchen area. A human bone, found in one of the walls, also disappeared without explanation.

Map 4, 7L (Doune). On A820, 19 Main Street, Doune, Stirling.
Hotel. (01786 841536 / www.dounehighlandhotel.co.uk)

A paranormal investigation was undertaken in November 2006 by Ghost Finders (www.ghostfinders.co.uk/highland_hotel_doune.html)

DOUNE OF ROTHIEMURCHUS

Doune, a mansion dating from the late 18th century, is a property of the Grants of Rothiemurchus, and was home to Elizabeth Grant, author of *Memoirs of a Highland Lady*.

The house was said to be haunted by the son of a laird, who suffered from episodes of madness. During one of these he reputedly strangled a servant girl on the stairs, then died himself after falling over the bannister. His ghost reportedly haunts the house, and activity is said to be concentrated in one of the bedrooms.

Map 2, 8G (Doune of Rothiemurchus). Off B970, 2 miles S of Aviemore, Rothiemurchus, Highland.
Open Apr-Oct. (01479 812345 / www.rothiemurchus.net)

DREADNOUGHT HOTEL, CALLANDER

The Dreadnought Hotel was built in 1802 by Francis MacNab, the chief of his clan: 'Dread nought' is the motto of the MacNabs. The Dreadnought is an imposing building, modified down the years, and used as a hotel; there has apparently been a hostelry here since the 17th century.

Francis MacNab had his seat at Kinnell House, near Killin, and lived in some style and eccentricity (and wickedness, according to some tales – see below), although he did not apparently have the funds to finance his lifestyle. He is depicted in Sir Henry Raeburn's impressive portrait of him, resplendent in full Highland dress. MacNab was succeeded by his nephew Archibald as chief, but Archibald escaped his circling creditors by fleeing to Canada.

The Dreadnought is said to be haunted by the ghost of a girl. There are at least two versions of the story behind the haunting. One is that she was a servant girl who was made pregnant by Francis MacNab, and he tossed her out of one of the windows on the upper floors to rid himself of her. A second that he walled up his wife somewhere in the building.

A second ghost is said to manifest itself by sobbing and weeping, heard coming from one of the bedrooms. One story is that an infant, an illegitimate child of

MacNab, was drowned in an old well in the basement of the hotel and eerie weeping can still at times be heard.

A third ghost is said to be that of MacNab himself.

Map 4, 7K (Callander). Off A84, Leny Road, Callander, Stirlingshire.
Hotel. (01877 330184 / www.oxfordhotelsandinns.com)

DREEL TAVERN, ANSTRUTHER
ILLUS PAGE III

Located on the High Street of the attractive seaside village, the Dreel Tavern is an atmospheric and friendly tavern, dating from the 16th century and a formerly a coaching inn.

There is a plaque commemorating the visit of James V, the story going that James was carried piggyback over the Dreel Burn by a beggar woman (it was usual practice in fishing communities for the womenfolk to carry their men out to the boats). The lass was rewarded by the king's purse, although some people have suggested that the king rode her rather more intimately. The woman is said to have given him a 'benison' (good wishes), saying 'May prick nor purse ever fail you'. This phrase is said to have inspired the formation of the 'Beggars' Benison of Anstruther', a secret society established in 1739, 'a Scottish society of an erotic and convivial nature composed of the Nobility and Gentry of Anstruther'. The society met in the now demolished Dreel Castle.

The Dreel Tavern is said to be haunted. There are accounts of an apparition of a man, dressed as a seafarer or pirate, which has been seen on more than one occasion sitting on a chair in a bedroom. Other manifestations in this chamber are reputed to include the unexplained movement of a bed (when someone was sleeping in it), and a shelf turning round by itself, although the ornaments on it did not fall off.

Other unexplained occurrences are said to be footsteps heard coming from the top floor although the area was unoccupied, as well as the noise of doors closing and the sounds of boisterous children playing, heard early one morning. Brass plates also fell from a wall with no obvious explanation, and half-seen movement or shadows have also been witnessed, after the bar had closed.

Map 4, 10K (Anstruther). Off A917, High Street West, Anstruther Wester, Fife.
Tavern. (01333 310727 / www.thedreeltavern.co.uk)

A paranormal investigation undertaken (www.paranormaldiscovery.co.uk)

DROVER'S INN, INVERARNAN
ILLUS PAGE III

Located in a lovely hill-clad spot to the north of Loch Lomond, The Drover's Inn is an atmospheric, memorable and intriguing hostelry, dating back to the 18th century. The inn was used by Highland drovers moving cattle down the banks of Loch Lomond to the markets of the south.

There are several accounts of ghosts at the Drover's Inn, perhaps the most disturbing is that several people sleeping in Room 6 have woken up to find that it feels as if they are lying next to a cold and dank body. The story is that a girl drowned in a burn and her corpse was laid out in that room.

Another tale is that a couple, who were sleeping in Room 2, woke up to find that there were the phantoms of a man, woman and lad standing at the end of their bed. The bogle of a cattle drover is reported to be occasionally seen in the hallways, and

Dreel Tavern, Anstruther (page 110)

Drover's Inn, Inverarnan (page 110)

Dryburgh Abbey
(page 114)

Duff House (page 115)

Dumfries House (page 116)

in the bar reputedly sometimes the sitting apparition of an old man is spotted, known as 'Old George'; his ashes are apparently kept in an urn in the inn.

There is also the story concerning a couple staying at the inn, who, when looking through photos in their camera, found ones of them sleeping in bed from the previous night.

Map 3, 6K (Inverarnan). On A82, 2 miles N of Ardlui, N end of Loch Lomond, Inverarnan, Stirling.
Inn. (01301 704234 / www.thedroversinn.co.uk)

DRUMLANRIG CASTLE

The large and stately towered mansion, dating mostly from the 17th century, incorporates part of an ancient castle. Drumlanrig was held by the Douglases, later Earls and Dukes of Queensberry, from the 14th century or earlier; James Douglas of Drumlanrig was involved in the death of Marion Carruthers at Comlongon Castle (see that entry). Bonnie Prince Charlie stayed at the castle in 1745, after his retreat from Derby, and his men sacked and damaged the building, including stabbing a picture of William of Orange, since repaired. Drumlanrig passed to the Scott Dukes of Buccleuch in 1810, with whose descendants it remains.

Three ghosts are believed to haunt the castle. One is reputed to be the spirit of Lady Anne Douglas, dressed in white, with her fan in one hand – and her head in the other. There is no story, however, about how she came to lose her head; indeed there is apparently no woman of that name who was beheaded.

Another bogle is said to be that of a young woman in a flowing dress, that is reputed to appear to people who are ill and bedridden in the castle.

The third is of a monkey, ape or other creature, witnessed in the Yellow Monkey Room.

Another story is that someone was murdered in one of the corridors, the 'Bloody Passage', and that the resultant spilt blood could not be washed off the floor.

There is also a strange story concerning William Douglas, Duke of Queensberry. Douglas obtained an evil reputation for his treatment of Covenanters. One tenant of his, while in Sicily, claimed that on the night Douglas died he saw a black coach bearing Douglas soar to the top of Mount Etna. Just to confirm the identity, a voice cried out: 'Open to the Duke of Queensberry', before the coach plunged into the steaming caldera, an indication that Douglas was on his way to hell.

The only thing that seems true about this tale is that the tenant did not think much of Douglas.

There is also a prophecy by Thomas the Rhymer about the castle – House of Hassock is another name for Drumlanrig:

When the Marr Burn runs where never man saw
The House of the Hassock is near to a fa'

This is said to have been fulfilled when Charles, 3rd Duke, diverted the Marr Burn to make a fountain and cascade south of the castle. His two sons died young. The Burn has since been returned to its original course.

Map 4, 7O (Drumlanrig). Off A76, 3 miles NW of Thornhill, Drumlanrig, Dumfries and Galloway.
Castle open Good Friday-Aug; country park open Good Friday-Sep. (01848 600283 / www.drumlanrig.com/)

DRUMMORAL

The lands of Drummoral were held by the MacCulloch family in the early part of the 17th century, and then by the Coltranes. One of the family was William Coltrane, Provost of Wigtown, who in May 1685 is believed to have been instrumental in the prosecution of the Wigtown Martyrs, when two women were tied to posts and drowned by the incoming sea. He was vilified by his Covenanter enemies, and it is said that when he died the windows of the house in which he perished were all ablaze, as if the place was consumed by fire, believed to show that Coltrane was being taken into the fiery pits of hell. The story also goes that his ghost began to haunt the area where he perished, his terrifying bogle reputed to be often spotted with fire snorting from its nostrils.

Map 4, 7Q (Drummoral). Off A750, 1 mile W of Isle of Whithorn, Drummoral, Dumfries and Galloway.

DRUMMORE CASTLE

Little or nothing remains of a 16th-century tower house owned by the Adairs of Kilhilt, which was habitable in 1684. There were significant remains, incorporated into the farm at Low Drummore, until the last part was demolished in 1963.

It is said that when the castle was first pulled down a skeleton and a spear were found sealed up in one of the walls, and materials from the castle were used to build Low Drummore. Mysterious noises then plagued the building, including a sound as if a thread was being snapped. The room where this occurred had to be abandoned for a while, until the last of the castle was demolished – since when the activity is believed to have ceased.

Map 3, 5Q (Drummore). Off B7041, 16 miles S of Stranraer, Low Drummore, Rhins of Galloway, Dumfries and Galloway.

DRUMTOCHTY CASTLE

Standing in acres of wooded grounds, Drumtochty Castle is a large castellated mansion dating from 1812, although the building may incorporate part of an old castle. The mansion was built for the Reverend J. S. Gammell of Countesswells, but was later used as a hospital in World War I, then as a hotel, then as a school from 1948 until 1968. The house was restored in the 1970s, and is now a residence again.

The building is said to be haunted by a 'Green Lady', and manifestations are reported to have been recently witnessed.

Map 2, 11H (Drumtochty). Off B966, 2 miles NW of Auchenblae, Drumtochty Castle, Aberdeenshire.
Available for weddings, events and accommodation. (01561 320169 / www.drumtochtyunlimited.com)

DRYBURGH ABBEY   ILLUS PAGE 112

A picturesque and substantial ruin by the banks of the Tweed, the Abbey was founded by David I as a Premonstratensian establishment, dedicated to St Mary. Most of the buildings date from the 12th and 13th centuries, and part of the church survives, as do substantial portions of the cloister, including the fine chapter house, parlour and vestry. The Abbey was burnt by the English in 1322, 1385 and 1545. Sir Walter Scott and Earl Haig are both buried here.

The abbey ruins are said to be haunted by ghostly monks, who in life had deceived a dying man into leaving them all his money. The unexplained sounds of chanting have also been reported.

Map 4, 10N (Dryburgh). Off B6356, 3 miles SE of Melrose, Dryburgh, Borders.
His Scot: Open all year, daily; closed 25/26 Dec and 1/2 Jan. (01835 822381 / www.historic-scotland.gov.uk)

DRYBURGH ABBEY HOTEL

Set on the banks of the wide Tweed in a lovely spot, and close to the fine ruins of the ancient abbey (see Dryburgh Abbey) is the Dryburgh Abbey Hotel. On the site of a much older building, the hotel is housed in a large and strapping castellated mansion, with a pink blush, and it stands in 10 acres of grounds.

A fair maiden, from what was then known as Mantle House, fell in love with one of the monks of Dryburgh Abbey, and the two soon became intimate but they were not sufficiently discreet. The abbot found out and, being a good Christian fellow, he had the poor lovestruck monk killed. When the maid discovered that her lover was slain, she was despairing, and she wandered down to the Tweed where she cast herself into the water and was drownded.

Her ghost, described as a 'Grey Lady', has reputedly been seen on the chain bridge over the Tweed and in outbuildings of the hotel. There is also a story that an apparition of the monk was seen several times in the early 19th century.

Disturbances apparently increased during building work.

Map 4, 10N (Dryburgh). Off B6356, 3 miles SE of Melrose, Dryburgh, Borders.
Hotel. (01835 822261 / www.dryburgh.co.uk)

DUCHAL CASTLE

Little remains of Duchal Castle, a stronghold of the Lyles, who were made Lords Lyle in 1440 and Lord High Justiciars of Scotland; the castle was besieged by James IV after the Lyles had joined a rebellion against him. The castle was abandoned for nearby Duchal House, which was built about 1768 and, when the old castle was being demolished for materials, it is said that human bones were found in one of the chambers on the upper floors.

The castle was said to have been haunted by the spirit of an excommunicated monk in the 13th century, apparently a very 'corporeal' ghost. The monk would stand on the walls of Duchal and shout and swear at the occupants. The ghost could not be got rid of – arrows melted when they hit the ghost – until a son of the laird, a particularly goodly youth, cornered the foul-mouthed bogle in the great hall. In the ensuing battle the son was killed and the hall wrecked, but the ghost departed and was not witnessed again.

One account also has the castle haunted by a 'White Lady'.

Map 3, 6M (Duchal). Off B788, 1.5 miles W of Kilmacolm, Renfrewshire.

DUFF HOUSE   ILLUS PAGE 112

Duff House, a fine classical mansion with colonnades and corner towers, dates from 1735 and was designed by William Adam for William Duff of Braco, later Earl of Fife. Adam and Duff fell out over the cost of building the house, and work stopped in

1741 – the subsequent (time consuming and expensive) legal action was eventually won by Adam. The house is now used to display works of art from the National Galleries of Scotland, and there is a programme of changing exhibitions, as well as musical and other events.

The building is said to have a 'Green Lady'.

Map 2, 11E (Duff House). Off A97, in Banff, Aberdeenshire
His Scot: Open Apr-Sep, daily; Oct-Mar, Thu-Sun; closed 25/26 Dec and 1/2 Jan.
(01261 818181 / www.historic-scotland.gov.uk)

DUMFRIES HOUSE
ILLUS PAGE 112

A large and stately pile set in hundreds of acres of parkland, Dumfries House is a symmetrical classical mansion, designed by John and Robert Adam, and dating from 1754-59.

The building is remarkably unchanged since it was constructed for William Dalrymple, 5th Earl of Dumfries, who died in his new house in 1768; the property later passed by marriage to the Crichton-Stuart Marquesses of Bute. The house was used by the army during World War II, but was then reoccupied by the family until the death of Dowager Marchioness of Bute in 1993. An appeal was begun and the house was purchased by the 'Great Steward's of Scotland's Dumfries House Trust' and the building is open to the public.

Dumfries House is said to be haunted by a smelly ghost, which makes its presence known by an unholy stench.

Another story regards a phantom coach. The Marquesses of Bute were related by marriage to the Hastings family. Whenever one of the Hastings family died, the story goes that a spectral coach would be seen or heard, approaching the doors of the place they were staying. One instance at Dumfries House was supposedly on the death of the 3rd Marquess of Bute in 1900, when his daughter heard the coach outside the house.

Map 4, 7N (Dumfries House). Off B7036, 2 miles W of Cumnock, Ayrshire.
Open end March-Oct, Thu-Mon for guided tours: tel to book except tour at 13.00.
(01290 425959 / www.dumfries-house.org.uk)

DUMFRIES PRIORY

Standing on Corbelly Hill above the burgh, the priory was established as a Benedictine nunnery of the Immaculate Conception in 1880 and part used to house a girls' school. The building was closed in 1988, and the nuns moved to Largs.

The road near the priory is said to be haunted by a headless horseman, reputed to be the phantom of a man called McGilligan. The story goes that he was galloping along but misjudged the height of a tree branch and was cleanly decapitated, his head bouncing along until it came to rest at the entrance to the priory.

Map 4, 8P (Dumfries). Off A75, 0.5 miles SW of town centre, Corbelly Hill, Maxwelton, Dumfries.

DUNANS CASTLE

Dunans Castle is an imposing baronial mansion, but was gutted by fire in recent years, although there are plans afoot to have it reroofed and restored. The lands were a property of the Fletchers from the 17th century or earlier, and their mausoleum is further downstream of Dunans Castle, standing on a wooded ridge. The castle is said to be haunted by a 'Grey Lady'.

Map 3, 5L (Dunans). Off A886, 7 miles S and W of Strachur, east of River Ruel, Glenruel, Dunans, Argyll.

DUNBAR CASTLE

Although once one of the most important castles in Scotland and in a fine location by the harbour, little remains of Dunbar Castle. The old stronghold has a long and turbulent history, changing hands between the English and Scots, and being successfully defended by the Scots for many months from January 1338.

The garrison on that occasion was led by 'Black Agnes', Agnes Randolph, Countess of Dunbar, daughter of Sir Thomas Randolph and wife of Patrick, 9th Earl of Dunbar and March; she would have been in her mid twenties at the time of the siege. She is said, by some, to have got her name because her skin was dark, although others have suggested it was because of her raven-black hair. Agnes behaved very bravely, both thwarting and taunting the English, and not even capitulating when the life of her own brother, who had been captured, was threatened. She reputedly said, after the English had withdrawn hastily and in disarray from the siege: 'behold of the litter of English pigs'. Agnes apparently lived into her sixties and is believed to be buried in a vault near the site of Mordington House, which stood a few miles to the north and west of Berwick upon Tweed.

A ghost of Black Agnes, known as 'Black Aggie', is said to have been witnessed in the area, although the apparition is reputedly only seen on clear nights.

Map 4, 11L (Dunbar). Off A1087, on N shore just W of harbour, Dunbar, East Lothian.
Access at all reasonable times – care should be taken as parts are dangerously ruined.

DUNDONALD CASTLE

In a prominent location and an imposing ruin, Dundonald Castle was built by the Stewarts in the 13th century, and is said to have been slighted in the Wars of Independence. Dundonald is particularly associated with Robert II, King of Scots, who died at Dundonald in 1390, and Robert III, who may have also died here, some 16 years later.

A paranormal investigation carried out at the castle apparently concluded that it was haunted.

Map 3, 6N (Dundonald). Off B730, 3.5 miles SE of Irvine, Dundonald, Ayrshire.
Open Apr-Oct, daily. (01563 851489 / www.dundonaldcastle.org.uk)

A paranormal investigation is to be undertaken by the Dunfermline Paranormal Research Fellowship

DUNFERMLINE PALACE   ILLUS PAGE 119

Set in the historic burgh of Dunfermline are the remains of the royal palace. The ruins are particularly impressive from Pittencrieff Glen, and consist of a range of buildings modelled into the palace from the guest range of the abbey. The palace had wide mullioned windows and elaborate vaulting, but had been unroofed by 1708.

The abbey was founded about 1070 by Queen Margaret, wife of Malcolm Canmore, and it was at Dunfermline that they had been married. Margaret was made a saint, and she and Malcolm were buried in the church. Abbot George Durie, the last abbot, was responsible for removing Margaret's head and taking it to the Continent, where it went to the Jesuits of Douai. The rest of their remains are said to have been sent abroad by Mary of Guise, and went to the church of St Lawrence at Escurial in the care of Philip II of Spain. Robert the Bruce's body – although not his heart – is interred in the Abbey Church. Other kings buried at Dunfermline include Edgar, Alexander I, David I, Malcolm IV, William the Lyon and Alexander III.

The church, domestic buildings of the abbey, and the remains of the palace are open to the public, as is the Abbey Church and Abbot House (see that entry).

There are stories that the palace and abbey buildings are haunted.

It is said that the apparition of a well-dressed lady has been seen wandering through the ruins, identified by some as the bogle of Anne of Denmark, who remodelled the palace in 1587. There is also said to be the white glowing ghost of a woman, observed looking down from the upper part of the palace, as well as another phantom, a dark hooded figure, spotted sometimes in the graveyard around the church.

Map 4, 9L (Dunfermline). Off A994, Monastery Street, Dunfermline, Fife.
His Scot: Palace and abbey open Apr-Oct, daily; Nov-Mar, Sat-Thu, closed Fri. (01383 739026 / www.historic-scotland.gov.uk)

DUNNOTTAR CASTLE

ILLUS PAGE 119

Crowning a sea-girt cliff-top promontory some 160 foot above the shore, Dunnottar Castle is arguably the most spectacular stronghold in Scotland, and impressive ruins of the many buildings remain. The way up to, and then through, the tunnel to the castle entrance is especially bracing and impressive, and external shots of the castle were used in the film *Hamlet* with Mel Gibson.

There was a stronghold here from early times, but the present castle was built by the Keith Earls Marischal, who held the property until 1716 when they were forfeited for their part in the Jacobite Rising. Famous visitors include Mary, Queen of Scots, Charles II, and William Wallace. Wallace captured Dunnottar in 1296 and is said to have burnt some 4000 Englishmen to death. In the 1680s more than 150 Covenanters were imprisoned in one of the vaults in appalling conditions, and nine died while 25 managed to escape down the cliffs.

Sightings of several ghosts have been reported here. The apparition of a girl, around 13 years old and dressed in a dull plaid-type dress, is said to have been witnessed in the brewery. She leaves by the doorway next to the building, but then vanishes.

Other ghosts are said to include a young deer hound, which faded away near the tunnel; a tall Scandinavian-looking man going into the guardroom at the main entrance, who then also vanished; and noises of a meeting coming from Benholm's Lodging when nobody was apparently present.

Map 2, 11H (Dunnottar). Off A92, 2 miles S of Stonehaven, Kincardine & Deeside.
Open all year, daily. (01330 860223 / www.dunnottarcastle.co.uk)

DUNOLLIE CASTLE

Standing on a prominent rocky ridge looking over the sea to Kerrera, Mull, Lismore and beyond, Dunollie Castle is an overgrown and ruinous stronghold, the oldest parts of which date back to the 13th century. The present castle was built by the

Dunfermline Palace (page 117)

Dunnottar Castle (page 118)

Dunrobin Castle (page 121)

Duns Castle (page 122)

Duntulm Castle (page 124)

Dunskey Castle (page 122)

Dunyvaig Castle (page 126)

MacDougalls of Lorn, one of the most powerful families in Scotland at that time, and bitter enemies of Robert the Bruce. A MacDougall force defeated Bruce at Dalry, nearly killing him; Bruce returned and ravaged MacDougall lands in 1309. In 1644 the castle was attacked, and three years later was besieged, sacked and torched by an army of Covenanters. Dunollie was attacked again in 1715 when the MacDougalls were fighting for the Stewarts during the Jacobite Rising. The MacDougalls built nearby Dunollie House to replace the old castle.

There are stories of a phantom piper or Highlander haunting the ruins, and the old castle is also said to have a 'Green Lady' or glaistig.

Map 3, 4K (Dunollie). Off A85, 1 mile N of Oban, Dunollie, Argyll.
Can be reached from a lay-by on the Ganavan road, but not from the drive to Dunollie House, which is NOT open to the public. Care should be taken.

DUNPHAIL CASTLE

All that remains of Dunphail Castle, a 14th-century stronghold of the Comyns, is the vaulted basement. The Comyns were besieged here in 1330 by the Regent Andrew Moray, after they had fled from Darnaway Castle. Moray managed to capture five of the garrison, including Alasdair Comyn of Dunphail, who had been out foraging. Moray had the men executed and their heads flung over the walls of the castle, reputedly with the words 'Here's beef for your bannocks'. The last of the Comyn garrison tried to flee, but were slaughtered by the Regent's men. In the 18th century, five skull-less skeletons were supposedly found buried near the castle.

Headless ghosts are said to haunt the castle, and tales of the sounds of fighting and groans have also been reported.

Map 2, 8E (Dunphail). Off A90, 6.5 miles S of Forres, Moray.

DUNROBIN CASTLE   ILLUS PAGE 119

Set in fine grounds overlooking the sea, Dunrobin dates from the 1300s and is a splendid 'fairy-tale' castle with a mass of turrets and spires. It was extended and remodelled about 1650, 1780 and in 1845-50, and is a huge building with some 189 rooms. There are fine formal gardens, designed by Charles Barry, architect of the Houses of Parliament.

The Sutherland family were created Earls of Sutherland in 1235, and had a castle here from the 13th century: Dunrobin may be called after Robert or Robin, the 6th Earl. The property passed by marriage to the Gordons, then to the Trentham Marquis of Stafford in the 18th century, who were made Dukes of Sutherland in 1833. They are remembered for their part in the Highland Clearances.

The upper floors of the old part of the castle are reputedly haunted by the spectre of Margaret, daughter of the 14th Earl of Sutherland. She fell in love with a fellow called Jamie Gunn, sometime during the 17th century, younger son of one of the Earl's men. But her father found out, and had her imprisoned in one of the attic rooms. Margaret pined and despaired; and Gunn decided to rescue her as her health was failing. A rope was smuggled to her attic room and Margaret tried to escape out of one of the windows, but her father burst into her room and startled her, and she fell to her death. It is said that one of the rooms she haunted has since been disused, although her moans and cries still come from the chamber where she was imprisoned, now known as the night nursery.

A different version of the story is sometime in the 15th century, the then Earl took a fancy to a young Mackay lass and imprisoned her in the chamber until she agreed to marry him. She managed to fashion a rough rope from her bed linen and began to climb down to freedom. But the Earl burst in on her, saw what she was doing and in a spurned pique cut the rope with his sword so that she fell to her death. This story bears more than a little resemblance to that of Ackergill Tower, but this is the version recorded in the guide book for Dunrobin. It also states that the ghost has been neither seen nor heard in living memory.

The apparition is described as a 'White Lady' in one account.

Disembodied footsteps are said to have been heard coming from Duchess Clare's Bedroom, even when the chamber is known to be empty. There is also a tale of an apparition of a man being spotted on a landing and disappearing through a closed door.

Map 2, 8D (Dunrobin). Off A9, 1.5 miles NE of Golspie, Dunrobin, Sutherland, Highland.
Open Apr-mid Oct, daily. (01408 633177 / www.dunrobincastle.net)

DUNS CASTLE
ILLUS PAGE 120

Set in a 1200-acre estate of wooded and landscaped grounds, Duns Castle is a magnificent castellated mansion which incorporates a 14th-century keep. There are fine walks, as well as a nature reserve and lake.

The castle may have been built by Thomas Randolph, Earl of Moray and nephew to Robert the Bruce, in 1320, but had passed to Home of Ayton by 1489. The building was damaged by the Earl of Hertford in 1547 during an English invasion. The property went to the Cockburns, then to the Hays of Drumelzier, with whose descendants it remains.

An apparition of Alexander Hay, who was killed at the Battle of Waterloo in 1815, is said to haunt the castle and to have been seen in the Yellow Turret room.

Map 4, 11M (Duns). Off A6112, 1 mile NW of Duns, Borders.
Accommodation available. Country park. (01361 883211 / www.dunscastle.co.uk)

DUNSKEY CASTLE
ILLUS PAGE 120

Set on a windswept and oppressive headland above the sea, Dunskey Castle is a ruinous tower house of the 16th century. It was held by the Adairs, and it was at Dunskey that the abbot of Soulseat Abbey was imprisoned and tortured to force him to sign away the abbey lands. The castle has been ruinous since the end of the 17th century, but was recently been put up for sale.

The castle was said to have had a brownie, and is also reported to be haunted by the ghost of a careless nursemaid, who dropped her charge from one of the windows to its death on the seashore far below.

Dunskey is also said to have a ghostly piper, the spirit of a jester who so angered the laird of the time, believed to be in the 14th century, that the jester was imprisoned in one of the vaults. The jester found a tunnel leading down and almost hidden, and hoping to find a way out entered the passageway. But he got completely lost in the tunnels below the castle and could not find a way out; he was not seen again, although eerie pipe music is sometimes said to be heard. It states in this account of the story that workmen, who were working on the water supply, found a large cavern from where, it was said, the eerie music was heard.

Map 3, 5P (Dunskey). Off A77, 5.5 miles SW of Stranraer, Dunskey, Portpatrick, Dumfries and Galloway.
View from exterior - climb and walk to castle from Portpatrick: care should be taken.

DUNSTAFFNAGE CASTLE

On a promontory in the Firth of Lorn, Dunstaffnage Castle is defended by a massive curtain wall, with round towers, and an altered gatehouse. A stronghold here was held by the kings of Dalriada in the 7th century, and was one of the places that the Stone of Destiny was kept. The present castle was built by the MacDougalls, but later passed to the Campbells after the castle was seized by Robert the Bruce in 1309. Other well-known visitors include James IV, and Flora MacDonald, who was briefly imprisoned here after helping Bonnie Prince Charlie.

The castle is said to be haunted by a ghost in a green dress, the 'Ell (or Elle)-maid of Dunstaffnage', also known as the Scannag. Her appearance is believed to herald events, both bad and good, in the lives of the Campbells. When she was seen to be smiling then there were happy events to come, but if she wept or was sad it augured trouble. The ghost is reported to be a gruagach and to be able to hand on handicraft skills, while at times the Ell-Maid could make the whole building shake as if it was caught in an earthquake. Very heavy disembodied footsteps have also been reported in the gatehouse, as well as loud bangs and thumps. When the castle was still inhabited, the Ell-Maid is also said to have playfully teased children while in their beds, this continuing over several generations.

Map 3, 4J (Dunstaffnage). Off A85, 3.5 miles NE of Oban, Dunstaffnage, Argyll.
His Scot: Open Apr-Oct, daily; Nov-Mar, Sat-Wed, closed Thu & Fri; closed 25/26 Dec and 1/2 Jan. (01631 562465 / www.historic-scotland.gov.uk)

DUNTARVIE CASTLE

Standing in a prominent position near to the M9, Duntarvie Castle is a large and long ruinous castle, mostly dating from the 16th century, although there was a stronghold here from long before then. Duntarvie was a possession of the Durham family in 1588 and they built or remodelled the present castle. The property passed to the Hamiltons of Abercorn, and then went to the Hope Earls of Hopeton, before being abandoned in about 1840. Duntarvie has been going through the process of restoration for many years, although this has been postponed when the place was recently put up for sale.

The story goes that the building is haunted by the ghost of the 'Marchioness of Abercorn', reputed to have been excommunicated and imprisoned (and to have died at Duntarvie) in the 1620s because of her adherence to the Catholic faith (she had already been jailed in Edinburgh where her health had suffered greatly). The bogle is said to have been spotted on the battlements of the castle and, during work on restoration, disembodied voices are said to have been heard here in the deep of the night.

Some elements of this story are wrong. The 'Marchioness of Abercorn' appears to be Marion Boyd, Countess of Abercorn (by marriage to James Hamilton, 1st Earl of Abercorn), who died at the Canongate in 1632 at around 50 years of age (although she was allowed to live at Duntarvie for some time after becoming ill during imprisonment for being a Catholic). The Hamiltons, however, were not made Marquesses of Abercorn until 1790 and Marion did not die at Duntarvie.

Map 4, 9L (Duntarvie). Off B8020 between B9080 and A904, 3 miles S and W of South Queensferry, Duntarvie, West Lothian.

DUNTRUNE CASTLE

Standing in a picturesque location on a rocky hillock by the banks of Loch Crinan, Duntrune was a property of the Campbells and dates from the 13th century. In 1792 the castle went to the Malcolms of Poltalloch, who still own it.

The castle is allegedly haunted by a ghostly piper. A MacDonald had been sent as a spy to try to capture the castle in 1615, but was discovered, and the only way he could warn his companions was to play the pipes, which he did and the attack was abandoned. The Campbells had both the piper's hands (or all his fingers) chopped off, and he was buried under the kitchen flagstones. From that time on the sound of ghostly bagpipes was often reported.

The ghost was thought to have been exorcised in modern times, when part of the basement was used as a church. A handless (or fingerless) skeleton was found sealed beneath the floor about 1870, and the remains were buried. However, the ghost became active in the 1970s, and unexplained knockings on doors were reported, as well as furniture and other objects being thrown about the rooms. Or so it is said.

Map 3, 4L (Duntrune). Off B8025, 6.5 miles NW of Lochgilphead, Duntrune, Argyll.
Holiday cottages available in grounds. (01546 510283 / www.duntrune.com)

DUNTULM CASTLE   ILLUS PAGE 120

Located in Trotternish on the northern extremity of Skye, Duntulm Castle stands on a headland overlooking the sea and the Outer Hebrides. Not much now remains of the castle, once the fine stronghold of the MacDonalds. The family moved to Monk-stadt from here in about 1730, itself now ruinous, reputedly because of the many ghosts here. They then built Armadale Castle in Sleat, to the south of the island.

At the turn of the 17th century, Hugh MacDonald, cousin to the then chief, Donald Gorm, devised a plot to gain the lands. The chief had no heirs, and Hugh planned to invite the chief to his own fortress, Caisteal Uisdean, some miles south of Duntulm, and there murder him and his immediate kin. Unfortunately for Hugh, he mixed up letters sent to the chief and to the proposed assassin. Hugh fled to North Uist, where he was besieged in the old stronghold of Dun an Sticar. He was finally captured, and then imprisoned in a vault at Duntulm. He was given salted beef and no water, and is reported to have died insane and raving from thirst. When the prison vault was opened many years later, his skeleton still grasped an empty jug in its parched jaws. His remains were not buried for some time, and his bones were kept as a warning to others, indeed his thigh bones and skull were then kept on display at the parish church at nearby Kilmuir, although they were finally buried in 1847. His ghostly groans and desperate cries have reputedly been heard at Duntulm Castle.

The ghost of the chief, Donald Gorm, brawling and drinking with phantom companions, has also been recorded in many tales.

Another apparition was allegedly that of Margaret, a sister of MacLeod of Dunvegan, and Donald's wife. She had lost an eye in an accident, but her husband threw her out, sending her back to Dunvegan on a one-eyed horse with a one-eyed servant and one-eyed dog. Her weeping ghost is said to haunt the castle.

A nursemaid is said to have dropped a baby out of one of the windows, onto the rocks below. Her terrified screams are said to be heard sometimes, as the poor woman was killed in reprisal, setting her upon the sea in a leaking boat.

Map 1, 2E (Duntulm). Off A855, 6.5 miles N of Uig, Duntulm, Isle of Skye, Highland.
View from exterior - care must be taken as dangerously ruined.

DUNURE CASTLE

Perched on a rock above the banks of the Firth of Clyde, Dunure Castle is now very ruinous but was once a fine house when it was a property of the Kennedys. In 1570, in a dispute with the Gilbert Kennedy, 4th Earl of Cassillis, Allan Stewart, commendator of nearby Crossraguel Abbey (also see that entry), was tortured and roasted in sop here until he signed away the lands of the abbey. Although he was eventually rescued, Stewart got no recompense except a small pension, and the Earl of Cassillis kept the lands (although, to be fair, much of the land given to the abbey down the centuries had come from the Earl's family).

Ghostly shrieks and the crackle of flames have reputedly been heard at Dunure, emanating from the chamber where Stewart was tortured, allegedly mostly heard on Sunday mornings.

Map 3, 5N (Dunure). Off A719, 5 miles NW of Maybole, Ayrshire.
Access at all reasonable times.

DUNVEGAN CASTLE

Standing on what was once an island in Loch Dunvegan, Dunvegan Castle has been continuously occupied by the chiefs of MacLeod from 1270. The MacLeods trace their ancestry back to Leod, a son of Olaf the Black, Viking King of the Isle of Man. His stronghold at Dunvegan was developed down the centuries into a large mansion and castle, and it is still owned by the chiefs of MacLeod.

Dunvegan is the home to the famous Fairy Flag, 'Am Bratach Sith' in Gaelic. There are many legends surrounding this piece of silk, which is now reduced in size (from pieces being removed and kept for luck) and somewhat threadbare.

One is that it was given to one of the chiefs by his fairy wife at their parting. This is said to have taken place at the Fairy Bridge, three miles to the north east, at a meeting of river and roads. The chief had married his wife thinking she was a mortal woman, but she was only permitted to stay with him for 20 years before returning to fairyland.

The flag, however, originates from the Middle East, and it has been dated between 400 and 700 AD, predating the castle by hundreds of years. The flag is believed to give victory to the clan whenever unfurled, and reputedly has done so at the battles of Glendale in 1490 and at Trumpan in 1578.

Worshippers were at Trumpan Church one Sunday when a raiding party of MacDonalds came ashore. They set fire to the thatched roof of the church. Most were burnt alive or slain, but one woman escaped and raised the alarm at Dunvegan. The MacLeods raised a small force, bringing with them the Fairy Flag. The MacDonalds were slaughtered at the subsequent battle after the Flag was unfurled.

The Fairy Flag was also believed to make the marriage of the MacLeods fruitful, when draped on the wedding bed, and to charm the herrings out of Dunvegan Loch when unfurled.

Belief in its power was such that during World War II pilots from the clan carried a picture of the flag as a talisman.

Map 1, 1E (Dunvegan). Off A850, 1 mile N of Dunvegan village, Skye.
Open Apr-mid Oct, daily; other times by appt; closed 21 Dec-3 Jan. (01470 521206 / www.dunvegancastle.com)

DUNYVAIG CASTLE

ILLUS PAGE 120

In a pretty spot on a bay by Lagavulin distillery, little survives of the scenic Dunyvaig Castle, except the ruin of a small 15th-century keep on top of a rock and the remains of a small inner and a larger outer courtyard. The castle belonged to the MacDonald Lord of the Isles, who had their main stronghold at Finlaggan, also on Islay. The Lord of the Isles was forfeited by James IV in 1493, and the castle then had a very stormy history, being besieged and changing hands often between the MacDonalds and their enemies. In 1598 the last MacDonald of Dunyvaig defeated the MacLeans of Duart at the Battle of (Traigh) Gruinart. He was, however, ordered to surrender the castle, and then forfeited in 1608. Islay fell to the Campbells of Cawdor in 1615, and the castle was occupied until about 1677, but was slighted soon afterwards, and the Campbells moved to Islay House. The ruin has been consolidated.

Dunyvaig is said to be haunted.

Map 3, 3M (Dunyvaig). Off A846, 2 miles E of Port Ellen, Lagavulin, Islay.
Access at all reasonable times - care should be taken.

DURRIS HOUSE

Durris House, an altered and extended tower house, was held by the Frasers from the 13th until the end of the 17th century. The house, divided into three, is still occupied.

A 'Green Lady' is said to haunt the castle, reputedly the wife of the Covenanter Fraser lord when the Royalist Marquis of Montrose torched the house on 17 March 1645. The poor woman is said to have been distraught, feeling that she was responsible after having cursed Montrose, and she drowned herself in a nearby burn. Her curse may have had some effect, however, as Montrose was finally defeated in 1650, captured, and then taken to Edinburgh where he was executed.

Map 2, 11G (Durris). Off B9077, 6.5 miles E of Banchory, Kincardine & Deeside.

EAGLE HOTEL, LAUDER

The hotel was originally a manse but in the early 19th century was converted into a coaching inn. The building is said to be haunted, although manifestations are apparently rarely witnessed.

Map 4, 10M (Lauder). Off A68, Market Place, Lauder, Borders.
Hotel. (01578 722255)

EARLSHALL, LEUCHARS

Earlshall, a fine courtyard castle with a main block of three storeys, was built by Sir William Bruce in 1546; unusually, he had survived the Battle of Flodden in 1513. The hall, on the first floor, has a large carved fireplace and panelled walls, and the second-floor gallery has a painted ceiling from the 1620s.

One of the family was Sir Andrew Bruce of Earlshall, known as 'Bloody Bruce', as he and his men killed Richard Cameron, a noted Covenanter and leader of the Cameronians, at Airds Moss in July 1680. Bruce then hacked off Cameron's head and hands, and took them back to Edinburgh, where they were tried for treason.

Earlshall is thought to be haunted by the ghost of Sir Andrew. Sightings of his apparition have been recorded, as have the ghostly sounds of heavy footsteps on one of the turnpike stairs, when nobody is about. Objects are also said to be moved about, and there is a story that a bed looked as if it had been slept in when the room it was in had been unoccupied for some time.

Another apparition is allegedly that of an old woman, believed to have been a servant.

Map 4, 10K (Leuchars). Off A919, E of Leuchars, Earlshall, Fife.
The gardens are occasionally open under Scotland's Gardens Scheme or by arrangement. (www.gardensofscotland.org)

EASTGATE SHOPPING CENTRE, INVERNESS

Some of the shops in the Eastgate Shopping Centre are said to be haunted, allegedly by the bogle of a former worker. Manifestations are reputed to include doors opening and closing by themselves, and light bulbs and fuses blowing for no apparent reason.

Map 2, 7F (Inverness). Off A82, Eastgate Shopping Centre, Inverness, Highland.

EDEN COURT THEATRE, INVERNESS

On the west bank of the River Ness, the Eden Court Theatre, which was opened in 1976, incorporates the building used as a bishop's palace, which was later converted into a residential pre-training centre for nurses. Eden Court was renovated and extended in 2007, and the theatre has a busy programme of drama, dance, music, comedy, musical theatre and film.

A 'Green Lady' has reputedly been witnessed here, the wife of one of the bishops; she is said to have hanged herself in the palace. The unexplained sounds of feet coming from unoccupied areas have also been reported.

Map 2, 7F (Inverness). Off A82, Inverness.
Theatre. (01463 239841 / www.eden-court.co.uk)

EDINAMPLE CASTLE

Edinample Castle, a fine Z-plan tower house, was built by Sir Duncan Campbell of Glenorchy – 'Black Duncan of the Castles' – around 1584.

The story goes that Campbell had ordered that the castle should have a parapet walk. The mason forgot to add this feature, but tried to show that it was possible to walk around the roof, as Campbell refused to pay him. Campbell, however, shoved the mason from the roof, so saving himself all the fee.

The apparition of the mason can reputedly be seen occasionally, still clambering around the roof.

Map 4, 7K (Edinample). Off A84, 1 mile SE of Lochearnhead, Edinample, Stirlingshire.

EDINBURGH CASTLE   ILLUS PAGE 129

Standing on a high rock in the middle of Scotland's capital, Edinburgh Castle was one of the strongest and most important fortresses in Scotland, and has a long and bloody history – only a little of which can be related here. The castle is the home to the Scottish crown jewels and to the Stone of Destiny, once held at Dunadd and then Scone – on which the Kings of Scots were inaugurated – and the castle is a fascinating complex of buildings with spectacular views over the city.

The oldest building is the small 12th-century chapel, dedicated to St Margaret, wife of Malcolm Canmore, probably built by her son, David I. The castle had an English garrison during the Wars of Independence, but was recaptured in 1313 when the Scots, led by Thomas Randolph, climbed the rock, surprised the garrison, and retook it. After the murder of the young Earl of Douglas and his brother at the 'Black Dinner' here in 1440, it was attacked and captured by the Douglases. In 1566 Mary, Queen of Scots, gave birth to the future James VI in the castle. The fortress also saw much action in Covenanting times and during the Cromwellian invasion and Jacobite Risings.

The castle is reputedly haunted by several ghosts.

A drummer, sometimes reported as being headless, has allegedly been witnessed. His apparition is said to be a warning that the castle is about to be besieged, and was first seen in 1650 before Cromwell attacked. Drums are reputedly heard more often than an apparition is seen. Manifestations were reported in 1960, although it is not clear who was about to besiege the castle (!).

A piper was sent to search a tunnel, believed to travel from the castle to Holyroodhouse one mile away at the end of the Royal Mile, but was never seen again. It is said that sometimes the faint sound of his pipes can still be heard.

The spectre of a dog, whose remains are buried in the pets' cemetery, reportedly haunts the battlements.

There are also stories of ghostly prisoners being witnessed in one of the castle vaults, and that the bogle of the wronged Janet Douglas, Lady Glamis, who was burned to death as a witch on what is now the castle esplanade in 1537, has also been seen here (see Glamis Castle).

Map 4, 9L (Edinburgh). Off A1, in the centre of Edinburgh (top of High Street/Royal Mile). **His Scot: Open all year, daily; times may be altered during Tattoo and state occasions; closed 25/26 Dec; open 1/2 Jan: tel for opening hours. (0131 225 9846 / www.historic-scotland.gov.uk)**

EDINBURGH FESTIVAL THEATRE, EDINBURGH

The theatre here is said to be haunted by the apparition of the Great Lafayette, Sigmund Neuberger. Lafayette was killed when part of the Empire Palace Theatre, dating from 1892, burned down in 1911, probably due to an electrical fault or because a gas lamp was knocked over by an escaping lion, although nobody is certain. The curtain was brought down but the mechanism failed and those behind the curtain were burnt to death. Two bodies were found, one believed to be the Great Lafayette, and the other perhaps his body double. The theatre was out of action for several months, but was restored, then remodelled in 1928 and then later used for bingo. The theatre was virtually rebuilt in the 1990s, and in 1994 reopened as the Edinburgh Festival Theatre, with a varied programme of performances including opera, ballet and music.

Since the renovation, however, an apparition of a black figure, believed to be Lafayette, has been seen several times, and to be felt at the spot where pictures of him are displayed.

Another ghost, said to be witnessed on the top floor at the entrance to the auditorium, is believed to be the sad bogle of a young woman. It is said that she is the ghost of a would-be dancer, who never managed to get on stage, but would enter-

Edinburgh Castle (page 127)

Edinburgh Filmhouse (page 131)

Edzell Castle (page 131)

129

Eilean Donan Castle (page 132)

Falkland Palace (page 134)

Falside Castle (page 134)

tain the audience before shows. The spot where she is witnessed is said to be very cold, and there is the unexplained smell of cheap perfume.

There are also many other reported manifestations, including the sounds of people fighting on the back stairs, perhaps as a result of a love triangle. The back upper circle, part of the original Empire and untouched, is said to be haunted by the ghost of female usher, who is said to have blown on the ear of a lad she liked. One seat is also said often to be occupied by the phantom of a well-dressed older man in a hat. One of the staff is said to have had a conversation with the ghost, believed to be that of a previous owner, who told the person that if he disapproved of the performances he would make it known.

Map 4, 9L (Edinburgh). On A7, 13-29 Nicolson Street, Edinburgh.
Theatre with bar and cafe. (0131 529 6000 / www.eft.co.uk)

EDINBURGH FILMHOUSE
ILLUS PAGE 129

The Edinburgh Filmhouse is located in a former church, which dates from 1830, although it was later rebuilt and then remodelled for use as cinemas and bar in the 1970s and '80s. The Filmhouse is the home of the Edinburgh International Film Festival, and is said to be haunted by the apparition of a woman, although there does not appear to be any story about the origins of the bogle.

Map 4, 9L (Edinburgh). On A702, 88 Lothian Road, Edinburgh.
Cinema with cafe/bar. (0131 228 2688 / www.filmhousecinema.com)

EDZELL CASTLE
ILLUS PAGE 129

Standing by the magnificent walled garden, ruinous Edzell Castle dates from the 16th century and was built by the Lindsay Earls of Crawford. Mary, Queen of Scots, held a Privy Council at Edzell in 1562. One story is that a Lindsay laird hanged the sons of a gypsy woman for poaching and she cursed him. His pregnant wife died that day, while he himself was devoured by wolves – all as foretold, of course.

The castle is said to be haunted by a 'White Lady', reputedly the spirit of Catherine Campbell, second wife of David Lindsay, 9th Earl of Crawford. She was thought to have died in 1578, but was only in a coma and was interred alive in her family vault. She eventually regained consciousness, but only after a sextant had tried to steal her rings by cutting off her finger. The unfortunate woman then died of exposure at the castle gates (although it is also said, in another version, that she lived for some time after the events).

The ghost has apparently been witnessed in recent times, including in 1986, and is described as being quite small with a white floral dress and a blur for a face; it is also said to exude a sickly smell or faint odour of scent. A photograph is said to have been taken of the bogle when it appeared at one of the windows. The phantom is also reputed to have been seen in the fine walled garden of the castle, as well as in the burial ground of Edzell Old Church, which is the location of the Lindsay Burial Aisle (also open to the public).

Map 2, 10H (Edzell). Off B966, 6 miles N of Brechin, Edzell, Angus.
His Scot: Open all year: Apr-Oct, daily; Nov-Mar, Sat-Wed, closed Thu & Fri; closed 25/26 Dec and 1/2 Jan. (01356 648631 / www.historic-scotland.gov.uk)

EGLINTON CASTLE

Eglinton Castle, a huge very ruined mansion, was built on the site of an old strong-hold of the Montgomery Earls of Eglinton. The family had a long and bitter feud with the Cunninghams of Glencairn. The castle here was burnt in 1528 by the Cunning-hams, and Hugh, 4th Earl of Eglinton, was murdered by them around 60 years later; in revenge, the Montgomerys killed every Cunningham they could find, cutting the murderer to pieces.

The castle was replaced by a large mansion in 1802 (also called Eglinton Castle), and it was here that the Eglinton Tournament was held in 1839, a magnificent medieval-style tournament. The house was, however, unroofed in 1925, and all that now survives is a single corner tower and some low walls.

The ruins stand in a public park, and the site is said to be haunted. There has been more than one paranormal investigation, although (scary though ghosts may be) it is the drink-fuelled local youth that have frightened off some investigators.

Map 3, 5M (Eglinton). Off B7080, 1.5 miles N of Irvine, Eglinton Park, Ayrshire.
Access at all reasonable times. (01294 551776 / www.north-ayrshire.gov.uk)

A paranormal investigation was undertaken by Spiritfinders Scotland (www.spiritfindersscotland.com) and by Ghost Hunters (www.ghosthunters.org.uk) and by Renfrewshire Ghost Hunters (www.teamrenfrewshireghosthunters.com) and by West of Scotland Paranormal Research (www.wospr.com).

EILEAN DONAN CASTLE   ILLUS PAGE 130

Eilean Donan stands in a tranquil unspoilt location at the mouth of Loch Duich on the road to Skye, and the castle is probably one of the most photographed and recognisable of Scottish strongholds. A strong tower, with walls up to 15 foot thick, and a courtyard stand on a small island, now joined to the mainland by a bridge. Although once quite ruinous, it was completely rebuilt between 1912 and 1932. Several films feature the castle, including *Highlander, Loch Ness, The Master of Ballantrae*, and more than one *James Bond* film.

Eilean Donan was long held by the Mackenzies, and sheltered Robert the Bruce in 1306. In 1331 Randolph, Earl of Moray, executed 50 men at Eilean Donan and spiked their heads on the castle walls. In 1511 the MacRaes became constables of the castle, and the MacRaes and Mackenzies were involved in the Jacobite Risings, and suffered heavy casualties in the Battle of Sheriffmuir in 1715. William Mackenzie, 5th Earl of Seaforth, garrisoned Eilean Donan with Spanish troops in the Rising of 1719, but three Government frigates battered it into submission. The castle surren-dered, and the powder magazine was then blown up, including 343 barrels of gun-powder, devastating the castle. The Spaniards, who numbered some 300 in all, were defeated at the nearby Battle of Glenshiel, along with an army of Scottish Jacobites, and the site is marked by an information board.

The ghost of one of the Spanish troops, killed at the castle during the siege or at the battle of Glenshiel, is said to haunt the castle. The ghost is said to carry its head under his arm.

Another apparition, Lady Mary, reputedly haunts one of the bedrooms.

Map 1, 4F (Eilean Donan). On A87, 8 miles E of Kyle of Lochalsh, Dornie, Highland.
Open mid Mar- early Nov, daily; gift shop, open all year. (01599 555202 / www.eileandonancastle.com)

ETHIE CASTLE

An impressive and picturesque building, Ethie Castle, dating from the 15th century, was for some of its long history a property of the Beatons. The castle was used by David Beaton when he was Abbot of Arbroath in the 1530s, and then when he was Archbishop of St Andrews and a Cardinal of the Roman Catholic Church. He was married to Marion Ogilvie, whose apparition is said to be seen at Claypotts (see that entry), and they had seven children, although his marriage was later annulled.

Beaton was a controversial character, having been involved in the burning of heretics, but he was himself brutally murdered in 1546 at St Andrews Castle (also see that entry) and his naked body hung from one of the windows. His body remained unburied for more than seven months, pickled in a barrel of brine.

His ghost was apparently witnessed at Ethie from shortly after his murder. The sound of his ghostly footsteps climbing a turnpike stair to a secret door in his own chamber have reportedly been heard, as well as sightings of his apparition. Manifestations have been reported in recent times. Other unexplained noises include the sound of something heavy being dragged across the floor.

Beaton's ghost is also said to haunt Melgund, Balfour, Blebo and St Andrews.

Another ghost was apparently that of a child, and activity, such as small footsteps, the sounds of playing and sobbing, was centred in a room where a skeleton of a child was later said to have been found. The entrance to this chamber is said to have been walled up and the child entombed inside. When the bones were buried, this haunting is believed to have stopped.

A further apparition is reputedly a 'Green Lady', who allegedly appears when one of the owners is about to die or misfortune is about to strike. Stories have her being seen in the walled garden.

Ethie passed to the Carnegies soon after Beaton's murder and they held the property until 1928. The building is still occupied and it is possible to stay at Ethie.

Map 4, 11J (Ethie). Off A92, 5 miles NE of Arbroath, Ethie, Angus.
Accommodation and convention facilities available. (01241 830434 / www.ethiecastle.com)

EVELICK CASTLE

Formerly a fine building, Evelick Castle is a substantial but ruinous castle, which dates from the 16th century. Evelick was long a property of the Lindsays, although not all of its history was happy. Thomas Lindsay was brutally murdered here by his step-brother, James Douglas, in 1682. Douglas stabbed Lindsay five times, held him under the water in a burn, and finally dashed his brains out with a rock. Douglas was tried and executed for the crime. The last Lindsay of Evelick was drowned in 1799.

There are stories of a 'White Lady of Evelick', the apparition of a woman in a white dress, believed to be the bogle of a daughter of the house. The ghost has reputedly been seen at Lady's Brig, which is on the road between Evelick and Kilspindie, near Balmyre, and on the road itself.

This may be the bogle of Leezie Lindsay, who traditionally ran off with a Highland laddie, although he then turned out to be a nobleman and a chieftain. She was the daughter of Sir Alexander Lindsay of Evelick, and the events are recorded in an old ballad.

Map 4, 9K (Evelick). Off A85, 6 miles E and N of Perth, 1.5 miles W of Kilspindie, Evelick, Perth and Kinross.

FAIRBURN TOWER

An impressive castle, Fairburn Tower is a substantial 16th-century tower house of the Mackenzies. The tower features in one of the Brahan Seer's prophecies, which predicted that when a cow managed to climb all way to the watch-chamber at the top of the tower, and there calve, that would herald the downfall of the Mackenzies of Fairburn. The line died out in 1850, and the cow's escapades became somewhat of an attraction for sightseers.

One ghost story involves one of the lairds. His apparition is said to have crossed the Conon Ferry, accompanied by the unfortunate ferryman, some hours after his death.

Map 1, 6F (Fairburn). Off A832, 4 miles W of Muir of Ord, Fairburn, Ross and Cromarty, Highlands.

FALKLAND PALACE
ILLUS PAGE 130

A magnificent Renaissance Palace, the palace is situated in the peaceful village of Falkland, and became a favourite residence of the Stewart monarchs, and was visited by James III, James IV, James V, Mary, Queen of Scots, James VI, Charles I and Charles II.

The remaining buildings consist of the complete gatehouse range, dating from the 15th century, defended by two large round towers with conical roofs, and a ruinous adjoining block at right angles. The impressive Chapel Royal, within the gatehouse block, has an unusual 16th-century oak screen and a painted ceiling of 1633. It is the fine tapestry gallery, however, that is said to be haunted by a 'White Lady', once seen travelling the length of the gallery and disappearing through a walled-up doorway. She has also been described as a 'Grey Lady', and is said (in life) to have pined away after waiting in vain for her lover to return from battle.

In the ruinous block is the restored cross house, which contains a refurbished room, reputedly the King's Room, where James V died in 1542, as well as the Queen's Room on the first floor.

David, Duke of Rothesay, heir of Robert III, was imprisoned at Falkland in 1402 and was starved to death, or was just plain murdered, by his uncle, Robert, Duke of Albany.

Map 4, 9K (Falkland). Off A912, 10 miles N of Kirkcaldy, Falkland, Fife.
NTS: Palace open early Mar-Oct, daily. (01337 857397 / www.nts.org.uk)

FALSIDE CASTLE
ILLUS PAGE 130

Standing dramatically on a high ridge and visible for miles around, Falside Castle is a tall L-plan tower house, dating from the 15th century, with turrets crowning the corners. For many years the castle was held by the Setons, but it was burnt by the English before the Battle of Pinkie in 1547, suffocating many of the occupants. Falside was restored from ruin in the 1970s and is still occupied.

There are stories of a 'Green Lady' haunting the castle. The bogle is said to be that of a lady of the house. Her husband had been killed in 1540 in a fight with the Hamiltons of Preston in a dispute about cattle. The brave lady rallied her people during the invasion by the English seven years later, and threw missiles down on the pillaging English forces. The English retaliated by cowardly setting fire to the castle and smoking out the inhabitants, killing most of those inside. The subsequent Battle of Pinkie was a disaster for the Scots, and many lords and men were slain.

Ghostly activity is said to be centred in the hall and the stairs leading up to the guest suite, where several strange feelings and weird experiences have been had. There are also reports of mysterious voices being heard coming from the hall, even though that chamber is empty at the time.

Map 4, 10M (Musselburgh). Off A6094 or A199, 2.5 miles SW of Tranent, Falside, East Lothian.

FASQUE

Set in many acres of fine parkland, Fasque, an impressive castellated mansion built in 1809, passed from the Ramsays of Balmain to the Gladstones in 1829, one of whom, William Ewart Gladstone, was Prime Minister four times between 1830 and 1851.

The house is said to be haunted by the ghost of Helen Gladstone, youngest sister of the Prime Minister, as well as by the spirit of a butler called MacBean.

Map 2, 10H (Fasque). Off B974, 5 miles NW of Laurencekirk, Fasque, Kincardine and Deeside, Aberdeenshire.
Organised groups of 12 or more can visit by appt only. (01330 850689 / www.fasque.com/fasque-estates.co.uk)

FEDDERATE CASTLE

Little remains of Fedderate Castle, once a large L-plan tower house, which dated from the 13th century. The castle was a stronghold of the Crawford family and then of the Gordons, and Fedderate was probably the last stronghold to hold out for the Jacobites in the Rising of 1689-90. The reduced condition of the building, however, is due to it being blown up to clear the site for agriculture and not because of the siege.

The castle is said to be haunted.

Map 2, 11E (Fedderate). Off A981, 2 miles NE of New Deer, Fedderate, Aberdeenshire.

FERGUSLIE PARK, PAISLEY

Ferguslie Park House was a fine old residence, built to replace an ancient castle, but it was later abandoned as a home and was then used as a hospital, known as Coats Hospital. The building has since been demolished.

During its use as a hospital, the house is said to have been haunted by the bogle of Lady Glen-Coats, which reportedly caused much fear among the staff. A hazy apparition was apparently seen on more than one occasion, in which could be seen the outline of a woman, bending over the beds of patients who were very sick, and always spotted after midnight. There were also many incidents involving bangs and bumps and unexplained noises.

People who died were carried up to the attic before being taken away by the undertaker. There was an old piano in the attic, and the story goes that it was often heard, tinkling away although without playing a tune, when a corpse was left there. This has also been put down to the ghost of Lady Glen-Coats.

The building was also said to have a 'White Lady', the apparition of a nursing sister, also known as the 'White Witch', and a well-known Paisley bogle.

Map 4, 7M (Paisley). Off A737, Ferguslie Park, W of Paisley, Renfrewshire.

FERNIE CASTLE

ILLUS PAGE 143

Situated in 17 acres of woodland with a loch, Fernie Castle is an imposing 16th-century tower house with later additions and extensions. The fine white-washed building has a large round tower with a conical roof at one corner, and the Keep Bar, located in a vaulted room in the old part of the building, dates from 1530. Fernie was held by many families, including by the MacDuffs, by the Balfours, by the Fernies and by the Arnots, and the castle is now a prestigious hotel. One feature is the tree house, located in woods and available to rent.

The West Tower of the building is said to be haunted. The story goes that a young woman eloped with her lover, and they intended to be wed. Her father, however, disapproved of her husband to be. The couple sought refuge in the castle, and hid in a small chamber in the West Tower. They were discovered by her father's men, and in the ensuing struggle the poor girl fell three floors from the tower to her death.

It is said that her apparition, a 'Green Lady' clad in a green dress with a high neck, has been spotted in some of the bedrooms, and is said to look sorrowful. Other manifestations include electrical equipment and lights switching themselves on and off, and unexplained knocking at doors, and a lad, a visitor to the castle, reported that he had been poked by invisible fingers.

There was a sighting of the bogle in around 1996.

It is believed that the ghost is searching for her lover.

Map 4, 9K (Fernie). On A914, 4 miles W of Cupar, Fernie, Fife.
Hotel. (01337 810381 / www.ferniecastle.demon.co.uk)

A paranormal investigation was undertaken in November 2005 by Scottish Paranormal Investigations (www.scottishparanormalinvestigations.co.uk)

FERNIEHIRST CASTLE

Ferniehirst Castle is an impressive Border stronghold, which dates from the 16th century, although it was altered in later centuries. This was a property of the Kerrs of Ferniehirst, but was seized by the English in 1523, and only recaptured 25 years later when the captain of the English garrison was beheaded. James VI attacked the castle in 1593 because of help given by the Kerrs to Francis Stewart, Earl of Bothwell, who had been accused of witchcraft (among many other things).

A 'Green Lady' is said to haunt a bedroom in the old part of the castle, and unusual occurrences were reported during the time the castle was used as a youth hostel. This is a story that is refuted, however.

Map 4, 11N (Ferniehirst). Off A68, 1.5 miles S of Jedburgh, Ferniehirst, Borders.
Open Jul, Tue-Sun. (01835 862201 / www.ferniehirst.com)

FETTERESSO CASTLE

Fetteresso Castle, a mansion dating from the 17th century, stands on the site of a 15th-century castle. Fetteresso was built by the Keith Earls Marischal, but was torched by the Marquis of Montrose in 1645. James VIII, the old Pretender, stayed here over Christmas 1715 during the Jacobite Rising.

The castle is believed by some to be haunted.

One ghost is reputedly a 'Green Lady'. An apparition is said to have been seen, and there are also reports of the sounds of feet and the swish of a skirt on the stairs. On one occasion the ghost is said to have had a baby in its arms, and to have disappeared into a wall, later shown to be a sealed-up doorway. On another occasion the sound of feet, followed by the dragging of something metallic along the floor of a passage, were reported.

The ghost is also reputed to haunt a house on the High Street of Stonehaven (also see Stonehaven), and there is an unlikely tale of a tunnel linking Fetteresso, the house in Stonehaven and Dunnottar Castle (see that entry) – one of many such tales.

Map 2, 11H (Fetteresso). Off A92, 1.5 miles W of Stonehaven, Kincardine & Deeside.

FEUARS ARMS, KIRKCALDY

The Feuars Arms opened in 1859, and is named after the 'Society of Feuars', a company of men who worked for the landowning Oswald family and collected 'feus', or rents, from their tenants. The pub has many original Victorian features with hand-made tiles, a marble tiled floor, gothic stained-glass windows, and a solid mahogany bar, the longest in Fife at 59-foot long – the men's toilets have solid marble pedestals and glass-walled cisterns.

The pub is said to be haunted, and activity seems to be concentrated in the basement, from where there have been mysterious noises, including running feet being heard although the stair is devoid of life. Items have also been moved without explanation, such as the valves for the beer taps being turned off during the night when the bar was closed.

Map 4, 9L (Kirkcaldy). Off A921, 66-68 Commercial Street, Bogies Wynd, Kirkcaldy, Fife.
Public House (01592 205577 / www.thefeuarsarms.co.uk)

A paranormal investigation was undertaken in August 2004 by Ghost Finders (www.ghostfinders.co.uk/feuarsarms.html) and in February 2005 by Scottish Paranormal (www.scottish-paranormal.co.uk).

FIDDLENAKED PARK

The park, which lay between Coatbridge and Airdrie, has been swallowed up by development, but was said to be haunted by a 'Grey Lady'.

The story goes that in the 1850s a well-to-do woman arrived at Coatbridge station and then walked across Fiddlenaked Park (later known as The Woodbine) towards Airdrie. She had asked for directions from a man she met, and she gave him some money for helping her. The man, thinking she was wealthy, decided to rob her, sneaking up behind her and hitting her on the head, but in doing so killing the poor woman. Her body was found the following morning.

Her ghost is then said to have begun to haunt the area.

Fiddlenaked Park is said to have been named after the tradition that, in the depths of night, it was the location of wanton cavorting of witches and other wicked folk.

Map 4, 8M (Airdrie). Off A810, between Coatbridge and Airdrie, Lanarkshire.

FINAVON CASTLE

Only ruins remain of Finavon Castle, once the strong and splendid castle of the Lindsay Earls of Crawford. David, 3rd Earl, and his brother-in-law Ogilvie of Inverquharity – badly wounded at Battle of Arbroath in 1446 – were brought back to the castle. The Earl soon died, and his wife suffocated Ogilvie, her brother, with a pillow to ensure the succession of her own son. Alexander Crawford, this son, was the 4th Earl, and called 'The Tiger' or 'Earl Beardie', a cruel and ruthless character.

On the Covin Tree, grown from a chestnut dropped by a Roman soldier, Crawford hanged Jock Barefoot, as an example for cutting a walking stick from one of its branches. Jock's ghost is said to have been seen here.

Crawford himself is said to haunt Lordscairnie and Glamis (see those entries).

Map 2, 10I (Finavon). Off A94, 4.5 miles NE of Forfar, Finavon, Angus.
Finavon Doocot: keys from the Finavon Hotel

FINLARIG CASTLE

In a fabulous location surrounded by hills, Finlarig Castle is a ruinous and overgrown Z-plan tower house, which stands in an atmospheric wooded location; nearby is a ruined mausoleum. The castle was built in the 17th century by Sir Duncan Campbell of Glenorchy, known as 'Black Duncan of the Cowl' or 'Black Duncan of the Castles'. Close by the castle is said to be a beheading pit, the story going that nobles were executed in the pit, while commoners were hanged on an oak tree. The pit is more likely to be a cistern or even a cesspit, but this does not make such a good story. Apart from this, it does seem unlikely that there were sufficient high-born folk needing their heads snuck off to warrant the digging of such a large pit.

The castle by some is said to be haunted. At least two paranormal investigations have been undertaken at Finlarig, although there is apparently no story behind the investigations.

Map 4, 7J (Finlarig). Off A827, 0.5 miles NE of Killin, W end of Loch Tay, Finlarig, Stirlingshire.
Access at all reasonable times: view from exterior as dangerously ruined.

A paranormal investigation was undertaken in May 2004 by Ghost Finders (www.ghostfinders.co.uk/finlarig.html) and in September 2004 by Spectre (www.freewebs.com/ukspectre/finlarigcastle.htm)

FINTRY INN

Located in the peaceful and picturesque village in the Strathendrick Valley, the Fintry Inn was established in the middle of the 18th century and is a cosy establishment with an open fire.

The inn is said to be haunted by a hazy apparition, although the identity of the ghost is not known.

Map 4, 7L (Fintry). Off B818 by junction with B822, 4 miles E of Balfron, 23 Main Street, Fintry, Stirlingshire.
Inn and restaurant; accommodation available. (01360 860224 / www.thefintryinn.com)

FLOORS CASTLE

Said to be the largest inhabited mansion in Scotland, Floors Castle dates from 1721, and was originally designed by William Adam for the Kerr 1st Duke of Roxburghe: Floors is still the home of the Duke and Duchess of Roxburghe. There is a walled garden, with fine herbaceous borders.

There are stories that the house is haunted by the ghost of Margaret Hay, 1st Duchess of Roxburghe, who is said to have disappeared in mysterious circumstances. Ghostly sobbing is reported to have been heard coming from the Long Gallery, and there were apparently sightings of the ghost as late as the 1950s.

A further tale is that the house is haunted by the ghost of a gardener, who is said to be felt – rather than seen – outside the main entrance.

Map 4, 11N (Floors). Off A6089, 1 mile NW of Kelso, Floors, Borders.
Open Easter- Oct. (01573 223333 / www.roxburghe.net)

FORDELL

Standing on the edge of a ravine, Fordell Castle is a 16th-century Z-plan tower house, long a property of the Hendersons.

A nearby mill – although the location may be at Fordel near Kinross – was said to be occupied by Cromwell's troops following the Battle of Inverkeithing in 1651. The soldiers interfered with the miller's wife and daughter, and the man poisoned them and then fled with his family. When the dead troops were discovered, the assistant miller was hanged for the crime, although he had nothing to do with the killings.

On some nights it is said that an apparition of his corpse can still be seen, swinging and creaking from an old oak tree.

Map 4, 9L (Fordell). Off B981, 1.5 miles N of Inverkeithing, Fordell, Fife.

FOREST HILLS HOTEL, AUCHTERMUCHTY

Once known as the Boar's Head and formerly a coaching inn, the Forest Hills Hotel is located at the Cross, in the old part of Auchtermuchty, and was first established in 1738. It stands opposite the historic townhouse and tolbooth, with its tall impressive tower and spire.

The hotel is said to be haunted, and several apparitions have reportedly been seen, including a woman dressed in an old-fashioned way in the back bar, a uniformed man observed repeatedly in the kitchen, and once a dark shadowed phantom in the function room. Other activity reputedly includes glasses being thrown from behind the bar, again in the function room, unexplained noises, and people feeling as if they have been touched.

Map 4, 9K (Auchtermuchty). Off A91 or B936, High Street, The Cross, Auchtermuchty, Fife.
Hotel. (01337 828318)

A paranormal investigation was undertaken (www.paranormaldiscovery.co.uk)

FORFAR

Nothing remains of this ancient royal castle, which was apparently defended by the loch. The castle was associated with Malcolm Canmore and Queen Margaret, and St Margaret's Inch, now a promontory since the loch was partly drained, is located in the loch. The stronghold had a long history before it was abandoned in the 1330s, after having changed hands several times between the Scots and English during the Wars of Independence.

The area around the Loch of Forfar is said to be haunted by the ghost of girl who was murdered by being buried alive after apparently being unfaithful.

There are also stories of a group of phantom men, being seen in the water from the waist up, as if they are drowning.

Map 4, 10J (Forfar). Off A926, to W of Forfar, Loch of Forfar, Angus.
Site accessible at all reasonable times.

FORT GEORGE

An outstanding example of a Georgian artillery fort, Fort William was built after the failure of the Jacobite Rising at the Battle of Culloden in 1746, and is named after the king. It was designed by the architect William Skinner, with work also from William and John Adam. By the time it was finished in 1769 it was not needed – the Duke of Cumberland had 'pacified' the Highlands efficiently in a bloody campaign 20 years earlier. The buildings could house nearly 2000 troops, and covers 16 acres.

The fort is said to be haunted by several ghosts, including by a ghostly piper and by a bogle known as 'Abernethy', which is said to have been witnessed in the fort jail and to be an unpleasant spook. The medical centre is reputed to be where a soldier hanged himself, and it is said that the creaking of a rope can be heard at times.

Map 2, 7E (Fort George). Off B9006, 10 miles NE of Inverness, Fort George, Ardersier, Highland.
His Scot: Open all year, daily; closed 25/26 Dec and 1/2 Jan. (01667 460232 / www.historic-scotland.gov.uk)

FORTINGALL

The village is a picturesque place with thatched cottages, and this was a religious centre from the 6th century. In the old kirkyard is an ancient yew tree, believed to be more than 3,000 years old, and in the church is a bell said to have been used by St Adamnan, biographer of St Columba, as well as a 7th-century font. Fortingall is reputed to be the birthplace of Pontius Pilate, the son of a Roman emissary and a local girl.

The village is reputedly haunted, at times, by a procession of phantom nuns.

Map 4, 8J (Fortingall). Off B846, 5 miles W of Aberfeldy, Perthshire.
Access to churchyard at all reasonable times.

FOUNTAINHALL, ABERDEEN

Fountainhall, an 18th-century house, is said to be haunted. It was home to Dr Patrick Copland, an eminent Professor at Marischal College, who died in 1822.

Manifestations were reported, including the sounds of heavy footsteps and unexplained knockings, crashes and banging. An explanation for the haunting is that one of the owners murdered his wife (she was said to be having an affair with a Scottish noble), and hid her body here.

Map 2, 12G (Aberdeen). Off B9119 or B983, Blenheim Place, Aberdeen.

FOUR MILE INN, ABERDEEN

The Four Mile Inn is said to be haunted, the ghost thought to be that of a former landlord, who ran the establishment in the 1950s. There are reports of unexplained footsteps and noises coming from unoccupied areas, especially an upstairs room. When closing up, staff are said to have repeatedly heard the footsteps, even though the room has been checked and locked. This has led the staff to recheck the room, only to return downstairs and for the footsteps then to begin again.

Map 2, 12G (Aberdeen). On A96, Inverurie Road, Bucksburn, Aberdeen.
Public house. (01224 712588)

FRENDRAUGHT CASTLE

Frendraught dates mostly from the 17th century and later, but may incorporate part of an old castle of the Crichtons. This was the scene of an infamous blaze in 1630, when several people were burned alive.

The Crichtons and the Gordon family had been feuding over land, which had led to not a little violence. Several of the Gordons, however, were staying at Frendraught with their hosts, Sir James Crichton and his wife, Elizabeth Gordon, when the building mysteriously caught fire. John Gordon, Lord Rothiemay, and John Gordon, Viscount Aboyne, the son of the Marquis of Huntly, were burned and killed, as well as others of their kinsfolk and servants, some dozen or so people, although Sir James Crichton escaped with all his family. Indeed, it is said that Crichton did nothing to try to save his guests, and even that the Gordons had been locked in.

Sir James was tried for their murders in April 1631 and, although he was acquitted, one of his servants, John Meldrum, was executed. Lady Rothiemay certainly believed in Crichton's involvement: she employed Highlanders to attack and plunder his lands and family. Lady Rothiemay was eventually imprisoned in 1635, although she was later released.

The castle is believed to be haunted by the ghost of Crichton's wife, Elizabeth Gordon, daughter of the Earl of Sutherland, who may have been involved in the torching of the castle. One story is that she disposed of the keys to the Gordons' chambers in the well, and in the 1840s, when the well was cleaned out, a set of keys were indeed found.

Her ghost has reportedly been seen, most often on the stairs, in the 18th and 20th centuries, and her apparition has been described as a dark woman wearing a white dress edged with gold. Other activity reputedly includes the sounds of arguing, footsteps coming down the stairs, and crashing sounds, as well as doors being locked and unlocked, opened or shut. Electrical equipment is also said to have been interfered with and, despite being switched off at night, a television, video and fan heater were found to be turned on the next morning.

The castle passed to the Morisons, who still occupy the building.

Map 2, 10F (Frendraught). Off B9001, 6 miles E of Huntly, Aberdeenshire.

FULFORD TOWER

There was an old mansion here, which incorporated part of a 14th-century castle called Fulford Tower. This was rebuilt and extended with materials from Old Woodhouselee (see separate entry) in the 1660s, and then again in 1796. This house was then renamed Woodhouselee, but the entire building was completely demolished in 1965. The property was held by the Purves family, but the mansion was later home to Patrick Tytler, an eminent Scottish historian, and the place was visited by Sir Walter Scott.

It is said that the mansion was haunted by the ghost of Lady Hamilton, apparently translated from Old Woodhouselee along with the materials, although this may be a mix up over names – or it could be that Fulford had its own bogle and the two stories have been confused.

Map 4, 9M (Fulford). Off A702, 2.5 miles N of Penicuik, Woodhouselee, Midlothian.

FYVIE CASTLE   ILLUS PAGE 143

Set in the rolling countryside is Fyvie Castle, one of the most outstanding castles in Scotland. The building consists of a massive tower house with very long wings, and it is adorned with turrets, dormer windows and carved finials, and corbiestepped gables. The castle was formerly built around a courtyard, but the north and east side were lost in the 18th century.

When the castle was first being built, stones were removed from church lands by demolishing a nearby chapel, but fell into a nearby river. The then laird refused Thomas the Rhymer shelter in the castle, and the Rhymer is said to have prophesied that unless the three stones were recovered the castle and estate would never descend in direct line for more than two generations. Only two of the stones were found, and the prophecy is said to have come true. One of the stones is in the charter room, while another is reported to be built into the foundations – and they are said to 'weep', oozing with water, when tragedy is going to strike the owners.

Fyvie was destined to have a succession of owners, and passed to the Prestons in 1402, then about 1433 to the Meldrums, then the Seton Earls of Dunfermline in 1596, then to the Gordon Earls of Aberdeen in 1733, and finally to the Leith family in 1889, each of whom added to the castle. Fyvie was put onto the open market in 1982, and is now owned by The National Trust for Scotland.

The castle is reputedly haunted by a 'Green Lady', the ghost of Lillias Drummond, wife of Alexander Seton, Earl of Dunfermline. She died on 8 May 1601, aged about 30, at Seton's house at Dalgety in Fife. Lillias had five children, all of whom were daughters and four of whom lived into adulthood, but her husband wanted a son and heir. One theory is that she was starved to death by her husband, or she may have died of a broken heart, or she simply grew ill and died (possibly because of so many births in a relatively short time) – as in many stories, details are confused. Whatever the truth of it, Seton married Grizel Leslie only six months after Lillias's death: in fact, he was contracted to Grizel only a few weeks later.

On their wedding night, 27 October, Seton and his new wife were staying in what is now known as the Drummond Room. They were plagued all night by sighing coming from the window, and in the morning found the following carved into the window sill, some 50 foot from the ground: 'D[ame] LILLIES DRUMMOND'. Although this seems far fetched, the writing can be seen and it is an unusual place for anyone to have their name carved, particularly as it faces outward.

Grizel did not have a happy time of things, as she too did not deliver the son Seton wanted, and she died only five years later. Seton married for a third time, and finally produced a son, Charles, who went on to become the 2nd Earl of Dunfermline. The line lasted only another generation, and James, the 4th Earl, was forfeited in 1690 and died without heirs. Lillias's daughters, however, all married into the great families of Scotland.

The appearance of Lillias's ghost is believed to be an ill omen for the resident family, and the ghost is recorded as being often spotted, on the main turnpike stair, from the 17th century onwards, sometimes disappearing into solid panelling. Her appearance is said to have manifested itself as a fully formed apparition in a green brocade dress with a candle and pearls, but also as a fuzzy patch of light or a glow. Her presence is also said to be heralded by the smell of roses, an event which has been noted in recent times, including in 2008 when a guide felt someone push past him although there was nothing there except the perfume. A guest also reported seeing the phantom of a woman in the Gordon bedroom.

Fernie Castle
(page 136)

Fyvie Castle (page 142)

George Heriot's School, Edinburgh (page 148)

Glamis Castle (page 149)

Glamis Manse (page 150)

In the 19th century Colonel Cosmo Gordon recorded that he had been shaken out of bed by invisible hands, and on another night a wind arose which blew off the covers from his own bed and his guests. Lillias is thought to have appeared before the death of Cosmo in 1879, and before that of Alexander Gordon, a few years later.

Lillias is also believed to haunt another former Seton castle, Pinkie House (also see that entry), in Musselburgh, although that identification is problematic, as she is said sometimes to be seen with the ghost of a boy.

Fyvie Castle is also reported to have a 'Grey Lady' or a 'White Lady', believed to be the spirit of a lass starved to death here. The ghost was at its most active in the 1920s and 1930s. When workmen were renovating one of the chambers, the gun room, in the castle, they found a secret chamber behind a wall, in which they uncovered the remains of a woman. When the skeleton was removed, disturbances increased until the bones were returned to the secret room – or so it is said. One account has a maid being woken from sleep to see an apparition of a lady in white-greenish flowing dress gliding across her bedroom, turn to look sadly at her, and then disappear through a closed door.

These two ghosts, 'Green Lady' and 'White Lady', may be one and the same, depending on the account.

Some say the castle also has a ghostly drummer, while others a trumpeter, the ghost of an Andrew Lammie. He is said to have fallen in love with Agnes, daughter of a local miller, but her parents had him banished or abducted, an occurrence in which the Gordon lairds were involved. His ghost is said to return and blow a trumpet when one of the Gordons is near death.

Map 2, 11F (Fyvie). Off A947, 8 miles S of Turriff and 1 mile N of Fyvie village, Fyvie, Banff & Buchan.
NTS: Castle open Apr-Jun & Sep-Oct, Sat-Tue (closed Wed-Fri); Jul-Aug, daily; grounds and garden open all year, daily. (01651 891266 / www.nts.org.uk)

A paranormal investigation was undertaken in November 2008 by East of Scotland Paranormal (esparanormal.org.uk)

Featured in Living TV's Most Haunted, *series six (2005).*

GAIRNSHIEL LODGE

In a wild, picturesque location, Gairnshiel Lodge, an attractive house with corbie-stepped gables, stands in four acres of grounds in the foothills of the Cairngorm mountains. It was used by Queen Victoria as a hunting lodge, and is now a comfortable, family-run establishment, available for exclusive use.

The lodge is said to be haunted by the apparition of an old woman, reputedly the spirit of one of the former owners.

The old military road, built because of the Jacobite Risings, runs past the building and crosses the River Gairn over a tall arched bridge. This was one of the main routes north from Braemar and Deeside across the mountains to Tomintoul. The sounds of feet, horses, carts and marching men have allegedly been heard here, even though there is nobody to be seen.

Map 2, 9G (Gairnshiel). On B976, 4 miles NW of Ballater, Kincardine & Deeside.
Available for exclusive use for small private parties. (01339 755582 / www.gairnshiellodge.co.uk)

GALDENOCH CASTLE

Galdenoch Castle, a ruinous tower house, was built by Gilbert Agnew, who was killed at the Battle of Pinkie in 1547.

The story goes that the son of the laird of Galdenoch was a Covenanter, and finding himself pursued by Royalist forces, took refuge at a farm, which was only inhabited by a farmer. The farmer became suspicious of the young Agnew, and tried to prevent him from leaving. Perhaps fearing that he was to be turned over to the authorities, Agnew shot the farmer, killing him. Agnew returned to Galdenoch, and no suspicion fell on him. The attack, however, was not to go unpunished.

From that time Galdenoch was haunted by the vengeful spirit of the farmer. Although no apparition was seen, all other manner of manifestations occurred. On one occasion the ghost seized Agnew's grandmother and ducked her in a freezing stream, and on another threw blazing coals from the fire, which set fire to an outbuilding. The ghost scorned people who tried to rid the castle of its presence.

The bogle was eventually exorcised by the mighty singing of a priest and a choir of local people.

Map 3, 5P (Galdenoch). Off B738, 6 miles W of Stranraer, Galdenoch, Dumfries and Galloway.

GALLOWAY ARMS HOTEL, CROCKETFORD

The old coaching inn, which mostly dates from 1856 (although there was an older establishment here) is a fine picturesque building in the village of Crocketford. The inn was visited by Robert Burns in 1793 and is a traditional welcoming hotel.

The building is said by some to be haunted by the ghost of Elizabeth Buchan, who died in 1791. The Buchanites were an apocalyptic Christian sect and were centred around her, and she was believed to be a character referred to in the *Book of Revelation* in the *Bible*. She founded a religious house here after having visions, and attracted a large following. Part of the premise of the sect was that they would be able to ascend to heaven without dying, but this failed to happen on the day ordained. Support for the Buchanites then withered, perhaps not surprisingly.

Map 4, 8P (Crocketford). By junction of A75 with A712, 7 miles NE of Castle Douglas, Crocketford, Dumfries and Galloway.
Hotel, restaurant and bar. (01556 690248 / www.gallowayarmshotel.co.uk)

GALLOWAY GAZETTE, NEWTON STEWART

The premises of the Galloway Gazette in Victoria Lane are said to have been haunted by a ghost known as 'Harry'.

Manifestations are reported to have included doors being found locked, open or closed without explanation, furniture moving by itself, lights turning on and off by themselves, interference with electrical equipment, mysterious heavy footsteps, disembodied voices, banging and rattling, and unusual smells. The staff also reported feeling a presence in the building.

The story goes that the activity began when a gravestone, with the name Harry Flynn, was brought into the building, after it had been found against the door to the cellar. Staff thought that the stone had fallen off a cart and, having gone missing, the stone would be claimed, but it never was and long resided at the premises.

Map 3, 6P (Newton Stewart). Off A714, Victoria Lane, Newton Stewart, Dumfries and Galloway.
Galloway Gazette. (01671 402 503 / www.gallowaygazette.co.uk)

GARLETON CASTLE

Nestling under the picturesque Garleton Hills, Garleton Castle is a partly ruinous courtyard castle, for many years a property of the Lindsays. Sir David Lindsay of the Mount, the well-known 16th-century playwright who was the author of *The Satire of the Three Estates*, is thought to have been born here.

The building was said to be haunted at the end of the 18th century by the apparition of a man, and the sounds of heavy footsteps were also reported. The spectre was said to be tall and pale, and wished to relate some tale to whichever mortal would listen. The then owner, however, would have nothing to do with the bogle, and the ghost withdrew when she demanded it did so. It is said that the apparition of the man has not been seen since, but that at times the sounds of unexplained footsteps can still be heard, thumping about during the night.

Map 4, 10L (Garleton). Off B1343, 1.5 miles N of Haddington, Garleton, East Lothian.

GARTH CASTLE

Standing on a steep crag, Garth Castle, a plain 14th-century tower, was built by Alexander Stewart, the Wolf of Badenoch. Nigel Stewart of Garth, a later owner, was by all accounts a wicked fellow. He seized Sir Robert Menzies in 1502 from nearby Weem and imprisoned him in the dungeon at Garth, threatening to torture him unless he signed away some of his lands. Stewart was also suspected of murdering his wife, Mariota, as she died in suspicious circumstances: a stone apparently struck her on the head in the ravine below the castle.

Sightings of her apparition have been reported in the area.

Stewart was imprisoned in Garth until his death in 1554, and the castle is still occupied, although it underwent a rather brutal restoration in the 1960s.

Map 4, 8J (Garth). Off B846, 6 miles W of Aberfeldy, Garth, Perthshire.

GARTLOCH HOSPITAL

Gartloch Hospital was built in 1889 as an asylum for people with mental health problems, with more than 500 beds, and it remains an impressive complex of buildings. The hospital was closed in 1992 and the site is to be redeveloped as a 'luxury village'.

The hospital was reputedly haunted by the apparition of a woman dressed in black, spotted on the stair of Ward One and accompanied by a chill atmosphere. It is said that the bogle would pass along a passage, before disappearing through a sealed-up door.

Map 4, 7M (Gartloch). Off B806, to E of Glasgow, 1 mile W of Gartcosh, Gartloch, Lanarkshire.

GEORGE AND ABBOTSFORD HOTEL, MELROSE

The present hotel probably dates from the beginning of the 19th century, but the George Inn seems to have been established by the mid 18th century and was a coaching inn. The inn was visited by Sir Walter Scott, along with William and Dorothy Wordsworth in 1803, and the then proprietor is mentioned in the introduction to Scott's *The Monastery*. At some time in the 19th century, 'Abbotsford', the home of Scott, was added to the name of the inn.

The building is said to be haunted, and the sounds of footsteps have reputedly been heard above rooms on the first floor, even though there are no occupied rooms in that area.

Map 4, 10N (Melrose). Off A6091, High Street, Melrose, Borders.
Hotel. (01896 822308 / www.georgeandabbotsford.co.uk)

GEORGE HERIOT'S SCHOOL, EDINBURGH ILLUS PAGE 144

George Heriot's School was founded in 1628 although not completed until 1659, and is housed in a fantastic towered and turreted courtyard building with a monumental clock tower. George Heriot was a fabulously wealthy man, being a goldsmith and banker to James VI, and he left his fortune to establish a hospital and charity school.

The school is said to be haunted by the bogle of a drummer boy, heard playing in the turret stairs in the mornings. The story goes the boy's task was to rise first and wake the students in the school by drumming. But one fateful day, goes the tale, he fell to his death, down one of the steep turret stairs, and from time to time the drumming is still heard, early in the morning.

Map 4, 9L (Edinburgh). Off A702 or A7, Lauriston Place, Edinburgh.
School. (0131 229 7263 / www.george-heriots.com)

GEORGE STREET, EDINBURGH

The elegant and exclusive street, which runs parallel to Princes Street, Edinburgh's main shopping thoroughfare, is reputed to be haunted by the phantom of Jane Vernelt. The story is that, early in the 20th century, she was given poor financial advice, which resulted in her losing her business and dying before her time.

It is said that her apparition has been spotted during the day several times, going back to her former premises.

Map 4, 9L (Edinburgh). Off A90, George Street, Edinburgh.

GEORGE STREET, GLASGOW

There are accounts of George Street being haunted.

Early in the morning, it is said, a witness saw two figures dressed as if from the 18th century. The men, who appeared to be deep in conversation (although nothing could be heard), were seen walking along the road, only to then fade and disappear. The figures have apparently been witnessed since.

Map 4, 7M (Glasgow). Off M8, George Street, Glasgow.

GEORGIAN HOUSE, EDINBURGH

This Georgian House is part of Robert Adam's elegant and splendid north side of Charlotte Square in Edinburgh's New Town. The lower floors of number 7 have been restored as to when the house was new, in about 1800, both the grand and the domestic areas. There is a fine display of china and silver, pictures and furniture, gadgets and utensils: everything of the period, from the essentially decorative to the purely functional.

The kitchen is said to be haunted, and the apparition of a girl has been spotted here on more than one occasion, suggested as being the phantom of a kitchen maid.

Map 4, 9L (Edinburgh). 7 Charlotte Square, Edinburgh.
NTS: House open early Mar-late Nov, daily. (0131 226 3318 / www.nts.org.uk)

GIGHT CASTLE

Pronounced 'Gecht', Gight Castle is a ruined castle of the Gordons, who were re-putedly a wicked lot: bad enough indeed to have practised the black arts - one account states that a nearby pool is where the Devil still cavorts with phantoms of the Gordons.

Catherine Gordon, heiress of Gight, married John Byron, but in 1787 had to sell the property to pay off his gambling debts. Their son was the famous poet George Gordon Byron (Lord Byron).

Ghostly pipes can reputedly be heard from a piper sent to explore a subterranean passage under the castle. His progress could be followed above ground by the music of his pipes, which eventually died away, and although the unfortunate piper was never seen again, it is said that his bagpipes can sometimes still be heard.

Map 2, 11F (Gight). Off B9005, 4 miles E of Fyvie, Aberdeenshire.

GIGHT HOUSE HOTEL, METHLICK

The hotel here, once a manse, is said to be haunted. The apparition of a man, thought to be the Reverend John Mennie who died in 1886, has been seen in the bedrooms and bar, which were in the former manse. Ghostly footsteps have been reputedly heard from unoccupied parts of the hotel, and a bathroom door was locked from the inside when nobody was in it.

The hotel appears to be closed at the time of writing.

Map 2, 11F (Methlick). Off B999, Methlick, Aberdeenshire.
Hotel. (01651 806389)

GLAISNOCK HOUSE

Located in a fine spot, Glaisnock House is a massive muscular mansion of four storeys, dating from 1833, and there are many rooms and reputedly 365 windows. The present mansion was built for James Allason, but the property passed to Cap-tain Robert Campbell around 1850. The estate was broken up in 1949, and the house was converted into a boys' boarding school, then in the 1970s into a base for outdoor activities. The mansion fell into disrepair, and in recent years it was reno-vated to become a 'European Centre for Creativity', but the trust behind the project collapsed.

The building is said to be haunted by a 'Green Lady', the spirit of a girl reputed to have been imprisoned in one of the many chambers of Glaisnock and to have died there. The ghost is said to have been seen in the house.

Map 4, 7N (Glaisnock). Off A76, 1 mile S of Cumnock, Glaisnock, Ayrshire.

GLAMIS CASTLE   ILLUS PAGE 144

Probably best known as one of the most haunted places in Britain, Glamis Castle is a magnificent building set in fine park land with an Italian garden. The massive keep towers over the countryside and has a wide turnpike stair, rising 143 steps from the basement to the battlements. There are later wings, and the building has a mass of corbelling, sculpture, turrets and pinnacles. The keep is vaulted on three floors, and houses 'Duncan's Hall', traditionally associated with Macbeth and Dun-can's death. Any connection, as at Cawdor, is probably only based on Shakespeare's play, as Glamis is not mentioned until 1264, some 200 years after the events. Glamis has long been held by the Lyon family, who were given the lands by Robert II in 1372. The family became Earls of Strathmore and of Kinghorne.

Janet Douglas was the beautiful widow of John Lyon, 6th Lord Glamis, although she remarried, wedding Walter Campbell of Skipness. Unfortunately for her, she was also the sister of Archibald Douglas, 5th Earl of Angus. This meant that she was hated by James V, who had a long-running vendetta with the Douglases. He had been ill treated and imprisoned in his youth by the Earl of Angus (who had married his mother, Margaret Tudor, after the death of James IV at Flodden in 1513).

James's spite was extended to many members of the Earl of Angus's family, and Janet was accused of both trying to poison the king, as well as on a false charge of witchcraft. The young woman defended herself eloquently, but it was to no avail: she was burned to death on Castle Hill in Edinburgh on 3 December 1537, after being imprisoned with her husband and her son John for so long that she had nearly gone blind. One description of her tells 'she was in the prime of her life, of a singular beauty, and suffering through all, though a woman, with a man-like courage'. Glamis was forfeited to the Crown, and John, her orphaned son, was also sentenced to death, although he was too young at the time for the execution to go ahead. Luckily for John, James V died in 1542 and John was pardoned and then went on to inherit his father's property, including Glamis Castle.

Janet's apparition, the 'Grey Lady of Glamis' is said to haunt Glamis, and to have been seen in the chapel and clock tower. In the chapel she is said to have been spotted several times, either sitting or praying. One sighting is said to have been made in 1716 when the Old Pretender was at Glamis; on another occasion the ghost was described as small figure through which the sun shone, making a pattern on the floor. Her bogle is also said to have been seen on the castle esplanade at Edinburgh (see that entry), near the place where she was executed.

The ghost of Alexander Lindsay, 4th Earl of Crawford, 'Earl Beardie', is alleged to haunt a walled-up room where he played cards with the Devil. Here he is compelled to play until the 'day of doom', and he was certainly a cruel and ruthless character. Indeed, one story is that his mother smothered her own brother so that he would succeed to the Earldom of Crawford. It is said that Crawford's ghost can also be seen at his castle of Lordscairnie (see that entry).

Other stories of ghosts and beasts abound and are widely reported: a little African boy, a 'White Lady' who haunts an avenue up to the castle, a tongueless woman, a party of Ogilvies walled up in Glamis, and a servant girl who was a vampire and drained one of her victims before being sealed up in the castle walls.

Map 4, 10J (Glamis). Off A94, 5.5 miles SW of Forfar, 1 mile N of Glamis village, Angus.
Open mid Mar-Dec, daily. (01307 840393 / www.glamis-castle.co.uk)

GLAMIS MANSE ILLUS PAGE 144

In the garden of Glamis Manse is a fine carved Pictish stone, with a cross and other carving on one side, Pictish symbols and figures on the other. The stone may have been associated with the nearby healing well of St Fergus, an 8th-century holy man, and the megalith is known by some as 'King Malcolm's Stone'. The area around the stone is said to be haunted by a grey figure, the apparition of some unknown person.

Not much remains of the old church of St Fergus, dating from the 12th century or earlier, except the south transept, which was used as the burial vault of the Lyon

Earls of Strathmore of nearby Glamis Castle (see that entry). A new church replaced this ancient building, and there is a landscaped trail, which leads down from the church to the healing well.

Map 4, 10J (Glamis). Off A94, Glamis village, Angus.

GLASGOW ROYAL CONCERT HALL

The Glasgow Royal Concert Hall, in the centre of the city, replaced St Andrew's Hall (which was burnt down in 1962) and this was opened in 1990 as a venue for stage shows, exhibitions, dancing and sports.

The building is reputed to be haunted, and manifestations are alleged to include objects being moved by themselves, and security staff spotting half-seen apparitions although nobody is present.

Map 4, 7M (Glasgow). Off M8, 2 Sauchiehall Street, Glasgow.
Concert hall, conference and exhibition centre and restaurant. (0141 353 8000 (box office) / www.glasgowconcerthalls.com)

GLASGOW ROYAL INFIRMARY

Glasgow Infirmary, dating from 1792, stands on the site of Glasgow Castle, the bishop's residence, with the fine medieval cathedral nearby – a stone marks the site of the old castle in the grounds.

The surgical block is reputedly haunted by a 'Green Lady' (or a 'Grey Lady'), one story being that she is the spectre of a nurse, who fell to her death down a stairwell while trying to prevent a patient from committing suicide. The ghost is said to be helpful, and to have been witnessed on numerous occasions, such as ascending a stair and walking down a corridor, before vanishing. It is not clear whether this is the same apparition which is claimed to have been seen, but cut off at the knee.

Another bogle is said to be known as 'Archie', and to be that of an old man, seen in Ward 27, and apparently talking to patients who are near death.

A spooky story is that a doctor, while responding to an emergency, was asked the way out by a person. The doctor did not have time to respond properly to the request, but when he got to the emergency he realised that the patient before him was the same person who had apparently asked him the way out.

Map 4, 7M (Glasgow). Off A8, 84 Castle Street, Glasgow.
Hospital. (0141 211 4000 / www.nhsgg.org.uk)

GLEN MORE, MULL

Glen More cuts through the middle of the island of Mull, overlooked by the 3000-foot mountain Ben More, and is the main route to Iona and the west of the island, used by pilgrims from medieval times, and travellers of later days.

The glen, however, is said to be haunted by a headless horseman.

The ghost story goes back to events in 1538. The MacLaines held the south and east of Mull (also see Lochbuie) and the son and heir of the 5th chief was Ewen of the Little Head. Ewen had been given an island dwelling in Loch Squabain as his residence, but his wife, a daughter of MacDougall of Lorn and being from an important clan, did not feel that the house or marriage settlement was sufficient for her needs. This led to conflict between father and son, and eventually open fighting. Their forces came to battle, but in the subsequent conflict Ewen was slain, his head being hewn clean off by an axe. His horse rode away down Glen More, his upright decapitated body still in the saddle, before coming to rest some two miles away.

Ewen's ghost, a headless horseman on a dun horse, sometimes described as wearing a green cloak, is said to be seen riding in Glen More when one of the MacLaines is about to die or suffer from a serious illness. Some accounts have him accompanied by a large black phantom hunting dog, and one account from 1909 has only the dog being seen (on the death of Murdo MacLaine). This ghostly dog is also said to haunt Lochbuie, having been both heard and seen.

The story goes that the apparition of Ewen of the Little Head has been seen three times in living memory on Mull, and was also spotted on the Island of Coll.

Map 3, 3K (Glen More). On A849, 8 miles SW of Craignure, Glen More, Mull, Argyll.
Access at all reasonable times.

GLEN SCOTIA, CAMPBELTOWN

Glen Scotia, a malt whisky distillery founded in 1832 in the Kintyre town of Campbeltown, is said to be haunted by a former owner, who despaired of life and drowned himself in Campbeltown Loch. Mysterious footsteps are said to have been heard crossing the maltings floor, even though nobody is apparently present.

Map 3, 4N (Campbeltown). Off A83, High Street, Campbeltown, Kintyre, Argyll.
Distillery.

GLENCOE

One of the most picturesque parts of Scotland, Glencoe is the site of the infamous massacre in 1692, executed by government forces under Campbell of Glenlyon. Thirty-eight members of the MacDonalds of Glencoe, including their chief Maclain, were slaughtered by men from the garrison at Fort William, who had been billeted on the MacDonalds. One of the sites of the massacre at Inverglen can be visited; as can the Signal Rock, reputedly where the signal to begin the massacre was given.

The glen is reported to be haunted by ghosts of the slaughtered MacDonalds.

Map 1, 5I (Glencoe). On A82, 17 miles S of Fort William, Glencoe, Highlands.
NTS: Site open all year; visitor centre, shop and cafe open early Jan-Feb, Thu-Sun (closed Mon-Wed); Mar-Oct, daily; Nov-mid Dec, open Thu-Sun (closed Mon-Wed); open between Christmas and New Year (check days). (01855 811307 / www.nts.org.uk)

GLENGORM CASTLE

In a picturesque location with fantastic views, Glengorm Castle is a fabulous castellated mansion of 1860 with many turrets and towers, built for John Forsyth. The story goes that Forsyth, thinking that the air had an unusual colour called the place 'Glengorm' ('blue glen'), but it is said the colour actually came from the smoke from crofters being burned out of their houses. Forsyth was apparently cursed by one of the crofters, told that he would not spend a single night in his new mansion, and Forsyth duly died in a riding accident before the castle was completed.

The building is believed to be haunted by a 'Green Lady'.

Map 1, 2I (Glengorm). Off B882, 4 miles NW of Tobermory, Glengorm Castle, Mull, Argyll.
Cafe and art gallery; self-catering apartments/B&B available. Market garden. (01688 302321 / www.glengormcastle.co.uk)

GLENLEE

Glenlee, much enlarged in 1822, was the home of the Miller family in the 18th century, two of whom were eminent judges, but by the end of the 19th century had passed to the Smiths.

The house is said to be haunted by a 'Grey Lady'. The apparition, clad in a grey silk dress, has reportedly been witnessed on several occasions, as have the sounds of its footsteps. Manifestations are mostly said to have taken place in the old part of the house. At least four sightings were reported in the 19th century, although during none of these was the observer apparently aware that, at the time, what they spotted was not a real person.

The story goes that this was the spirit of a Lady Ashburton, wife of a Lord Glenlee (although it has not been possible to ascertain either which Lady Ashburton or which Lord Glenlee). Lady Ashburton is said to have murdered her husband by poisoning him (reportedly because he was infested with lice), but was then poisoned herself by their butler, so that he could rob her.

Map 4, 7P (Glenlee). Off A762, 2 miles NW of New Galloway, Glenlee, Dumfries and Galloway.

GLENLEE (TALL SHIP), GLASGOW   ILLUS PAGE 157

The *Glenlee* was built in 1896 at Port Glasgow, and is a three-masted barque, some 240-foot long and constructed from steel. The ship circumnavigated the world four times before being bought by the Spanish navy in 1922, when it was subsequently used as a training vessel. The ship was purchased by the Clyde Maritime Trust, was restored and brought to Glasgow, where she was opened as a visitor attraction. The *Glenlee* features exhibitions, events and activities, as well as a nautical souvenir shop.

Several strange occurrences have been reported on the *Glenlee*, including half-seen apparitions spotted around the stairs, staff feeling as if they are being watched or someone is behind them, and unexplained changes in temperature.

Map 4, 7M (Glasgow). Off A814, 100 Stobcross Road, Glasgow.
Open Mar-Oct, daily 10.00-17.00; Nov-Feb 11.00-16.00. (0141 222 2513 / www.glenlee.co.uk)

A paranormal investigation was undertaken in February 2007 by the Ghost Club (www.ghostclub.org.uk) and was apparently featured in an episode of 'Ghost Towns'.

GLENLIVET

The Battle of Glenlivet was fought on 3 October 1594 between the government forces of the Earl of Argyll with about 10,000 men and the Catholic forces led by the Marquis of Huntly and the Earl of Errol with a much smaller force, perhaps as few as 2,000 troops. Despite the superior numbers, it was Huntly who won the day by his use of artillery and cavalry, and the government forces were routed.

On the anniversary of the battle the ghost of a headless horseman is reputed to be seen, the phantom of a man called MacAllister, who was allegedly beheaded by cannon fire at the onset of the fighting.

Map 2, 9F (Glenlivet). Near B9009, 3 miles E of Glenlivet village, Moray.

GLENLUCE

The house of Gilbert Campbell, in the village, was said to be haunted by a polter-geist in 1655. Disturbances included objects being thrown at the house, clothes being shredded, bedclothes being pulled from the beds, all when nobody was apparently present. The activity stopped as suddenly it had started.

Campbell is thought to have been cursed by Alexander Agnew, a tinker, after he had insulted him, and the activity apparently stopped at the same time that Agnew was hanged.

Map 3, 5P (Glenluce). Off A75, Glenluce, Dumfries and Galloway.

GLENMALLAN

A house here was said to have been haunted by the apparition of a woman, lying on a bed with her face turned to the wall. The ghost was apparently witnessed by a girl staying in the house in 1875.

The story goes that the woman was the wife of a former owner. He was a drunkard and beat his wife, and she died of her injuries.

Map 3, 5L (Glenmallan). On A814, 3 miles N of Garelochhead, Glenmallan, Argyll.

GLENSANDA CASTLE

Glensanda Castle, also known as Caisteal Mernaig, is one of the most remotely situated castles by road in Scotland, and the ruin stands on a rock at the mouth of a loch on the west side of Loch Linnhe. The lands belonged to the MacMasters, but they passed to the MacLeans in the 15th century, and it was Ewen MacLean of Kingairloch who built the old stronghold in about 1450.

The castle is said to have had a 'Green Lady' or gruagach.

Map 3, 4J (Glensanda). Off (by track) A884, 5 miles S of Lochaline, W side of Loch Linnhe, Glensanda, Highland.

GLOBE INN, DUMFRIES

The Globe Inn has been a hostelry since 1610, and Robert Burns visited the pub often. There is some fine 18th-century panelling, and the bedroom he used has been preserved. Other visitors to the Globe include Robert Louis Stevenson, J.M. Barrie, Rudyard Kipling and Andrew Carnegie.

The inn is said to be haunted by the ghost of Helen Park (Anna in Burns's poem), who worked in the establishment in the 18th century, and lived in the upstairs room. Helen had a daughter, Elizabeth, by Robert Burns in 1791 and, although Helen died soon afterwards, Burns brought up Elizabeth in his own household.

Helen's apparition has reputedly been witnessed in the upstairs room, along with unexplained noises, and there was a sighting of the ghost on a staircase in 1996, clad in an old-fashioned full skirt and rushing down the steps. In one account the ghost is described as being a 'White Lady', and is said to be more active when Burns is being celebrated. Other manifestations are reported to be people feeling as if they are being pulled, and lights going on by themselves.

Map 4, 8P (Dumfries). Off A756, 56 High Street, Globe Inn, Dumfries, Dumfries and Galloway. **Public house. (01387 252335 / www.globeinndumfries.co.uk)**

GOLDEN LION, STIRLING

The Golden Lion was built in 1786, and the hotel, bar and brasserie are located in the heart of the historic burgh. The hostelry was visited by Robert Burns.

The hotel is said to be haunted.

Map 4, 8L (Stirling). Of A811 or B8052, 8-10 King Street, Stirling.
Hotel. (01786 475351 / www.thegoldenlionstirling.com)

GORRENBERRY TOWER

There was a tower house at Gorrenberry, which was held by the Elliots, but nothing survives. The tower is said to have had a brownie or a mischievous spirit called a Shellycoat (because his coat was covered in shells, so that he rattled when he moved).

Map 4, 10O (Gorrenberry). Off B6399, 6 miles N of Newcastleton, Gorrenberry, Borders.

GRANDTULLY CASTLE

An impressive and well-preserved fortress, Grandtully Castle consists of a Z-plan tower house of the Stewarts, later altered and extended. The castle was visited by the Marquis of Montrose and Bonnie Prince Charlie.

After defeat at the Battle of Killiecrankie in 1689, the story goes that a soldier serving in the forces of William and Mary killed an officer in one of the turrets. The blood staining the floor is said to be impossible to wash off.

One further tale is that the castle was haunted by a Redcap, often an unpleasant bogle that frequented places where violence had been done. The Redcap is described as a hunched old man with long gnarled fingernails and seen wearing a red cap, the cap being dipped in human blood. Attacking unwary sleepers, the Redcap is said to renew the colour of its cap by dipping it in the blood of its victims. The Redcap can be driven off by the hilts of a sword or dagger (as long as they are cross-shaped) or by a Christian prayer. The Redcap that haunts Grandtully is reputed to be much more benign, however, and to bring luck to the castle (perhaps a brownie).

Map 4, 8J (Grandtully). Off A827, 2.5 miles NW of Aberfeldy, Grandtully, Perthshire.

GRANGE HOUSE, EDINBURGH

Grange House was a splendid old mansion, dating from the 16th century or earlier, but it was completely demolished in 1936. Bonnie Prince Charlie stayed here in 1745. The old house reputedly had many ghosts, one of whom was a miser, who rolled a phantom barrel of gold through the corridors and passageways.

Map 4, 9L (Edinburgh). Off A7, 1.5 miles S of Edinburgh Castle, Grange, Edinburgh.

GRANGEMUIR HOUSE

There was a castle or old house at Grangemuir, which was owned by the Scotts in the 16th century: Elie was made a Burgh of Barony for William Scott of Grangemuir in 1598-99. The present house dates from about 1807, but stands on the site of a much older building, which was occupied by the Bruce family, who held the lands in the 18th century. The property later passed to the Douglases, but it was sold in 1931 and the house is now ruinous, after being used as an old persons' home, and stands in a caravan park.

Grangemuir was reputedly haunted by the ghost of a pretty girl called Buff Bare-foot, named so because she wore no footwear. When she was a baby, she had been found abandoned, with nothing except a bag of gold. But she grew into a very attractive lass.

Buff had at least two admirers (one a son of the family who owned Grangemuir), but her affections appear to have become a bone of contention. The poor girl ended up murdered, although the exact circumstances are not certain, there being more than one version of the story. Her killer was captured, while her other suitor committed suicide.

There were then reputedly many manifestations at Grangemuir, not least the sound of heavy footfalls in the building, made by unseen bare feet; her apparition was also observed. The disturbances were apparently so frightening that they caused the old house to be abandoned, and the new building was put in its place.

The builders were careful enough, however, not to reuse any of the materials from the previous dwelling, just in case her bogle managed to re-establish itself in the new house along with the old materials.

There are some accounts, however, that still have the sound of her bare feet being heard in the vicinity of Grangemuir.

Map 4, 10K (Grangemuir). Off A917, 1 mile N of Pittenweem, Grangemuir, Fife.
Chalets. (01333 450314)

GREENKNOWE TOWER ILLUS PAGE 157

Built on a small hill in a fine position with an avenue of old trees, Greenknowe Tower is an L-plan tower house, rising to four storeys and with turrets at three of the corners. The tower is dated 1581, and still has its iron yett (gate). Greenknowe passed by marriage from the Gordons to the Setons of Touch, who built the tower. It was acquired by the Pringles of Stichill in the 17th century, one of whom, Walter Pringle, was a noted writer and Covenanter. It later passed to the Dalrymples, who occupied it until the middle of the 19th century, although it is now ruinous.

There are reports that the tower is haunted.

Map 4, 10N (Greenknowe). On A6105, 7 miles NW of Kelso, 0.5 miles W of Gordon, Green-knowe, Borders.
His Scot: Access at all reasonable times. (www.historic-scotland.gov.uk)

GREENLAW

Greenlaw is an imposing classical mansion, dating from 1741, which rises to three storeys. The entrance is reached by a wide imposing staircase, but the mansion is an empty shell after being gutted in a fire in the 1970s. The lands were a property of the Gordons.

The mansion is said to have been haunted by the ghost of an old woman, clad in grey.

Map 4, 7P (Greenlaw). Off B795, 1.5 miles NW of Castle Douglas, Greenlaw, Dumfries and Galloway.

GREENLAW HOUSE, GLENCORSE

Greenlaw House, which incorporated a 17th-century laird's house, was remodelled from 1804 into a large barracks and prison that could hold up to 6,000 prisoners from the Napoleonic wars. The building served as the military prison for Scotland

Glenlee *(Tall Ship)*, Glasgow *(page 153)*

Greenknowe Tower (page 156)

Hailes Castle (page 161)

Hermitage Castle (page 163)

His Majesty's Theatre, Aberdeen (page 165)

from 1845 to 1888. In 1875 Greenlaw was extended to become the army depot for south-east Scotland, but the house was completely demolished and the site is occupied by later buildings.

The ghost of a young woman, said to be Morag Mackintosh, is reported to have been seen at a spot called 'Lover's Loup (Leap)', at a gorge above the River Esk. The story goes that she had been cavorting with one of the French prisoners imprisoned at Greenlaw. Her father had her imprisoned and, while incarcerated, her French lover was murdered, died or moved elsewhere. When the girl was released, she found her lover gone, and then threw herself into the river at 'Lover's Loup'. Her ghost is also said to have been seen in the Frith Wood, running dishevelled through the trees towards the spot from which she leapt, or just standing weeping.

Map 4, 9M (Glencorse). Off A701, Glencorse Barracks, N of Penicuik, Midlothian.

GRESHORNISH HOUSE

Set in ten acres of gardens and wooded grounds in a tranquil spot, the fine old house dates from the middle of the 18th century, although it was extended about one hundred years later and is now a comfortable residence and hotel. The lands were held by the MacLeods, and it was Kenneth MacLeod, a wealthy fellow, who did much to improve the house in the 1840s.

The house is reputed to have a haunted room and a ghost.

Map 1, 2E (Greshornish). Off A850, 1.5 miles N of Edinbane, Greshornish, Isle of Skye, Highland. **Hotel. (01470 582266 / www.greshornishhouse.com)**

GREYFRIARS KIRKYARD, EDINBURGH

Built in the garden of the dissolved Franciscan friary (hence the name 'Greyfriars') this was the first post-Reformation church built in Edinburgh, and was completed in 1620, although altered in the following centuries. The National Covenant was signed here in 1638, a bill asserting the rights of the people over the king to decide on their own form of worship. The historic kirkyard has a variety of interesting gravestones and monuments, including the open area known as the Covenanters' Prison to the south of the kirkyard, where prisoners held after the Battle of Bothwell Brig were imprisoned in 1679 after the Covenanters had been defeated by government forces. Dark deeds were undoubtedly done by both sides during this troubled period, but the unbridled slaughter in the kirkyard, purported by many 'authorities' to have happened here, is grossly exaggerated.

The kirkyard is reputedly the setting for various supernatural manifestations, attributed to either the souls of prisoners who died here or to the bogle of Sir George MacKenzie of Rosehaugh. He was an eminent judge who dealt (harshly, according to his enemies, who gave him the title 'Bloody' Mackenzie') with Covenanters and who died in 1691; his tomb is one of those in the 'prison'. While Sir George is undoubtedly a controversial figure to many, it is simply not clear why any supposed activity should be attributed to him. If, for example, his spirit was so powerful as to injure and perhaps even kill visitors to the 'prison', why did it not protect his own tomb in 2002 when it was desecrated by two youths, who went on to throw about a skull, perhaps even his own. The youths had to be punished by more earthly authorities and were the first people prosecuted for despoiling a sepulchre in some 100 years. The 'manifestations' have been documented in a book

The Ghost that Haunted Itself which was written by Jan-Andrew Henderson (who started the City of the Dead tour).

Many people have reported being touched or injured while visiting the area (most on ghost walks), including being pushed, having their hair pulled, being knocked over, bruised, scratched, cut and many even fainting. Other strange occurrences are reputed to be the sighting of an apparition in white, strong smells, and unexplained knocking and other noises, and activity has apparently extended even to houses around the graveyard. Some reports have as many as 450 people being affected, 140 fainting or passing out, and even an unexplained death of an apparently healthy 24-year-old woman; in 2003 a fire burnt out Mr Henderson's house and this has also been suggested as being caused by the angry bogle. If this is all true, perhaps it might be an idea to leave the bogle in peace...

City of the Dead Ghost Tours (www.blackhart.uk.com / 0131 225 9044) organise tours including the kirkyard.

Map 4, 9L (Edinburgh). Off A7, Greyfriars Place, near Museum of Scotland, Edinburgh. **Church open during summer months (www.greyfriarskirk.com); kirkyard open all year. (0131 226 5429 / www.greyfriars.org)**

Paranormal investigations have been undertaken by Ghost Finders (www.ghostfinders.co.uk) and by Paranormal Encounters Group (www.p-e-g.co.uk) and in July 2003 and in October 2005 by Scottish Paranormal Investigations (www.scottishparanormalinvestigations.co.uk).

GREYFRIARS, DUMFRIES

Nothing remains of Greyfriars, a Franciscan friary founded in 1266, probably by Devorgilla of Galloway. It was in the church of the Friary, before the altar, that John Comyn was stabbed to death by Robert the Bruce and his men. A plaque on a wall in Castle Street commemorates the event.

There is also a story that the ghosts of Robert the Bruce and his accomplices in the murder of John Comyn have been seen at the site.

Map 4, 8P (Dumfries). On A701, Dumfries.
Site only; access to plaque at all reasonable times.

GUTHRIE CASTLE

Standing in 150 acres of mature woodland, Guthrie Castle is an imposing castle and mansion, extended and remodelled in Victorian times. The original tower was built by the Guthries around 1470, and the building is very picturesque with towers, turrets, battlements and corbiesteps. Sir David Guthrie, 1st laird, was Armour Bearer to James II and Lord High Treasurer of Scotland. The Guthries got into a long and bloody feud with the Gardynes, which led to both families losing their lands but, while the Guthries managed to recover theirs, the Gardynes never did. The Guthries held the property until 1984.

The castle is said to have a very kind ghost, the spirit of one of the Guthrie ladies or one of their servants, dressed in black and with a large bunch of keys. The benign bogle is believed to be concerned with the welfare of guests. There has not apparently been a sighting of the ghost for many years, but there are said to have been other manifestations.

Map 4, 10J (Guthrie). Off A932, 6.5 miles E of Forfar, Guthrie, Angus.
Accommodation available and venue for weddings. (01241 828691 / www.guthriecastle.com)

H M FRIGATE *UNICORN*, DUNDEE

H M Frigate *Unicorn* is one of the oldest British warship still afloat, and was launched in 1824 for the Royal Navy at Chatham dockyard. The frigate had 46 guns and was one of the foremost warships of her day (although she was never involved in battle, being used as a supply ship for most of her active service).

The ship has several reports of eerie occurrences, including the spotting of an apparition of a man in naval uniform, seen crossing the upper deck during the day. Other manifestations are reputed to be unexplained footsteps, coming from the upper deck, although there was nobody apparently present to make them, visitors and staff being touched by invisible hands or even having their hair pulled, and a bookcase being knocked over and the contents tipped out on the deck. During the filming of *Most Haunted* here, it is also claimed that objects were thrown at the presenters (a discerning bogle, perhaps?).

Map 4, 10K (Dundee). Off A92, Victoria Dock, Dundee, Angus.
Open Apr-Oct, daily; Nov-Mar, Wed-Sun. (01382 200900 / www.frigateunicorn.org)

A paranormal investigation was undertaken in April 2007 by Ghost Finders (www.ghostfinders.co.uk/hm_frigate_unicorn.html) and in October 2005 by Paranormal Investigation Scotland (www.paranormalinvestigationscotland.co.uk/ hmfrigateunicorn.htm) and by Spiritfinders Scotland (www.spiritfindersscotland.com) and in November 2007 by Borders Paranormal Group (www.bordersparanormal.co.uk)

Featured in Living TV's Most Haunted, *series eight (2006).*

HADDO HOUSE

Haddo House, a massive classical mansion with two sweeping wings, was first built in 1731-6 and designed by William Adam, although it was later altered. The apparition of Lord Archibald Gordon is said to have been seen in the Premier's Bedroom. He was the youngest son of the 1st Marquis of Aberdeen and Temair, and was killed in a car accident, one of the first to die in such a way.

The house stands on the site of an old castle. In 1644 Sir John Gordon of Haddo, who had been in the army of the Marquis of Montrose, was captured after being besieged here for three days. He was imprisoned in 'Haddo's Hole' in St Giles Cathedral, before being executed by beheading. The castle was then destroyed.

Map 2, 11F (Haddo). Off B9005, 10 miles NW of Ellon, Haddo, Aberdeenshire.
NTS: Open Apr-Jun, Fri-Mon (closed Tue-Thu); Jul-Aug, daily; Sep-late Oct, Fri-Mon (closed Tue-Thu); garden and grounds open, daily.. (01651 851440 / www.nts.org.uk)

HAILES CASTLE   ILLUS PAGE 157

In a lovely location above the River Tyne, Hailes Castle is a scenic ruin. The remains consist of a keep, extended by ranges and towers in later centuries, with a thick wall protecting the landward side. There are two pit prisons, although why Hailes needed two is not clear.

Hailes was long a Hepburn property, and was besieged and captured several times during its history. Patrick Hepburn became Earl of Bothwell, but was killed at the Battle of Flodden in 1513, and James, 4th Earl, brought Mary, Queen of Scots, here after abducting her in 1567. By 1700 the property had been sold to the Dalrymples of Hailes, and they abandoned the old castle for the mansion of Newhailes (also see that entry), near Musselburgh. In 1835 Hailes was being used as a granary, but it is now in the care of Historic Scotland.

Like many other places, Hailes is said to have an underground passage, which in this case appears to have led under the river, or even to Traprain Law.

One of the pit prisons is said to be haunted by the spirit of a man imprisoned and starved to death because he had fallen in love with the laird's wife.

And there are also reports of a 'White Lady', seen in the gateway to the castle.

Map 4, 10L (Hailes). Off A1, 4 miles E of Haddington, 1.5 miles W of East Linton, Hailes, East Lothian.
His Scot: Access at all reasonable times. (www.historic-scotland.gov.uk)

A paranormal investigation was undertaken in May 2004 by Ghost Finders (www.ghostfinders.co.uk/hailescastle.html) and in July 2007 by Scottish Society of Paranormal Investigation and Analysis (www.sspia.co.uk)

HALLGREEN CASTLE

Hallgreen Castle dates from the 14th century, and is an L-plan tower house which was held by the Dunnet family and then by the Raits. During restoration, it is said that a secret passage and stair was found, leading up from the dungeon to the hall.

Several ghosts are said to haunt Hallgreen Castle. One is reputed to be that of a woman who reputedly killed herself after the death of her child, another a cloaked man who is witnessed in the hall and is known as 'The Watcher', while two others are a pair of servant girls, witnessed in the old kitchen in the basement. One gruesome story is that the body of a child was thrown into the well and was never recovered; the unexplained sobbing of a child has been reported.

Map 2, 11H (Hallgreen). Off A92, east of Inverbervie, Hallgreen, Kincardineshire.

HARVIESTOUN CASTLE

Harviestoun Castle was a grand castellated mansion, dating from 1804 and then enlarged and altered around 50 years later. By 1965, however, it had been gutted and five years later it was blown up and demolished. Nothing remains except gate lodges and stables. There was an earlier house on the site, which Robert Burns had visited in 1787, and it was here he had the inspiration for his poem, 'The Banks of Devon'.

Craufurd Tait inherited the property from his father in 1800, and bought Castle Campbell from the Duke of Argyll. Tait did much else to improve his estate, but by 1822 he was in financial difficulties and, although he put the property on the market, he did not manage to sell it. He died ten years later, and was buried in what is now known as Tait's Tomb, which stands by the A91 before Dollar. There are stories that the area around the tomb is haunted, with apparitions of people and vehicles, some which have reputedly caused accidents.

Map 4, 8L (Harviestoun). Off A91, 1 mile E of Tillicoultry, Harviestoun, Clackmannan.

HAWKHEAD HOSPITAL

Hawkhead Hospital, built 1932-5 in art-deco style as an infectious diseases hospital, was said to be haunted by a 'Grey Lady', the spectre of a ward sister murdered by one of her patients. The hospital has been closed, and some of the buildings are to be converted into residences, while houses are to be built in the grounds.

The hospital stood on the site of a castle, which was once surrounded by wooded parks and gardens, a property of the Ross family from the middle of the 15th until the 19th century.

Map 4, 7M (Hawkhead). Off A726, 1 mile E of Paisley, Hawkhead, Renfrew.

HAZLEHEAD ACADEMY, ABERDEEN

Hazlehead Academy was established more than 100 years ago, but the current comprehensive school dates from the 1960s.

The stage area and drama department are said to be haunted. The apparition of a boy, dressed as if from the 1960s, has been reported on more than one occasion, as have unexplained voices and noises, such as knocking, coming from the walls, and the chains of the curtain rattling on their own. Other manifestations are reputedly people feeling as if they have been touched by unseen hands, cold spots, and folk feeling foreboding or very gloomy for no reason.

Map 2, 12G (Aberdeen). Off B9119, Hazlehead Academy, Groats Road, Hazlehead, Aberdeen. **School. (01224 310184 / www.hazleheadacy.aberdeen.sch.uk)**

HERMITAGE CASTLE

ILLUS PAGE 158

One of the most impressive and oppressive of Scottish fortresses, Hermitage Castle is a large brooding fortress in a bleak location. The old stronghold has a long and eventful history, and there are many stories of murders and diabolic deeds, so much so that the weight of all the wickedness perpetrated has, perhaps, made the castle sink into the ground. More prosaically, there are a series of ditches and banks by the castle, built to defend the fortress against artillery.

There are tales of at least three ghosts.

In the 13th and early 14th centuries the castle was a property of the Soulis family, who held lands on both sides of the border. William Soulis (or perhaps his father, Nicholas) is said to have been a warlock (having been a pupil of Michael Scott in the Eildon Hills), and he is reputed to have seized children and slaughtered them within the walls, using their blood in evil rites. Soulis became virtually indestructible, having magical armour: iron weapons were of no use against him. According to one account, after consultation with Thomas the Rhymer, the local people eventually took matters into their own hands and seized Soulis, encasing him in lead and binding him with ropes of sand. Soulis was taken to Ninestane Rig – a stone circle some 1.5 miles north-east of the castle – and boiled in a cauldron until the metal was molten and Soulis was melted away into nothing.

William Soulis, however, (who had a distant claim to the Scottish crown) is recorded in historical sources as having been imprisoned in Dumbarton Castle for supporting the English; his family were certainly forfeited in 1320 and he lost the castle and lands.

Ghostly screams and cries have reportedly been heard from the victims of Soulis, and his own terrifying bogle is said to haunt the castle and area around Hermitage, according to one version, appearing every seven years and returning to the underground chamber, where he slaughtered his victims. In this vault is said to be buried a fantastic treasure.

The castle later passed to the Douglases, and William Douglas, 'The Knight of Liddesdale', a devious fellow, was one of those who resisted Edward Balliol in the

1330s after the English had placed Balliol on the throne. Douglas did, however, seize Sir Alexander Ramsay of Dalhousie at his devotions in St Mary's Church in Hawick. Ramsay had taken Roxburgh Castle for the Scots, had found favour, and was made Sheriff of Teviotdale, an office that Douglas coveted. Ramsay was imprisoned in a dungeon at Hermitage, and starved to death, although a trickle of corn from a granary agonisingly prolonged his life.

Ramsay's spirit is said to have been seen and heard at Hermitage.

In 1353 Douglas's plotting caught up with him and he was ambushed and slain by his godson, another William, when he attempted to block the latter's promotion to the lordship of Douglas.

The castle did not stay with the Douglases, and in 1492 it was exchanged with Patrick Hepburn, Earl of Bothwell, for Bothwell Castle in Clydesdale. In 1566 James Hepburn, 4th Earl of Bothwell was stabbed and badly wounded in a skirmish with the Border laird 'Little Jock' Elliot of Park (Elliot was shot by Hepburn and killed). As Bothwell recovered, he was paid a visit by Mary, Queen of Scots, who had been at Jedburgh.

Mary made only a brief stay and she returned to Jedburgh that same day but, having fallen from her horse on the return journey, made herself so ill that she nearly died. After much intrigue, Mary and Bothwell were married, although he was implicated in the murder of Darnley, her previous husband. Their marriage was a disaster: Mary was defeated in battle and fled to imprisonment and eventual execution in England, while Bothwell escaped to Norway.

His end was not a happy one. He was incarcerated in the Danish fortress of Dragsholm and there died: his mummified corpse survives at the castle (or did so for a long time), and his ghost is said to have been witnessed at Dragsholm (which is now a hotel).

It is, however, an apparition of Mary, in a white dress, that is said to haunt Hermitage. It is not clear why Mary would grace Hermitage with her ghostly presence, as it played such a small part in her life, but hers is a busy bogle.

Map 4, 10O (Hermitage). Off B6399, 5 miles N of Newcastleton, Hermitage, Borders.
His Scot: Open Apr-Oct, daily. (01387 376222 / www.historic-scotland.gov.uk)

HILLHEAD UNDERGROUND STATION, GLASGOW

The underground station is reputed to be haunted, there being several stories regarding the apparition of a pretty woman, dressed in evening wear, being seen on the platform and also being heard singing, apparently quite happily.

The phantom is then said to disappear into one of the tunnels.

Map 4, 7M (Glasgow). On A82, Byres Road, Hillhead, Glasgow.
Underground station.

HILTON HOTEL, GLASGOW

The Hilton Hotel is reputed to be haunted, and one story is that the apparition of a woman with long blonde hair has been witnessed in a chamber on the 13th floor. The bar is also said to be the scene of eerie occurrences, such as glasses being thrown across the room or moving by themselves; the phantom of a man has reportedly been spotted here, too.

Map 4, 7M (Glasgow). Off M8, 1 William Street, Glasgow.
Hotel. (0141 204 5555 / www.hilton.co.uk/glasgow)

HIS MAJESTY'S THEATRE, ABERDEEN ILLUS PAGE 158

His Majesty's Theatre, a fine building dating from 1906 holding an audience of up to 1470, was fully renovated in the 1980s and then again in 2005, and features a range of popular productions, including musicals, drama and dance.

The theatre is said to be haunted by the spirit of a stagehand, John Murray, known as 'Jake', who was killed messily in 1942 by a stage hoist during a circus performance. Manifestations are believed to include objects being mysteriously moved or hidden by themselves, including on one occasion when a member of staff was painting some scenery and had his paint brush repeatedly moved (until the member of staff told the ghost to stop). Footsteps have also allegedly been heard from unoccupied areas, witnessed in 2005 during the last renovation.

An apparition of Jake has also reputedly been seen, said to be that of a man dressed in a brown coat, which then faded away.

The foyer is said to be haunted by a 'Grey Lady', while a phantom of a bar maid has reportedly been witnessed in the Stalls Bar.

Another spectre is allegedly that of a man with a top hat, spotted in the Royal Box enclosure – and even on the stage during performances.

Map 2, 12G (Aberdeen). Off B986, Rosemount Viaduct, Aberdeen.
Theatre. (01224 641122 (box office) / www.hmtaberdeen.com)

HOBKIRK

An attractive building in a pleasant spot, the present church dates from 1869, although it incorporates some ancient masonry. The present Hobkirk stands on the site of a much older church, which is mentioned from the 13th century, but may date from even earlier. There are some old memorials in the burial ground, and the name comes from 'Hope Kirk', 'hope' being a sheltered valley.

In the 18th century it is said that the then church was haunted, and that it had to be exorcised by a priest.

Map 4, 10O (Hobkirk). Off A6088 or B6357, 6 miles E of Hawick, 1 mile S of Bonchester Bridge, Hobkirk, Borders.
Church. (www.hobkirk.org)

HOLYROODHOUSE, EDINBURGH ILLUS PAGE 169

Standing near Holyrood Park and the impressive mass of Arthurs Seat, Holyrood-house is a fine palace, set around a courtyard, and incorporates a 16th century block built out of the guest house of the Abbey. Original interiors survive in the old block, and the ruins of the abbey church adjoin.

Holyrood Abbey was founded by David I around 1128 as an Augustinian establishment dedicated to the Holy Cross, and it was sacked in 1322, 1385, 1544 and 1547 by the English.

David Rizzio, Mary, Queen of Scots's secretary, was repeatedly stabbed and murdered in her presence by men led by her husband, Lord Darnley, and a plaque marks the spot. One story is that Rizzio's copious amount of blood stained the floor and could not be washed off, no matter what was done.

Bonnie Prince Charlie stayed here in 1745 during the Jacobite Rising, and Butcher Cumberland later made it his headquarters. The palace is the official residence of the monarch in Scotland.

A 'Grey Lady', thought to be the spirit of one of Mary's companions, has reputedly been seen in the Queen's Audience Chamber, although one account described the apparition as being very faint. Ghostly footsteps are said to have been heard in the long gallery, which has portraits of Scottish monarchs from earliest times, most of the portraits being painted entirely from the imagination of the artist.

Map 4, 9L (Edinburgh). Off A1, at foot of Royal Mile, Edinburgh.
Open all year, daily (closed some dates: check with Palace) (0131 556 5100 / www.royalcollection.org.uk)

HOPETOUN HOUSE

Standing in extensive parkland by the Firth of Firth, Hopetoun House is a large palatial mansion, which dates from 1699, and was built by the architect William Bruce for the Hope family. Sir Charles Hope, made Earl of Hopetoun in 1703, had the house remodelled by William Adam from 1721, the work being continued by John and Robert Adam.

The ghost of a dark-cloaked man is said to have been seen on one of the paths in the grounds, and to be a harbinger of death or misadventure in the Hope family.

There are also accounts of uncanny occurrences in the restaurant, which was formerly the stables. The apparition of a man is said to have been spotted several times, and was identified from a photograph as being the phantom of a coach driver who had worked at the house in the 1900s. Another apparition has reputedly been seen in the staff lavatories in the main house.

Map 4, 9L (Hopetoun). Off A904, 6 miles E of Linlithgow, Hopetoun, West Lothian.
Open mid Apr-end Sep (check exact dates). (0131 331 2451 / www.hopetounhouse.com)

A paranormal investigation was undertaken in January 2005 by Ghost Finders (www.ghostfinders.co.uk/hopetounhouse.html)

HOUNDWOOD HOUSE

Houndwood House incorporates an old tower house, but the building was remodelled and castellated in the 19th and 20th centuries. The lands were originally held by Coldingham Priory – the monks are believed to have had a hunting lodge here – but were acquired by the Homes after the Reformation.

The house is said to be haunted by a ghost called 'Chappie'. Manifestations were reported in the 19th century, including unexplained heavy footsteps, knocking and rapping, and deep breathing and moans. The apparition of the lower part of a man, dressed in riding breeches, was said to have been witnessed in the grounds outside the house. The story goes that a man was killed by a party of soldiers in the 16th century, and then apparently cut in half.

The sounds of ghostly horses have also been reported here, perhaps linked to a visit to the house by Mary, Queen of Scots.

Map 4, 11M (Houndwood). Off A1, 3 miles SE of Granthouse, Houndwood, Borders.

HOUSE OF DUN   ILLUS PAGE 169

House of Dun is a fine sparse classical mansion, built in 1730 by the famous architect William Adam for David Erskine, Lord Dun. There are formal gardens with woodland and parkland, as well as a 19th-century walled garden; the present mansion replaced an old stronghold of the Erskines, a fragment of which survives.

Dun had passed to the Erskines by 1375. The old castle was the scene of a notori-ous case of poisoning, reputed witchcraft and murder in 1613, when the young John Erskine, heir to Dun, and his brother Alexander were poisoned by Robert Erskine, their uncle, and their three aunts in a dispute over property. The older boy died in agony, while Alexander survived after a severe illness, and eventually succeeded to the lands. Robert Erskine and two of his sisters were executed, while the third had to go into exile. The Erskines held the property until 1980, when it passed to The National Trust for Scotland.

There are many tales of the house being haunted. Manifestations are alleged to include apparitions, one of which is said to be that of a little girl skipping, another an austere man, and unexplained noises, one instance of which lasted for more than 30 minutes.

A 'White Lady' is also said to have been witnessed in one of the bedrooms of the flats in the house.

Map 2, 11I (House of Dun). Off A935, 3 miles NW of Montrose, Angus.
NTS: House open April-late June, Wed-Sun (closed Mon-Tue); late Jun-Aug, daily; Sep-Oct, Wed-Sun (closed Thu-Fri). (01674 810264 / www.nts.org.uk)

A paranormal investigation was undertaken in August 2006 by the Ghost Club (www.ghostclub.org.uk)

HOUSTON HOUSE

Standing on a woody ridge in 20 acres of grounds, Houston House is an early 17th-century L-plan tower house, to which has been added wings around a rectangular courtyard. The lands were originally held by the Houstons, one of whom, Sir Peter Houston, was killed at the Battle of Flodden in 1513. The property passed to the Sharp, or Shairp, family about 1569. Archbishop James Sharp, from the family, was murdered at Magus Muir in 1679. Houston was sold by the family in 1945, the build-ing extended in the 1960s, and the house is now used as a hotel.

According to some accounts, one of the rooms of the old part in the house is reputedly haunted.

Map 4, 8M (Houston). Off A899, Uphall, Houston, West Lothian.
Hotel. (01506 853831 / www.macdonaldhotels.co.uk/houstounhouse/)

HOWLET'S HOUSE, LOGANLEA

Howlet's House was an old dwelling, fortified and sturdy, with very thick walls and a vaulted basement. One tale recounts that one of the owners, although old, re-turned unexpectedly with a young and fetching new wife. For a while they appear to have been happy, but eventually the attractions of a young servant lad tempted her away from the prune of her husband. The young wife and servant lad then disappeared, with a sum of money, but soon afterwards phantoms of the couple were reported in the area.

The bodies of the young woman and lad were eventually unearthed and, when they were properly buried in consecrated ground, the disturbances stopped.

It seems the old farmer discovered they were having an affair and murdered them both, then fled the area.

Map 4, 9M (Loganlea). Off A702, 3 miles NW of Penicuik, Loganlea, Midlothian.

HUNTER'S TRYST, EDINBURGH

Hunter's Tryst, an old coaching inn, much altered and extended in recent years, is said to be haunted by a 'White Lady'.

The apparition is said to have been seen by customers in several of the rooms.

Map 4, 9L (Edinburgh). Off B701, Oxgangs, Edinburgh.
Public house and restaurant. (0131 445 1797)

HUNTINGTOWER CASTLE ILLUS PAGE 169

Standing on the outskirts of Perth, Huntingtower is an impressive and slightly gloomy pile which dates from the 15th century and was long held by the Ruthvens. Some rooms have fine original painted ceilings, mural paintings and plasterwork, as well as decorative beams in the hall.

Mary, Queen of Scots, visited the castle in 1565. In 1582 William Ruthven, 1st Earl of Gowrie, abducted the young James VI – in what became known as the 'Raid of Ruthven' – and held him at Huntingtower. James escaped during a hunting trip and had the Earl beheaded in 1585.

Gowrie's ghost is said to haunt the West Bow (see that entry) in Edinburgh.

In 1600 John, 3rd Earl of Gowrie, and his brother, Alexander, Master of Ruthven, were slain at Gowrie House in Perth by James VI and his followers, following the 'Gowrie Conspiracy', a possible plot to murder the king. Their bodies were posthumously hanged, drawn and quartered, which must have been messy. The Ruthvens were forfeited, their name proscribed, and the castle (originally called Ruthven Castle) renamed Huntingtower.

The castle and grounds are said to be haunted by a 'Green Lady', also known as 'My Lady Greensleeves'. Her footsteps have reputedly been heard, along with the rustle of her gown, and she has reportedly appeared on several occasions, sometimes as a warning of death, sometimes to help passers-by – including an ill child and a man being robbed. Indeed her appearance is said to herald events, both bad and good, depending whether the bogle was seen weeping or laughing.

There was a sighting of the ghost in one of the small chambers on the second floor in the 1970s, made by two visitors.

Map 4, 9K (Huntingtower). Off A85, 2 miles NW of Perth, Huntingtower, Perthshire.
His Scot: Open all year: Apr-Oct, daily; Nov-Mar, Sat-Wed, closed Thu & Fri; closed 25/26 Dec and 1/2 Jan. (01738 627231 / www.historic-scotland.gov.uk)

ILLIESTON HOUSE

Reached by a tree-lined drive, Illieston House is an altered T-plan tower house of two storeys and an attic with dormer windows and corbiestepped gables. The kings of Scots are said to have had a hunting lodge here, which was used often by James II and James IV, but by the 17th century the property was held by the Ellis family (the name being from 'Elliston'). The house is still occupied and in good condition, although it was roofless in 1856.

A ghostly horseman, shrouded in black and with a naked skull for a head, is said have been seen riding from Illieston down tracks towards the nearby waterfalls on the River Almond.

Map 4, 9M (Illieston). Off B7015 or B7030, 2 miles SE of Broxburn, Illieston, West Lothian.

Holyroodhouse (page 165)

House of Dun (page 166)

Huntingtower Castle (page 168)

Inn at Lathones (page 171)

Inverawe House (page 173)

INCHBUIE

Inchbuie, an island in the impressive Falls of Dochart, was used as a burial ground by the MacNab clan. Their walled burial enclosure is at the north-east end of the island, and there are several old memorials and effigies, including a medieval stone slab.

One story is that the burial ground is haunted by the last person to be interred at Inchbuie.

Map 4, 7J (Inchbuie). By A827, in Killin, Stirling.
Access possible: key from the Breadalbane Folklore Centre.

A (brief) paranormal investigation was undertaken in May 2004 by Ghost Finders (www.ghostfinders.co.uk/clanmcnab.html)

INCHDREWER CASTLE

Inchdrewer Castle was built by the Ogilvies of Dunlugas in the 16th century, and the family were made Lords Banff. The then Lord Banff was murdered here in 1713 after returning home from Edinburgh. He was probably slain by his own servants, who had been robbing him, although the castle was torched to destroy the evidence. One source had his ghost haunting the building.

The castle is also said to be haunted by the spirit of a lady, who reputedly takes the form of a white dog.

Map 2, 10E (Inchdrewer). Off B9121, 3 miles SW of Banff, Aberdeenshire.

INDIA STREET, EDINBURGH

One of the houses in the street, dating from the 1820s, is reputedly haunted. An apparition has often apparently been seen in the hall, a few feet above the present floor level, but it is ill-defined and transparent.

Map 4, 9L (Edinburgh). Off A90, 0.5 miles N of Edinburgh Castle, Edinburgh.

INN AT LATHONES   ILLUS PAGE 170

The Inn at Lathones is an old coaching inn, which dates back to early in the 17th century, the oldest part of the building being the stables. The front house was built later in that century, and above the fireplace is a wedding stone with the initials of Iona Kirk and Ewan Lindsay, who were married in 1718 and ran the inn for many years. The story goes that the couple were so in love that when Iona died the stone cracked, and her husband followed her to the grave a short time later.

The stables are said to be haunted by a 'Grey Lady' and her horse, and she is said to be a friendly bogle; it is not clear whether this ghost is responsible for the grey swirling mist which has apparently been observed above the beds in some of the rooms. Other activity is reported to include doors and windows opening and closing by themselves and fire irons moving from one side of a fireplace to another, and also swinging to and fro by themselves. The unexplained sound of a baby crying has also reputedly been heard, coming from an empty upstairs office.

Map 4, 10K (Lathones). On A915, 5 miles SW of St Andrews, Lathones, Fife.
Inn with bar, restaurant and accommodation. (01334 840494 / www.theinn.co.uk)

A paranormal investigation was undertaken by Paranormal Discovery (www.paranormaldiscovery.co.uk)

INVERARAY CASTLE

Standing near the banks of Loch Fyne by the planned village of Inveraray, Inveraray Castle is a large towered mansion, begun in 1743, then remodelled by William and John Adam. Inveraray has long been the seat of the Campbells, Earls then Dukes of Argyll, and the present mansion replaced an ancient stronghold which stood nearby. Famous visitors include James V, Mary, Queen of Scots, and the Marquis of Montrose (who burnt the place).

Several ghost stories are recorded in various places about Inveraray, although these are refuted. The old castle was said to be haunted by a ghostly harper, one of Montrose's victims in the attack in 1644. The bogle is said to be clad in Campbell tartan and to mostly be seen or heard by the Duchesses, and only rarely by the Dukes. Harping is said sometimes to be heard when one of the Duke's is near death or during their funeral.

The library is also reputedly haunted, and strange noises and crashes have reportedly been heard there.

Other ghosts include a spectral birlinn, which is reputedly seen when one of the Campbells is near death, seen in 1913 on the death of Archibald Campbell, as well as gatherings of ravens; and the ghost of a young servant, who was murdered by Jacobites, is said to haunt the MacArthur room.

The apparitions of Redcoats, some of Cumberland's men, are said to have been seen marching on the road through Glen Aray, not far from the castle.

Map 3, 5K (Inveraray). Off A83, N of Inveraray, Argyll.
Open Apr-Oct, daily. (01499 302203 / www.inveraray-castle.com)

INVERARAY JAIL

Inveraray Jail was founded in 1820, and served as the court house and prison for Argyll, some 6,000 people being tried and sentenced, and then imprisoned, in the jail. The court was housed in a fine classical building and there were two prison blocks with an exercise area. The jail was closed in 1889, although the court went on sitting into the 1950s. Since 1989 the court and jail have been a museum and tourist attraction, with a reconstruction of life in the prison, including custodians in period costume, re-enacted trials, and furnished cells.

The jail is said to be haunted, and there are numerous reports of apparitions and other eerie manifestations; the building has had a series of paranormal investigations.

Map 3, 5K (Inveraray). On A83, Church Square, Inveraray, Argyll.
Open all year, daily, except 25-26 Dec and 1 Jan. (01499 302381 / www.inverarayjail.co.uk)

A paranormal investigation was undertaken in May 2005 by Spectre (www.freewebs.com/ ukspectre/inverarayjail.htm) and in April 2005 by Ghostfinders (www.ghostfinders.co.uk/inverarayjail.html) and in July 2005 by Paranormal Investigation Scotland (www.paranormalinvestigationscotland.co.uk/inveraryjail.htm) and by Spiritfinders Scotland (www.spiritfindersscotland.com) and in February 2008 by the Scottish Society of Paranormal Investigation and Analysis (www.sspia.co.uk) and in September 2005 and in April 2006 by Scottish Paranormal Investigations (www.scottishparanormalinvestigations.co.uk)

INVERAWE HOUSE ILLUS PAGE 170

Inverawe House, a fine harled and whitewashed mansion in a pretty spot, may incorporate a castle of the 14th century. Inverawe was a property of the Campbells, and Mary, Queen of Scots, is said to have visited.

The house is thought to be haunted by a 'Green Lady', said to be the ghost of Mary Cameron of Callart (although she has been called 'Green Jean'), who married the then laird, Diarmid Campbell. Campbell rescued Mary from the plague at Callart, but he died in 1645 after the Battle of Inverlochy, while fighting against the Marquis of Montrose, and he is buried at Ardchattan Priory. Mary died after him, and her ghost is said to haunt the house.

The phantom has supposedly been seen in the Ticonderoga Room, and there are reports of the ghost in the 20th century, including in 1912 when loud screams were heard coming from the Ticonderoga Room, perhaps because at that time the room had been cleared. The ghost was described as being about 16 years of age with beautiful gold hair and wearing a green dress. On another occasion, in 1967 the bogle is said to have turned someone over in bed, who woke to find himself alone. Alternatively she is said to have been seen in the servant's quarters and on a stair, which she climbs before disappearing. There have also been sightings away from the house, one when a shepherd reported seeing the ghost moving through his sheep, the sheep parting to let the ghost through, and another when several men working on the nearby hydroelectric scheme see the bogle walking along the road towards Inverawe House, before vanishing in front of them.

There were also two sightings in 2001 during renovations to the house, and it is reported that disturbances became much worse during building work. Other manifestations, reported in recent times, are said to include doors opening and closing, sometimes loudly, by themselves, unexplained noises, disembodied footsteps running on the stairs, and items going missing only to turn up later.

The 'Green Lady' is reputed to be a friendly ghost, and to have helped people on several occasions; some say she only appears to members of the Campbell family.

Another ghost story is said to be that of Duncan Campbell, who died at Ticonderoga in Canada in 1758. Duncan unwittingly sheltered his foster-brother Donald's murderer, and the spectre of Donald appeared to remonstrate with Duncan, finally telling him that, 'We shall meet again at Ticonderoga'. Duncan had no idea what this might mean, until he joined the army and fought in Canada, being mortally wounded at Ticonderoga. One account has Duncan, however, living in Glasgow until 1760, although he did die of wounds received at the battle.

Map 3, 5K (Inverawe). Off A85, 1 mile NE of Taynuilt, Inverawe, Argyll.
Smokery and visitor centre, country park, accommodation available in grounds.
(0844 8475 490 / www.smokedsalmon.co.uk)

INVEREY CASTLE

There was a castle at Inverey, which was demolished in 1689 after the Battle of Killiecrankie. John Farquharson of Inverey, the 'Black Colonel', was a Jacobite, and that year had defeated a force attacking Braemar Castle (see that entry), which he then burnt. He is said to have summoned servants by firing a pistol, but his home was torched when the Rising failed, although he escaped with his life.

Farquharson left strict instructions that he wished to be buried at Inverey, alongside his mistress, who had predeceased him. His wife ignored his wishes and had him interred in St Andrew's churchyard at Braemar. His coffin then, reputedly, appeared above ground three times, despite having been buried. The story goes that, his wife, perhaps still unsure whether this was just some unpleasant practical joke, was then visited by his angry ghost, which terrorised her and the family. She gave up and had him taken and buried at Inverey.

Another tale is that some years later his grave was despoiled, and two men each took one of his teeth as souvenirs, until his wrathful bogle appeared to them both, and they then quickly returned the teeth to Farquharson's coffin.

Farquharson's ghost is said to have been witnessed at Braemar Castle, where a lit candle is allegedly left as a sign of his presence.

Map 2, 8G (Inverey). Off A93, 4.5 miles W of Braemar, Kincardine & Deeside.

INVERGARRY CASTLE

Perched on the 'Rock of the Raven', the slogan of the family, Invergarry Castle is an impressive ruinous tower house of the Clan Ranald branch of the MacDonalds. The old stronghold has an eventful history, and was burnt in 1654 by Cromwell, changed hands several times during the Jacobite Risings, and was finally torched by the 'Butcher' Duke of Cumberland after being visited by Bonnie Prince Charlie. The Glengarry Castle Hotel stands on the site of a later mansion.

The old castle is said to have had a brownie, although possibly a 'Green Lady' or gruagach.

Map 1, 5H (Invergarry). Off A82, 7 miles SW of Fort Augustus, Highlands.
Glengarry Hotel – open end Mar-beg Nov. Ruin can be seen from grounds of hotel – the interior of the castle is in dangerous condition. (01809 501254 / www.glengarry.net)

INVERNESS CASTLE

Virtually northing survives of the medieval royal castle of Inverness, once one of the most important fortresses in Scotland and with a long turbulent history of sieges and intrigue. The castle was in a poor state of repair when used by government forces before the Battle of Culloden in 1746, and the building was blown up by retreating Jacobites. An impressive baronial building of 1835, housing the Sheriff Court and police, stands on the site of the old castle.

It is said that Malcolm Canmore destroyed a stronghold of Macbeth at Inverness in 1057, and that an apparition of Duncan, dressed in all his kingly finery, has been seen walking along the banks of the Ness near the site of the castle (presumably based on Duncan being murdered here, as described in Shakespeare's Scottish play).

Map 2, 7F (Inverness). Off A82, Inverness, Highland.
Exhibition open in summer.

INVERQUHARITY CASTLE

Inverquharity Castle was built by the Ogilvies about 1420. One of the family, Alexander, was smothered at Finavon Castle by his sister in 1446, while another Alexander was captured after the Battle of Philiphaugh in 1645, while fighting for the Marquis of Montrose, and he was beheaded in Glasgow.

Inverquharity is said to have been haunted by a Sir John Ogilvie. Desiring the beautiful daughter of the local miller John White, Ogilvie had her father hanged when she refused him, then raped her and her mother. The local priest prayed for vengeance, and Ogilvie was struck down dead, although his ghost is said to have so plagued the castle that it had to be abandoned. Such is the story, anyway.

Map 2, 9I (Inverquharity). Off B955, 3.5 miles NE of Kirriemuir, Inverquharity, Angus.

IONA

Situated on the beautiful and peaceful island of Iona, the abbey occupies the site of St Columba's monastery, founded in 563. Columba is believed to have converted the Picts of mainland Scotland to Christianity, and died in 597. His shrine, within the Abbey buildings, dates from the 9th century.

The abbey was abandoned after raids by the Norsemen, and one ghost story dates from this time. It is said that apparitions of longships and their marauding Norsemen crew have been seen at White Sands, reputedly the spot where Vikings slew the abbot and 15 monks in 986. They then went on to plunder and burn the abbey buildings.

Other tales relate that monks have also been seen at other places on the island, dressed in brown robes. These ghostly presences are believed to have been caused when many of the stone crosses, said to mark their graves, were cast down and thrown into the sea during the Reformation. The appearance of the monks is said to be accompanied by strange twinkling blue lights. Although much was lost, the magnificent St Martin's Cross and St John's Cross, the latter a replica (the original is reconstructed and displayed in the Infirmary Museum), stand just outside the church, and the Infirmary Museum houses a splendid collection of sculptured stones and crosses, one of the largest collections of early Christian carved stones in Europe.

Many of the early Kings of Scots are buried in 'Reilig Odhrain', Oran's cemetery, by the 'Street of the Dead' – as well as kings of Ireland, France and Norway: 48 Scottish, 8 Norwegian and 4 Irish kings, or so the tales go. Among the kings buried here are both Duncan and Macbeth, as well as the Lords of the Isles. The chapel of St Oran also survives.

The Abbey was re-established by Queen Margaret, wife of Malcolm Canmore, in the 11th century, and it flourished until the Reformation when it was abandoned and the buildings became ruinous, although the church was used into the 17th century. The abbey church was rebuilt from 1899-1910, and the cloister was restored in 1936 for the Iona Community, and it is possible to stay at the Abbey.

Also on the island is the Sithean Mor, the Fairy Mound, and it is said that soft music can often be heard coming from the knoll.

Map 3, 2K (Iona). Off unlisted road, Iona, Argyll.
His Scot: Open all year, daily – ferry from Fionnphort (£), no cars on Iona. Walk to abbey. (0131 668 8800 / www.historic-scotland.gov.uk)

JEDBURGH CASTLE JAIL AND MUSEUM

The Castle Jail stands on the site of an ancient castle, which was occupied by the English from 1346 until 1409, when it was retaken by the Scots and demolished. The Castle Jail, built in 1823 and now a museum, is a Howard reform prison, and the only one of its kind now remaining in Scotland. The museum recreates life in the jail using costumed figures and replica prison furniture, and there are displays on local history in the Gaoler's House.

Malcolm the Maiden died at the old castle in 1165. Alexander III was married to the young and beautiful Yolande de Dreux in the hall of the castle in 1285, after his first wife and children had predeceased him. A ghostly apparition at the marriage feast warned of Alexander's impending death. This was a terrifying figure, clad in a hooded shroud and with a death mask, like a grinning corpse. At first it was thought that the figure was part of some joke or sick entertainment, but when the figure was tackled and wrestled to the ground, all that was left was the shroud and ghastly mask. The ghostly apparition was apparently witnessed several times, and was always the harbinger of death.

The prediction, of course, came true when, not long afterward, Alexander fell with his horse from a cliff and was killed at Kinghorn (also see Kinghorn Castle) on his way to 'see' his new bride.

The jail buildings are also said to be haunted, and there are many reports of apparitions and unexplained manifestations, including a phantom piper, who has been witnessed on the battlements, and many mysterious lights. The jail has had several paranormal investigations, and during filming for *Most Haunted* several strange incidents were reported, not least pebbles being thrown at one of the investigators, furniture being moved about, equipment stopping working for no reason in the same spot, and the mysterious sounds of breathing.

Other manifestations which have been reported over the years include unexplained footsteps, breathing or whistling, feeling as if someone or something is pushing past, the sounds of cell doors being closed or creaking, mysterious lights and flashing lights, smoke, and extremely uncomfortable or unpleasant feelings.

Map 4, 11N (Jedburgh). Off A68, Castlegate, Jedburgh, Borders.
Open late Mar-Oct, daily. (01835 864750 / www.scotborders.gov.uk)

A paranormal investigation was undertaken in May 2008 by the Ghost Club (www.ghostclub.org.uk) and in May 2005 and September 2006 by Borders Paranormal Group (www.bordersparanormal.co.uk)

Featured in Living TV's Most Haunted, Series eleven (2008).

JOHNSTONE LODGE, ANSTRUTHER

Johnstone Lodge, a townhouse of 1829, was said to be haunted. In the 19th century it was the home of a George Dairsie, who married Princess Tetuane Marama, a Tahitian princess. The two lived here, although she found the climate inhospitable, and when she died she was buried in the kirkyard, a memorial on the south wall of the church commemorating her. After her death, the apparition of Tetuane was reported in many of the rooms of Johnstone Lodge, as well as on a balcony, and she has been described as a 'Black Lady'.

The building has been converted into flats.

Map 4, 10K (Anstruther). Off A917, Kirk Wynd, Anstruther, Fife.

JOHNSTOUNBURN HOUSE

Johnstounburn House, a romantic old mansion, probably dates from 1623 or earlier, although it was altered and extended in later years, including in 1863 when it was given a large castellated block. The lands were held by the Johnstones from around 1250, but had gone to the Borthwick family by the beginning of the 17th century or earlier. Johnstounburn passed to the Browns, and then to the Ushers from 1884, who were noted whisky blenders. The house was used as a hotel for some years but is now a private residence again.

There is reputedly a tunnel from the building to Soutra Hill, which is about two miles away.

The house is said to have a ghost, the spirit of a lady, although it is said to be gentle rather than especially frightening, and there are accounts of a strange presence in one of the bedrooms.

Map 4, 10M (Johnstounburn). Off B6368, 8 miles SE of Dalkeith, 0.5 miles S of Humbie, Johnstounburn, Midlothian.

KAIMHILL SCHOOL, ABERDEEN
At least one account has the primary school haunted by the apparition of a lady clad in grey and with a veil obscuring its face.

Map 2, 12G (Aberdeen). Off A90, Pitmedden Road, Kaimhill, Aberdeen.
School. (01224 316356)

KEAVIL HOUSE HOTEL
The mansion dates from 1873, although it replaced an earlier building, and the lands were held by the Lindsays in the 17th century and then later by the Barclay family. After World War II, Keavil was used as the Martha Frew's Children Home, but this closed and the building is now a fine hotel.

The house is said to be haunted by the ghost of a boy, unexplained footsteps having reputedly been heard in the corridors, as well as by the ghost of a lady. The boy is said to have been one of those who lived here during the time the building was used as a children's home.

Map 4, 9L (Keavil). Off A944, 2 miles W of Dunfermline, Keavil, Crossford, Fife.
Hotel. (01383 736258 / www.keavilhouse.co.uk)

KELLIE CASTLE
ILLUS PAGE 183

A splendid and imposing castle with a magnificent garden famous for its old roses, Kellie dates from the 16th and 17th centuries and was built by the Oliphants. The property passed to the Erskines, then in 1878 was leased by James Lorimer, who proceeded to restore it. Indeed, the ghost of Lorimer is said to have been seen, seated in one of the corridors. (Sir) Robert Lorimer, his son, the famous architect and garden designer, spent most of his childhood here.

A turnpike stair in the castle is reputedly haunted by the ghost of Anne Erskine, who is said to have died when she fell from one of the upstairs windows, presumably committing suicide. It is not clear who this Anne was, although the wives of both the 3rd and the 4th Earl (who held the property in the 17th century) were called Anne, nor is the reason why she chose to end her life recorded. Her apparition is rarely reported, but it is said that her footsteps have often been heard on the stair. Indeed, it is even reported that a pair of dainty red shoes can sometimes be seen hastily ascending the stairs, although there are no legs or body to go with them.

In 1970 Kellie passed into the care of The National Trust for Scotland.

Map 4, 10K (Kellie). Off B9171, 4 miles N of Elie, Kellie, Fife.
NTS: Castle and garden open early Apr-May, Fri-Tue (closed Wed & Thu); Jun-Aug, daily; Sep-Oct, Apr-May (closed Wed & Thu). (01333 720271 / www.nts.org.uk)

KELVIN HOUSE HOTEL, GLENLUCE

Located in the heart of the quiet village, the Kelvin House Hotel was built in 1770, and is a comfortable and welcoming hotel.

The building is said to be haunted by a ghost, spotted dressed in a deerstalker and accompanied by a smell of sandalwood.

The bogle is reputed to be friendly rather than frightening.

Map 3, 5P (Glenluce). Off A75, 53 Main street, Glenluce, Wigtownshire, Dumfries and Galloway.
Hotel. (01581 300303 / www.kelvin-house.co.uk)

KELVINGROVE ART GALLERY AND MUSEUM, GLASGOW

The excellent gallery, located in a magnificent building of 1901 which was recently refurbished, has a fabulous collection of art and sculpture, including works by Giorgione and Rembrandt, the French Impressionists, Post-Impressionists, and Scottish artists from the 17th century to the present day. One area is devoted to the 'Glasgow Style', with furniture by Charles Rennie Mackintosh, and others. There are also exhibits on archaeology, ethnology and natural history, including Scottish wildlife.

The building is said to be haunted, and there are stories of the phantom of a woman dressed in a ball gown being spotted on one of the upper stairs. Her identity has not been established, but it is said that the apparition is not frightening.

Map 4, 7M (Glasgow). Off M8, Argyll Street, Kelvingrove, to W of centre of Glasgow.
Open all year, Mon-Sat 10.00-17.00, Sun 11.00-17.00; closed Christmas and New Year. (0141 287 2699 / www.glasgow.gov.uk)

KEMBACK HOUSE

Kemback House, a handsome old house, probably dates from the beginning of the 18th century, but it was altered in 1907. The present house replaced an earlier building, possibly a castle or fortified house, which was a property of the Schivas family, and before that the Grahams.

Nearby Dura Den, the 16th-century Dairsie Bridge and the house are said to be haunted by a 'White Lady'. She is believed to be the wife of the Schivas laird in the troubled times of the 17th century. Her husband was a Covenanter, had taken refuge in a cave in Dura Den, and was being hunted by the authorities. She brought him food, but she was eventually arrested, although she would not betray the whereabouts of her husband. The poor woman was taken to Dairsie Bridge, and there hanged. A chamber in Kemback House is known as the 'White Lady's Room'.

An alternative identity has been given to her as the wife of Miles Graham, who held the property in the 15th century. He was involved in the murder of James I in 1437 and, again in this version, she was interrogated as to where he was hiding. She did reveal his hiding place, after great sufferance, and he was executed and she soon also died.

The Schivas family lost the property in the 17th century, and Kemback was then held by the Makgills until 1906. The house is still occupied.

Map 4, 10K (Kemback). Off B939, 3.5 miles E of Cupar, Kemback, Fife.

KEMPOCK STONE, GOUROCK

The Kempock Stone, which is about six foot tall, is also known as Granny Kempock's Stone, as it bears some resemblance to a cloaked and hooded old women. The stone was used by fishermen in rituals to try to ensure good weather, fair winds and a good catch of fish. People would walk around the stone seven times, carrying a basket of sand; the same ritual was used by betrothed and newly married couples for good luck and a productive marriage.

In 1662 several women, including the 18-year-old Mary Lamont (or Lawmont), were accused of trying to throw the stone into the Clyde (to destroy boats and ships), which would have been some feat, along with, rather less dramatically, attempting to steal milk by employing magic. Mary was also accused of dancing around the stone, accompanied by the Devil. She and several other women were accused of witchcraft, and were apparently executed.

There are stories, that sometimes on the night of a full moon, ghostly figures can be seen, circling the stone.

Map 3, 5L (Gourock). Off A770, 2.5 miles W of Greenock, Kempock Point, Gourock, Renfrewshire.
Access at all reasonable times.

KILBRYDE CASTLE

Built in the 16th century, Kilbryde Castle is an attractive L-plan tower house, incorporating older work and extended in around 1877. Kilbryde was once held by the Graham Earls of Menteith, but was sold to the Campbells in 1669, one of whom, Sir Colin, Lord Aberuchill, was prominent in his activities against Rob Roy MacGregor. Despite his best efforts, he had to pay blackmail to be left alone by the MacGregors. The house is still occupied by the Campbells, and the gardens, which have been restored and developed, are open to the public.

One story is that the castle and the grounds near the old chapel were haunted by a 'White Lady'. The story goes that Sir Malaise Graham, the Black Knight of Kilbryde, was romantically entwined with Ann Chisholm of Cromlix. Graham grew weary of his lady, and the tale goes that he cruelly murdered her and buried her body in Kilbryde Glen.

Her ghost, an apparition in a white blood-stained dress, is said to have been seen in the glen, near the old chapel and at a window of the castle, and her restless bogle did not find peace until her remains were found and properly buried.

Map 4, 7L (Kilbryde). Off A820, 3 miles NW of Dunblane, Kilbryde, Stirlingshire.
Garden open to the public all year by appt only and occasionally as part of Scotland's Gardens Scheme; castle not open. (01786 824897 / www.gardensofscotland.org)

KILCHRENAN

A cup-marked stone here is reputedly where a monk was sacrificed in early Christian times. An apparition of his decapitated body has reportedly been spotted here.

Map 3, 5K (Kilchrenan). Off B845, 1 mile E of Kilchrenan, Argyll.

KILDALTON CASTLE

Kildalton Castle is a large castellated mansion with a tall tower, and dates from the 1860s with no older origins. The mansion was held by the Ramsays, and is now apparently derelict.

The story goes that the Ramsays were cursed by an old woman after they had had the local crofters forcibly emigrated to the Americas. John Ramsay and his wife are said to have died soon afterwards; the estate was soon bankrupted.

The castle is said to be haunted, and there is a report of an apparition seen in the grounds.

Map 3, 3M (Kildalton). Off A846, 6 miles E of Port Ellen, 2.5 miles E of Ardbeg, Kildalton, on S coast of island of Islay, Argyll.

KILLIECRANKIE

On 27 July 1689 the Jacobites, led by John Graham of Claverhouse, Viscount Dundee, defeated a government army and were victorious at the Battle of Killiecrankie. Claverhouse, however, was mortally wounded at the battle, and the Jacobites disbanded after failing to capture Dunkeld. At Killiecrankie is the 'Soldier's Leap', where one government soldier escaped from Jacobite forces by jumping across the River Garry. An exhibition in the visitor centre features the battle, with models and maps, and there are also displays on natural history.

There are many reports of manifestations at the battle site, including a red glow that covers the area on the anniversary of the battle. Others claim to have had visions of the battle or its aftermath.

Dundee, himself, is said to have had a visitation of a bloodied man, gore dripping from his head, on the night before the battle. The apparition apparently said: 'Remember Brown of Priesthill!' Brown of Priesthill was executed by Dundee in 1685 because he was a Covenanter who refused to acknowledge the authority of James VII. This was taken afterwards to be a warning of Dundee's impending death.

Dundee's apparition, itself, is said to have appeared to Lord Balcarres at Edinburgh Castle, about the time he died.

Incidentally, Dundee was said by his Covenanter enemies to be a warlock, and therefore could only be killed using silver. Their assertion was that he had been killed by a silver bullet or by a musket ball hitting one of the silver buttons on his tunic and forcing itself into his flesh.

Map 2, 8H (Killiecrankie). On B8079, 3 miles N of Pitlochry, Perthshire.
NTS: Site open all year; visitor centre open Apr-Nov, daily. (01796 473233 / www.nts.org.uk)

KILMANY

Just to the north and west of Kilmany village is Ghoul's Den, a picturesque ravine which has been planted with trees and from where there are fine views. The area is said to be haunted by one or more 'White Ladies', as well as by other apparitions.

It is not clear, however, how far back the use of 'Ghoul's' is, as in a book of the late 19th century the word is spelt 'Goales'.

Map 4, 10K (Kilmany). Near A914, 4 miles N of Cupar, Ghoul's Den, to the W of Kilmany, Fife.

KILMARNOCK HOUSE

Situated on what is now a car park, Kilmarnock House was an old town house, dating from 1650, and was owned by the Boyd Earls of Kilmarnock, who had their main castle further north at Dean. The Boyds were made Earls of Kilmarnock in 1661, but in 1746 William, the 4th Earl, was beheaded in London after fighting for the Jacobites at the Battle of Culloden; his property and titles were forfeit. There is a strange story regarding a premonition of his death at Dean (see that entry)

During his trial in London, his wife, Anne Livingstone (from a staunchly Jacobite family herself), stayed at Kilmarnock House, walking in the garden and waiting for news. These gardens are now Howard Park, and a tree-lined avenue is known as Lady's Walk. Anne, herself, died the year after her husband, at the age of 38, and it is reported that her ghost has been witnessed in the park.

Kilmarnock House was long occupied, although by 1909 it was being used as an industrial school; in 1935 it was finally demolished, and the site is occupied by a car park.

Map 3, 6N (Kilmarnock). Off A77 or A71, between Marnock Street and Nelson Street, Kilmarnock, Ayrshire.

KILMICHAEL COUNTRY HOUSE HOTEL

In the secluded Glen Cloy, Kilmichael House is a small symmetrical mansion, dating from the 18th century, and the house stands on land given by Robert the Bruce in 1307 to by the MacLewis or MacLewie family. Their descendants, the Fullartons, were in possession by the middle of the 16th century and they held the house into the 20th century. The building is now used as a luxurious five star hotel.

The building is said to be haunted by a 'Grey Lady', and the bogle has reputedly been witnessed in some of the rooms.

Map 3, 5N (Kilmichael). Off A841, 1 mile SW of village of Brodick, Glen Cloy, Isle of Arran.
Hotel. (01770 302219 / www.kilmichael.com)

KILMORY CASTLE

Located in fine grounds and gardens, Kilmory Castle is a large and impressive castellated mansion, with parts said to date from the 14th century. The property was held by Paisley Abbey, but passed to the Lamonts (briefly), before coming to the Campbells in 1575, who held the estate until 1828. Kilmory then passed by marriage to the Orde family, who built much of the present rambling mansion, and the castle now houses the local council headquarters.

The castle is said to be haunted by a 'Green Lady'.

Map 3, 4L (Kilmory). On A83, 1 mile S of Lochgilphead, Kilmory, Argyll.
Garden: open all year, daylight hours; closed Christmas and New Year; castle not open. (01546 604360 / www.argyll-bute.gov.uk/content/leisure/heritage/kilmory)

KILSPINDIE CASTLE

Nothing remains of Kilspindie Castle, an ancient stronghold, which was completely demolished in 1840. William Wallace and his mother are supposed to have taken refuge here, according to a poem by Blind Harry. Much later the castle was a property of the Lindsays.

There is a tale of a 'White Lady' haunting Kilspindie, as well as legends of a green serpent.

Map 4, 9K (Kilspindie). Off A90, 7 miles E of Perth, at or near Kilspindie.

KIMBERLEY HOTEL, OBAN

On the site of an older house, the fine baronial mansion was built in 1885 by the Cowan family, who had been pioneers in diamond mining. The name of the mansion comes from Kimberley in South Africa and, after use as a maternity hospital, the building is now a hotel.

The hotel is said to be haunted by a 'Grey Lady', a friendly ghost, although there is no story as to her origin. Several sightings have been reported, including in recent times, as have disembodied voices.

Map 3, 4K (Oban). Off A85, 13 Dalriach Road, Oban
Hotel. (01631 571115 / www.kimberley-hotel.co.uk)

KINCARDINE COMMUNITY CENTRE

The community centre is housed in an old church building, dating from the 19th century, which was converted to use as a school early in the 20th century. In the 1980s the building was renovated for community use.

The community centre is said to be haunted. Reports of strange occurrences include half-seen apparitions flitting around corridors, unexplained noises and voices, a clock repeatedly falling from a wall without explanation, and a piano playing by itself when nobody was near it. The activity is said not to be malicious.

Map 4, 8L (Kincardine). Off A977, Anderson Lane, Kincardine, Fife.
Community centre.

A paranormal investigation was undertaken by Paranormal Encounters Group (www.p-e-g.co.uk).

KINDROCHIT CASTLE

Little remains of a once strong castle, for many years held by the Drummonds. The place was reputedly destroyed by cannon in the 17th century, after the plague had struck, so that the occupants could not escape.

The story goes that, after the Jacobite Rising of 1745-46, a way into one of the old vaults was found. A Hanoverian soldier was lowered in, hoping to find treasure, but fled when he found a phantom party seated around a table piled with skulls. Later excavations failed to find the ghostly company or any skulls, but the exquisite Kindrochit Brooch was unearthed and the walls were traced.

Map 2, 8G (Kindrochit). Off A93, by car park, S of Braemar, Kincardine and Deeside.
Access at all reasonable times.

KINGCAUSIE

Pronounced 'Kincowsie', Kingcausie, a modern mansion, incorporates a 16th-century tower house of the Irvines of Kingcausie, and is still owned by the same family.

The house is said to be haunted by the ghost of a two-year-old child. James Turner Christie, the infant, fell down the stairs from his nanny's arms and was

Kellie Castle (page 177)

Kinnaird Head Castle (page 187)

Kylesku Hotel (page 191)

Lauriston Castle, Edinburgh (page 193)

Leith Hall (page 194)

killed. The pattering of child's footsteps have reputedly been heard several times when there is nobody about.

The Chinese Room is also said to be haunted, and the bedclothes are said to have been violently flung off one of the occupants.

Map 2, 11G (Kingcausie). Off B9077, 1.5 miles SE of Peterculter, Aberdeenshire.

KINGHORN CASTLE

There was an ancient royal stronghold in Kinghorn, dating from the 12th century, but nothing of it now remains.

It was at the castle that Yolande de Dreux, the young and beautiful wife of Alexander III, awaited him one stormy night in 1286. Alexander had been in Edinburgh but he decided, although the weather was stormy, to make the hazardous trip across the Forth at Queensferry and then along the coast to Kinghorn. But Alexander got separated from his entourage and he fell, along with his horse, from cliffs close to the castle and was killed: a monument marks the spot where his broken body was found. It is said that the ghost of Yolande, a 'Grey Lady', has been seen in the area of the castle, and also in the Kingswood (also see that entry), still searching for him (although she has also been described as a 'Green Lady'). In truth, Yolande did not die until 1330, when she was well into her sixties, and only after she had remarried and had at least six children with the Duke of Brittany.

The property passed to Sir John Lyon of Glamis, Chancellor of Scotland, towards the end of the 14th century, a descendant of whom was made Earl of Kinghorn(e) in 1606.

Map 4, 9L (Kinghorn). Off A921, 3-5 Burt Avenue, Kinghorn, Fife.

KINGSHOUSE HOTEL, BALQUHIDDER

The popular hotel stands in a pretty spot near the village of Balquhidder, the burial place of Rob Roy MacGregor. Kingshouse is the site of a hunting lodge of the monarchs of Scotland, and the present building is believed to date from the 16th century and to have been used by James VI. The hotel stands on the route of a military road and was used to accommodate soldiers when the route was being constructed. In 1799 it was commissioned as a 'King's House' (hence the name), with six government troops providing escorts for cattle drovers and travellers.

The building is said to be haunted.

Map 4, 7K (Balquhidder). By A84, at turn-off for Balquhidder, 2.5 miles E of Balquhidder, Kingshouse, Stirling.
Hotel and holiday cottages. (01877 384646 / www.kingshouse-scotland.co.uk)

KINGSWOOD HOTEL, KINGHORN

The Kingswood Hotel, which dates from around 1850, was originally built as a country residence by the Johnstones, who were plantation owners from Jamaica. The building is now a hotel.

At one time, a young girl reported being harassed by ghostly manifestations, including something pinching her bottom. She also said she had seen the apparition of a woman in a white flowing dress.

There are also stories of a 'Grey Lady' being seen in the area in the 1960s, particularly around the main road and at a bus stop on the opposite side of the road

from the hotel. One motorist reported having to brake sharply to avoid the apparition. It is also said that the ghost got onto a bus and went upstairs, although a
subsequent search of the vehicle could find no passengers. It is reputed that the
apparition was seen often.

The monument which marks where Alexander III fell from his horse to his death is
near the hotel, and some stories have his young wife, Yolande de Dreux, as the
ghost which haunts the area (but also see Kinghorn Castle).

Another version is that this is the spirit of a woman who once lived in a cottage
behind the Kingswood Hotel; she hanged herself from a tree on the Kinghorn Road.

Map 4, 9L (Kinghorn). On A921, 1 mile E of Burntisland, Kinghorn Road, Kingswood, Fife.
Hotel. (01592 872329 / www.kingswoodhotel.co.uk)

KING'S ARMS HOTEL, DUMFRIES

Standing near the junction of English Street with the High Street, the King's Arms
Hotel was allegedly haunted by the ghost of a young woman in Victorian garb, a
'Grey Lady'. The story goes that she was the widow of Captain Robert Stewart, who
was killed during the French Revolution in the 18th century, and that she died of a
broken heart at the age of only 24.

The hotel was demolished many years ago, and the site is occupied by shops,
although there was a report in 1996 of ghostly activity in one of the shops adjacent
to the site.

Map 4, 8P (Dumfries). Off A75, Dumfries, Dumfries and Galloway.

KING'S ARMS HOTEL, LOCKERBIE

Frequented by many famous Scots, including Bonnie Prince Charlie and Sir Walter
Scott, the King's Arms Hotel is believed to be one of the longest established hostel-
ries in Lockerbie, dating as it does from the 17th Century.

The building is reputed to be haunted. Manifestations are reported to include
strange smells, noticed in some areas of the hotel: the odour of rose water or
lavender, or antiseptic. In some of the guest bedrooms there have also been several
instances of items being found wet without explanation, such as a pillow, beds and
a duvet, and guests reported that the taps in their bathroom (both sink and bath)
came on by themselves late at night; on another occasion, someone cleaning the
room had a similar experience.

A guest reported hearing banging, as if a window was being repeatedly opened
and closed in the adjoining room, but the chamber was not occupied at the time; a
couple about to be married woke up and found that the bride's dress has been
taken out of the wardrobe, and its protective bag, and had been thrown on the
floor.

Other manifestations have also been recorded, including a wooden spoon moving
by itself in the kitchen, half-seen apparitions, and a guest reporting that, on waking, they had seen the phantom of a woman in a crinoline dress.

Map 4, 9P (Lockerbie). Off M74, 29 High Street, Lockerbie, Dumfries and Galloway.
Hotel. (01576 202410 / www.kingsarmshotel.co.uk)

*A paranormal investigation was undertaken in January 2006 by Scottish Paranormal
Investigations (www.scottishparanormalinvestigations.co.uk)*

KINNAIRD CASTLE

Located in 1300 acres of walled parkland, Kinnaird, an impressive if glowering 19th-century mansion, incorporates part of an ancient castle. Kinnaird has been a property of the Carnegie Earls of Southesk family for more than 600 years, and they still live here.

One story connected with the castle is that the corpse of James Carnegie, the 2nd Earl of Southesk, who died in 1669, was reportedly taken by a ghostly black coach driven by black horses. Carnegie is said to have studied in Padua, where he allegedly learnt black magic, and to have lost his shadow to the Devil. A similar story is told of Alexander Skene of Skene House (also see that entry).

More prosaically, Carnegie was made Sheriff of Forfarshire after the Restoration in 1660; he appears to be another victim of Covenanter vilification.

Map 2, 10I (Kinnaird). Off A934, 5.5 miles W of Montrose, Kinnaird, Angus.
Accommodation available. (01674 810240 / www.southesk.co.uk)

KINNAIRD HEAD CASTLE ILLUS PAGE 183

In an open location by the sea, Kinnaird Head Castle consists of an altered massive 15th-century keep, the walls of which are harled and whitewashed. The Wine Tower, standing about 50 yards away, is a lower tower, now of three storeys, all of them vaulted. It is said to have been so called as it was used as a wine cellar for the main castle, and probably its predecessor.

This was a property of the Frasers of Philorth. Sir Alexander Fraser built the harbour at Fraserburgh – the town was originally called Faithlie – and came near to bankrupting himself, and had to sell much of his property in 1611. A lighthouse was built into the top of the castle in 1787, and the outbuildings were built around it in 1820 by Robert Stevenson, grandfather of Robert Louis Stevenson. It now forms part of a lighthouse museum (01346 511022; www.lighthousemuseum.org.uk).

Sir Alexander is said to disapproved of his daughter Isobel's lover, and had the poor man chained in a sea cave below the Wine Tower to teach him a lesson. Fraser miscalculated, however, and the poor man drowned. When Isobel found her dead lover, she threw herself to her death in the water or she cast herself from the top of the Wine Tower.

An apparition is said to been seen by the Wine Tower whenever there is a storm, the desperate phantom of Isobel, still searching for her sweetheart. In another version, Isobel's lover is alleged to have been a piper, and it is said at times his pipes can still be heard skirling up from the cave.

Kinnaird Head Castle is also alleged to be haunted, visitors reporting that they felt as if they were being watched and also experiencing sudden drops in temperature. There are also stories of footsteps being heard coming from unoccupied areas, and the apparition of what appeared to be a fisher-woman being spotted here.

Map 2, 12E (Kinnaird Head). Off A98, N of Fraserburgh, Banff and Buchan, Aberdeenshire.
His Scot: Open all year, daily except closed 25-26 Dec and 1-2 Jan. (01346 511022 / www.lighthousemuseum.org.uk/www.historic-scotland.gov.uk)

KINNEIL HOUSE

Set in a public park, Kinneil House, dating from the 16th century, is a fine old mansion with original paintings in two of the rooms. The lands were long held by the Hamiltons. John Hamilton, 4th Earl of Arran, was Governor for Mary, Queen of Scots, until 1554, and then led her party until 1573 – he built a large tower here. As a result, the house was sacked, and part blown up with gunpowder, but it was later rebuilt. The building was occupied by Cromwell's forces in 1650, from when the ghost story is said to originate.

The house and the policies around it are said to be haunted by a 'White Lady', garbed in a white nightdress, the ghost of Ailie or Alice, Lady Lilburne, the young wife of a Cromwellian colonel billeted here in the 1650s or (according to another version of the tale) the mistress of the Duke of Hamilton. If the latter was the case, she cannot have been a contented lass, as the first Duke was executed in 1649 by Cromwell and the second Duke died at the Battle of Worcester two years later. After having tried to escape repeatedly without success, Ailie was locked in one of the upper chambers with no hope of release. She finally despaired, and cast herself from the window into the Gil Burn, some 200 foot below (or into the sea, which would be some feat even for a supernatural entity, as the sea is some distance away). Her forlorn screams and weeping are said still to be heard on dark winter nights, and her spectre is reputed to be seen, haunting the spot in the glen where she died. An account from the 19th century also reports that her ghost was seen at the place from where she had jumped, and that the house was plagued by unexplained heavy footfalls, as if the bogle was wearing boots, heard stomping about the stairs, corridors and chambers.

Map 4, 8L (Kinneil). Off A993, 5 miles E of Falkirk, 1 mile SW of Bo'ness, Kinneil, West Lothian. **His Scot: Access at all reasonable times – view from exterior. (0131 668 8800 / www.historic-scotland.gov.uk)**

KIRK OF SHOTTS

The present Kirk of Shotts dates from the 1820s and is still the parish church, and this replaced an earlier building of 1450 or earlier, which was dedicated to St Catherine of Sienna. There is a spring known as Kate's Well near the present church.

The road that runs past the church, Canthill Road, is said to be the scene of several sightings of an apparition, dressed in a dark cape and with a carriage hat. On one occasion, it is claimed, the phantom stepped out in front of a car, apparently went over the roof, and then got back to its feet and vanished, greatly discomfiting the driver. The phantom had apparently been witnessed on several other occasions, another driver having to swerve to miss the ghost, and pedestrians are also alleged to have seen the bogle.

One story is that the spirit is that of William Smith, a Covenanter, who is buried in the grave yard. His memorial reads: 'Here lies the bones of William Smith who lived in Moremellen and who with others fought at Pentland Hills in defence of Scotland's Covenant in 1666 and was murdered on his return home near to this place'.

The burial ground is also said to have a 'Grey Lady', reputedly witnessed on more than one occasion, and blamed for blurred grey streaks which appeared in photographs being taken for a church calendar.

Map 4, 8M (Kirk of Shotts). Off B7066, 2 miles NW of Shotts, Canthill Road, Lanarkshire.

KIRK OF ST NICHOLAS, ABERDEEN

The 'Mither Kirk' of Aberdeen, the church dates from the 12th century, and there has been a church here from early times. The church was divided in two after the Reformation, then largely rebuilt. The East Kirk dates from 1752, the West from 1830s, while the central tower and spire are from later in the 19th century, built after a fire destroyed the old belfry. The congregations were united in 1980. St Mary's Chapel, in the crypt, survives from the 15th-century church, and Sir John Gordon, executed after the Battle of Corrichie in 1562, is interred here. There is also fine 17th-century embroidery.

The adjoining graveyard has many table-tombs and memorials, dating from as early as the 17th century.

The area has a reputation for being haunted. In 1982 two men witnessed the apparition of a woman, garbed in a long white dress and veil. She was said to have black hair, and to have disappeared at the corner of the church.

Map 2, 12G (Aberdeen). Off A956, Back Wynd off Union Street, Aberdeen.
Open May-Sep, Mon-Fri, other times by appt; kirkyard open all year, daily. (01224 643494 / www.kirk-of-st-nicholas.org.uk)

KIRK O' FIELD, EDINBURGH

This is the site of the house where Henry Stewart, Lord Darnley, second husband of Mary, Queen of Scots, and his servant, were suffocated in 1567 after the building had been blown up using gunpowder. Darnley was buried in the church of Holyrood Abbey.

Some stories have his ghost haunting the area.

Map 4, 9L (Edinburgh). Off A7, Old College, University of Edinburgh, Edinburgh.

KIRKCONNEL HALL

Little remains of an ancient tower house here, a property of the Irvines, who came here from Kirkconnel, near Springkell, in 1609. By the old ruin is Kirkconnel Hall, an attractive mansion dating from 1870, standing in more than four acres of gardens. The hall was a property of the Arnott family, one of whom was physician to Napoleon Bonaparte, but it is now used as a hotel.

The building is said in some old stories to be haunted, and there are tales of an apparition being seen, known as the 'Ha' Ghost', and this is reputed to be a noisy bogle. The tale goes that the ghost was especially active when one of the Arnott family was near death.

Map 4, 9P (Kirkconnel). Off B725, NW of Ecclefechan, Kirkconnel, Dumfries and Galloway.
Hotel. (01576 300277 / www.kirkconnelhall.co.uk)

KIRKDALE BRIDGE

One story tells how a gypsy murdered a young lady near Kirkdale Bridge, and that afterwards her ghost, in a white dress, was repeatedly seen around midnight, with half of her head missing. The bogle, it was said, would wander along to road for some way before disappearing at a track to Kirkdale Bank.

Map 4, 7Q (Kirkdale). On A76, 4 miles W and S of Gatehouse of Fleet, Kirkdale Bridge, Dumfries and Galloway.

KIRKTON JEAN'S HOTEL, KIRKOSWALD

Kirkton Jean's Hotel stood on the Main Road of Kirkoswald and was an old coaching inn, dating from 1792, before it was closed. The establishment was originally called The Star Inn but was renamed after Jean Kennedy, 'Kirkton Jean', who is one of the characters in Burns's famous poem, 'Tam o' Shanter'; her house was incorporated into the inn and was used as the restaurant. The building is being renovated as part of a larger development of a hotel, whisky shop and museum. The village is associated with several other of Burns's contemporaries, and Soutar Johnnie's Cottage in the village is open to the public.

The inn was said to be haunted, although reported manifestations were limited to a door in the loft of the restaurant repeatedly opening and closing by itself.

Map 3, 5O (Kirkoswald). On A77, Main Road, Kirkoswald, Ayrshire.

KNIPOCH HOTEL

Located in a fine position overlooking Loch Feochan, the Knipoch Hotel is a long extended building, which stands on the site of an older house. Knipoch was a property of the Campbells, and was the scene of the murder of John Campbell of Cawdor in 1592: Campbell was shot by a musket as he sat by the fire. The murder was part of an argument in the Campbell clan over who had control over the young Earl of Argyll. The murderer, Patrick Og MacKellar, was later captured and hanged.

Campbell's ghost was said at one time to haunt Knipoch.

Map 3, 4K (Knipoch). On A816, 6 miles S of Oban, Knipoch, Argyll
Hotel. (01852 316251 / www.knipochhotel.co.uk)

KNOCK CASTLE

In a fine spot with great views, Knock Castle is a small and ruinous tower house with turrets and shot-holes. The property was held by the Gordons during a feud with their rivals, the Forbeses, which came to its conclusion in the 1590s. Henry Gordon, 2nd of Knock, was slain in a raid, while the seven sons of Alexander (Alasdair), the next laird, when out cutting peats (on Forbes's land), were surprised, seized and summarily beheaded by Alexander Forbes of Strathgirnock. To make things even worse, their severed heads were tied to their peat-spades. All this after another son of Alexander Gordon had already been slain after he had fallen in love with Forbes's daughter.

When the news reached Knock, and their father heard of their terrible deaths, he was so shocked that he fell down the turnpike stair of his own tower, broke his neck, and was also slain. Alexander Forbes of Strathgirnock was summarily executed for the deed in his own house by Alexander Gordon of Abergeldie, who fell upon the house at Strathgirnock and slaughtered all those involved.

The tower is said to be haunted by the unhappy bogle of Alexander Gordon of Knock.

Map 2, 9G (Knock). Off B976, 1.5 miles W of Ballater, just E of Knock, Aberdeenshire

KNOCKDERRY CASTLE

Perched at the edge of a rocky outcrop, Knockderry Castle, a mansion of 1855 which was enlarged in 1896 by the architect William Leiper, is said to have been built on the basement of a small castle or watch-tower, dating from the Norse occupation of the area in the 13th century.

The house is said to be haunted by ghosts associated with the dungeon of the castle.

Map 3, 5L (Knockderry). Off B833, 1 mile N of Cove, Loch Long, Dunbartonshire.

KNOCKHILL

Knockhill is an elegant two-storey symmetrical mansion, dating from 1777. It was a property of Andrew Johnstone of Knockhill, who was transported to the West Indies for his part in the Jacobite Rising of 1745-46; he returned in 1777.

At one time the mansion was said to be haunted by the ghost of a man shot dead by the butler, who thought him a robber and had apparently challenged him; this is believed to have occurred in 1829. The intruder, called Bell, had in fact been in love with one of the maids, and had been visiting her secretly.

His ghost then began to haunt the house.

Map 4, 9P (Knockhill). Off B723, 4 miles S of Lockerbie, 1.5 miles W of Ecclefechan, Knockhill, Dumfries and Galloway.

KYLESKU HOTEL   ILLUS PAGE 184

By the sea in a remote and rugged part of the west coast of Sutherland is the Kylesku Hotel, an old coaching inn which dates from 1680. It stands by the former ferry, although the road now crosses by a bridge, and is a friendly family-run hotel.

The inn is said to be haunted by the ghost of a fisherman. The story goes that a party was being held in the attic, above the bar, after a barrel of whisky had been washed ashore following a wreck in the Minch. The company were in good spirits, but were becoming rowdy, and the Sabbath was approaching. What happened next is not clear – some may have felt it was time for the party to break up – but, after an argument, two fishermen, father and son, ended up in a brawl. The older man tumbled down the ladder from the attic and broke his neck. But before he died he cursed his son, saying he would return to get his revenge. The son was soon killed at sea, but his father's ghost did not rest.

An apparition is said to appear near the entrance to the snug on the anniversary of the fisherman's death, although the last appearance is said to have been in 1950.

Map 1, 5B (Kylesku). Off A894, 9 miles SE of Scourie, Kylesku, Sutherland, Highland.
Hotel. (01971 502231 / www.kyleskuhotel.co.uk)

LAGG

Lagg Tower is a ruined 16th-century tower house of four storeys, which formerly had a courtyard with outbuildings. The lands were held by the Griersons from 1408, and they built the tower.

Sir Robert Grierson of Lagg was made a baronet of Nova Scotia in 1685, and was prominent in prosecuting Covenanters. In 1685 he surprised an illegal Coventicle and, after killing some of the worshippers (reputedly by rolling them down a hill in a spiked barrel), including James Clement, denied them a Christian burial, at least according to stories told afterwards. A granite monument marks the spot where the Covenanters were slain.

Later Grierson went on to become a Jacobite, for which he was fined and imprisoned. Grierson, himself, is buried in the cemetery of the old parish church at Lagg. He died in 1733 in his 70s, and was so fat that one wall of his house in Dumfries had to be demolished to extract him from it. All sorts of stories were told about him by his critics and Covenanter enemies. His spit could burn holes where it fell; when he placed his feet in water he made it boil; wine would turn to congealed blood when it was given to him.

On the night Grierson died, sailors on a ship on the Solway Firth are reputed to have seen a terrifying phantom chariot (or state-coach), drawn by six horses, accompanied by lightning and dark clouds and peels of thunder, along with a whole entourage of outriders, footmen, torch-bearers and other figures. This chariot is said to have taken Grierson off to hell (presumably, because of his corporeal bulk, it was a substantial vehicle). A further story is that a black and fearsome raven accompanied Grierson's coffin from Dumfries to his burial, and could not be driven off, whatever the mourners tried. And yet another that the horses used to pull the hearse dropped dead as soon as they reached the cemetery.

Like others of his contemporaries, it does seem, however, rather unlikely that Grierson quite warranted this demonic reputation.

Map 4, 7O (Lagg). Off B729, 7 miles SE of Moniaive, Lagg, Dumfries and Galloway

LAGG HOTEL

The picturesque whitewashed hotel, built in 1791 and an excellent hostelry, is set in a fantastically lovely spot in a dell where the road crosses the Kilmory Water; the hotel has eleven acres of fine gardens.

One story is that the hotel is haunted by the ghost of a laird who sold his soul to the Devil.

Map 3, 4N (Lagg Hotel). On A841, Lagg, south of Isle of Arran, Ayrshire.
Hotel. (01770 870255 / www.lagghotel.com)

LAINSHAW HOUSE

Nothing remains of an old castle of the Montgomerys, which was replaced by Lainshaw House, a classical mansion built around 1800. Lainshaw passed from the Montgomerys and was sold to William Cunningham in 1779, one of Glasgow's 'tobacco lords'. The house was latterly used as an old people's home, but is apparently to be converted into flats with houses built in the grounds.

Lainshaw was said to have a 'Green Lady', reputed to be the apparition of Elizabeth Cunningham, wife of Montgomery of Lainshaw. Along with many Cunninghams, she is thought to have been involved in the plot in 1586 which resulted in the savage murder of one of her husband's family, Hugh Montgomery, 4th Earl of Eglinton (and then the severe retribution against the Cunninghams in retaliation).

Her ghost, a 'Green Lady', is said to have been witnessed, wearing a green dress and carrying a candle. The rustle of her dress has also reportedly been heard.

Map 3, 6M (Lainshaw). Off B769, 1 mile SW of Stewarton, Lainshaw, Ayrshire.

LARGIE CASTLE

Little survives of Largie Castle, an ancient stronghold, except some fragments built into a later farm, High Rhunahaorine, the buildings of which are now also very ruinous. The property was held by the MacDonalds of Largie (or Clan Ranaldbane, the Ranald Bane in question had distinguished himself in battle at Inverlochy in 1431), descendants of the Lords of the Isles, from the middle of the 15th until the 20th century. The castle is said to have been razed by the Covenanter general David Leslie in 1647, and Flora MacDonald was related to the family and visited Largie several times. The family moved to 'new' Largie Castle, 0.5 miles north-east of Tayinloan, and had a burial vault at the Old Parish Church at nearby Killean.

The old castle is said to have had a brownie, which also frequented the MacDonalds' house on the island of Cara, south of Gigha (see Cara House).

Map 3, 4M (Largie). Off A83, 17 miles SW of Tarbert, Argyll.

LAST DROP TAVERN, EDINBURGH

The name comes from its site in the Grassmarket and the pub's proximity to the spot where public executions once took place. Although a cosy and popular place, the Last Drop is said to be haunted, and manifestations are reputed to have included a disembodied voice in the cellar calling out staff's names when nobody else was about, and objects, including glasses, moving or falling from shelves by themselves.

One story is that the ghost is the spirit of a girl murdered in the 18th century, and the bogle is said to have been active in recent times.

Map 4, 9L (Edinburgh). Off A7 or A702, Grassmarket, Edinburgh.
Public house. (0131 225 4851)

LAUDALE HOUSE

Laudale House, a three-storey mansion, is said to be haunted. The sounds of something heavy, perhaps a body in armour, being dragged across the floor, are reportedly heard, but nothing can be found to explain the noises.

One tale is that it was to Laudale that the body of Angus Mor was brought. Angus had murdered the young chief of the MacIans, and was himself slain in battle in Glen Dubh, near Kinlochaline, by a force of Camerons and of MacLeans.

Map 1, 3I (Laudale). Off A884, south side of Loch Sunart, Lochaber, Highland.

LAURISTON CASTLE, EDINBURGH   ILLUS PAGE 184

Set in 30 acres of a parkland and gardens near the picturesque village of Cramond, Lauriston Castle is an imposing building, and consists of a tower house dating from the 16th century and a later mansion. The mansion has a fine Edwardian-period interior and impressive chimneys.

The old tower was built by the Napiers of Merchiston in the 1590s, one of whom, John Napier, was the inventor of logarithms. The property passed through several families, until the last owners, the Reids, gave it to the city of Edinburgh in 1926.

The ghostly sound of feet have reportedly been heard in the castle.

Map 4, 9L (Edinburgh). Off B9085, 3 miles W of Edinburgh Castle, Cramond Road South, Davidson's Mains, Edinburgh.
Open for guided tours Apr-Oct, Sat-Thu; Nov-Mar, Sat & Sun; grounds open, daily.
(0131 336 2060 / www.edinburgh.gov.uk/internet/A-Z/AZ_lauriston_castle)

LAWERS

On the banks of Loch Tay in a grand spot beneath the mountain of Ben Lawers was an old house or castle at the abandoned village of Lawers. The old house is said to have been destroyed around 1645, only to be replaced by a new house, although there are no traces of this building. There was a village, mill and church here, some crumbling remains of which survive. Lawers was long held by the Campbells, and this branch of the clan rose to inherit the Earldom of Loudoun. Their main seat was moved to nearer Crieff at Fordie or Fordew.

This was the home in the 17th century of the Lady of Lawers (her first name has not apparently been recorded), the Stewart wife of John Campbell of Lawers, who made prophecies, many of which reputedly came true (as in the events described apparently happened, not they were correctly predicted). There are also tales of a ghost haunting the site of the village, known as the 'White Lady of Lawers', said to be her bogle.

Map 4, 7J (Lawers). By A827, 8 miles E of Killin, on N shore of Loch Tay, Lawers, Perthshire.
It is possible to visit the remains of the village.

LEARMONTH GARDENS, EDINBURGH

In the 1930s, the story goes that this house in Learmonth Gardens was occupied by Alexander Hay Seton, baronet of Abercorn and Armour Bearer to the monarch. Alexander and Zeyla, his wife, visited Egypt in 1936 and, when visiting an excavation, Zeyla took a bone from a tomb and brought it back with them to Edinburgh.

A series of strange manifestations occurred after they were back, and the couple grew to believe that they had been cursed by taking the bone. There were unexplained footsteps, crashes and noises from unoccupied areas, which continued for weeks, and then also sightings of a robed apparition, wandering the house.

One night Alexander heard all sorts of commotion and found that the locked room in which the bone was kept had been ransacked, and this was then repeated in another chamber. Alexander finally had the bone exorcised and then burnt into ash, although the tale is that he still thought himself cursed and that bad luck hounded him and his wife for the rest of their lives.

Map 4, 9L (Edinburgh). Off A90, Learmonth Gardens, Edinburgh.

LEARMONTH HOTEL, EDINBURGH

Standing on Queensferry Road, the Learmonth Hotel, now a Travelodge, was said at one time to be haunted by a poltergeist. Doors reputedly opened and closed, and even unlocked, themselves. Electrical equipment, such as kettles and hair driers, have been known to switch themselves on and off, and unexplained whistling is said to have been heard in empty corridors.

Map 4, 9L (Edinburgh). Off A90, 18-20 Learmonth Terrace, Edinburgh.
Hotel. (0871 9846 415 / www.travelodge.co.uk)

LEITH HALL ILLUS PAGE 184

Set in 286 acres of grounds, Leith Hall is a courtyard mansion with yellow-washed walls and small drum towers. It was a property of the Leith family from 1650, or earlier, until 1945, when it was given to The National Trust for Scotland.

Guests in 1968 reported manifestations in their bedroom, including the sounds of a woman's laugh and a party going on when nobody else was apparently there.

Sightings of the apparition of a man, bandaged about the head, were also reported. The ghost is thought to be of John Leith, who was killed in a brawl or a duel on 25 December 1763 and died from a head wound. Indeed, the person who reputedly saw the ghost thought it greatly resembled a portrait of Leith, which hung in the house.

Another ghost is said to be that of a woman, dressed as if from the 18th century, while the apparition of a man in a military uniform is alleged to have been spotted in the grounds. This bogle is reputed to be that of the last Leith owner, who died in a motorcycle accident.

Other spooky manifestations have been reported, such as footsteps from unoccupied areas, unexplained music of pipes and drums, the sounds of doors being slammed, heard in the deep of night, and of a woman and children laughing, and the odour of camphor and of food, smelt in the bedrooms. Extreme changes in temperature and a foreboding atmosphere have also been recorded, as have people feeling as if they have been touched when nobody else is present.

Map 2, 10F (Leith Hall). Off B9002, 8 miles S of Huntly, 3.5 miles NE of Rhynie, Leith Hall, Aberdeenshire.
NTS: House and tearoom not open at time of writing; garden and grounds, open all year. (01464 831216 / www.nts.org.uk)

Featured in Living TV's Most Haunted, *series three (2003).*

LENNOXLOVE

Originally known as Lethington, Lennoxlove is a stately pile in fine grounds, and incorporates an altered L-plan tower house, with work from the 14th century, and later additions and extensions. The lands were a property of the Maitlands from around 1350, one of whom, William Maitland of Lethington, was secretary to Mary, Queen of Scots. He was taken prisoner after Edinburgh Castle was captured in 1573 and died, possibly after being poisoned, soon afterwards.

In 1947 Lennoxlove passed to the Duke of Hamilton, since when it has been the family seat. Among the treasures it contains are the death mask of Mary, Queen of Scots, a sapphire ring given to her by Lord John Hamilton, and the casket which may have contained the 'Casket Letters' .

The building is said to be haunted, and there are reports that ghostly music has been heard on more than one occasion, coming from a piano playing by itself in the Blue Room of the ancient part of the castle. The piano was once played by Chopin, and the story goes that it was given to Susan, Duchess of Hamilton, in 1828 (before Lennoxlove was owned by the Hamiltons; Chopin played the piano at the now demolished Hamilton Palace) and it is her bogle which is how playing with phantom fingers (although her ghost would needed to have translated along with the piano). The music is said, however, not to be tuneful, just random notes in no particular order.

Map 4, 10M (Haddington). Off A1, between B6369 and B6368, 1 mile S of Haddington, Lennoxlove, East Lothian.
Open Easter-Oct for tours, check days before setting out; booked tours outwith these times by appt. (01620 828608 / www.lennoxlove.com)

LIBERTON HOUSE, EDINBURGH

Liberton House, built by William Little, Provost of Edinburgh, around 1605 is an L-plan tower house, now harled and orange-washed. The name Liberton comes from 'lepers' town': the leper colony which was once located near here. The house is reputedly haunted, and a photograph taken at the beginning of the century purports to show the image of an apparition of a man not seen when the photograph was taken. Other spooky manifestations are reported to be electrical equipment, including a fan heater and the burglar alarm, switching themselves off and on.

Map 4, 9L (Edinburgh). Off A701, 3 miles SE of Edinburgh Castle, Liberton, Edinburgh.

LINLITHGOW COURTHOUSE

The Court House is an attractive Tudor-style building of 1863, which housed the Sheriff Court, and is built on the site of the town house of Sir James Hamilton of Finnart. Hamilton was the illegitimate son of the Earl of Arran, and he had a glittering but brief career. Among other offices, he held the Captain of Linlithgow Palace but he was executed in August 1540 after firing a missile at James V in Linlithgow.

It was from this town house that James Hamilton of Bothwellhaugh shot and assassinated Regent Moray (James Stewart, Earl of Moray), in 1572, and a plaque on the outside of the courthouse commemorates the event. The sheriff court is to be moved to Livingston.

The court house is said to be haunted.

Map 4, 8L (Linlithgow). On A803, High Street, Linlithgow, West Lothian.

LINLITHGOW PALACE   ILLUS PAGE 201

Once a splendid palace and still a spectacular ruin, Linlithgow Palace consists of ranges of buildings around a rectangular courtyard, and may include 12th-century work. There is a fine carved fountain in the courtyard, which has been recently restored and can be seen working. The palace was used by the Stewart monarchs, and has a long and eventful history.

A castle here was captured by Edward I of England in 1301 during the Wars of Independence, but was recaptured by the Scots driving a cart under the portcullis. It was rebuilt by James I at the beginning of the 15th century, and the work continued under James III and James IV. Mary, Queen of Scots, was born here in 1542. The palace was last used by Charles I in 1633, although his son, James, Duke of York, stayed here before succeeding to the throne in 1685. In 1746 General Hawley retreated here after being defeated by the Jacobites at Falkirk. The soldiers started fires to dry themselves, and the palace was accidentally set blaze. It was never restored.

The palace is said to be haunted by a 'Blue Lady', who walks from the entrance of the palace to the door of the nearby parish church of St Michael. This is said to take place in the morning, around nine o'clock, usually in April, although apparently also in September. The sound of the rustling of her dress has also been reported, and the apparition is said to vanish a few feet from the wall of the church.

Queen Margaret's bower, at the top of one of the stair-towers, is reputed to be haunted by the ghost of either Margaret Tudor, wife of James IV, or Mary of Guise, wife of James V, depending on the version (although neither seems likely). The ghost is said to be awaiting the return of its husband. One account describes the ghost as a 'White Lady', and had her presence also announced by a whiff of perfume.

There is a further story that the ghost of Mary, Queen of Scots, has been spotted, as if praying, in the chapel of the palace.

Map 4, 8L (Linlithgow). Off A803, in Linlithgow, West Lothian.
His Scot: Open all year, daily; closed 25/26 Dec and 1/2 Jan; fountain operates Jul-Aug, Sun. (01506 842896 / www.historic-scotland.gov.uk)

LINTHILL HOUSE

Standing near the meeting place of the Eye and Ale Waters, Linthill is an ancient house, with an L-plan tower house dating from the 17th century or earlier at its core. The building has a very steep roof pitch and corbiestepped gables, and enjoys fine views over Eyemouth and out to sea.

Linthill was a property of the Homes. On 12 August 1751, Margaret, the widow of Ninian Home of Linthill, was brutally murdered by her servant, Norman Ross. Ross had been robbing his mistress, and she caught him in the act; he attacked her and then jumped from a window, breaking his leg. Ross was caught and imprisoned, and Margaret died three days after the attack. Ross was tried and then executed, and he is the last man in Scotland also to be mutilated and hung in a gibbet afterwards. Margaret is buried in the apse of the old church at Bunkle, about three miles north of Duns, although her funeral procession set off without her body.

One story is that Ross's bloody hand prints from the murder cannot be washed off; and that unexplained banging can be heard coming from one of the upstairs rooms, along with the sound of an unseen carriage drawing up to the house.

Map 4, 12M (Linthill). Off B6355, 1.5 miles SW of Eyemouth, Linthill, Berwickshire, Borders.

LION AND UNICORN, THORNHILL

In an attractive whitewashed building, the Lion and Unicorn is a traditional country house hotel, which dates from the 17th century. There is a huge open fireplace, dated 1635, in one of the dining rooms. Visitors to the hotel have included Rob Roy MacGregor, when this part of Scotland was the domain of cattle drovers and thieves, and (in more settled times) Elizabeth Taylor in 1980.

The building is said to be haunted by a 'Green Lady', known as 'Annie', garbed in a green dress but apparently rarely witnessed. The bogle is described as a kind and happy ghost.

Map 4, 7L (Thornhill). On A873, 8 miles W of Stirling, Main Street, Thornhill, Stirling.
Hotel. (01786 850204 / www.lion-unicorn.co.uk)

LITTLEDEAN TOWER

Littledean Tower has a sinister tale regarding one of the Kerr lords of the 17th century. The ruinous castle consists of a rectangular block, to which was added a large distinctive D-plan tower, and the old stronghold dates from the 16th century.

A ghostly horseman, the spirit of one of the Kerr lords, the 'Deil of Littledean', is said sometimes to be seen near the castle, galloping madly through the woods and fields as if pursued by some unseen terror.

The story goes that he was a cruel man – as, in many other ghost stories, he was a persecutor of Covenanters – who scorned his wife and his servants, and spent his nights drinking and brawling with others of like mind. One night, while out riding after an argument with his wife, he came to a clearing in the woods, where there was the cottage of an attractive young woman. The laird began cavorting with the girl, and for some time the affair continued, although the laird was far from discreet: Kerr even gave the girl one of his wife's rings.

Then one night Kerr returned having been pursued by witches disguised as hares, which had launched themselves at him, and it was only by attacking them with his sword that he managed to fend them off. One hare had its front leg severed and the others had then abandoned the attack.

The paw had become trapped in his belt, but when he looked more closely he found that the paw had turned into a girl's arm, and on the finger was the ring he had given his lover. Kerr rode off and tried to dispose of the arm, but he met his erstwhile lover, finding that she had her arm severed. The girl, revealed as a witch, cursed him, telling him he would never be free of her.

Kerr tried in vain to get rid of the arm – stabbing it, throwing it away or even burning it could not rid him of it. Then one morning Kerr did not appear. On investigation, he was found dead, throttled, finger marks clawed around his neck.

Thomas Wilkie, who died in 1838, wrote of the *Scottish Hare Witch*, regarding a Harry Gilles of Littledean (although no family of that name apparently owned the tower). In his tale the laird has an encounter with hares, severing a paw, which then turns into a woman's arm. He was then able to identify a witch because she had a bleeding stump which matched the limb that he had severed. The story of the 'Deil of Littledean' seems to be based on this tale.

Andrew Kerr of Littledean was one of the Commissioners of a witchcraft accusation in 1662 (about the time of the story), regarding a Bessie Morrison and Grizel Murray, but they had already confessed to witchcraft.

Map 4, 11N (Littledean). Off A699, 6.5 miles W of Kelso, Littledean, Borders.

LOCH LEVEN HOTEL, BALLACHULISH

In a fine loch-side spot hemmed in by mountains, the hostelry was established here in the 17th century as a coaching inn and stands at a crossing point at Ballachulish of Loch Leven. The ferry was originally a rowing boat which plied the narrow sound, although this has since been replaced by a bridge.

The building is said to have a ghost, witnessed in a haunted room as well as in the public bar and the function suite.

Map 1, 4I (Ballachulish). On A82, 1.5 miles W of Onich, North Ballachulish, Loch Leven, Highland.
Hotel. (01855 821236 / www.lochlevenhotel.co.uk)

LOCH OF LEYS

Once on an island which has since been drained, nothing remains of a castle of the Burnetts. Alexander Burnett of Leys married Janet Hamilton in 1543, and acquired a sizeable dowry of church lands. With this new wealth, the couple built nearby Crathes Castle (also see that entry), and abandoned Leys.

The old castle at Loch of Leys was reputedly haunted. Alexander Burnett fell in love with Bertha, a relative who was staying with his family. His mother, Agnes, was dismayed for she had other plans for her son and she poisoned Bertha. But Bertha did not rest after her death, and Agnes was apparently frightened to death by Bertha's spectre – or perhaps by her own conscience.

A phantom is said to still appear on the anniversary of Bertha's death.

Map 2, 11G (Loch of Leys). Off A980, 1 mile N of Banchory, Aberdeenshire.

LOCHAILORT INN

The Lochailort Inn was said to be haunted, and manifestations included the apparition of a woman in a blue dress. There has been an inn on the site from 1650, but after a fire in 1994 and the rebuilding of the hotel, there have been no further reported disturbances.

Ghostly bagpipes are allegedly heard in the glen from a phantom piper of the Jacobite Rising of 1745-46.

Map 1, 3H (Lochailort). By A830, 22 miles W of Fort William, Lochailort, Highland.
Hotel. (01687 470208 / www.lochailortinn.co.uk)

LOCHBUIE   ILLUS PAGE 201

In a beautiful situation on a rocky crag by the seashore at Lochbuie, Moy Castle is a plain and somewhat dour tower house, which is ruinous but complete to the wallhead. The castle was abandoned in 1752 for nearby Lochbuie House, a large Georgian mansion with later wings. Lochbuie was long a property of the MacLaines, who held the property into the 20th century.

The then chief, and his son and heir, Ewen of the Little Head, fought in 1538 over the latter's marriage settlement. Ewen was decapitated in the subsequent battle in Glen More (see that entry), and his ghost, the headless horseman, is said to have been seen riding the glen when one of the MacLaines is about to die or misfortune is going to strike. Sometimes the bogle is said to be accompanied by the phantom of a black hunting dog.

Indeed the dog is also said to have been witnessed at Lochbuie House, reportedly being both heard and seen.

Map 3, 3K (Lochbuie). Off A849, 10 miles SW of Craignure, Lochbuie (Moy), Mull.
View from exterior.

LOCHHOUSE TOWER

Lochhouse is a strong tower house, dating from the 16th century, and a property of the Johnstones of Corehead. The tower was restored from ruin in about 1980 and is occupied.

The tower is reputedly haunted by the ghost of Lillias Johnstone, the beautiful sister of one of the lairds. She fell in love with Walter French of nearby Frenchland Tower. Her brother and French argued, leading to a murderous quarrel during which Johnstone was slain. French fled abroad and, when he returned, he married a daughter of Maxwell of Breckonside.

Lillias would take no other man, and after her death her ghost returned to haunt Lochhouse.

Map 4, 8O (Lochhouse). Off A701, 1 mile S of Moffat, Lochhouse, Dumfries and Galloway.

LOCHLEVEN CASTLE

ILLUS PAGE 201

Standing on an island in the picturesque Loch Leven, the castle consists of a tower house and courtyard, dating from the 14th century. Andrew of Wyntoun wrote his *Original Chronicle of Scotland* at the priory of St Serf's on the largest island in the loch.

During the Wars of Independence, having been seized by the English, the castle was stormed by William Wallace, who swam out to the island and surprised the garrison.

Mary, Queen of Scots, was imprisoned here from 1567 until she escaped the next year. She signed her 'abdication' here, although it is not clear how willing she was to do so, and she is said to have miscarried during this period.

Her ghost reputedly still haunts the castle, one of more than a dozen places she is said to haunt.

Map 4, 9L (Lochleven). Off B996, 1 mile E of Kinross, Loch Leven, Perthshire.
His Scot: Open Apr-Oct, daily – includes boat trip from Kinross. (07778 040483 (mobile) / www.historic-scotland.gov.uk)

LOCHNELL HOUSE

Lochnell House is a large baronial mansion, added to and extended down the centuries, although it incorporates part of a 17th-century block in one wing. Lochnell was built by the Campbell family, but suffered a serious fire about 1859, and only part was subsequently restored. At Ardchattan Priory (also see that entry) is the Lochnell Aisle, which dates from 1620 and is where many of the Campbells were buried. Lochnell is now held by the (Douglas Blair) Cochrane Earl of Dundonald.

The house is said to have had a brownie (possibly a 'Green Lady' or gruagach), and ghostly music has reportedly been heard here.

Map 3, 4J (Lochnell). Off A828, 4 miles N of Oban, Lochnell, Argyll.

LOCHRANZA

Set in a lovely spot to the north of Arran, the village is said to be haunted by a phantom piper, reported to be the ghost of a man who died in the hills above Lochranza. The unexplained sounds of pipes are reputed to have been heard several times in the area.

Among the many attractions in the village are Lochranza Castle, a fine ruinous stronghold, and the Isle of Arran Distillery.

Map 3, 4M (Lochranza). Off A841, 10 miles N of Brodick, Lochranza, Isle of Arran, Ayrshire.

LOGIE HOUSE, DUNDEE

Nothing survives of an old mansion, which was demolished at the beginning of the 20th century, a property of the Read family from a least a hundred years earlier.

The mansion was thought to be haunted by a 'Black Lady', reputedly an Indian princess captured by one of the family while they were working for the East India Company. Read had brought her to Logie, but kept her imprisoned, and there she died.

Her ghost was then reported to have haunted the area.

Map 4, 10K (Dundee). Off A85 or A923, 1 mile S of Dundee Law, Dundee.

Linlithgow Palace (page 196)

Lochbuie (page 199)

Lochleven Castle (page 200)

Lunan Lodge (page 204)

Meggernie Castle (page 209)

Meldrum House (page 210)

LORDSCAIRNIE CASTLE

Once standing on an islet in a loch, Lordscairnie Castle is a stark ruinous tower, dating from the 15th century and later. This was a property of the Lindsay Earls of Crawford, and was probably built by Alexander, the 4th Earl, 'Earl Beardie', also known as the 'Tiger Earl'.

His ghost can reputedly be seen playing cards here with the Devil on the stroke of midnight on New Years' Eve – although this may be a translation from Glamis (see that entry and also Finavon Castle).

There are also stories of a great treasure being buried at Lordscairnie.

Map 4, 10K (Lordscairnie). Off A913 or A914, 3 miles NW of Cupar, Lordscairnie, Fife.

LOUDOUN CASTLE

Loudoun Castle, a large ruined castellated mansion, incorporates an old tower house into the impressive building. The property was owned by the Campbells, one of whom was John Campbell, Chancellor of Scotland and Earl of Loudoun from 1641. The castle was used by Belgian troops during World War II, but was accidentally torched and gutted in 1941. The ruin is now the centre piece of a theme park.

There is a story of an underground tunnel leading from Loudoun to Cessnock Castle.

Loudoun was reputedly haunted by a 'Grey Lady', who was apparently often seen before its destruction in 1941, and is said to have been witnessed since. The ghost of a hunting dog, with glowing eyes, is also believed by some to roam the area.

There are also tales of a ghostly piper, as well as the apparition of a monk, who can allegedly be heard saying 'Pax Vobiscum' (Latin for 'Peace be with you').

Map 4, 7N (Loudoun). Off A77, 4 miles E of Kilmarnock, 1 mile N of Galston, Loudoun, Ayrshire.
Loudoun Castle Park open, Apr-Aug: check days with park. (01563 822296 / www.loudouncastle.co.uk)

LUFFNESS HOUSE

Standing by the sea near the picturesque village of Aberlady, Luffness House consists of an old tower house, although parts date from the 13th century, with later additions and modifications. It was once a large strong and splendid castle.

The property was given to the church in memory of Sir David Lindsay, who was slain while on crusade, and a Carmelite friary was built nearby in his memory before 1293. Some of the church survives, in which is the weathered the stone effigy slab of a crusader, probably of the founder himself. The property passed to the Hepburn Earls of Bothwell after the Reformation, and was visited by Mary, Queen of Scots. Luffness was sold to the Hope Earls of Hopetoun in 1739, and remains with their descendants.

One strange story is that the massive door of one of the angle towers – the only way into the chamber – is said to have locked itself. When the room was investigated through one of the gunloops, the key was found to be on a table in the middle of the room. There was no other way into the room.

Map 4, 10L (Luffness). Off A198, 1 mile E of Aberlady, Luffness, East Lothian.

LUNAN LODGE, MONTROSE

ILLUS PAGE 202

Set on a hill with excellent views across Lunan Bay, Lunan Lodge is an attractive building, first built as a manse and dating from the 18th century. The lodge stands in two acres of secluded grounds, and has long had a reputation for being haunted

There are many reported manifestations, including a pretty maid spotted as often as three times a week, a man in plus fours who is reputed to shout at guests, a stable boy, and a presence witnessed on the stairs. Other activity is reputed to include bangs and clanks, often heard at night, and unexplained singing coming from unoccupied areas.

Map 4, 11J (Lunan Lodge). Off A92, 3 miles S of Montrose, N of Lunan, Angus.
B&B. (01241 830679 / www.lunanlodge.co.uk)

A paranormal investigation was undertaken in December 2006 and in February 2007 by Ghost Finders (www.ghostfinders.co.uk/lunan_lodge.html) and by Ghost Hunters Scotland (www.ghosthunters.org.uk).

LUNDIN LINKS HOTEL

Lundin Links Hotel dates from 1898, and is a fine Tudor-style building; it replaced an earlier inn on the site, which dated from the early 17th century.

The building is said to be haunted by the spirit of Mrs Cameron, a former hotel housekeeper in the 1920s or '30s, who lived (and died) in Room 22. The story goes that her bogle makes the journey from this room to the reception area in order to check everything in the hotel is in order. Although no apparition is seen, the sounds of disembodied footsteps have often been heard, along with sounds of jangling keys; lights have also been mysteriously turned off or on, and windows opened or closed.

Her ghost is believed to be a good-hearted bogle.

Map 4, 10L (Lundin Links (L.Links)). Off A915, Largo Road, Lundin Links, Fife.
Hotel. (01333 320207 / www.lundin-links-hotel.co.uk)

MACDUFF'S CASTLE

Macduff's Castle, a ruinous but picturesque stronghold by the sea, was held by the Wemyss family. In 1666 the Countess of Sutherland, who was a daughter of the 2nd Earl of Wemyss, lodged her children here during the plague in Edinburgh.

The castle is said to be named after the MacDuff Thanes or Earls of Fife, who may have had an older stronghold here, and other owners included the Livingstones, the Hamiltons, and the Colvilles, before the property returned to the Wemyss family in 1630.

The ghost of a woman, the 'Grey Lady' reputedly haunts the castle. She is thought to be Mary Sibbald, who ran off with a gypsy laddie but was accused of thievery. A court found her guilty, and she was sentenced to be whipped, but the punishment appears to have killed the poor woman.

Her ghost is also said to haunt Wemyss Caves, as the trial took place in the Court Cave.

Map 4, 9L (Macduff's). Off A955, E of East Wemyss, Macduff's Castle, Fife.
View from exterior.

MACHERMORE CASTLE

Machermore Castle, a tall and imposing mansion with towers, turrets and dormer windows, incorporates an old tower house. There is a tale that the castle was originally to be built on higher ground at another site, but the foundations were mysterious removed each night, leading the laird to believe that there was super-natural intervention. So the castle was built at its present spot. Reputedly, a hoard of gold, hidden in a kettle, is secreted somewhere under the floor of the castle.

Machermore was held by the MacDowalls, although by 1866 the property had passed to the Dunbars. The building is now used as a nursing home.

At one time the castle was said to be haunted by a 'White Lady', although it is reputed that few have ever spotted the ghost. In the chamber known as Duncan's Room was said to be a bloody handprint, which could not be removed from the floor, whatever was done: even replacing the floor boards did not work as the hand print returned. This room was also the scene of other manifestations, such as the rustling of a dress, mysterious footsteps, and noises like a drawer being opened and shut.

Map 3, 6P (Machermore). Off A75, 1 mile SE of Newton-Stewart, Machermore, Dumfries and Galloway.
Nursing home. (01671 402 216 / www.machermore.co.uk)

MAIDEN'S WELL, GLENQUEY

The Maiden's Well, a small pool and a stone, stands by the old drove road which led up from Dollar across the Ochil hills to Glendevon. The well is said to be haunted by the spectre of a young woman, which by day resided in the well but at night would venture forth. Anyone foolish enough to sleep near the well was risking death as the girl's bogle would steal away their life. One story is that the maid in question was imprisoned in Castle Campbell, and was only occasionally allowed to venture out of the old fortress's walls to the well to drink.

Map 4, 8L (Glenquey). Off A823 or A91, on track between Castle Campbell and Glendevon, 1.5 miles N of Castle Campbell, 0.5 miles S of Glenquey Reservoir, Clackmannan.

MAINS CASTLE, DUNDEE

Located in Cairds Park, Mains Castle is an impressive courtyard castle, dating from the 15th century with ranges of buildings forming three sides of a courtyard, while the last side is completed by a high wall. The property was held by the Douglas Earls of Angus from the 14th century, but passed in 1530 to the Grahams, and they built most of the existing castle. One of the family, Sir David Graham, nephew of Cardi-nal Beaton, was executed for plotting to restore Catholicism to Scotland in around 1592. The property was sold to the Erskines in the 19th century, then to the Cairds, before being given to the City of Dundee. Although ruined and derelict for many years, it has been restored and part is used as a restaurant.

The building is said by some to be haunted, and manifestations are believed to include unexplained voices, running feet, and the sound of furniture being moved.

Map 4, 10K (Dundee). Off A929, to N of Dundee, E of Caird Park, Mains, Dundee.
Restaurant. (01382 456797)

A paranormal investigation was undertaken in March 2008 by Ghost Finders (www.ghostfinders.co.uk/mains_castle.html)

MAINS CASTLE, EAST KILBRIDE

Mains Castle was a property of the Lindsays of Dunrod until 1695. One of the family, along with Kirkpatrick of Closeburn, helped 'mak siccar' by slaying John Comyn after he had been stabbed by Robert the Bruce in 1306. A later Lindsay, while curling on the ice of a nearby loch, was angered by one of his servants, and had a hole cut in the ice and the man drowned by forcing him under the ice.

The castle is reputedly haunted by the ghost of a woman strangled by her jealous husband after he found her with another man; the story goes that she was the sister of the 12th-century King of Scots, William the Lyon. Her not-so-gallant lover escaped out of a window on knotted sheets, leaving her to her fate, and she was too slow and was throttled by her furious husband.

Her apparition, and that of the knotted sheet, are both said to have been witnessed.

Map 4, 7M (Mains). Off B873, 1 mile N of East Kilbride, Mains, Lanarkshire.

MANDERSTON

Standing in 56 acres of the gardens and policies, Manderston is a fine Edwardian mansion, part of which dates from the original house of 1790, and the building features the only silver staircase in the world.

The present mansion stands on the site of a castle.

Manderston was a property of the Homes. Sir George Home of Manderston was involved in a witchcraft accusation involving his wife and Alexander Hamilton (also see Penkaet Castle). The lady was cleared, but Hamilton implicated many others and himself, and he was executed in Edinburgh in 1630.

The house was virtually rebuilt between 1903-5 for Sir James Miller, a millionaire racehorse owner, whose family had acquired the property in 1890. The Channel 4 series *The Edwardian House* was filmed at Manderston.

Some stories have the house haunted by the apparition of a woman on the main stairs, the ghost identified in one account as Lady Eveline, Sir James's wife.

This tale, however, has been refuted.

Map 4, 11M (Manderston). Off A6105, 1.5 miles E of Duns, Manderston, Borders.
Open mid May-end Sep, Thu and Sun; Bank Holiday Mons (late May and Aug); other times group visits by appt. (01361 882636 / www.manderston.co.uk)

MANSFIELD CASTLE HOTEL, TAIN

Mansfield Castle, which is now a fine hotel, was probably first built in the 1870s for Thomas Darling, who had purchased the property from the Ross or Rose family. In 1890 the property was bought by the Fowlers, and the owner was Provost of Tain for some 12 years. The Fowlers extended and refurbished the house inside and out, with the addition of the tall tower. Mr Fowler died in 1930, and then his wife some eight years later.

It is her ghost that is said to haunt the building, although the bogle is reputed to be interested in the welfare of the house and to be more active when changes are being made.

The ghost is reported not to be frightening or unpleasant.

Map 2, 7D (Tain). Off A9 (B9174), Scotsburn Road, Tain, Ross.
Hotel. (01862 892052 / www.mansfieldcastle.co.uk)

MARLFIELD HOUSE

Marlfield House, a somewhat stark symmetrical mansion, was remodelled in the mid 18th century and later, possibly by William Adam, but is said to incorporate part of an ancient castle. The property was held by the Bennetts in the 17th century, but passed to the Nisbets.

The house is reputed to be haunted by a ghost which pushes past people in one of the passageways. The bogle is said to have been active in recent years.

Map 4, 11N (Marlfield). Off B6401, 5.5 miles S of Kelso, Marlfield, Borders.

MARY KING'S CLOSE, EDINBURGH

Lying just off the Royal Mile beneath the City Chambers, which was designed by the architects John and Robert Adam in 1753, lies Mary King's Close, the remains of a narrow old street, bordered by tenements on each side, which formerly rose to some seven storeys. The Close is thought by some to be called after the daughter of Alexander King, the owner of the place and a wealthy advocate, and a woman named Mary King did live here in the middle of the 17th century.

The inhabitants of the Close were devastated by plague in 1645, and the buildings were sealed off. Some years later, because of overcrowding elsewhere in the Old Town, the close was reoccupied, but had reputedly become haunted. Apparitions were seen frequently, including disembodied men and headless animals, and eventually the buildings were abandoned again. The upper floors were then demolished, while the lower part was sealed over, and the City Chambers were constructed on top.

The spirit of the young girl, who looks around the age of five or six and is clad in a dirty dress, is said to haunt a chamber in the complex, and she has been called 'Annie' by visitors (many toys have been left for her in the room where she is said to be witnessed). Other ghosts are reputed to be that of a dog, as well as that of a tall thin woman, clad in a black dress, witnessed quite recently.

Other disturbances include cameras flashing for no apparent reason, and not working in parts of the close.

Map 4, 9L (Edinburgh). Off A1, 2 Warriston's Close, High Street, under City Chambers, Edinburgh. **Open all year, daily except 25 Dec. (08702 430160 / www.realmarykingsclose.com)**

Paranormal investigations have been undertaken by Ghost Finders (www.ghostfinders.co.uk)

Featured in Living TV's Most Haunted, *series four (2004) and* Most Haunted Live, *(2006) and the Sci-Fi Channel's* Ghost Hunters International

MARY QUEEN OF SCOTS HOUSE, JEDBURGH

Set by a formal garden which is now a public park, Mary Queen of Scots House is an altered 16th-century T-plan tower house of three storeys. Mary, Queen of Scots, stayed in a chamber on the second floor. She was very ill and lay for many days near to death after her visit to James Hepburn, Earl of Bothwell, at Hermitage Castle (also see that entry) in 1566. Above Mary's chamber is another similar room where the Queen's Four Marys are thought to have stayed. The building is open to the public, and houses a museum displaying exhibits relating to the visit by Mary to Jedburgh.

The building may be haunted, at least according to a well-known medium and psychic investigator.

Map 4, 11N (Jedburgh). Off A68, in Jedburgh, Borders.
Open early Mar-Nov, daily. (01835 863331 / www.scotborders.gov.uk/outabout/visit/ museums/)

MARYCULTER HOUSE

Picturesquely situated on the south bank of the Dee, Maryculter House Hotel is located in five acres of woodland and landscaped gardens. Although altered and extended, it is substantially a 17th-century house of the Menzies family, who held the property from 1535 or earlier. The house stands on the site of a preceptory (priory) of the Knights Templar, founded by Walter Bisset around 1230. Vaulted cellars from the preceptor's (prior's) house are built into the hotel, notably under the cocktail bar. The foundations of the nearby Templar's church and adjacent burial ground, which was used by the parish until 1782, can also be traced and are located opposite reception car park.

One of the Templars was Godfrey Wedderburn of Wedderhill. Godfrey went on Crusade, but he was badly wounded and was only nursed back to health by a beautiful Saracen woman, with whom he formed a close but chaste bond. When he had recovered, he returned to Maryculter.

Years later the Saracen woman travelled to Maryculter to find her old friend. The preceptor did not believe such a relationship, even an innocent one, could be permitted, and Godfrey was forced to kill himself. The Saracen woman plunged a knife into her own chest, but as she did so called down a curse – and a lightning bolt struck down the Preceptor, and fried him, leaving a scorched hollow where he had been. This hollow, the 'Thunder Hole' (which was formerly much deeper) can still be seen.

It is said that Godfrey and the Saracen were buried side by side, but that his apparition returns to ride over the hill of Kingcausie, while the ghost of the beautiful Saracen woman has been seen in the woods.

Map 2, 11G (Maryculter). Off B9077, South Deeside Road, 8 miles SW of Aberdeen.
Hotel. (01224 732124 / www.maryculterhousehotel.com)

MEDWYN HOUSE

Medwyn House, a fine mansion, incorporates parts of a 15th-century building, which was used as a coaching inn, known as the Brighouse Inn (the main road to Edinburgh used to follow a course nearer to the house). One innkeeper, James Wedderspuine, is reputed to have been involved in the murder of David Rizzio. The lands were purchased in three lots from 1802, and in the 19th century Medwyn was a property of the Forbes family, and was home to John Hay Forbes, Lord Medwyn and a Senator of the College of Justice, who was an eminent judge and died in 1854. The original building was developed and extended by Lord Medwyn into an attractive mansion, and the house was put up for sale quite recently for offers of more than £975,000.

The sounds of ghostly horses and a coach are said to have been heard near the house.

Map 4, 9M (Medwyn). Off A702, 0.25 miles NW of West Linton, Medwyn, Borders.

MEGGERNIE CASTLE ILLUS PAGE 202

In a scenic location, Meggernie Castle, a handsome 16th-century tower house, was built by Colin Campbell of Glenlyon, but passed to the Menzies of Culdares, then to the Stewarts of Cardney.

The rather grim ghost story dates from when the castle was held by the Menzies family. One of the lairds had a beautiful wife, but he was a jealous husband and suspected his wife of straying and of showing undue interest in other men. In a fit of rage, he attacked and then murdered the poor woman in one of the upper chambers in the ancient part of the castle. Menzies chopped her body in two, hoping to dispose of it later, and hid her remains under the floorboards, or disposed of them in a chest in a closet, depending on the version. Menzies then left for the continent, and when he returned excused his wife's disappearance by claiming she had drowned when they were away.

He then returned to the gruesome task of disposing of her body. He managed to bury her lower half, but was then apparently murdered himself, perhaps by one of his wife's family or friends.

From then on odd things began to happen at Meggernie, and the chamber where the manifestations were centred is said to have been abandoned at one time. The apparition of the top half of a woman's body, seen in a pink glow, was said to haunt the upper floors; while the lower half, in a blood-stained dress, was reputedly seen on the ground floor, and in the grounds near the family burial ground, including an avenue of trees. There were recorded sightings in 1869 and in 1928, and also the sounds of disembodied footsteps and mysterious banging and knockings, which have been reported in recent times.

During renovation, the upper bones of a skeleton were reportedly discovered, but the haunting continued even after the skeleton was buried.

The ghost is also said to have hotly kissed visitors to Meggernie in 1869, waking them from sleep, but this particular story was a matter of some debate, and doubt was thrown on the credibility of at least one of the witnesses.

Map 4, 7J (Meggernie). Off B846, 8 miles N of Killin, Meggernie, Perthshire.

MEGGINCH CASTLE

Surrounded by woodlands, evocative Megginch Castle has been a property of the Drummonds from 1646, although the building dates from the 15th century. There are extensive gardens with 1000-year-old yews, a 16th-century rose garden, kitchen garden, topiary and a 16th-century physic garden. The courtyard of the castle was used for filming part of the film version of *Rob Roy* with Liam Neeson in 1994. This is a little ironic as the Drummonds of Megginch tried to hunt down Rob Roy MacGregor, but were – of course – unsuccessful.

One of the rooms in the old part of the castle is said to be haunted by the whispering of two gossiping women, coming from a former nursery. The story is that the whispering is mostly heard after guests have visited, and that the sounds stop as soon as anyone tries to approach or when the door to the chamber is opened.

Map 4, 9K (Megginch). About 8 miles E of Perth, E of A85, Megginch, Perthshire.
Castle not open; gardens open Apr-Oct, Wed only; Jul, daily; other times by prior arrangement. (01821 642222)

MELDRUM HOUSE

ILLUS PAGE 202

Standing in 15 acres of landscaped park land, Meldrum House is a sprawling mansion with round towers. It incorporates an ancient castle, dating from as early as the 13th century, and part of the basement is vaulted. Meldrum was a property of the Meldrum family until about 1450 when it passed to the Setons, then from 1670 to the Urquharts, then latterly to the Duffs. The house was altered down the centuries, including removing the upper storey, and is now used as a hotel and golf club.

The house is traditionally believed to be haunted by a 'Green Lady', who has reputedly been seen many times. Recent reports, however, have her clad in white, or this may be another ghost, and she has been identified by some as Isabella Douglas. Sightings of this apparition have been reported several times, as recently as 1985 when the bogle reputedly gave a male guest a cold kiss during a thunder storm. Another sighting was of the apparition walking along an upstairs corridor. It was believed by some that this spectre only appeared to children when they were alone. Afterwards, the children would report that a lady in a white dress had been taking care of them.

One account states that the ghost behaves differently when content, moving slowly and serenely, or when angry, when it is much quicker and more chilling (and showing some characteristics of a gruagach). It is also said by some that this bogle (or perhaps another) scratches the chest of men staying in Room 3, provided they are from one of three families that owned Meldrum, namely Meldrum, Seton or Urquhart (although no mention is made of the Duffs, in this account).

Map 2, 11F (Meldrum). Off A947, 1 mile N of Oldmeldrum, Aberdeenshire.
Hotel. (01651 872294 / www.meldrumhouse.co.uk)

MELGUND CASTLE

An impressive and interesting building, Melgund Castle is an L-plan tower house and hall-block, which dates from the 16th century. Although ruinous for a long time, the main part has been restored in recent years.

Melgund was held by the Cramonds, but the property passed to the Beatons. The castle was built by Cardinal David Beaton, Archbishop of St Andrews and Chancellor of Scotland, and Margaret Ogilvie, his mistress (or wife: they married before he was made a Cardinal and they had seven children together); there is a panel at Melgund bearing their heraldic shields. Beaton was murdered on 29 May 1546 at St Andrews Castle (also see that entry), although Marion continued to live here after his murder, until she herself died in 1575; she is buried in the Ogilvie Aisle of Kinnell Church, near Friockheim (and is said to haunt Claypotts Castle, although this seems unlikely – see that entry). Beaton, himself, remained unburied for more than seven months after his death, preserved in a barrel of brine in one of the vaults at St Andrews Castle, until he was finally laid to rest in a 'dunghill'.

Melgund passed to the Gordon Marquis of Huntly in the 17th century, then to the Maules, and then to the Murrays, later Murray Kynmonds, then to the Elliot Earls of Minto and Viscounts Melgund, whose descendants held it until 1990.

The ghost of Cardinal Beaton reputedly haunts the castle, one of several places his spirit is said to frequent (see Ethie Castle, St Andrews Castle, Balfour House and Blebo House).

Map 2, 10I (Melgund). Off B9134, 4.5 miles SW of Brechin, Melgund, Angus.

MELLERSTAIN

Mellerstain is a magnificent castellated mansion, designed by William and Robert Adam, and dating from the 18th century. There are fine interiors and a terraced garden, and the house stands in 200 acres of parkland.

The lands of Mellerstain are mentioned in 1451, and were held by several families before in 1642 going to the Baillies. The family were Covenanters and were ruined after the Restoration, although their fortune was restored with the overthrow of James VII. Mellerstain was built for George Baillie of Jerviswood, and was home to Lady Grisell Baillie (nee Hume), well known for her *Household Book*. The property is now owned by the Baillie-Hamiltons, Earls of Haddington.

Ghostly footsteps have been reported coming from empty rooms, and one story is that a guest woke to find the apparition of a woman wearing a cap, leaning over his bed. The manifestations are said to be friendly rather than frightening.

Map 4, 10N (Mellerstain). Off A6089, 5.5 miles NW of Kelso, Mellerstain, Borders.
Open Easter weekend (Fri-Mon), then May, Jun & Sep, Sun, Wed and Bank Hol Mon; Jul & Aug, Sun, Mon, Wed & Thu; Oct, Sun only; groups at other times by appt. (01573 410225 / www.mellerstain.com)

MELROSE ABBEY   ILLUS PAGE 219

An elegant and picturesque ruin, Melrose Abbey was founded as a Cistercian house by David I about 1136, and was dedicated to the Blessed Virgin Mary. The church is particularly well preserved, while the domestic buildings and the cloister, except for the Abbot's House, are very ruinous.

The Abbey was sacked by the English in 1322, 1385 and 1545. The heart of Robert the Bruce is buried in the nave, as are the remains of Alexander II and Joanna, his wife, as well as many of the powerful Douglas family. Sir Michael Scott of Balwearie, the 13th-century scholar and reputed warlock, is also said to be interred on the south side of the chancel. The area is supposed to radiate unease.

The spirit of a monk was reputed to haunt the cloister area. This wicked fellow is said to have led a life of violence and sin, despite his vows, and to have become a vampire, who returned to his tomb each night after venturing abroad for blood. The monk apparently attacked the abbess of a nearby convent.

He was finally laid to rest when another monk waited for him to emerge from the tomb, then beheaded him with an axe.

Map 4, 10N (Melrose). Off A7 or A68, in Melrose, Borders.
His Scot: Open all year, daily; closed 25/26 Dec and 1/2 Jan. (01896 822562 / www.historic-scotland.gov.uk)

MELVILLE CASTLE

Standing in a 50-acre wooded estate, Melville Castle is a symmetrical castellated mansion of three storeys with round corner towers, designed by James Playfair and dating from the 18th century. The mansion replaced an old castle, which had been visited by Mary, Queen of Scots.

The property took its name from a Norman baron called de Malavilla in the 12th century, and was held by the Melvilles, and then later by the Rennies, before passing by marriage to Henry Dundas, 1st Viscount Melville. Dundas was a very powerful man in Scotland, and there is a memorial to him in the gardens of St Andrew Square in Edinburgh. Melville Castle was used as a hotel but, although only abandoned in the 1980s, soon became derelict. In recent years, the building has been restored and became a hotel again.

The castle is reputedly haunted by the spirit of possibly Elizabeth Rennie, Dundas's wife, or perhaps another spectre of Mary, Queen of Scots. During renovation, an apparition of a woman was seen to walk through a wall, later found to be a blocked-up door. An apparition is also said to have been witnessed going through the entrance to the library bar.

Map 4, 9M (Melville). Off A7, 1.5 miles W of Dalkeith, Melville, Midlothian.
Hotel. (0131 654 0088)

MELVILLE GRANGE

The farmhouse here is said to be haunted, and the apparition of a girl dressed in white has been reported. The story goes back 700 years (perhaps to the 1330s) to when there was a farm (grange) here, belonging to Newbattle Abbey. The grange was used as a rendezvous by a young noble women, Margaret Heron of nearby Gilmerton, and a monk (or the abbot) from the abbey. The girl's father, Sir John, learned of their dallying, and forbad them to meet. The girl met the monk for the last time at the farm to part from him forever, but her father followed her and, when she would not respond to his threats, burnt the grange down around them, killing them both in the flames. The events are recounted in 'The Grey Brother', a poem written by Sir Walter Scott, and Margaret is also said to haunt Newbattle Abbey (see that entry), where her apparition is described as a 'Grey Lady'.

Map 4, 9M (Dalkeith). Off A720, 1 mile W of Dalkeith, Melville, Edinburgh.

MENIE HOUSE

Menie House, a two-storey Jacobean-style house of about 1840, incorporates an 18th-century house at one corner, and stands on the site of a 14th- or 15th-century castle. Menie was long a property of the Forbes family. A prestigious (and controversial) golf course and holiday complex are to be built here by Donald Trump.

The castle is said to be haunted by a 'Green Lady', the bogle of a housemaid, who is reported to have been seen in the basement of the old part of the house and is always witnessed wearing a green dress.

Map 2, 12F (Menie). Off A92, 2 miles north of Balmedie, Aberdeenshire.
Accommodation available, sporting estate. (01358 742885/743092 / www.meniehouse.com)

MERCAT CROSS, EDINBURGH

It was at Edinburgh's Mercat Cross, parts of which date from the 15th century, that ghostly apparitions are reported to have read the lists of dead at the Battle of Flodden, some months before the disastrous battle or on the eve in 1513, depending on the account. The list began with James IV, then went through the nobles and commoners. This was witnessed by a Richard Lawson, a merchant in the burgh, but the poor man collapsed on hearing his own name and appealed to be spared. If this was a warning, it remained unheeded, as was a similar portent at Linlithgow. James IV led his large army into England, and at Flodden was killed with 15 earls, 70 lords, hundreds of lairds and as many as 10,000 men.

Lawson is said to have survived the battle, despite the portent.

The sighting of the apparition of one of the old town guard, a Highlander with a grey beard, has been reported in Parliament Square.

Map 4, 9L (Edinburgh). Off A1, Royal Mile, W of St Giles Cathedral, Edinburgh.
Accessible at all times.

MINARD CASTLE

Set in fine countryside on the west side of Loch Fyne, Minard Castle is a grand baronial mansion, which dates from the 18th century, although then the house was known as Knockbuie and was held by the Campbells. The building was extended and remodelled with a new castellated front in the mid 19th century. By then it was a property of the Lloyds, who were related to the former Campbell owners, and they held the property until the 1940s. Minard became a hotel, but was sold to the Gayre family in 1974, and is now a private residence again.

The building is said by some to be haunted.

Map 3, 4L (Minard). Off A83, 8 miles NE of Lochgilphead, Minard Castle, Argyll.
B&B (Apr-Oct) and self-catering accommodation available. (01546 886272 / www.minardcastle.com)

A paranormal investigation was undertaken in November 2005 by Paranormal Investigation Scotland (www.paranormalinvestigationscotland.co.uk/minardcastletwo.htm)

MONALTRIE HOTEL, BALLATER

Standing on the north bank of the River Dee, the former hotel, a large Tudor-style building of about 1860 and later, was alleged to be haunted.

The hotel closed in recent years and the building has been converted into flats.

Map 2, 9G (Ballater). On A93, Bridge Square, Ballater, Aberdeenshire.

MONCRIEFFE ARMS, BRIDGE OF EARN

An old hotel here, which is now an elderly people's home, is said to be haunted. Manifestations are alleged to include the sound of footsteps on floorboards, even though areas are carpeted, and the sound of weeping coming from unoccupied areas, thought to be from one of the upstairs passages. In the 1970s the owner reported finding a bathroom door locked with sounds of someone having a bath, only to find some seconds later that the door was open and nobody was in the room.

Map 4, 9K (Bridge of Earn). Off A912, Bridge of Earn, Perthshire.

MONKTONHALL HOUSE, MUSSELBURGH

Monktonhall House, a small symmetrical mansion of three storeys, appears to date from the 18th century. This was presumably a property of the church at one time, but in the 17th century the lands were held by the Sharps of Stoneyhill and then by the Earls of Wemyss.

One story has the building haunted by the bogles of monks, and another manifestation is said to be the unexplained smell of cooking meat wafting through the building.

Map 4, 10M (Musselburgh). On B6415, to the S of Musselburgh, Monktonhall, East Lothian.

MONTGREENAN HOUSE

Montgreenan House, dating from 1817, replaced an older classical mansion, and was designed by Alexander 'Greek' Thompson. The house was built for the Glasgow family, who made their wealth through a shipping company based in the West Indies. The house has been used as a hotel since 1982.

One of the rooms of the house is said to be haunted, although the manifestations are reputed to be mischievous rather than frightening.

There was apparently a bishop's palace near the house, and the Abbot of Kilwinning was shot at the gate of that building in 1591.

Map 3, 6M (Montgreenan). Off A736, 3.5 miles NE of Kilwinning, Montgreenan, Ayrshire. **Hotel. (01294 850005 / www.montgreenanhotel.com)**

MONTROSE AIR STATION MUSEUM

Montrose airfield was established in 1913, making it one of the oldest in the country, and five years later was used for training American pilots. In World War II many others were trained here, including Commonwealth, Polish, Czech, American, Russian, Turkish and the Free French. The airfield was bombed by German bombers in 1940, and hangars and a mess were destroyed. The airfield was abandoned by the RAF in 1957

A museum, housed in the buildings, displays wartime memorabilia, comprising historic photographs, uniforms, mementoes and archive material. Aircraft are also on display, including a Seahawk 131, as well as a Bofors gun, a Commer airfield control van and Whirlwind XJ723.

The aerodrome is said to be haunted. There are several reports of a phantom biplane here, thought to be from a crash which happened soon after the airfield was opened, as well as the sound of an aeroplane being heard over the airfield when no craft are present.

Other manifestations include the apparition of an airman in flying gear, again reported several times, and the unexplained sounds of footsteps in and around the buildings, as well as the sound of a door handle rattling. During its time as a vehicle testing centre, doors were also said to open and close by themselves.

Map 2, 11I (Montrose). Off A92, Waldron Road, Broomfield, NW of Montrose on Links, Angus. **Open all year, Wed-Sun; parties other times by arrangement. (01674 678222 / www.rafmontrose.org.uk)**

A paranormal investigation was undertaken in June 2004 and in July 2005 by the Ghost Club (www.ghostclub.org.uk) and by Paranormal Research Scotland in 2008.

During the Ghost Club investigation, several people heard prolonged knocking, towards the end of the session. At first it was thought that this might be a ghostly manifestation until it was realised that one of the investigators was missing and had been locked in a toilet some time before.

MONYMUSK CASTLE

Monymusk Castle is a fine and impressive tower house, which dates from the 16th century (although parts may be much older), with later additions. The lands were originally owned by the priory of Monymusk, and the Monymusk Reliquary, a casket containing the relics of St Columba, was long kept at the priory. The Reliquary was carried before the Scottish army at Bannockburn in 1314, and is now held at in the

Museum of Scotland. The lands were held by the Forbes family after the Reformation, and then by the Grants from 1711.

The castle is said to have several ghosts, one being that of a man reading in the library, who would disappear when approached. There are also stories of a 'Grey Lady', who is alleged to appear from a cupboard in the nursery, check any children present and then leave, and the phantom of a pale lady, who crossed one of the upper rooms and bathroom. Another bogle is reputed to be the 'Party Ghost', a red-haired man, dressed in kilt, sporran, laced shirt and silver-buttoned jacket, that would apparently barge through party guests, and could later be heard laughing, joking and running on the stairs by guests in the upper chambers.

Map 2, 11G (Monymusk). Off B993, 6.5 miles SW of Inverurie, Monymusk, Aberdeenshire. **Walled garden, garden centre and cafe. Church open all year. (01467 651543 / www.monymusk.com)**

MOORINGS BAR, ABERDEEN

Located at Trinity Quay by Aberdeen harbour, the Moorings Bar was established in 1965, and was the first hostelry in Aberdeen to have a jukebox. The bar is reported to be haunted, and strange occurrences have been reported, such as the movement of objects including chairs, mops and a knife, taps being mysteriously turned off in the cellar, and doors being held closed although there is apparently nobody there. The apparition of a man, spotted apparently working in the cellar, is thought to be that of a Canadian airman called Ted who was employed at the bar.

An unfriendly disembodied voice has also been reported, which has been linked to the removal of a price list of the 1970s from a wall in the cellar, which is thought to have angered this particular bogle.

Map 2, 12G (Aberdeen). Off A956, Trinity Quay, off Virginia Street, Aberdeen. **Public bar. (01224 587602 / www.myspace.com/themooringsbar)**

MORRONE LODGE

The lodge, a substantial building with excellent views, was used for team-building exercises and outward-bound courses, but this has closed and the house has been converted for use as a dwelling.

The lodge is said to be haunted, and there are stories that apparitions were seen in the dormitories, described on one occasion as being spotted at the foot of a bed and described as a tall man in a dark jacket and with a large moustache. Unexplained movements and noises were also reported, coming from an upper but unoccupied bunk, by sleepers in the bed below. Sleepers also recalled feelings as if they were being forced down into their beds. Other reputed manifestations included unexplained noises, such as footsteps from unoccupied areas, and an uncomfortable and foreboding atmosphere.

Map 2, 8G (Morrone). Off A93, to the W of Braemar, Chapel Brae, Morrone, Aberdeenshire.

MUCHALLS CASTLE

Muchalls Castle was built by the Burnetts in the early 17th century and is an imposing courtyard castle, which incorporates earlier work. The uncrowned James VIII stayed here in 1716 during the Jacobite Rising, although by then the cause was deemed hopeless and he soon fled back to France.

The castle is thought to be haunted by the ghost of young female servant, a 'Green Lady', who is said to have been drowned in a cave used for smuggling at the Gin Shore (and a mile from Muchalls), which formerly could be reached by an underground stair from the wine-cellar. She had been awaiting her lover, one of the crew of a ship, in the cave, but fell into the water and was lost.

Her ghost, clad in a green gown, has reportedly been seen in one of the rooms, sitting in front of a mirror arranging her hair, one sighting being in the 1970s, when she was spotted in an old-fashioned lime-coloured dress; the ghost faded away when the room was entered. Another sighting, this time in 1906, had the ghost clad in a yellowish frock, although again the phantom was looking in a mirror. The room the ghost was observed in is also said to be especially cold at times. In a third sighting, the then owner saw the ghost cross the former dining room and then disappear into what appeared to be a cupboard. This was, however, later found to be the opening into a secret passage.

Map 2, 11H (Muchalls). Off A92, 4 miles NE of Stonehaven, Kincardine & Deeside.

MURDOSTOUN CASTLE

Set in 37 acres of grounds, Murdostoun Castle is a large house which incorporates an ancient keep and is now used as a hospital.

Murdostoun was once a property of the Scotts, and Sir Michael Scott, heir of Murdostoun, fought at the Battle of Halidon Hill in 1333, and was slain at Durham 13 years later. The property passed through other families until in 1856 was sold to Robert Stewart, Provost of Glasgow, who was responsible for getting Glasgow's water supply from Loch Katrine. Murdostoun was the first building to have electric light in Scotland.

The castle is said to be haunted by a 'Green Lady', seen in the East Dressing Room, although it has not apparently been witnessed for many years.

Map 4, 8M (Murdostoun). Off A71, 1 mile N of Newmains, Murdostoun Castle, Lanarkshire.

MURROES CASTLE

Built on sloping ground above the Sweet Burn, Murroes Castle is a fine tower house, with a long main block and a centrally projecting round tower with a conical roof. A low-roofed chamber is called the 'Goblin Hall'. Murroes was a property of the Fotheringhams from the 14th century, although by the end of the 19th century the house had been converted to house farm labourers. The castle was restored in 1942 and is occupied.

The castle is said to be haunted by a 'White Lady', known as the 'Lady in White'. The unexplained sounds of feasting are said to have been heard coming from the Goblin Hall when nobody is about.

Map 4, 10J (Murroes). Off B978, 2.5 miles N of Broughty Ferry, Murroes, Angus.

MUSEUM OF CHILDHOOD, EDINBURGH

One of the first museums of its kind, the Museum of Childhood was reopened in 1986 after major expansion and reorganisation. The museum has a fascinating and extensive collection of toys, games and belongings of children through the ages.

The museum, however, is said by some to have been built on the site of a building sealed up during the plague in Edinburgh, trapping woman and children inside and leaving them to die. During the night, the sounds of ghostly children weeping are reputed to sometimes be heard.

Map 4, 9L (Edinburgh). Off A1, 42 High Street (Royal Mile), Edinburgh.
Open all year, daily. (0131 529 4142 / www.cac.org.uk)

MUSEUM OF FLIGHT, EAST FORTUNE

The Museum of Flight, which is located on a former airship base and RAF airfield, has many points of interest, not least that it was from here that Airship R34 flew to New York and back during its record-breaking flight of 1919. Aircraft on display include a Supermarine Spitfire Mk 16, De Haviland Sea Venom, Hawker Sea Hawk and Comet, as well as a Concorde.

There are several accounts of ghostly activity at the museum, including the smell of tobacco smoke in one of the hangars, even although nobody has been smoking. Less frequently, the apparition of a man in flying gear has also been spotted, in different hangars. Unpleasant feelings have also been recorded in many places.

Map 4, 10M (Haddington). Off A1, 3 miles NE of Haddington, East Fortune Airfield, East Lothian.
Open Apr-Oct, daily (0131 247 4238 / www.nms.ac.uk/flight)

A paranormal investigation was undertaken in August 2005 and in June 2006 by the Ghost Club (www.ghostclub.org.uk)

MUSEUM OF TRANSPORT, GLASGOW

The museum, housed in the 1920s' Kelvin Hall, features a reconstruction of a Glasgow street from the 1930s, with the Regal Cinema, underground station, and reconstructed shop fronts. Other exhibits include buses, and trams, which were last used in 1962, as well as Scottish-made cars, fire engines, horse-drawn vehicles, cycles and motorcycles, a walk-in car showroom and steam locomotives.

Parts of the museum have a reputation for being haunted, not least the reconstructed street, and there are reports of apparitions being seen, one reported as being the tall phantom of a man with a trilby hat. Other manifestations include unexplained noises, including children's voices, disembodied walking and running footsteps, the sounds of a foot being dragged across the cobbles, and the screams of a girl. Apparitions have also apparently been seen in other areas, including in the car showroom, and the underground station area is said to have an especially unpleasant atmosphere at times.

In the cinema several seats have been found in the down position on many occasions, despite having return springs; indeed this happened to seven seats while a paranormal investigation was in progress. Electrical appliances are also said to turn themselves off and on, and there are also reports of dark apparitions being spotted.

Map 4, 7M (Glasgow). Off A814, Kelvin Hall, Bunhouse Road, Glasgow.
Open all year, daily except 25-25 Jan and 1-2 Jan. (141 287 2720 / www.glasgow.gov.uk)

A paranormal investigation was undertaken in January 2005 by Ghost Finders (www.ghostfinders.co.uk/transportmuseum.html) and in March 2005, in March 2007 and in February 2008 by the Ghost Club (www.ghostclub.org.uk) and by Spiritfinders Scotland (www.spiritfindersscotland.com)

MYRTON CASTLE

Built on a 12th-century motte, Myrton Castle is a ruinous tower house of the 16th century. Sir Alexander MacCulloch of Myrton burnt Dunskey Castle in 1503, and was James IV's Master Falconer. The property was sold to the Maxwells in 1685, and they built Monreith House, a large country mansion, close by in 1791; the family have a mausoleum in Kirkmaiden churchyard at the village of Monreith.

An old story is that, when this parish was united with Glasserton, the pulpit and bell were removed from Kirkmaiden church and were to be transported by sea across Luce Bay to a church of the same name near the Mull of Galloway. A strange storm blew up and the boat foundered, sinking the pulpit and bell. The story goes that on the approaching death of any descendant of the MacCullochs of Myrton (or presumably the owners of the property), the wraith-bell rings out from the depths of Luce Bay.

Map 3, 6Q (Myrton). Off B7021, 6 miles W and N of Whithorn, Myrton, Dumfries and Galloway.

NEIDPATH CASTLE   ILLUS PAGE 219

Nestling on the side of steep gorge overlooking a bend of the River Tweed, Neidpath Castle dates from the 14th century, and consists of a substantial tower house with a small courtyard. There is a dark pit prison which is only reached from a hatch in the floor above.

The property belonged to the Frasers, one of whom was Sir Simon Fraser. He was one of the Scottish leaders who defeated the English three times at Roslin in 1302, but he was later captured and executed. The castle passed by marriage to the Hays. In 1650 it was garrisoned against Cromwell and held out longer than any other fortress south of the Forth. In 1686 it was sold to the Douglas Duke of Queensberry, and later passed to the Earl of Wemyss and March, with whose descendants it remains.

Neidpath is reputedly haunted by the ghost of a young lass, the 'Maid of Neidpath', who was written about by Sir Walter Scott, although there are said to have been manifestations in recent times. The ghost is believed to be that of Jean Douglas, the youngest of the three daughters of Sir William Douglas, Earl of March. She was born in 1705, and fell in love with the son of the laird of Tushielaw, which was owned by the Scott family. Her father did not think her lover, although a man of property, was of high enough birth for an Earl's daughter and forbad them to marry. The lad was sent away from the area, and the Earl hoped that Jean would forget him. The girl was devastated and her health deteriorated. Her lover eventually returned, but by then she had become so ill that he no longer recognised her. Wounded to the core by this final slight, she died of a broken heart. Her ghost then began to haunt Neidpath, waiting for her lover to return to her in death as he had not in life.

Sightings of Jean's ghost report that she is clad in a full-length brown frock with a large white collar. Doors are said to open and close by themselves, unexplained noises have been reported, and objects move by themselves, including on one occasion a wooden plank.

Map 4, 9N (Neidpath). Off A72, 1 mile W of Peebles, Neidpath, Borders.
**Open Easter, then May-Sep, Wed-Sat, 10.30-17.00, Sun 12.30-17.00, closed Mon &
Tue. (01721 720333)**

Melrose Abbey (page 211)

Neidpath Castle (page 218)

New Lanark (page 221)

Newark Castle, Selkirk (page 222)

Newhailes, Musselburgh (page 224)

Newton Castle (page 224)

NEW ASSEMBLY CLOSE, EDINBURGH

The former bank is located in the close on the south side of the High Street, and was built in 1814, although it incorporates the 18th century assembly rooms (after which the close is named). The bank was closed in 1847, and the building has been used for a variety of purposes, including as a children's home, as the Edinburgh Wax Museum, and as a restaurant, before coming to the Faculty of Advocates.

The building is said to be haunted by a bogle heard whispering and seen shuffling about the cellar. During its use as the wax museum, there were many accounts of customers being pushed and touched by invisible hands with exceptionally chilly areas in the building. The place where activity was most experienced was reputedly the 'Chamber of Horrors' exhibit.

Map 4, 9L (Edinburgh). Off A1, New Assembly Close, High Street (Royal Mile), Edinburgh.

NEW CENTURY THEATRE, MOTHERWELL

The Rex Cinema dated from 1936 but incorporated part of the New Century Theatre, which was opened as a variety hall in 1902. The cinema was closed in the 1970s, and the building was then used for amusements, as a snooker club and as a nightclub, before being demolished in 1995.

The New Century was said to be haunted by a ghost, 'Oscar', the story going that a man had committed suicide by jumping from the gallery into the stalls.

Map 4, 7M (Motherwell). Off A721, Windmillhill Street, Motherwell, Lanarkshire.

NEW LANARK   ILLUS PAGE 219

Surrounded by woodlands and close to the Falls of Clyde, this cotton-spinning village (a World Heritage site) was founded in 1785 by David Dale, and made famous by the social pioneer Robert Owen, his son-in-law. The visitor centre has the ride the 'New Millennium Experience', and there is also access to the mills, Millworker's House, Village Store and Robert Owen's House. There is a fine walk to Falls of Clyde. Originally an 18th-century mill in the village, the New Lanark Mill Hotel has many original features, including Georgian windows and barrel-vaulted ceilings, and there are said to have been ghostly shenanigans.

Apparitions have been seen throughout the village, and there are reports of other spooky activity, including disembodied crying and footsteps, and unexplained crashing and banging coming from parts of the place.

The house, located over the village shop, is reputedly haunted by the apparition of young woman, dressed in a tartan cloak and black hat. She has been witnessed by several children on different occasions, and is said to have disappeared through a sealed door.

Another alleged sighting is the apparition of Robert Owen, spotted smiling at his desk in the building that used to be his house. A phantom was also reported, seen climbing the stairs, and other activity is claimed to include the sounds of children laughing and disembodied footsteps.

The Institute Building is said to be haunted by a young man with light gold hair, and other apparitions have also been spotted here, while the phantom of an old lady has been seen out in the street.

Map 4, 8N (New Lanark). Off A73, 1 mile S of Lanark, New Lanark, Lanarkshire. Access to village at all times. Visitor centre open all year, daily except closed

Christmas Day and New Year's Day. (01555 661345/01555 667200 / www.newlanark.org (or www.robert-owen.com))

A paranormal investigation was undertaken in October 2005 by Ghost Finders (www.ghostfinders.co.uk/newlanark.html) and in May 2004 by the Ghost Club (www.ghostclub.org.uk) and in April 2007 by Borders Paranormal Group (www.bordersparanormal.co.uk)

Newark Castle, Port Glasgow

Standing on a spit of land into the sea, Newark Castle is a solid and impressive building, dating from the 15th century, and forming three sides of a courtyard, the remaining side was formerly enclosed by a wall.

Newark was long associated with the Maxwells. In the 1580s one of the family, Patrick Maxwell, was involved in the murders of two members of the Montgomerys of Skelmorlie, the murder of Patrick Maxwell of Stanely, and the assassination of Hugh Montgomery, 4th Earl of Eglinton, during a series of feuds. He was married to Margaret Crawford for some 44 years and had 16 children, although he is said to have beaten and mistreated his wife, and for many years kept her imprisoned in one of the chambers. She eventually managed to escape, and fled to Dumbarton, where she ended her days in poverty.

The castle is said to be haunted by the ghost of Margaret Crawford. Her bogle is reputed to be seen looking out from the windows, and one story is that in recent years an unexplained apparition was seen in wedding photos.

In 1668 the property was sold to the city of Glasgow so that a new harbour could be built, the name being changed from Newark to (New) Port Glasgow.

Map 3, 6L (Port Glasgow). On A8, 3 miles E of Greenock, Newark, Port Glasgow, Renfrewshire.
His Scot: Open Apr-Oct, daily. (01475 741858 / www.historic-scotland.gov.uk)

Newark Castle, Selkirk

ILLUS PAGE 220

Standing in the grounds of the mansion of Bowhill, Newark Castle is a ruinous 15th-century castle with the remains of a courtyard. It has an eventful history, but is the site of a cruel massacre in 1645.

The Marquis of Montrose was defeated at the Battle of Philiphaugh and, while he escaped, most of his small army was slaughtered by the forces of the Covenanter General David Leslie. This was not enough for the Covenanters. Campfollowers were brought to Newark – mostly Irish women, many of them pregnant – and were then shot, stabbed, slashed or bludgeoned to death. The castle and area are said to be haunted by the folk butchered here, and their cries and moans have reputedly been heard.

Other prisoners, again mostly women and children, were taken to the market place in Selkirk, and there later also shot.

Map 4, 10N (Newark, Selkirk). Off A708, 3 miles W of Selkirk, in the grounds of Bowhill, Borders.
Park open Easter-end Aug; house open Jun, Thu & Sun, 13.00-16.00; Jul, daily 13.00-17.00; Aug, Tue & Thu 13.00-16.00; tel to confirm; other times by appt for educational groups. (01750 22204 / www.bowhill.org)

NEWARK CASTLE, ST MONANS

Standing above the shore of the Firth of Forth, Newark Castle or Newark of St Monans is a very ruinous castle, which dates from the 15th century but was altered and extended down the years.

St Monans was originally a property of the Kinloch family, but passed to the Sandilands of Cruivie. The Sandilands became bankrupt and sold the castle in 1649 to the Covenanter General Sir David Leslie. Leslie served under Gustavus Adolphus, and joined the army of Covenanters in 1643. He fought at Marston Moor the following year and defeated the Marquis of Montrose at Philiphaugh in 1645 (see Newark Castle, Selkirk), as well as leading a bloody campaign up the western seaboard of Scotland in Argyll and the Highlands. However, he was defeated by Cromwell at Dunbar 1650, and was captured at the Battle of Worcester the following year, after which he spent nine years in the Tower of London. After being released, he was made Lord Newark, and he died in 1682. The castle passed to the Anstruthers, then to the Bairds of Elie.

The castle is reputed to be home to a 'Green Lady', the ghost of Jean Leslie, daughter of Sir David Leslie, and the swish of her dress has been reported. Caves below the castle are believed to have been used for smuggling, and it is possible that the ghost was invented to keep people away.

'Green Ladies' are hardly unusual in Scotland's castles, however.

Map 4, 10L (Newark, St Monans). Off A917, 2 miles E and N of Elie, 0.5 miles W of St Monans, Fife.
View from exterior. (www.inverie.com)

NEWBATTLE ABBEY

Newbattle Abbey was founded in 1140 by David I, as a Cistercian house dedicated to the Blessed Virgin Mary, and became a very rich establishment. The abbey was visited by Alexander II – Marie de Coucy, his wife, was buried here. Newbattle was burned by the English in 1385, 1544 and 1548. The Kerrs acquired the abbey after the Reformation, having been commendators, and were made Lords Newbattle in 1591, and then Earls of Lothian in 1606. They demolished most of the abbey, and greatly altered the little that was left – the vaulted undercrofts of the dormitory and reredorter survives, as well as the warming house along with fine plasterwork and wood carving. The building is now an adult education college.

There are stories of a 'Grey Lady' haunting the grounds, said to be the spectre of Margaret, daughter of John Heron of Gilmerton. She fell in love with one of the monks of the abbey in the 14th century, but the affair was discovered by the lady's father and he forbad them to meet again. They arranged to see each other one last time to say goodbye at their meeting place at Melville Grange (also see that entry), a farm owned by the abbey, but Margaret's father followed them to their tryst and torched the grange, burning both of them to death.

There are also said to be phantom monks, seen in the grounds of the abbey.

Map 4, 9M (Newbattle). Off B703, 1 mile SW of Dalkeith, Newbattle, Midlothian.
Adult education college; open for tours end May-Aug, Sun only. (0131 663 1921 / www.newbattleabbeycollege.ac.uk)

NEWHAILES, MUSSELBURGH
ILLUS PAGE 220

In landscaped parkland and woodland overlooking the Forth, Newhailes is a plain and somewhat dour, stark and glowering symmetrical mansion, built in 1686 by the architect James Smith and extended around 1750. There are fine rococo interiors, including the library, and there is a good collection of paintings and portraits.

The property was formerly known as Whitehill, but the name was changed to Newhailes when the property was purchased by Sir David Dalrymple, calling it after his East Lothian estate of Hailes (also see Hailes Castle). Newhailes was visited by many leading figures of the Scottish Enlightenment.

The house is said to be haunted.

Map 4, 10M (Musselburgh). On A6095, Newhailes Road, Musselburgh, East Lothian.
NTS: House and visitor centre open Easter, then May-Sep, Thu-Mon (closed Tue & Wed); estate open all year, daily. Guided tours for visiting house, maybe sensible to reserve a place. (0131 653 5599/ 0844 4932125 / www.nts.org.uk)

NEWSTEAD, MELROSE

The Roman fort was built to defend where Dere Street (approximately the A68), an important route, crossed the Tweed on its way north. The fort was named Trimontium, after the three peaks of the Eildon Hills, which lie to the south, and was built by the Emperor Agricola in the first century AD. Not much is to be seen today, except a flattened area and some remains of the defensive ditches, as well as matching camps nearby.

In Melrose is an exhibition about the fort, the Trimontium Exhibition, which has displays illustrating life on the frontier of the Roman empire and many fascinating exhibits from Newstead.

There are accounts that there have often been mysterious noises at Newstead, usually heard in the early evening, described as sounding as if some kind of building is being constructed: hammering, sawing and banging. The sound of horns has also been reported, along with marching feet.

Map 4, 10N (Melrose). Off B6361, 1 mile E of Melrose, E of Newstead, Borders.
Roman fort. (www.trimontium.org.uk)

NEWTON CASTLE
ILLUS PAGE 220

Newton and Ardblair Castles are said to share the same ghost, the sorrowful Lady Jean Drummond. Newton was a property of the Drummonds, who feuded for many years with the Blairs of Ardblair. George Drummond and his son William were murdered in 1554 by a band of local lairds. Several of those involved were tried and outlawed, and two were executed for the slaying.

A 'Green Lady' reputedly haunts Newton, the sad and tragic apparition of Lady Jean, dressed in green silk, who searches for her love. Lady Jean fell in love with one of the Blairs of Ardblair, but appears to have died of a broken heart when she was betrothed to another man, drowning herself in a local marsh. An old (and long) ballad recounts the tale, and has Jean involved with fairies, who gave her the green gown, the colour of the fairies and generally believed to be unlucky.

The castle was plundered in 1644 by the Marquis of Montrose, then burnt by Cromwell five years later, although the garrison is said to have survived by sheltering in the vaulted basement, while the castle burned around them. Newton later passed to the Macphersons, is in good condition and is still occupied.

Map 4, 9J (Newton). Off A923, NW of Blairgowrie, Newton, Perthshire.

NICKY TAMS BAR AND BOTHY, STIRLING

In the heart of the historic burgh of Stirling, Nicky Tams is an atmospheric and popular free house and bar.

The bar is said to be haunted, and manifestations are believed to include half-seen apparitions or shadowy figures, people feeling as if they have been touched, and unexplained voices when nobody is about. Glasses are also reported to have fallen from a shelf by themselves, and gas cylinders for beer are found to have been turned off. An event which is supposed to have prompted the spooky happenings was the discovery of the photo of a clergyman, perhaps from Victorian times, which had been hidden in a niche in a wall and was found by workmen during renovations in 1999. The photo is on display behind the bar.

Map 4, 8L (Stirling). Off B8052 or A811, Baker Street, Stirling.
Public house. (01786 472194 / www.myspace.com/nickytams)

A paranormal investigation was undertaken in March 1999 by Paranormal Encounters Group (www.p-e-g.co.uk).

NICOL EDWARDS, EDINBURGH

Nicol Edwards is a popular and atmospheric pub in the Old Town of Edinburgh, and is named after a Lord Provost of the city in the 16th century, who reputedly was a miser and left a great treasure somewhere within the walls. The hostelry features three bars over three levels: the Main Bar and Mary Queen of Scots Lounge, the Scots Bar and the music box, and the Vaults Bar and Banqueting Hall.

It is this latter area which is said to be the most haunted part of the pub, and there are numerous accounts of mysterious occurrences, affecting both staff and customers. One story is that a boy got trapped in one of the chimneys and suffocated, and his bogle has been witnessed in the building.

Map 4, 9L (Edinburgh). Off A7, Niddry Street, South Bridge, Old Town, Edinburgh.
Public house. (0131 556 8642 / www.nicoledwards.co.uk)

Featured in Living TV's Most Haunted Live, *(2006).*

NIDDRY STREET VAULTS, EDINBURGH

Described by some as the 'Most Haunted' place in Scotland, the vaults are contained within the foundations of the 19 stone arches of South Bridge, which spans the dip over the Cowgate and was built in 1788. Tenements were built on each side of the bridge, rising many storeys, and the vaults were used for a variety of purposes, including as workshops, storage, and for dwellings places, but were eventually abandoned, except for use as air raid shelters during World War II. In the 1990s the vaults were cleared out and opened up for visitors, and there are many reports of bogles and supernatural activity.

The Niddry Street Vaults are said to be haunted by a poltergeist, which is claimed to be mostly witnessed in one of the large vaults and to have attacked visitors, especially females. There are said to have been many sightings and supernatural occurrences. The 'haunted vault' can be visited, although cameras, torches and electrical equipment are reputed to have been damaged or drained of power in this chamber.

In another chamber is what is alleged to be a pagan temple, a circle of stones on the floor. The temple is reported to have been disused because of bad things happening, and people are not supposed to go into circle as this may cause them harm or ill luck.

Map 4, 9L (Edinburgh). Off A1, off the Royal Mile, Niddry Street, Edinburgh.
Auld Reekie Tours (leave from Tron Kirk). (0131 557 4700 / www.auldreekietours.com)

A paranormal investigation was undertaken in May 2008 by Scottish Society of Paranormal Investigation and Analysis (www.sspia.co.uk).

Featured in Living TV's Most Haunted, *series three (2003),* Most Haunted, *series eleven (2008), and Living TV's* Most Haunted Live *(2006).*

NIVINGSTON HOUSE HOTEL
Standing in 12 acres of secluded and landscaped gardens is the former Nivingston House Hotel. It nestles at the foot of the picturesque Cleish hills, and was housed in a mansion dating from 1725 with later extensions. The hotel has closed.

The building is said to be haunted, and since 1980 there have supposedly been at least three sightings of an apparition of an old woman, dressed in night clothes. The ghost allegedly leaves one bed chamber and enters another chamber, now a bedroom but formerly a bathroom. It was the room from where the ghost leaves that a former owner reputedly shot himself in the early 1900s. Other alleged manifestations include the sound of footsteps and doors closing when there is nobody about; the noises always come from the same part of the building.

Map 4, 9L (Nivingston). Off B9097, 3 miles SW of Kinross, Cleish, Perthshire.

NOBEL HOUSE, LINLITHGOW
The office in Nobel House is reputedly haunted, and staff have reported seeing the apparition of an old man, hearing a man's voice when nobody was about, and have experienced other activity, such as books flying off a shelf. The disturbances became so bad that in 2006 the company chairman brought in a priest and historian to see if he could sort out the problem.

The office is believed to have been built on the site of an explosives factory, which was damaged by an explosion during World War I. It is thought that two female workers and a male foreman were killed in the blast, and one explanation for the haunting is that it was caused by the bogle of the foreman.

Map 4, 8L (Linlithgow). On A803, Nobel House, Linlithgow, West Lothian.

NOLTLAND CASTLE
A strong and grim stronghold in a remote location, Noltland Castle is a large ruined 16th-century Z-plan tower house, built by Gilbert Balfour. Balfour was Master of the Household to Mary, Queen of Scots. He acquired the property by marrying Margaret Bothwell, whose brother was the Bishop of Orkney and granted the lands to Balfour. Balfour had been involved in the murders of Cardinal David Beaton in 1546, for which he was imprisoned and became a galley slave, and Henry Stewart, Lord Darnley

in 1567. He supported Mary after she fled to England, but when her cause became hopeless he fled Scotland, and served in the Swedish army until his death, being executed for treason against the Swedish king, in 1576. The castle was abandoned about 1760 and is ruinous.

A death in the Balfour family was reputedly heralded by a ghostly howling dog, the 'Boky Hound', while births and marriages were announced by an eerie spectral light. The castle is also said to have had a brownie, the spirit of an old man which helped folk in need, beaching boats or clearing roads, and is said to have been well liked by the Balfour family.

The brownie is reported to have only left when the castle was abandoned.

Map 2, 10C (Noltland). Off B9066, NE side of island of Westray, Orkney.
His Scot: Open: tel 01856 841815 (Skara Brae). (01856 841815 / www.historic-scotland.gov.uk)

NORWOOD HALL, ABERDEEN

Set in seven acres of wooded grounds, Norwood Hall is a fine mansion with an imposing staircase. The house was rebuilt in 1881 for the Ogston family, and stands near the site of Pitfodels Castle, which was on high ground slightly to the south-east. Pitfodels was held by the Reids, but passed by marriage in the 16th century to the Menzies family. Norwood Hall is now a prestigious family-owned hotel.

The building is reputedly haunted by two ghosts.

One is said to be the apparition of the mistress of Colonel James Ogston, and her ghost has supposedly been seen on the main stair. The story is that the poor woman despaired after Ogston would not leave his wife and she waits for his return.

The other bogle is believed to be Ogston himself, and it is described as the apparition of an elegant gentleman. It has reportedly been seen in the dining room in recent times, when it went from the wine cupboard across the chamber, stopping for a brief moment in front of the log fire, before going through to the kitchen.

Map 2, 12G (Aberdeen). Off A93, Garthdee Road, Cults, Aberdeen.
Hotel. (01224 868951 / www.norwood-hall.co.uk)

OLD CASTLE INN, DUNDONALD

The Old Castle Inn is said to be haunted. Manifestations are believed to have included several female staff feeling as if they have had their bottoms pinched or as if someone is pushing past them. There are also reports of unexplained footsteps and other noises. On one occasion, although securely placed on a gantry, 12 jugs of water all flew off by themselves, and the CO_2 for the beer had switched itself off. Activity is said to have increased since the building was renovated.

Map 3, 6N (Dundonald). On B730, 29 Main Street, Dundonald, Ayrshire.

A paranormal investigation is to be undertaken by the Dunfermline Paranormal Research Fellowship.

OLD KING'S HIGHWAY, ABERDEEN

Located by the Green, originally the market place for Aberdeen, the Old King's Highway is a public house which was originally established as a hostelry in 1741.

The building is said to be haunted. There are reports of objects being moved about, disembodied voices, and areas being unexpectedly cold and foreboding, as well as the alleged sightings of two apparitions: a man and a lady, spotted near the windows at the front of the establishment.

Map 2, 12G (Aberdeen). Off A93 or A9013 (Union Street), 61 The Green, Aberdeen.
Public house. (01224 210952)

A paranormal investigation was undertaken in July 2008 by East of Scotland Paranormal (esparanormal.org.uk/reports/okhreport.html)

OLD MANSE, LAIRG

The Old Manse, which has been demolished, was said to have been haunted by the Reverend Thomas MacKay, who had been the minister. He died peacefully in his sleep in 1803, but his apparition is alleged to have been seen in 1827 and later, and his ghost is believed to still haunt the site.

Map 2, 7D (Lairg). Off A836, Lairg, Sutherland, Highland.

OLD POST HORN INN, CRAWFORD

The inn dates from 1744 but was closed some years ago and is now derelict, is said to be haunted by at least three ghosts.

One is reputed to be that of a young girl, who was killed by a coach in Main Street and who was the daughter of an innkeeper. Her apparition was reputedly seen in the dining room, which was originally the stables, and the ghost is said to have moved the chairs around and to sometimes have been heard singing to itself.

Another phantom is reportedly that of a coachman, spotted wearing a dark cloak, who is believed to have died in snow during 1805.

There are also accounts of the phantom of a five-year-old girl, hanged for stealing bread. Her ghost has reportedly been seen in the neighbouring countryside, as well as occasionally in the inn.

Ghostly Roman legionnaires are also said to have been seen, marching up the main street. However, they can only be seen from the knees up as the level of the road in Roman times was lower than it is today.

Map 4, 8N (Crawford). Off M74, Crawford, Lanarkshire.

OLD RECTORY GUEST HOUSE, CALLANDER

Nestled under the Callander Crags in the holiday village of Callander, this Victorian villa, formerly used as an inn, is now a guest house.

The building is said to be haunted by the ghost of a highwayman, which is reputedly witnessed in the kitchens, although there are no recent reports of activity.

Map 4, 7K (Callander). On A84, Leny Road, Callander, Stirling.
Guest house. (01877 339215 / www.theoldrectoryincallander.co.uk)

OLD SMUGGLERS INN, AUCHENCAIRN

The old inn stands in the peaceful village of Auchencairn, but was the haunt of smugglers, being both near the coast and a convenient stopping off place on the old route through Galloway.

The building is said to be haunted by a bogle, which is known as 'Old Gladys'.

Manifestations are alleged to include unexplained footsteps, electrical equipment and lights being switched on and off, and objects being moved about, including a powder compact being lifted from a handbag while on the floor. There are also reports of the sighting of an apparition in one of the rooms, and, when Border Television was recording at the inn, a shadowy figure was later seen on the footage even although nobody had noticed anything spooky at the time. The ghost is said to be displeased when anyone takes its favourite position at the fire.

The inn is closed, apparently temporarily, at the time of writing.

Map 4, 8Q (Auchencairn). On A711, Auchencairn, 6 miles S of Castle Douglas, Dumfries and Galloway.
Hotel - temporarily closed at time of writing. (01556 640331)

OLD SWAN INN, PAISLEY
The Old Swan Inn is said to be haunted.

Map 4, 7M (Paisley). Off A737, 20 Smithhills Street, Paisley, Renfrewshire.
Public house. (0141 587 2641)

A paranormal investigation was undertaken in March 2007 by Spiritfinders Scotland (www.spiritfindersscotland.com)

OLD WOODHOUSELEE CASTLE
An old castle here, which is now very ruinous, was owned by the Hamiltons of Bothwellhaugh, and has a tragic ghost story.

The story goes that one winter night a favourite of the Regent Moray turned up at Woodhouselee, and threw Lady Hamilton and her child out into the snow, in only their night wear. The infant died from the cold and Lady Hamilton went mad with despair, weeping herself to death. Her sad ghost, dressed in white, was frequently reported, searching through the castle and countryside for her child. At one time her ghost is said to have been often seen on cold moonlit nights. Her bogle is usually described as a 'White Lady', but it has also been called a 'Green Lady'.

Her husband, James Hamilton of Bothwellhaugh, shot and killed Regent Moray at Linlithgow in 1570, possibly as an act of revenge for his wife and child, then fled Scotland (although another account has this Lady Hamilton alive as late as 1609).

The castle was demolished in the late 17th century, and much of the stone was used to build Woodhouselee at Fulford (also see that entry), itself now gone. Lady Hamilton's ghost is said to have translated to this new house, but this may be a confusion over names.

Map 4, 9M (Old Woodhouselee). Off B7026, 1.5 miles NE of Penicuik, Old Woodhouselee, Midlothian.

ORAN MOR, GLASGOW
ILLUS PAGE 235

Previously used as the Kelvinside Free and Parish Church and as a Bible Institute, the Oran Mor (Gaelic for 'big song') was built in 1862 but was converted in 2002 into a cultural centre and meeting place with a night club, bars, restaurants and an event space.

The minister of the church between 1868 and 1907 was Walter Ross Taylor, and a story is that his body is one of two buried in the walls of the building.

Several mysterious events have taken place here, including disturbing presences being felt by staff, chairs being moved by themselves, and an office door being found open several times, despite not only being closed but also having been locked.

Map 4, 7M (Glasgow). On A82, Byres Road, Great Western Road, Glasgow.
Cultural centre, bars, restaurants, nightclub and private event space. (0141 357 6200 / www.oran-mor.co.uk)

A paranormal investigation was undertaken in April 2006 by Ghost Finders (www.ghostfinders.co.uk/oran_mor.html)

ORD HOUSE

With 60 acres of the gardens and woodlands, the handsome and stylish Ord House dates from about 1810, but has a date stone of 1637 and may incorporate work from the 17th century. Ord was a property of the Mackenzies, but the building is now a fine hotel.

The house is said to have the bogle of a lady, an apparition which has been witnessed both in corridors and sitting at the end of a bed in one of the rooms. The sounds of unexplained footsteps have also reputedly been heard. The ghost has also been blamed for removing pictures, presumably because of a dislike for them, and propping them neatly and unbroken against walls.

Map 2, 7E (Ord). Off A832, 1 mile W of Muir of Ord, Ord House, Ross and Cromarty, Highland.
Hotel. (01463 870492 / www.ord-house.co.uk)

OVERTOUN HOUSE

Overtoun House is a large baronial mansion, dating from the mid 19th century, and built for James White, a successful chemical manufacturer. The house stands on the site of an old castle, once held by the Colquhouns. The house and some of the lands were given over to the people of Dumbarton in 1939, after which Overtoun was used as a maternity hospital until 1970. It is now a Christian Centre for Hope and Healing, and the estate around the house is open to the public with formal gardens and a nature trail.

The house is said to be haunted by the apparition of a woman, dressed in Victorian style.

There are also strange stories regarding Overtoun Bridge, claiming that more than 50 dogs have jumped to their deaths from the bridge in the last 50 years.

Map 3, 6L (Overtoun). Off A82, to E of Dumbarton, Milton, via Milton Brae, Overtoun, Dunbartonshire.
Park open all year, daily. (www.overtounhouse.com)

A paranormal investigation was undertaken in 2005.

O'BRIEN'S, GLASGOW

O'Brien's, formerly Graham's Bar, is a small public house.

The building is said to be haunted by the spirit of an little old woman lady, witnessed shrouded in a tartan shawl which hides her face, seen sitting by the fireplace.

Map 4, 7M (Glasgow). Off M8, 37-45 Saltmarket, Glasgow.
Public House (0141 552 0567.)

PAISLEY ABBEY

Paisley Abbey is an impressive and evocative church, dating from the 13th century, with a very long and interesting history. Founded as a priory in 1163 by Walter, son of Alan, Steward of Scotland, this replaced an ancient Christian establishment, dedicated to St Mirren. The priory was elevated to an abbey in 1219, and the abbey church was restored in the 20th century and is used as the parish church.

In the abbey is preserved the stone effigy of Marjorie, daughter of Robert the Bruce, as well as the tomb of Robert III. The Barrochan Cross, dating from as early as the 8th century and decorated with warriors and human figures, is also housed here.

Some stories have the church haunted by the apparitions of monks.

Map 4, 7M (Paisley). Off A726 or A737, Paisley, Renfrewshire.
Open all year, Mon-Sat. (0141 889 7654 / www.paisleyabbey.org.uk)

PAISLEY ART INSTITUTE

Opposite the University of Paisley and founded in 1876, the Paisley Art Institute is located in Paisley Art Gallery, a fine building in the style of a Greek temple, which was paid for by the famous Coats family of Paisley. They, along with other industrialists, donated many works of arts to the gallery.

The building is said to be haunted. Manifestations are said to include the sound of heavy footsteps coming from an empty and locked room, as well as disembodied whispering. It is also said that very heavy clays were mysteriously moved one night, although nobody was present. It then took three people to return the clays to their proper place.

Map 4, 7M (Paisley). Off A726 or A737, High Street, Paisley, Renfrewshire.
Art Institute. (www.paisleyartinstitute.org.uk)

PANNANICH WELLS HOTEL, BALLATER

The former hotel here, a historic inn which dates from 1760, has had guests including Lord Byron and Queen Victoria. John Brown, Queen Victoria's manservant, worked in the hotel before going on to serve the queen.

The building and the neighbouring area are said to be haunted by a 'Grey Lady', the phantom of a young and slim woman, seen dressed in a grey blouse and long dark skirt, perhaps the ghost of a Victorian maid. The ghost is reported to have been seen quite often and to be friendly.

Other alleged disturbances include unexplained noises such as disembodied breathing, and the moving of furniture and the opening of doors when nobody is apparently present, as well as the smell of violet perfume. This latter manifestation may be from a separate ghost, said to have been witnessed in Room 1.

A further apparition is said to be that of a young boy, observed begging for water.

Map 2, 9G (Ballater). On B976, South Deeside Road, 1.5 miles E of Ballater, Kincardine & Deeside.

PAVILION THEATRE, GLASGOW

The Pavilion Theatre was opened in 1904 and is housed in a plush building with a sumptuous Louis XV style interior; it is one of the few privately run and unsubsidised theatres left in Britain. The Pavilion features a varied programme of popular shows, plays and pantomimes, and many famous people have entertained here, including Harry Lauder, Sarah Bernhardt and Charlie Chaplin (then unknown).

There are stories of the bogle of a woman being seen in one of the boxes, and the phantom of a girl being spotted in an upper dressing room. A chair in the stalls is often alleged to be found in the down position, as if someone invisible was sitting on it. One tale is that a member of staff heard the sounds of piano coming from the main auditorium, but on investigation found the theatre was empty, dark and unoccupied; there was also no piano in the building.

The stories are completely refuted by management, who state there is no paranormal activity here, and the theatre should NOT be contacted about the supernatural.

Map 4, 7M (Glasgow). Off M8, 121 Renfield Street, Glasgow.

PEAR TREE, EDINBURGH

The Pear Tree is a fine hostelry in an atmospheric building with a large walled beer garden, and was built in 1747 as a private residence. This was the birthplace in 1826 of Andrew Usher, who is thought to have been the first producer of blended whisky. His elder brother founded the Usher brewing business, and in 1896 Andrew gave money to build the famous Usher Hall on Lothian Road. The Pear Tree became a pub in 1982.

The building is said to have a ghost.

Map 4, 9L (Edinburgh). Off A7, 38 West Nicolson Street, Edinburgh.
Public House. (0131 667 7533)

PEARCE LODGE, GLASGOW

Pearce Lodge was the original gateway of the Old College of the University of Glasgow, and it was moved to its present site in the 1980s and many salvaged materials were used in the rebuilding.

The lodge is reputed to be haunted, one manifestation said to be the mysterious sound of piano music. The lodge is also said to have a 'Grey Lady', spotted dressed in a grey coat and hat, and reported to have been seen in 1989 when the bogle is said to have walked up to the entrance where it then vanished. The apparition was reported to be dressed in an old-fashioned style and to have had a 'shiny' face.

Map 4, 7M (Glasgow). Off A82 or A814, University of Glasgow, Glasgow.

PENKAET CASTLE

Standing in a walled garden, Penkaet Castle has been the property of several families, but was held by the Lauders from 1685 until 1922. The castle, although altered and extended in later centuries, incorporates a 16th-century tower house.

One ghost is said to be the spectre of Alexander Hamilton. He was a beggar, who was accused of witchcraft after cursing the lady of the house and her eldest daughter. They both soon died from a mysterious illness, after they had thrown Hamilton off their property. He was executed in Edinburgh, and his ghost is said to have been witnessed near the castle.

Another is reported to manifest itself by banging doors and moving furniture. It may be the spirit of John Cockburn, who had apparently committed – or been the victim of – a murder. The sounds of disembodied footsteps and the dragging of a heavy object, as if across the floor, have also apparently been heard.

A four-poster bed, once slept in by Charles I, is reputedly haunted, as it often appears to have been used – some say by a manifestation of the king himself – although it has not actually been slept in.

Ghostly activity was reported in the 20th century – the house was investigated in the 1920s, when many unexplained noises and events were recorded, although the investigation was not as thorough or reliable as it might be today.

Map 4, 10M (Penkaet). Off A6093, 1 mile SW of Pencaitland, Penkaet Castle, East Lothian.

PERTH THEATRE

Perth Theatre is Scotland's most successful repertory theatre, established in 1935, and it is housed in a fine building of 1898, which was rebuilt after a fire in the 1920s.

The theatre is reputedly haunted by a 'Grey Lady', seen since the fire in 1924. Other manifestations are said to include seats slamming down and then springing back up.

One strange occurrence was when a production of Shakespeare's *Macbeth* was being shown at the theatre. Actors and staff reported hearing a caged-door lift ascending to the third floor during performances, and the lift doors opening and footsteps as somebody got out. The lift, however, had not been used for years and the electricity had reputedly been disconnected.

Map 4, 9K (Perth). Off M90, 185 High Street, Perth.
Theatre. (01738 621031 / www.horsecross.co.uk)

PINKIE HOUSE

Now part of a private school, Pinkie House is a grand mansion consisting of an L-plan tower house of the 16th century at its core, along with many alterations and extensions from later centuries. Noteworthy visitors include Charles I and Bonnie Prince Charlie.

The ghost story dates from when the house was held by the Setons. Alexander Seton was 1st Earl of Dunfermline and Chancellor to James VI. He altered the house in 1613, and died here nine years later.

The house is said to be haunted by a 'Green Lady', who some have identified as Lillias Drummond, his first wife, who died in 1601 after giving Seton four daughters but no son as an heir. The manner of her demise is a matter of some debate, but Seton did marry again only months after her death. Her appearance bodes ill for the family, and she also reputedly haunts Fyvie (also see that entry).

Her ghost, or another, is sometimes said to be accompanied by a child, claimed to be that of a lad, which does not tie in as Lillias did not have a son...

There have apparently been no manifestations in recent years.

Map 4, 10M (Musselburgh). Off A199, Loretto School, Pinkie House, E end of Musselburgh, East Lothian.
School. (0131 653 4444 / www.lorettoschool.co.uk)

PITCAIRLIE HOUSE

Pitcairlie, a house of about 1730 which was remodelled about 1740 and again in 1815, incorporates a very altered 16th-century Z-plan tower house. The house stands in 120 acres of parkland and woodlands.

Pitcairlie was a property of the Abernethy family, but passed by marriage to the Leslies in 1312. One of the family was David Leslie, the Covenanter general (see Newark Castle, St Monans). The family became bankrupt, and Pitcairlie was eventually sold in the mid 18th century to the Cathcarts, with whose descendants it remained until the 20th century. The house is still occupied as a family home.

The building is said to have a 'Green Lady'.

Map 4, 9K (Auchtermuchty). Off B936, 2 miles N of Auchtermuchty, Pitcairlie, Fife. **Holiday self-catering accommodation available. (01337 827418 / www.pitcairlie-leisure.co.uk)**

PITCAPLE CASTLE

Located in some 70 acres of parkland, Pitcaple Castle is a handsome Z-plan tower house, with a main block and projecting round towers at opposite corners. The castle dates partly from the 15th century and, although ruinous by the end of the 18th century, was restored in the following century. Charles II visited Pitcaple, and the then laird was killed at the Battle of Worcester in 1651. The castle later passed by marriage to the Lumsdens, and it is occupied by their descendants.

When a robin is found in the castle, it is reputedly the harbinger of bad news and the herald of death. A robin was discovered when the laird was killed at the Battle of Worcester in 1651. A recent recorded instance was in 1978, when a robin apparently heralded the death of one of the family.

Map 2, 11F (Pitcaple). Off A96, 4 miles NW of Inverurie, Aberdeenshire. **Accommodation available, up to 10 guests in castle; houses available to let. (01467 681204 / www.pitcaplecastle.co.uk)**

PITREAVIE CASTLE

Pitreavie Castle is an altered early 17th-century U-plan tower house, which was remodelled in later centuries into a large and impressive mansion. The tower was built by the Wardlaws of Balmule, who acquired the lands in 1608, and the family had a burial vault in Dunfermline Abbey.

The Battle of Inverkeithing (or Pitreavie) was fought nearby in 1651. A Cromwellian force routed a Royalist army, mostly made up of Highlanders, with the loss of 1600 killed and 1200 taken prisoner. A party of MacLeans, many of them wounded, sought refuge in the castle, but were dispersed by missiles cast from the battlements. The MacLeans are said to have cursed the Wardlaws for their poor treatment – the laird of Pitreavie died 18 months later, and the family had lost the property within some 50 years.

Ghost stories apparently date from this event. The building reputedly has both a 'Green Lady' and a 'Grey Lady', while the phantom of a headless Highlander was reported in the vicinity of the castle. The apparitions of the ladies were most often witnessed in the wee hours of the night.

The property was sold in 1703, and by the mid 19th century Pitreavie was empty and abandoned. Restored, remodelled and enlarged in 1885 by the Beveridge family, it was later owned by the Royal Navy and then by the Royal Air Force, but was put up for sale when the base was closed. The castle has been converted into six luxury apartments.

Manifestations were reported from when the building was in use by the RAF, included a WAAF being pushed down stairs by an invisible force, a cleaner being

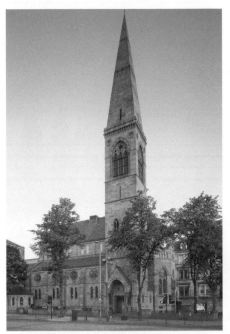

Oran Mor, Glasgow (page 229)

Preston Tower (page 240)

Renfrew Victory Baths (page 247)

Rammerscales (page 245)

Rosslyn Chapel (page 250)

Rosslyn Chapel (page 250)

grabbed by the shoulder although nobody else was present, and phone calls being received from a room which was known to be empty.

There are also tales of the apparition of a WAAF being seen.

Map 4, 9L (Pitreavie). Off A823, 2 miles S of Dunfermline, Pitreavie, Fife.

PITTENWEEM TOLBOOTH TOWER

The old tolbooth tower is a strong and squat building, surmounted by a balustraded wall walk and a hexagonal steeple, which was added about 1630. The tower rises to five stories and dates from the 16th century, and is built on part of the site of Pittenweem Priory. The ground floor is vaulted and has no connection with the upper floors, and the tower is adjacent to the parish church. The tower is believed to have been used as a prison and for incarcerating those accused of witchcraft.

Janet Corphat (Cornfoot) was one of those accused of witchcraft in 1704, after a local man complained that he had been made ill and went on to denounce his neighbours. Janet had been implicated by the confession of another accused person, but she managed to escape from her prison in the tower and she fled Pittenweem and reached Leuchars, near St Andrews. Here, however, she was apprehended and she was sent back to Pittenweem and imprisoned.

The poor woman was then dragged from the tower by a mob, and taken down to the beach, was tied up and then beaten with stones and stakes to make her confess. When she refused, a door was placed over her and stones and rocks piled on top. She still would not confess, so this was repeated and then a horse and sledge were ridden over her until she was crushed and dead.

This appalling act was utterly illegal but, although the Privy Council ordered all those involved to be brought to the tolbooth in Edinburgh, nobody was subsequently prosecuted. Thomas Brown, another of those accused, died in captivity, reputedly from starvation, while a further accused was banished from the parish.

It should be said that even at the time these evil acts were widely condemned, and it was one of the events that soon saw a change in the witchcraft law.

Since the tower has been opened for tours there have been a series of reported spooky manifestations, including unexplained voices, the sounds of a fight going on in an upper floor when a subsequent search revealed nobody there, witnessed by more than a dozen visitors, and sightings of an apparition of a man in a black gown as well as a large ball of red light.

One visitor said that she felt as if she was being stabbed by a pole and tortured.

Map 4, 10K (Pittenweem). Off A917, Pittenweem, Fife.

PITTODRIE HOUSE

Set in 200 acres in the foothills of the impressive and foreboding hill of Bennachie, Pittodrie House was once a property of the Erskines, and incorporates an old tower house. The building was extended in later centuries, including after it had become a hotel.

A chamber which was formerly used as a nursery is said to be haunted, the story going that a servant had died after falling down a stair during a fire. Other manifestations are reputed to include unexplained footsteps, cries and screams, and the smell of burning: all centred on the old stair. Indeed, one story has the apparition of a flame-haired servant lass throwing itself down the staircase once a year, reported to be on Halloween, although it is not clear from the story whether it is the hair which is aflame or whether the bogle has red hair. There are also reports of an apparition being seen in the library.

Another tale is that a phantom carriage with a single horse has been seen going riding along the driveway.

Map 2, 11F (Pittodrie). Off A96, 5 miles NW of Inverurie, Pittodrie, Aberdeenshire **Hotel. (01467 681444 / www.macdonaldhotels.co.uk/Pittodrie/)**

PLACE OF BONHILL

Place of Bonhill was described as a mysterious old house, and the building incorporated an ancient castle into the later mansion. The whole building was demolished in 1950, and the site is occupied by Vale of Leven school. The property was originally held by the Lennox family, but Bonhill passed to the Lindsays in the 15th century, then to the Smolletts around 200 years later.

One story is that a tunnel led down from a hidden entrance behind the drawing-room fireplace, and it was believed to go to the banks of the River Leven, but nobody had used it for as long as anyone could remember. In 1785 a piper was sent to explore the passage, but he vanished without trace. Afterwards, it was said, faint phantom pipe music was often heard from within the walls.

Map 3, 6L (Bonhill). Off A8, S of Alexandria, Dunbartonshire.

PLAYHOUSE THEATRE, EDINBURGH

The theatre, which was built in 1927-9 and can hold 3000 people, is said to be haunted by a ghost called 'Albert'. His apparition has reputedly been seen, apparently often, and his ghost is said to be friendly but mischievous. It is believed that Albert is the bogle of a maintenance man, killed in a backstage accident.

The theatre stands near Gallowlea, where Major Thomas Weir, whose house was in the West Bow (see that entry), was strangled and burnt for crimes including incest.

Map 4, 9L (Edinburgh). On A1, 18-22 Greenside Place, Edinburgh.
Theatre. (0131 524 3333 / www.edinburghplayhouse.org.uk)

PLOTCOCK CASTLE

In a bend of Plotcock Glen, little survives of an overgrown tower house of the Hamiltons. The tower is said to have been used as a prison.

There are tales of the lands around here being haunted by ghosts and by witches.

Map 4, 7M (Hamilton). Off A723 or W of B7078, 4 miles S of Hamilton, Lanarkshire.

POLDEAN

There was an old tower house at Poldean, a property of the Bells and of the Johnstones, but there are no remains and the location of the site is not even certain. When Poldean was held by the Johnstones, it is said to have been plagued by a bogle, with manifestations including unexplained noises, drums and trumpets, apparitions, and a phantom naked arm. The story is that, in the 1650s, English troops occupying the tower house were terrified by the ghostly manifestations.

Map 4, 8O (Poldean). Off A708, 3 miles S of Moffat, Poldean, Dumfries and Galloway.

POLLOK HOUSE, GLASGOW

Nestling in a country park with fine woodland and shrubbery, the impressive and elegant Pollok House was first built about 1750, and was then remodelled and extended in 1890. The present mansion replaced an ancient castle, which had a ditch and drawbridge. This was originally a property of the Polloks, but passed by marriage to the Maxwells in the mid 13th century and they held Pollok for some 600 years. Pollok was gifted to the City of Glasgow in 1966, and the Burrell Collection is situated within the grounds. The house is open to the public, and houses the Stirling Maxwell collection of Spanish and European paintings, furniture, ceramics and silver.

The building is said, by some, to be haunted.

Map 4, 7M (Glasgow). Off B768, Pollok Country Park, Pollokshaws area of Glasgow.
NTS: Open all year, daily; closed 25-26 Dec and 1-2 Jan; country park open all year, daily. (0141 616 6410 / www.nts.org.uk)

POOSIE NANSIE'S TAVERN, MAUCHLINE

Robert Burns was a patron of Poosie Nansie's Tavern, and the building dates back to the 18th century and is still open as an atmospheric hostelry. Poosie Nansie was the name Burns gave Agnes, the wife of George Gibson, who owned the establishment in Burns's time. Burns used many of the regulars and their revelry in the cantata known as *The Jolly Beggars*.

The building has long had a reputation for being haunted. The sound of a young child weeping has been reported, coming from the dining room, even though nobody was apparently there. Glasses are said to have fallen from shelves without explanation, and spirit optics have emptied by themselves. Several staff members have also reported feeling an uncomfortable 'presence' in the tavern.

Map 4, 7N (Mauchline). Off A76, 21 Loudoun Street, Mauchline, Ayrshire.
Public house. (01290 550316)

A paranormal investigation is to be undertaken by Spiritfinders Scotland (www.spiritfindersscotland.com).

POWIS HOUSE, ABERDEEN

Powis House is a two-storey mansion, which dates from 1802, and the present building replaced an ancient castle. The lands were held by the Frasers of Powis, possibly from the early 16th century, but passed to the Leslies, and then to the Burnetts in 1781, who held the property until 1866 or later. The grounds were used to build a housing estate in the 1930s, and Powis House is now used as the Powis Community Centre.

The basement of the house is said to be haunted by the ghost of a young girl, and there are reports that an apparition has been seen there, as well as in the attic. The story goes that the lass died from scarlet fever, or was perhaps pushed down the turnpike stair to the basement. The ghost was named 'Annie' by people who work at the centre, and other manifestations are said to include a heater being repeatedly turned on despite the room it was in being locked, and unexplained footsteps on the main stair.

There is also an account of the bogle of a woman with long dark hair, an indistinct face, and a pale or white dress, being seen at one of the windows, bathed by a strange blue illuminance.

It is not clear if the two apparitions are linked, although there are stories of the phantom of a woman, sometimes spotted with a baby in its arms, the young girl (mentioned above), and the voice of a man being heard when nobody was present.

Map 2, 12G (Aberdeen). Off A956, Powis, Old Aberdeen, to N of Aberdeen.
Community Centre.

A paranormal investigation was undertaken in December 2008 by East of Scotland Paranormal (esparanormal.org.uk)

Premier Lodge, Edinburgh

Located in a tall tenement building in the historic Grassmarket is the Premier Lodge, and the hotel is said to be haunted.

The phantom of a woman, dressed as a maid from Victorian times, is reported to have been spotted several times where guests have breakfast, and one account has a man waking to see the apparition of a woman at the end of his bed.

Map 4, 9L (Edinburgh). Off A1, 94-96 Grassmarket, Edinburgh.
Hotel. (0870 7001370 / www.travel-lodge-hotels.co.uk)

Preston Tower

ILLUS PAGE 235

Standing in fine gardens but still a somewhat grim and brooding edifice, Preston Tower is a strong L-plan tower of six storeys, perhaps with work from as early as the 14th century. At the end of that century, Preston passed by marriage to the Hamiltons, with whom it was to have a long association, and they probably built the tower. Preston was torched in 1544, and then in 1650 by Cromwell. The tower was consolidated in 1936, purchased by The National Trust for Scotland in 1969, and is under the guardianship of the local council. It was repaired in 2004-5.

The tower is reputed to have a 'Green Lady'.

Map 4, 10L (Prestonpans). Off A198, SE of Prestonpans, Preston, East Lothian.
NTS: Gardens open all year, daily dawn to dusk - tower: the tower may be viewed from the exterior. (01875 810232)

Prestonfield House, Edinburgh

Prestonfield House, an elegant mansion, was built (or rebuilt) in 1687 for Sir James Dick of Braid, who was Provost of Edinburgh. Prestonfield had earlier been a property of the Hamiltons, and in 1646 Sir James Hamilton of Prestonfield was made hereditary keeper of the nearby Holyrood Park and of Holyroodhouse. The Hamiltons exploited their position by extracting thousands of tons of the stone from the park until 1831 when the House of Lords put a stop to their activity. Prestonfield was burnt out in 1681 by a Protestant mob, and the new house was built for the Dick family, who held the property for almost 300 years. Prestonfield has been used as a hotel since 1958.

One story is that a phantom horse-drawn carriage often comes along the main drive, early in the morning, and then vanishes at the doors of the house.

Map 4, 9L (Edinburgh). Off A68, S of Holyrood Park, Prestonfield, Edinburgh.
Hotel. (0131 225 7800 / www.prestonfield.com)

PRESTONPANS COMMUNITY CENTRE

Prestonpans Community Centre is built on the former site of the Schaws Hospital, a school for poor boys. This institution, in turn, was replaced by the Mary Murray Institute, a school for destitute girls and young women.

Mary Murray's ghost is said to haunt the building, and to have been witnessed in the present community centre.

Map 4, 10L (Prestonpans). Off B1361, Preston Road, Prestonpans, East Lothian.
Community centre. (01875 813349)

PRINCES STREET, EDINBURGH

The West End is said to be haunted by a weeping woman, the bogle of one Moira Blair. The story goes that her husband had been murdered in the area. The poor woman found his body, and in distress stumbled into the road and was killed by a coach and horses.

Sounds of her weeping have also been reported in Princes Street Gardens and in St John's Church, and her apparition has also allegedly been seen.

Map 4, 9L (Edinburgh). On A1, Princes Street, Edinburgh.
Accessible at all times.

PRINCE'S HOUSE, GLENFINNAN

The Prince's House Hotel, set in a beautiful and remote part of Scotland on the road between Fort William and Mallaig, is a small former coaching inn, and the building dates from 1658. It was nearby, and the site marked by a tall monument, that Bonnie Prince Charlie raised his father's standard and so started the Jacobite Rising of 1745-46. At one time the house is recorded as being owned by the 'tallest land-lord in Scotland', said to be six foot and seven inches tall.

The building is said to be haunted by both a 'Grey Lady', reputed to be seen on the stairs, and by a bearded Highlander, who has allegedly been observed wandering the building. Neither ghost is said to be frightening.

Map 1, 4H (Glenfinnan). Off A830, Glenfinnan village, Highland.
Hotel and restaurant. (01397 722246 / www.glenfinnan.co.uk)

PROVAN HALL

Standing in the grounds of Auchinlea Park, Provan Hall is a fine old house which dates from the 15th century, and is enclosed by a walled courtyard with an arched gateway. The lands were owned by Glasgow Cathedral, but by the 16th century had been acquired by the Baillie family, who built the house. The property later passed by marriage to the Hamiltons. The property was sold to the City of Glasgow in 1667, and in 1935 it was given to The National Trust for Scotland.

Provan Hall is said to be haunted by the ghost of Reston Mathers, seen on the stair of Blochairn House, and dressed in a white suit and black bowler hat.

There is also reputed to be a 'White Lady'. She is believed to be the apparition of the wife of one of the lairds. The poor woman was murdered along with her son, reputedly in one of the first-floor chambers, and her ghost has allegedly been seen and heard at the gate, calling for her lad.

There are stories that staff have heard unexplained noises in the building (even believing that they are being burgled), and have felt as if they were being touched by icy invisible fingers.

Map 4, 7M (Provan Hall). Off B806 or M8, 3.5 miles W of Coatbridge, Provan, Lanarkshire. **NTS: Managed by the City of Glasgow Council. Open all year, Mon-Fri except Dec 25/ 26 and Jan 1/2, and when special events in progress: tel to confirm. (0141 773 1202 / www.eastglasgow.co.uk/provanhall/)**

A paranormal investigation was undertaken in May 2005 and in June 2007 by the Ghost Club (www.ghostclub.org.uk)

PROVAND'S LORDSHIP, GLASGOW

Provand's Lordship, the oldest house in Glasgow with steep roofs and corbiestepped gables, dates from 1471 and was built by Bishop Muirhead as part of St Nicholas's Hospital. The building also housed the Prebend of Balornock or Provand, and hence the name (also see Provan Hall). There are period displays and furniture, as well as a recreated medieval herb garden.

There are stories that the building is haunted, and manifestations are reputed to include objects being moved around by themselves, the sounds of unexplained footsteps being heard around the building, and some areas being extremely and suddenly cold.

Map 4, 7M (Glasgow). Off M8, 3 Castle Street, opposite the Cathedral, Glasgow. **Open all year, daily except closed 25-26 Dec and 1-2 Jan. (0141 552 8819 / www.glasgow.gov.uk/)**

PROVOST SKENE'S HOUSE, ABERDEEN

Provost Skene's House is a fine fortified town house, and dates from about 1545. Magnificent 17th-century plaster ceiling and wood panelling survives, and the painted gallery features a unique cycle of tempera wall and ceiling painting depicting Christ's life. The house is home to a museum, and rooms include a suite of Georgian chambers and an Edwardian nursery.

The house was a property of George Skene of Rubislaw, a wealthy merchant and provost of the city, from 1669. The Duke of Cumberland stayed here for six weeks in 1746 on his way to Culloden and the defeat of the Jacobites.

The building is said to be haunted, including by the apparition of a woman spotted in the parlour room in the 17th-century part of the building, believed by some to be the bogle of Elizabeth Aberdour, wife of Matthew Lumsden (who owned the house in the 17th century: their initials and the date 1626 are carved on one of the dormer window pediments). Another phantom has allegedly been seen in the original kitchen: a woman dressed in an old-fashioned manner with a bonnet.

Other manifestations are reported, not least ghostly footsteps, reputedly heard following people using the turret stair, and the doors into the painted gallery apparently being held closed by invisible hands. Visitors to the house have also reported being touched or jostled by unseen hands, and the building reputedly sometimes has an uncomfortable or even foreboding atmosphere.

Map 2, 12G (Aberdeen). Off A9103, 45 Guest Row, off Broad Street, Aberdeen. **Open all year, Mon-Sat; closed 25/26/31 Dec and 1/2 Jan. (01224 641086 / www.aagm.co.uk)**

QUEEN MARGARET DRIVE, GLASGOW

The former BBC headquarters on Queen Margaret Drive was partly housed in a fine edifice dating from 1869, which was originally built as a country house. In 1884 the house was acquired by Queen Margaret College, the first college for women in Scotland, and some ten or so years later it was here that Britain's first women's medical school was founded, designed by architects including Charles Rennie Mackintosh. The BBC became established here in 1936, but recently vacated the building, moving to Pacific Quay, and the five-acre site is to be redeveloped.

The story goes that the apparition of a woman dressed in a long-sleeved frock with a stiff white collar has been spotted in the corridors of the building during the night. It is also said that some areas have such bad feelings that some members of staff could not tolerate them and refused to work there.

Map 4, 7M (Glasgow). Off A82, Queen Margaret Drive, Great Western Road, Glasgow. **(Former) BBC headquarters.**

A paranormal investigation was undertaken in August 2007 by Borders Paranormal Group (www.bordersparanormal.co.uk)

QUEENSBERRY HOUSE, EDINBURGH

Queensberry House is an imposing old mansion house, at the foot of the Royal Mile, and now forms part of the buildings which make up the Scottish Parliament, being used as offices for, among others, the Presiding Officer. The building probably dates from 1681, and was held by the Dukes of Queensberry, hence the name. Having been bought by the Board of Ordnance in 1803, it was then used as a barracks, as a 'House of Refuge for the Destitute', and as an old people's home until 1996. The building was then restored and renovated, including replacing all the floors and returning the roof pitch as to when the house was first built.

The story goes that James Douglas, 2nd Earl of Queensberry, had a son who suffered from bouts of insanity and was kept locked in his chamber at Queensberry House for his own (and others') protection. During the troubles around the Treaty of Union in 1707, the son escaped and had free run of the building, as all the family and staff were occupied outside. All that is, except for a lad who was working in the kitchen, tending the fire.

The motive is not clear (although perhaps mad hunger drove him), but Queensberry's son seized the unfortunate lad, tied him to a spit and then roasted him over the great kitchen fire. It is said that when the family returned, they found the house filled with a terrible stench and the remains of the lad, scorched and blackened, still tethered to the spit.

The story goes that the apparition of the kitchen lad has been witnessed in the building, and often the unexplained smell of charring meat wafts through the chambers.

Map 4, 9L (Edinburgh). Off A1, 64 Canongate, Royal Mile, Edinburgh. **Part of the Scottish Parliament buildings. (www.scottish.parliament.uk)**

RAASAY HOUSE

On the long and picturesque island of Raasay (which lies just off Skye), Raasay House dates from 1747 and replaced an old tower house of three storeys, called Kilmaluag Castle. The island was held by the MacLeods of Raasay, who were Jacobites: Bonnie Prince Charlie was briefly sheltered on Raasay in 1746. The island was sacked in retaliation and every dwelling on Raasay was torched, plus the islanders' boats were holed and 280 cows and 700 sheep were slaughtered. In 1846 the 12th and last chief of MacLeod had to sell the property, and the island went through many years of underinvestment, depopulation and poor management, but things have improved in recent years.

Raasay House, an outdoor centre with accommodation and a cafe, was being renovated, however, when it suffered a serious fire in January 2009.

Raasay House is said to be haunted, manifestations are reputed to have been experienced in four of the rooms, and a spectral dog to have been witnessed in the kitchen. The apparition of a Dr Green is reported to have been seen on the stairs. There is also reputed to be the bogle of a piper, a MacCrimmon: it is believed that the ghost has never been seen but at times the sounds of pipes are said to be heard.

Map 1, 2F (Raasay House). Off minor road, Clachan, Isle of Raasay, Highland.
Outdoor centre with cafe and accommodation. (01478 660266 / www.raasay-house.co.uk)

Radisson SAS Hotel, Edinburgh

Located on the Royal Mile in the heart of the Old Town, the large and bustling hotel dates from the late 1980s and is built in a Scottish vernacular style which well matches many of the other nearby buildings.

The hotel stands on the site of old tenements, and there are stories that the building is haunted by the ghosts of plague victims. It is said that apparitions have been seen, sprawled on the floor of the laundry room, and that these phantoms fade away if approached.

Map 4, 9L (Edinburgh). Off A1, 80 High Street, The Royal Mile, Edinburgh.
Hotel. (0131 557 9797 / www.radissonsas.com)

Ragged Hospital, Edinburgh

The Ragged Hospital (or School) was located in a building dating from 1850, and was founded by Dr Guthrie. The school has long been shut and the building is now derelict, although plans are afoot to incorporate the former school into the Camera Obscura (also see that entry).

The building is said to be haunted, and some have suggested that the adjacent Camera Obscura is also being plagued by bogles from here.

Map 4, 9L (Edinburgh). Off A1, Ramsey Lane, Castlehill, Edinburgh.

A paranormal investigation was undertaken in June 2007 by Ghost Finders (www.ghostfinders.co.uk/camera_obscura.html) and in February, in May and in July 2008 by Scottish Society of Paranormal Investigation and Analysis (www.sspia.co.uk)

Rait Castle

Rait Castle is a striking ruinous hall-house, dating from the 13th century but altered in the 16th and 17th centuries. The building is mostly complete to the wallhead, and was a property of the Raits, but later passed to the Comyns or Cummings.

The tale (although there is more one version) goes that in 1524, when the castle was held by the Cummings, they invited the Mackintoshes here for a feast, possibly a wedding banquet, but planned to murder their guests. The Mackintoshes apparently learned of the plan and came heavily armed, and managed to flee from Rait after killing many of their treacherous hosts. The Cumming laird was furious – he suspected his daughter had betrayed his plan, as she was in love with one of the Mackintoshes – and he pursued the terrified girl through the building.

The girl tried to escape out of an upstairs window, but her father hacked off her hands with his sword as she hung from a window ledge, and she fell to her death. Her ghost, sometimes known as the 'Wraith of Rait', a handless phantom in a white blood-stained dress, then began to haunt Rait.

The Cumming laird and his followers were, themselves, apparently slain at Balblair in retribution.

Rait passed to the Mackintoshes, then to the Campbells of Cawdor, and there are plans afoot to clear and consolidate the ruins; work has recently begun.

Map 2, 8E (Rait). Off B9101, 2.5 miles S of Nairn, Rait, Highland.
View from exterior. (www.saveraitcastle.org)

RAMMERSCALES HOUSE

ILLUS PAGE 235

Standing on a high slope of the Torthorwald Hills, Rammerscales is a fine 18th-century mansion, with magnificent views over Annandale. In Adam style and mostly unaltered, Rammerscales was built for Dr James Mounsey in the 1760s, but is now a property of the Bell Macdonald family, having been purchased by James Bell, a sugar merchant from Glasgow, in the 1790s. It houses rare contemporary art and a library with 600 volumes, and there are extensive and attractive grounds with walled gardens.

The house is said to be haunted by the ghost of Dr James Mounsey, who had been physician to Czar Peter of Russia and died in 1773. Disturbances are said to be centred in the library, and evacuees from Glasgow, during World War II, were apparently so scared of the ghost that they chose to sleep in the stables.

Map 4, 9P (Rammerscales). On B9020, 3 miles SW of Lockerbie, Dumfries and Galloway.
Guided tours for parties of 25 or more. (01387 810229 / www.rammerscales.co.uk)

RAMSAY GARDEN, EDINBURGH

Ramsay Garden is a fine, fanciful and intricate building at the top of Castlehill in the shadow of the castle, and dates from the 18th century, although it was much altered in the 1890s. The building is named after Allan Ramsay, the father of the famous portrait painter.

One account has Ramsay Garden haunted by the frightening apparition of a hunch-back, reputed to be in the style of the late 18th century. The bogle is said to have been seen more than once, dragging a large wooden chest after it.

Map 4, 9L (Edinburgh). Off A1, Ramsay Gardens, Castlehill (Royal Mile), Edinburgh.

RAMSHORN THEATRE, GLASGOW

The Ramshorn Theatre is housed in an atmospheric Gothic church of 1826, which itself replaced an older church on the site, and the adjoining burial ground has some interesting old memorials. The theatre has a varied programme of music and drama, and is the University of Strathclyde's drama centre.

The building is reputed to be haunted by a bogle of a woman, which is called 'Edie', spotted in the toilets (where the vestry for the church was located). Other manifestations are said to be the sound of unexplained footsteps heard around the building, and strong but mysterious smells.

Map 4, 7M (Glasgow). Off A8, Ingram Street, Glasgow.
Theatre. (0141 548 2542 / www.strath.ac.uk/culture/ramshorn/)

RATHEN CHURCH

The present church, dating from 1870, replaced a much older building, of which the south and west wall and the remains of an aisle survive. The church here was given to the Abbey of Arbroath by Marjorie, Countess of Buchan, and in 1328 Robert the Bruce granted the benefice to the College of Old Machar.

The old church was believed to be haunted at one time, the story originating from the 1640s. The sounds of singing and musical instruments were heard coming from the loft of the building, when there was nobody present there.

The eerie phenomena was attributed to the ongoing battle between the Royalist Marquis of Montrose and Covenanter Earl of Argyll.

Map 2, 12E (Rathen). Off A92, 3 miles S of Fraserburgh, Banff & Buchan.
Open at all reasonable times.

RAVENSCRAIG STEEL WORKS

The Ravenscraig Steel Works, which once covered a large site and employed thousands of men, was built by the firm Colvilles to meet the demand for steel following World War II. The plant was closed in the 1990s, and the cooling towers and iconic gas-holders were finally demolished in 1996. The whole site, more than 1,000 acres, is being redeveloped into a new town and parkland, with retail, leisure, residential and commercial building.

The plant was said to be haunted by the ghost of a worker decapitated in an accident; the bogle is reported to have been seen several times beside one of the furnaces.

Map 4, 7M (Motherwell). Off A723 or A721, to E of Motherwell, Ravenscraig, Lanarkshire.
New town development. (www.ravenscraig.co.uk)

RAVENSPARK ASYLUM, IRVINE

Ravenspark was first built in 1857 as the Cunninghame Combination Poor House, but was soon used to house people diagnosed with mental health problems. In 1892 it was said that corpses of paupers, who died here, were being buried in a mass grave in the grounds. The asylum was converted to a hospital in the 1930s, with wards for the elderly, for psychiatric patients, and for the 'mentally defective'. The hospital was closed in 1996, and the site is to be redeveloped, retaining the facade of the main building, with some 117 flats and houses.

Ravenspark is said to be haunted, believed to be by the spirits of patients. Manifestations are reported to include unexplained footsteps, whispering and disembodied voices, and doors sounding as if they are being shut loudly.

Map 3, 6N (Irvine). On B779, Sandy Road, to NW of Irvine, Ravenspark, Ayrshire.

Paranormal investigations have been undertaken by Ghost Hunters Scotland (www.ghosthunters.org.uk) and by Spiritfinders Scotland (www.spiritfindersscotland.com)

RAVENSWOOD HOTEL, BALLATER

Set in expansive grounds by the picturesque River Dee, the Ravenswood Hotel dates from around 1820 and was a private residence until the 1970s.

The building is reputedly haunted. One ghost is said to be that of a woman, who was only ever apparently heard over an intercom when babies are staying in the hotel – she may have been a nursemaid. The kindly ghost is reputed to care for infants and children.

The other is said to be the apparition of an old man with a white beard, dressed like a sailor in a sweater, the arms rolled up to his elbow, sightings of which have been reported on the stair and in two of the bedrooms. Some believe that this is the bogle of the man who built the house and the original owner.

Map 2, 9G (Ballater). Off A93, Ballater, Kincardine & Deeside.
Hotel. (01339 755539)

RED CASTLE

Standing on a strong position above a steep ravine, Red Castle (also known as Edradour Castle) is a ruinous but an impressive L-plan tower house, which incorporates some of a 12th-century castle. The property had several owners before coming to the Mackenzies in 1570, and they built most of the present castle. The castle was used to house troops in World War II, but the building soon became derelict after the war and it is in a dangerously ruined condition.

The castle is said to be haunted.

Map 2, 7E (Red Castle). Off A832, 3.5 miles E of Muir of Ord, N shore of Beauly Firth, Redcastle, Ross and Cromarty, Highland.

RED LION INN, ELGIN

The former Red Lion Inn is an old merchant's house of three storeys, dating from 1688 and with an arcaded front, corbiestepped gables, and lower wings at the rear. In the 18th century it was used as an inn, and it was visited by Dr Samuel Johnson, although he was not happy with the food and 'found reason to complain of a Scottish table', the only occasion on his journeys in Scotland that he decided to do so. The inn has since been divided into separate dwellings.

There are reports that the building is haunted, and that phantom piping can sometimes be heard, coming from the second floor.

Map 2, 9E (Elgin). Off A96, 42-46 High Street, Elgin, Moray.

RENFREW VICTORY BATHS   ILLUS PAGE 235

Housed in an attractive building with an ogee-domed tower, the swimming baths were built in the 1920s, and still retain many contemporary features, such as the 25-yard pool, cubicles around the pool, arched doorways, memorabilia, and a viewing gallery, as well as more modern facilities, including a sauna suite, dance studio and beauty treatment area.

The baths are said to be haunted by two ghosts. The first is reputed to be a 'White Lady', who is apparently witnessed in a chamber under the pool which is used for storage. The bogle has been described as wearing a white, floaty dress, and the witness observed the phantom for some seconds before it faded away. The apparition has apparently been spotted several other times.

The second ghost is reported to be that of a small lad, who is believed to have died at the baths in the 1920s. A member of the staff reported that he had even taken a recording of the lad's apparition, on his mobile phone, after he had spotted it going by and then 'floating' up stairs towards the viewing gallery. The story goes that the lad had been given a German helmet and that he had worn it while diving from the highest board. The helmet snapped his head back and broke his neck.

Map 4, 7M (Renfrew). Off A741, Inchinnan Road, Renfrew.
Swimming baths. (0141 886 2088 / www.renfrewshireleisure.com)

RING CROFT OF STOCKING, AUCHENCAIRN

The haunting of Ring Croft of Stocking near Auchencairn in the parish of Rerrick, the house of Andrew Mackie, is a well-documented case of poltergeist activity in 1695, witnessed by many people and recorded by the local minister. The activity did not last for very long but was very intense, and involved not just the Mackies but their neighbours (and even the minister at first hand), when they visited.

All sorts of strange things happened. Mackie's cattle were let out of his cowshed, stones and other objects were thrown about, items disappeared only to be found later. The disturbances intensified: Mackie and others were hit with an invisible stick and dragged across the floor, stones and other items were thrown at folk, there were thumps and bangs, peats were thrown about and set alight, a rough voice was heard. The manifestations seemed to be worse on the Sabbath or when the family were praying together.

Mackie's wife disturbed a slab in the threshold of the house, and under it found the remains of a man. Disturbances then became even worse, despite the intervention of more ministers and an investigation into how the body had come to be under the entrance of the house (no explanation was found, nor culprit discovered).

Then, after about three months, the haunting suddenly stopped.

One explanation is that the house was reputedly built where a body had been found, believed to be a victim of murder, but why the ghost should have so afflicted Mackie, his family, neighbours and ministers has never been established.

Map 4, 8Q (Auchencairn). Off A711, near Auchencairn, Dumfries and Galloway.

RING O' BELLS PUB, ELDERSLIE

The Ring o' Bells, formerly known as the Wallace Tavern, is housed in an attractive old building, dating from early in the 19th century and with a turnpike stair.

The building is said to be haunted, manifestations reputed to include the phantoms of men clad in black cloaks and the unexplained sounds of horses' hooves.

The story is that around the 1850s a horse-drawn coach overturned by the pub, killing at least one of the passengers as well as the horses.

Map 4, 7M (Paisley). Off A737, 2 miles W of Paisley, 181 Main Road, Elderslie, Renfrewshire.
Public house. (01505 322053)

ROCKHALL

Rockhall, a much-altered tower house of the 16th century, was occupied at the end of the 17th century by Sir Robert Grierson of Lagg, an infamous prosecutor of Covenanters. One story is that a phantom black coach and horses were sent by the

Devil to fetch Grierson to hell after his death, all this witnessed by a ship on the Solway Firth (see Lagg).

Grierson's pet monkey, killed by his servants after his death, is said to haunt the building and reputedly can be heard at times blowing a silver whistle.

Map 4, 9P (Rockhall). Off A75, 6 miles E of Dumfries, Rockhall, Dumfries and Galloway.

ROSSDHU HOUSE

Rossdhu House is a large and attractive Adam-style mansion, which was built for the Colquhouns of Luss in 1772, standing in a fantastic spot on the shore of Loch Lomond. The mansion replaced Rossdhu Castle, which is now very ruinous and dated from the 15th century. The house was built using materials from the castle, and is now the clubhouse for the Loch Lomond Golf Club.

The lands were a property of the Colquhouns of Luss from the 13th century. The old castle was visited twice by Mary, Queen of Scots, and James Colquhoun led his clan to defeat in a battle with the MacGregors in Glen Fruin in 1603. The new house was visited by Johnson and Boswell in 1773. Lady Helen, wife of Sir James Colquhoun, 25th laird of Luss, was quite peeved when Johnson trudged through her spanking new drawing room, water and mud dripping from his boots, after he had been out on a boat on Loch Lomond.

The house is said to be haunted by the bogle of Lady Helen. She was very house proud in life, and her ghost reputedly returns to watch over the house she loved. The spirit has been most often reported in the staff quarters.

Map 3, 6L (Rossdhu). Off A82, 2 miles S of Luss, near Rossdhu House, near shore of Loch Lomond, Dunbartonshire.
Golf club house; accommodation is available. (01463 655555 / www.lochlomond.com)

ROSSHALL HOSPITAL, GLASGOW

The baronial mansion was built for the Rosses of Hawkhead, and dates from the end of the 19th century, although the building was later altered and extended and is now a private hospital.

One story is that the hospital is haunted by the phantom of a woman who died some years ago during an operation. The apparition is said to have grey hair, and to quickly vanish away after being spotted.

Map 4, 7M (Glasgow). On A736, 221 Crookston Road, Glasgow.
Private hospital. (0141 882 7439 / www.bmihealthcare.co.uk/rosshall)

ROSSLYN CASTLE

Standing in the picturesque glen high above the River Esk, Rosslyn Castle was once the magnificent fortress of the Sinclair Earls of Orkney and then of Caithness. Although much is now ruinous, part of the building is still habitable and the remains are very atmospheric.

A ghost story dates from the Wars of Independence in 1302, when an English army was heavily defeated by the Scots near the castle. A spectre of a dog, the 'Mauthe Dog', killed with its English master after the battle, reputedly haunts the castle, and its howling has been reported on several occasions.

The Sinclairs fought for Bruce at Bannockburn in 1314, and Sir Henry Sinclair was one of the nobles to add his seal to the Declaration of Arbroath six years later. Sir

William Sinclair set out on a Crusade with Robert the Bruce's heart, and was killed fighting the Moors in Granada in 1330.

A wondrous treasure is said to be buried beneath the vaults of the castle, guarded by a unearthly 'White Lady', a spirit of one of the Sinclair ladies. The story is that she can only be woken and the treasure found by blowing a trumpet when standing on the correct step of one of the staircases.

The apparition of a knight in black armour, riding a black horse and with his visor down, is reputed to have been seen on at least three occasions in recent times.

Map 4, 9M (Rosslyn). Off B7006, 2 miles S of Loanhead, Roslin, Midlothian.
Accommodation is available through the Landmark Trust for holidays for up to seven people. (01628 825925 / www.landmarktrust.org.uk)

ROSSLYN CHAPEL   ILLUS PAGE 236

Situated in the sylvan wooded Roslin Glen and overlooking the River Esk is the magnificent Rosslyn Chapel, which stands overlooking Rosslyn Castle. The chapel, dedicated to St Matthew and intended to be a Collegiate Church, was founded by William Sinclair, Earl of Orkney, in 1446. It was never completed: only the choir and parts of the transepts were built. The roof is vaulted and there are a mass of flying buttresses to carry the weight.

The chapel is richly and exuberantly carved with Biblical stories, and has the largest number of 'Green Men' found in any medieval building. In the burial vault beneath the floor are many of the Sinclairs of Rosslyn and their kin, at one time laid out in full armour without coffins. Ghostly flames were said to be seen here when one of the Sinclairs was about to die, although these did no damage to the building.

In recent years the chapel has been linked by some authors to the Holy Grail as well as to the Knights Templars (although perhaps the White Lady of Rosslyn Castle and her fabulous treasure are a better bet). This latter association is somewhat tenuous, however, as the Knights Templar were suppressed in 1312 and the chapel was not begun until the middle of the 15th century. Some claim, William Sinclair, the chapel's builder, was Grand Master of the Knights Templar, who were by now an 'underground organisation'. Whatever the truth of it, the chapel features in the *Da Vinci Code* by Dan Brown, and part of the movie with Tom Hanks was filmed at the chapel in September 2005.

The chapel is also reputedly haunted by the ghost of the apprentice, who carved the famous Apprentice Pillar and traditionally was murdered by his teacher.

Apparitions of monks or priests have also been reported in recent times, both in the chapel and outside the building. One report described a ghost clad in a black robe, another in a grey robe, so presumably these are different bogles...

Map 4, 9M (Rosslyn). Off A701, 6 miles S of Edinburgh, Roslin, Midlothian.
Open all year, daily, except closed 25-26 Dec and 31 Dec-1 Jan. (0131 440 2159 / www.rosslyn-chapel.com)

ROTHESAY CASTLE   ILLUS PAGE 255

Standing in the seaside town on the picturesque island of Bute, Rothesay Castle, dating from the 12th century, consists of a circular curtain wall with four round towers. The ruinous stronghold is surrounded by a wet moat, while a large gate-house block was added in the 15th century.

The castle was attacked and captured by Norsemen in the 1230s, and a ghost story dates from this time. According to a 19th-century ballad, the castle is haunted by a Lady Isobel, her apparition seen on the 'Bloody Stair', behind the chapel. Her family were killed by Norsemen, and rather than submit to marriage with a Viking she stabbed herself to death. One account describes the ghost as a 'Green Lady'.

Rothesay was long held by the Stewarts, and was besieged on many occasions. Robert II and Robert III, who may have died here in 1406, both visited often. In 1401 Robert III had made David, his son, Duke of Rothesay, a title since taken by the eldest son of the kings of Scots and currently held by Prince Charles.

It did not do David much good, however, as he was starved to death at Falkland Palace (also see that entry) by his uncle and rival, Robert, Duke of Albany.

Map 3, 5M (Rothesay). Off A845, Rothesay, Bute.
His Scot: Open all year: Apr-Oct, daily; Nov-Mar, Sat-Wed, closed Thu & Fri; closed 25/26 Dec and 1/2 Jan. (01700 502691 / www.historic-scotland.gov.uk)

ROTHIEMAY CASTLE

Although a grand and imposing castle with turrets, towers and spires, and having a long and intriguing history, Rothiemay Castle was completely demolished in 1956. The building may have dated from as early as the 14th century, but it had been remodelled and extended down the years into a massive mansion. The original castle was built by the Abernethys, after they had been given the lands by David II in the 14th century.

Rothiemay was later sold to the Gordons. In 1630 William Gordon of Rothiemay, and others, were burned to death at the castle of Frendraught (see that entry) in suspicious circumstances. In revenge, Gordon's widow, Lady Rothiemay employed Highlanders to attack and harry Crichton's lands and family; Lady Rothiemay was eventually imprisoned in 1635. Rothiemay passed to the Duffs in 1741, and then to the Forbeses.

There are ghost stories associated with the castle.

One bogle was said to be that of an old woman, an apparition of which, clad in a plaid shawl, was observed sitting by a fire.

Another ghost was believed to be that of Lieutenant Colonel J. Foster Forbes, which was seen several times after his death, including by his grandchildren.

Other manifestations reputedly included the weeping of children, arguing coming from an unoccupied room, and unexplained footsteps in an empty corridor.

Map 2, 10F (Rothiemay). Off B9118 or B9117, 5.5 miles N of Huntly, Rothiemay, Moray.

ROXBURGH CASTLE

This was once one of the most important strongholds in Scotland, although not much now remains, and the old fortress saw much action in the long wars with England. Mary, sister of Robert the Bruce, was suspended in a cage from the walls by the English, although she was eventually released. In 1460 James II was killed when one of the cannons, with which he was bombarding the castle, blew up beside him, although Roxburgh was then stormed and demolished. A holly tree between Floors and the River Tweed is said to mark the spot where James was killed.

A ghostly horseman is reputedly sometimes seen riding towards the castle.

Map 4, 11N (Roxburgh). Off A699, 1 mile W of Kelso, Roxburgh, Borders.
Access at all reasonable times.

ROXBURGHE HOUSE

ILLUS PAGE 255

Roxburghe House Hotel, formerly known as Sunlaws, dates mostly from 1853 and replaced a previous house which had been destroyed by fire. The hotel stands in a tranquil location in 200 acres of gardens and wooded park land. Sunlaws was a property of the Kerrs of Chatto, and Bonnie Prince Charlie was entertained here in November 1745. The house was used to hold German prisoners of war during World War II, the property was acquired by the Duke of Roxburghe in 1969, and the building is now an exclusive hotel.

The hotel is said to have several ghosts.

One is reported to be the apparition of a woman, a 'Green Lady', who is clad in green. She allegedly walks the area on the ground floor, covering the corridor from the kitchen, through to the inner hall and then along the path leading out from the conservatory up to the Chinese bridge. The story goes that she is searching for her baby. The ghost has been seen several times in living memory.

Another ghost is reputedly that of a soldier. The apparition may be one of those imprisoned here during the war, or one of the family who formerly lived at the house as many of them were in the military. The ghost has been witnessed on the top floor of the house, which is currently only used for storage space. The apparition is dressed in brown, military-style clothing.

A third manifestation is felt rather than seen, and one of the rooms has had a strange aura from time to time. A guest in 1990 reported that she awoke suddenly at night with a strange sensation, as if something cool was brushing down her entire body.

The administration offices, housed in the old laundry in the oldest part of the building, are also said to be haunted.

Map 4, 11N (Roxburghe). Off A608, 3 miles S of Kelso, Borders.
Hotel. (01573 450331 / www.roxburghe.net)

ROYAL ALEXANDRA INFIRMARY, PAISLEY

The Royal Alexandra Infirmary dates from about 1900, and the original building is an interesting mix of both baronial and art nouveau styles. The hospital serves Paisley and the surrounding area with maternity, accident and emergency, and many other services.

At least one account states that the hospital is haunted. Manifestations are said to include footsteps coming from an unoccupied loft, as well as the sounds of whispering and running water coming from wards where all the patients were apparently asleep. Beds are also reputed to have been mysteriously pushed away from walls and elevated, and there is also a report of the apparition of man dragging something behind him, which might have been a body bag.

Map 4, 7M (Paisley). Off B775, Corsebar Road, Paisley, Renfrewshire.
Hospital. (0141 887 9111)

ROYAL CIRCUS HOTEL, EDINBURGH

The Royal Circus was built in 1823 as part of Edinburgh's New Town, and is an elegant sweep of houses in a long crescent overlooking the Royal Circus gardens. The hotel is a fine establishment located in the crescent, and there are stories that the building is haunted by the apparition of a beautiful woman, dressed in white but with black hair, spotted moving along in the corridors.

Map 4, 9L (Edinburgh). Off A90, 19-20 Royal Circus, Edinburgh.
Hotel. (0131 220 5000)

ROYAL HOTEL, AUCHTERMUCHTY

The Royal Hotel is believed to be haunted.

The story goes that a previous owner committed suicide in one of the rooms, and since then unexplained activity has been reported in that chamber, as well as the alleged sightings of an apparition in the main hallway. The hotel has been closed in the last few years.

Map 4, 9K (Auchtermuchty). Off A91, 5 miles W of Cupar, Cupar Road, Auchtermuchty, Fife.

A paranormal investigation was undertaken in June 2004 by Ghost Finders (www.ghostfinders.co.uk/royalhotel.html)

ROYAL HOTEL, COMRIE

The Royal Hotel, in the pleasant Perthshire village of Comrie, is housed in a building dating from about 1800.

The building is said to be haunted by a 'Green Lady', an elegant apparition sighted in a long flowing green cloak. The bogle is said to been seen searching the corridors for her love, who was lost in a blizzard, and is reputedly a friendly ghost.

Map 4, 7K (Comrie). Off A85, Melville Square, Comrie, Perthshire.
Hotel. (01764 679200 / www.royalhotel.co.uk)

ROYAL HOTEL, COUPAR ANGUS

The Royal Hotel, which dates from the middle of the 19th century, is said to be haunted.

Map 4, 9J (Coupar Angus). Off A94, The Cross, High Street, Coupar Angus, Perthshire.
Hotel. (01828 627549)

A paranormal investigation was undertaken in June 2005 by Paranormal Investigation Scotland (www.paranormalinvestigationscotland.co.uk/royalhotelsecondvisit.htm)

ROYAL HOTEL, CUPAR

The former hotel, which was built in the 19th century, is said to be built on the site of a graveyard associated with the Dominican friary of St Katherine, founded in 1348 by Duncan Earl of Fife. The lands were given to the burgh in 1572, and a small part of the church survived in the 19th century, but nothing now remains.

The hotel was said to be haunted by the ghost of one of the friars, seen most often in the function rooms, while other manifestations reputedly included objects moving by themselves. A sighting of the ghost was made in 1978 in an empty room, when the hooded apparition was apparently seen walking silently across the floor, and other manifestations are said to have been sudden drops in temperature and the mysterious moving of cutlery and other objects. Another sighting of the ghost was allegedly made in the function room, when it was observed in a strange eerie light. The ghost vanished through a wall and the light was extinguished at the same time; this was accompanied by extreme cold.

The ghost had apparently been seen twice before in the same location.

The hotel is now used as flats for old folk.

Map 4, 10K (Cupar). Off A91, St Catherine Street, Cupar, Fife.

ROYAL LYCEUM, EDINBURGH

The Royal Lyceum Theatre, dating from 1883 but remodelled in 1992 with a glass foyer, has a fine Victorian interior, and is the venue for many excellent plays, drama and comedy. The building is said to be haunted by the apparition of a woman in a blue dress, seen in an upper gallery which is not open to the public during the performance of a play. The bogle has been identified by some as that of Ellen Terry, who was at the first performance of the theatre. A second ghost is claimed to be that of a shadowy figure, seen in the lighting gantry above the stage.

Map 4, 9L (Edinburgh). Off A1, 30B Grindlay Street, Edinburgh.
Theatre with bar. (0131 248 4848 / www.lyceum.org.uk)

ROYAL MILE, EDINBURGH

The Royal Mile is the street which runs down through the Old Town from the castle, through Castlehill, the Lawnmarket, the High Street and the Canongate to Holyrood.

The street is said to be where a harbinger of ill omen for the city was sometimes seen, in the form of a phantom coach tearing up the Royal Mile. This black coach was reported to be drawn by galloping black horses breathing fire, and to be full of mourners dressed in black.

Map 4, 9L (Edinburgh). Off A1, Royal Mile, Edinburgh.

RUTHVEN BARRACKS   ILLUS PAGE 255

The present building, a barracks built to defend against the Jacobites, stands on the site of an ancient stronghold. Ruthven was held by Alexander Stewart, Earl of Buchan and the Wolf of Badenoch, at the end of the 14th century. Stewart, who was an unruly fellow, was one of the sons of Robert II. When he was excommunicated by the Bishop of Moray, he burnt Forres and Elgin in revenge, including the cathedral.

One tale has him as an even darker character. The story goes that Stewart practised witchcraft, but in 1406 a dark visitor challenged Stewart to a game of chess. In the morning he and his men were found dead, for Stewart had played with the Devil and lost. The phantoms of Stewart and his followers reputedly repeat their grisly doom and haunt the place.

So the story goes. Stewart, however, was buried in Dunkeld Cathedral, having died in his sixties, and his fine stone effigy survives in the church.

Map 2, 7G (Ruthven). Off A9, 1 mile S of Kingussie, Ruthven Barracks, Badenoch, Highland.
His Scot: Access at all reasonable times. (01667 460232 / www.historic-scotland.gov.uk)

SADDELL CASTLE

Saddell Castle consists of an altered 15th-century keep and a range of 18th-century outbuildings, which replaced the original courtyard. The castle stands on what were the lands of Saddell Abbey, founded by Reginald, son of Somerled. Angus Og Mac-

Rothesay Castle (page 250)

Roxburghe House (page 252)

Ruthven Barracks (page 254)

*Scone Palace
(page 259)*

*Scottish Fisheries
Museum
(page 260)*

Scotland's Secret Bunker (page 259)

Donald is said to have sheltered Robert the Bruce here in 1306. The castle was later held by the Ralston family as tenants of the Campbells, and the castle was replaced by the 18th-century Saddell House.

Saddell Castle is said to be haunted. A 'White Lady' is reputed to walk the battlements, and the castle also reportedly has a ghostly monk, who appears to have translated, with much of the stone, from Saddell Abbey.

Map 3, 4N (Saddell). Off B842, 8 miles N of Campbeltown, Kintyre.
Can be rented through the Landmark Trust for holidays for up to eight people. (01628 825925 / www.landmarktrust.org.uk)

SALTOUN HALL

Saltoun Hall incorporates part of a strong castle, dating from as early as the 12th century. The lands were a property of the Abernethy Lords Saltoun, but were sold in the 17th century to Sir Andrew Fletcher, who was prominent in resisting the Union of Parliaments of Scotland and England in 1707. The hall is still occupied but has been divided into separate dwellings.

The hall is reputedly haunted by a 'Grey Lady'.

Map 4, 10M (Saltoun). Off B6355, 5 miles SW of Haddington, Saltoun, East Lothian.

SALUTATION HOTEL, PERTH

One of the oldest hotels in Scotland and dating from 1699, the Salutation Hotel was visited by Bonnie Prince Charlie in 1745 during the Jacobite Rising.

His apparition, wearing green tartan, is said to have been seen in one of the bedrooms.

Map 4, 9K (Perth). Off M90, 34 South Street, Perth.
Hotel. (01738 630066 / www.strathmorehotels.com/salu_site/)

SANDWOOD BAY

The picturesque sands here are reported to be haunted by a bearded sailor, as is a nearby cottage on Sandwood Loch, the apparition having been witnessed on several occasions, including in recent times. The phantom is clad in a brass-buttoned dark tunic, sailor's cap and boots. One story suggests that the ghost is that of a seaman drowned when his ship sank and his body was washed up in the bay.

Map 1, 5A (Sandwood). Off B801, 8 miles N of Kinlochbervie, Sandwood Bay, Sutherland, Highland.
Accessible at all times.

SANDYFORD PLACE, GLASGOW

One of the houses in Sandyford Place, which dates from the middle of the 19th century, is reported to be haunted. The apparition of a man has reputedly been spotted lying in a bed and the bogle appears to be choking. One occupant claimed to have seen the ghost along with a phantom noose, spotted hanging from the ceiling. The house is now used as an office, and there are apparently no recent reports of activity.

Map 4, 7M (Glasgow). Off A814 or A82, Sandyford Place, Glasgow.

SANQUHAR CASTLE

Sanquhar Castle is a ruinous 13th-century castle of the Crichton family, and two ghosts reputedly haunt the crumbling walls.

One is the 'White Lady', which is believed to be the spirit of a young golden-haired woman, Marion (MacMath?) of Dalpeddar (also see that entry), who is said to have disappeared in 1590. She may have been murdered by one of the Crichton lords, and a skeleton of a girl was reportedly found in 1875-76, face down in a pit, during excavations. Her appearance was said to bode ill for the Crichtons.

The other ghost is allegedly that of John Wilson, who was hanged unjustly in 1597 by Robert Crichton, 6th Lord Sanquhar. Wilson was an innocent messenger who got embroiled in a dispute between Crichton and Sir Thomas Kirkpatrick.

His bogle manifests itself with groans and the rattling of chains.

The headless body of a man was also found around the 1840s, under the floor of one of the castle vaults.

Map 4, 8O (Sanquhar). Off A76, 0.25 miles S of Sanquhar, Dumfries and Galloway.
Open all year: ruins are in a poor state of repair and great care should be taken.

SANQUHAR KIRKYARD

Abraham Crichton of Carco, an unpopular, miserly and apparently ruthless land-owner, who was Provost of Sanquhar, died bankrupt in 1741. He had wanted to remove materials from the derelict church of Kilbride. As he was in the process of demolishing the church, a storm blew up and thunder frightened his horse. Crichton tumbled from the saddle and was dragged along the ground all the way to Dalpeddar, dying an excruciating death.

His ghost is then said to have haunted Sanquhar churchyard, where he was buried. Crichton is said to have been a very rich but miserly man, despite being declared bankrupt, and his ghost is reported to have returned to try and prevent his hoard of money being found. His bogle is said to have repeatedly terrified passers-by until it was exorcised by a priest, after which it was not witnessed again.

This is not the only ghost linked to the Crichtons which is associated with Dalpeddar (see Dalpeddar and Sanquhar Castle).

Map 4, 8O (Sanquhar). Off A76, Sanquhar, Dumfries and Galloway.

SARACEN HEAD, GLASGOW

Located in the centre of Glasgow, the original Saracen Head (or 'Sarry Heid', as it is known) was built in 1755 and stood over the road from the present pub. The hostelry has much character and an eventful history, not least it is home to the skull of the last reputed witch to be executed in Scotland, which is on display in a glass case.

The pub is reputed to be haunted by a former publican called Angus, and there has been unexplained activity in recent times, said to be caused by the bogles of former drinkers.

Map 4, 7M (Glasgow). Off A8 or A89, 209 Gallowgate, Glasgow.
Public house. (0141 552 1660)

A paranormal investigation was undertaken in May 2005 by Ghost Finders (www.ghostfinders.co.uk/saracenhead.html) and by Spiritfinders Scotland (www.spiritfindersscotland.com)

SAUGHTON HOUSE, EDINBURGH

Saughton House was burnt down in the 1950s and was then demolished, although it has been an attractive old fortified house. The site of the house is occupied by a garden.

Saughton originally belonged to the Watsons, but passed to the Ellis family, who built the house, and later to the Baillies, then to the Bairds. The building was used as a private lunatic asylum, before being bought by the local council, after which the grounds were turned into a park. The 1908 Scottish National Exhibition took place in the policies, although only a footbridge from the exhibition now survives.

The house was said to have had a 'Green Lady', which is still, reportedly, occasionally spotted in the garden.

Map 4, 9L (Edinburgh). Off A71, 3 miles W of Edinburgh Castle, Saughton Park, Edinburgh.

SCONE PALACE

ILLUS PAGE 256

Standing in 100 acres of fine gardens and woodlands, Scone Palace is magnificent and stately mansion, dating from 1802, although it incorporates older work, possibly part of the Abbot's Lodging. The property has long been owned by the Murray Earls of Mansfield.

The palace stands on the site of an abbey founded here in the 12th century, and the Kings of Scots were inaugurated at the Moot Hill from the 9th century up to Charles I in 1651. The Stone of Destiny, also called the Stone of Scone, was kept here, until taken to Westminster Abbey by Edward I in 1296 – although this was returned to Edinburgh Castle in 1996, exactly 700 years later.

The palace is said to be haunted by ghostly footsteps, heard in the south passage. Although the passage has a wooden floor, it allegedly sounds as if the footsteps are walking down a stone one.

Map 4, 9K (Scone). Off A93, 2 miles N of Perth, Scone, Perthshire.
Open Apr-Oct, daily; other times by appt. (01738 552300 / www.scone-palace.co.uk)

SCOTIA BAR, GLASGOW

The Scotia Bar, with a long and colourful history, was first founded at the end of the 18th century, and continues today as a popular hostelry for those with an interest in music, literature or politics.

The pub is said to be haunted, the story going that a former publican hanged himself in the cellar.

Map 4, 7M (Glasgow). Off A736, A737 or A739, 112-114 Stockwell Street, Glasgow.
Public house. (0141 552 8681 / www.scotiabar.net)

A paranormal investigation was undertaken in March 2007 by Spiritfinders Scotland (www.spiritfindersscotland.com)

SCOTLAND'S SECRET BUNKER, TROYWOOD

ILLUS PAGE 256

The bunker, which is some 100-foot underground, was built in the 1950s to house government operations in the event of a nuclear war. Everything was included within the bunker, including an operations room, cinema and restaurant. The entrance was concealed in what appeared to be a farm house, and a tunnel led through blast-proof doors and into the bunker. Furniture and other items seen in the bunker are authentic, including the Tote board showing aircraft and anti-aircraft gun status. The bunker was decommissioned in 1993, and it was sold and then opened to visitors.

There are several accounts of hauntings in the bunker, including sightings of an apparition of a uniformed person, seen at one spot in the bunker. Other activity is said to include unusual changes in temperature, including cold spots, and both staff and visitors reporting that they feel very drained.

Map 4, 10K (Troywood). Off B940, 6 miles SE of St Andrews, 4 miles N of Anstruther, Troywood, Fife.
Open Apr-Oct, daily. (01333 310301 / www.secretbunker.co.uk)

A paranormal investigation was undertaken in April 2008 by the Ghost Club (www.ghostclub.org.uk) and by Spiritfinders Scotland (www.spiritfindersscotland.com) and by in August 2005 Alba Paranormal Investigations (www.albaparanormal.com/ secretbunker.htm)

SCOTSMAN HOTEL, EDINBURGH

Housed in an impressive and elaborate building rising many storeys, the Scotsman Hotel was the former offices and printing works of The Scotsman newspaper, and its associated publications, until that organisation moved to a new site near Holyrood. The hotel is a luxury five star boutique establishment, with the bar and brasserie housed in the fabulous wood-panelled reception room; the press room is now occupied by a gym.

The building is said to be haunted by a several ghosts, including a phantom printer and the bogle of a forger.

Map 4, 9L (Edinburgh). Off A7, 20 North Bridge, Edinburgh.
Hotel. (0131 556 5565 / www.theetoncollection.com)

SCOTTISH FISHERIES MUSEUM, ANSTRUTHER   ILLUS PAGE 256

The Scottish Fisheries Museum is grouped around a cobbled courtyard at the harbour, and has extended into an old boatyard alongside. Among the many attractions are the boats, both real and model, and a fisherman's cottage. The museum buildings incorporate an abbot's lodging of Balmerino Abbey, dating from the 16th century, and a merchant's house of 1724, and other parts are built on the site of a chapel, inn and cooper's workshop.

The museum buildings are said to be haunted, and a dark apparition by a boat in the yard has been reported, as well as unexplained footsteps coming from an unoccupied area. The door into the fisherman's cottage is reported at times to be unusually difficult to open, as if someone was pushing it from the other side, even though the cottage was empty. It is also said that poltergeist-type activity was experienced in the Days of Sail exhibit. This may have been associated with a pair of boots, which had been taken from the cottage, as the odd occurrences are said to have ceased when the boots were returned to the cottage.

Map 4, 10K (Anstruther). Off A917, St Ayles, Harbour Head, Anstruther, Fife.
Open all year, daily; closed 25/26 Dec & 1-2 Jan. (01333 310628 / www.scotfishmuseum.org)

A paranormal investigation was undertaken by Paranormal Discovery (www.paranormaldiscovery.co.uk)

Scottish Mining Museum, Newtongrange
Based at the historic Lady Victoria Colliery, the mining museum features tours, led by ex-miners, of the pit-head, Scotland's largest steam winding engine, and a full-scale replica of a modern underground coalface.

Parts of the museum are said to be haunted.

Map 4, 9M (Newtongrange). On A7, 10 miles S of Edinburgh, Newtongrange, Midlothian.
Open all year, daily. (0131 663 7519 / www.scottishminingmuseum.com)

A paranormal investigation was undertaken by Alba Paranormal Investigations www.albaparanormal.com/scottishminingmuseum.htm)

Scourie Lodge
Set in a sheltered spot in the rugged north-west coast of Scotland, Scourie Lodge (or House) dates from the first half of the 19th century and was built by the Duke of Sutherland for his wife, but she did not like Scourie and never lived here. The lodge was then used as a factor's house for the Scourie estate, and was visited by Gladstone, J.M. Barrie and the Queen Mother. There are fine gardens, and bed and breakfast accommodation is available.

Scourie had been held by the Mackays, and Hugh Mackay of Scourie led the government forces that were defeated at the Battle of Killiecrankie in 1689; he then went to Holland where he was killed at Steinkirk three years later.

The lands went to the Earls and then Dukes of Sutherland, and the lodge was used by Evander MacIver, who was their factor for some 60 years and is infamous for his part in the Highland Clearances. He died in 1903 at the age of 90 years, and his ghost is said to haunt the building.

Map 1, 5B (Scourie). Off A894, Scourie, Sutherland, Highland.
B&B: open Mar-end Oct. (01971 502248 / www.scourielodge.co.uk)

Settle Inn, Stirling
Located in the ancient St Mary's Wynd, The Settle Inn is Stirling's most enduring hostelry and dates from 1733. The atmospheric cellar lounge is arched in stone, and there is a huge old fireplace.

There are tales that the place is haunted, and that manifestations seem to be focused on the cellar and stair down to it. Members of staff have reported feeling as if they are being pushed down the stairs. Unexpectedly frigid areas are reputed to be felt in the inn, which move around the place, and there are also stories of phantom drinkers, dressed in an old fashioned way, being seen in the hostelry, although they vanish when observers look away.

Map 4, 8L (Stirling). Off B8052 or A811, 91 St Mary's Wynd, Stirling.
Public house. (01786 474609 / www.stirling.co.uk/settleinn/index.htm)

A paranormal investigation was undertaken in December 2008 by Spiritfinders Scotland (www.spiritfindersscotland.com/settleinn.htm)

Shankend
There is said to have been an old mansion at Shankend, which overlooked the Waverley railway line, but nothing now remains of the mansion or the railway. During World War I the house is believed to have been used to house German POWs,

who were working on the farm, and several are said to have died in a cholera outbreak in 1917 and to have been buried locally.

Their ghosts are reported to haunt the area, and one manifestation is said to cause feelings of extreme foreboding and even dread.

Map 4, 100 (Shankend). Off B6399, 5 miles S of Hawick, Shankend, Borders.

SHEEP HEID INN, EDINBURGH

The fine old inn has been established here for many centuries, perhaps from as early as 1360, and the hostelry was visited by Mary, Queen if Scots, and James VI, who gave the then innkeeper a ram's head snuff box, much adorned and decorated. This was preserved at the Sheep Heid until the 19th century when it was sold; a copy replaced the original, while the original is now at Dalmeny House.

It was at the inn that in 1724 the funeral cortege of Maggie Dickson, who had been hanged for infanticide, rested before taking her body back to her home at Fisherrow. Noises were heard coming from the coffin and, when it was opened, it was found that the woman was still alive and was soon revived fully, earning her the nickname 'Half-Hangit Maggie'. Having been hanged the once, she was deemed to have undergone her punishment and she went on to live a long life, although she had to remarry her 'widowed' husband, as she had been pronounced dead.

Some people believe the Sheep Heid is haunted, and a former landlord, known as 'The Major', is said to have been witnessed in the bar, while the skittle alley is reported to be haunted by the bogle of a small girl.

Map 4, 9L (Edinburgh). Off A1, 43-45 The Causeway, Duddingston, Edinburgh.
Public house and skittle alley. (0131 661 7974 / www.sheepheid.co.uk)

SHIELDHILL

Set in rolling hills and six acres of wooded park land, Shieldhill is a large mansion and incorporates an ancient castle at its core. The oldest part may date from as early as 1199, but the building was extended often in following centuries.

Shieldhill was a property of the Chancellor family, although they only moved back here after their house at Quothquan was destroyed. The family supported Mary, Queen of Scots, and fought for her at the Battle of Langside in 1568. Unfortunately this put them on the losing side, and Quothquan was burnt to the ground – so much so that no trace remains. The Chancellors only left Shieldhill in the 20th century, and since 1959 the mansion has been a country house hotel.

The building is said to be haunted by a 'Grey Lady', the ghost of the young and good-looking daughter of one of the Chancellor lords. She is said to be seen wrapped in a grey cloak.

There are several versions of the story associated with her, and details are different.

One is that the poor girl was raped by soldiers returning from a battle in the 1650s, and became pregnant, but the child was cruelly taken from her at birth and left to die (and that she was driven to suicide). Another that was made pregnant by a gamekeeper's son, and her baby was born dead and then buried without her permission. The girl wept herself to death. A third that she fell to her death while trying to elope with her lover, a gamekeeper, or a fourth that her father forbad her to see him and she committed suicide.

Whatever the origin, her ghost has apparently been seen in recent times, walking towards the burial place in the grounds of the hotel, and especially in one of the rooms (which is available to guests). She is mostly seen in the old keep and uses the original stone stair to move from floor to floor. Unexplained footsteps and thumps during the night have also been reported, as have chairs moving by themselves and television channels changing independently.

There have also been reports of another bogle, said to be the spirit of a butler and to have been witnessed in the last couple of years.

Map 4, 8N (Shieldhill). Off B7016, 3 miles NW of Biggar, Quothquan, Lanarkshire. **Hotel. (01899 220035 / www.shieldhill.co.uk)**

A ghost hunt was held in April 2009 here by Shieldhill Clairvoyance and Ghost Hunt (www.northwestspiritseekers.co.uk)

SHIELDS ROAD UNDERGROUND STATION, GLASGOW

The underground station was opened in 1897, and is said to have a 'Grey Lady', the phantom of a woman carrying an infant in its arms, seen on the platform. The apparition is then said to leap from the platform, still holding the child, during which a scream is then heard, along with the weeping of an infant.

Map 4, 7M (Glasgow). Off M8 or A77, 326 Shields Road, Glasgow.

SKAILL HOUSE

Standing close by the important Neolithic village of Skara Brae, Skaill House is the most complete 17th-century mansion house in Orkney. The mansion was built for Bishop George Graham in the 1620s and has fine gardens. A dozen skeletons were excavated from near the house in 1996, and human remains were also found beneath the stone flags of the hall floor, suggesting that the house was built on a burial ground.

The building is reputedly haunted. Manifestations are said to have included the sound of feet coming from unoccupied areas, and the apparition of an old woman. Other spooky occurrences have been reported, including a dog getting into such distress one night in the small hours that it hid under the bed and howled in distress, and a heavy weight, as if someone invisible was sitting on a bed, which seemed to get up at the same time as the occupier of the bed.

Map 2, 9C (Skaill). Off B9056, 6 miles N of Stromness, Skaill, Breckness, Orkney. **Skaill House open Apr-Sep, daily. (01856 841501 / www.skaillhouse.com)**

SKELLATER HOUSE

Skellater House is a somewhat stark T-plan house with dormer windows, which dates from around the end of the 17th century. The building was restored in the 1970s, and was recently put up for sale.

Skellater was long a property of the Forbes family. George Forbes was a Jacobite and fought at Culloden in 1746, while John Forbes married a Portuguese princess, rose to become a Field Marshall in the Portuguese army, and died in Brazil in 1809.

One ghost story is that a rent collector was slain at the main doorway of the house, and his bogle is said to haunt the spot where he was murdered.

Map 2, 9G (Skellater). Off A944, 3 miles S and W of Strathdon, Skellater, Aberdeenshire.

SKENE HOUSE

Skene House, an extensive castellated mansion, incorporates an old castle, and was a property of the Skene family from 1318 until 1827. One of the family, Alexander Skene of Skene, who died in 1724, was said to be a warlock, although his only crime appears to have been to study on the Continent. He is said not to have had a shadow, and to have been responsible for defiling graves and all sorts of wickedness. A phantom carriage, occupied by himself and the Devil, is said to ride across the Loch of Skene at midnight on New Year's Eve, only to sink before it reaches the shore.

A similar story is told of James Carnegie, Earl of Southesk, whose castle was at Kinnaird (see that entry).

Map 2, 11G (Skene). Off A944, 4 miles NW of Westhill, Aberdeenshire.

SKIBO CASTLE

The present Skibo Castle dates from the 19th century, but it stands on the site of an ancient castle. This castle was reputedly haunted by the ghost of a young woman.

The story goes that a local girl visited to Skibo one day, when it was only occupied by the keeper of the castle, but she was never seen again. She was assaulted then murdered by the man, and from then on the apparition of a dishevelled, partially-dressed girl was witnessed, running through the building, and unexplained cries and screams were heard. Years later during renovations, a woman's skeleton was found hidden behind a wall. When the remains were buried, the hauntings ceased.

The castle was owned by the Bishops of Caithness until 1565, but later passed to the Grays. The Marquis of Montrose was imprisoned here after being captured at Ardvreck Castle. Jean Seton, wife of Robert Gray of Skibo, hit one of Montrose's guards with a leg of meat, and the family were fined.

The present house was built for Andrew Carnegie in 1898. Carnegie was born in Dunfermline in 1835 but emigrated to America when he was a teenager, and made a fortune from railways, and iron and steel. He was one of the richest men of his time, but gave away most of his money, Dunfermline benefiting particularly.

The castle now houses an exclusive country club, the Carnegie Club.

Map 2, 7D (Skibo). Off A9, 4 miles W of Dornoch, Skibo, Sutherland, Highlands.
Exclusive country club. (01862 894600 / www.carnegieclubs.com)

SKIPNESS CASTLE   ILLUS PAGE 267

With fine views over the Kilbrannon Sound to Arran, Skipness Castle is a solid castle of enclosure with a curtain wall surrounding a tower house and ranges of buildings. The first castle was probably built by the MacSweens around 1247, which was rebuilt by the MacDonalds, but in 1499 Skipness was acquired by the Campbell Earl of Argyll. The castle was besieged unsuccessfully by Alaisdair Colkitto MacDonald in the 1640s, but was abandoned at the end of the 17th century, then being used as a farm steading. In 1898 the farm was removed, and the ruins consolidated. Near the castle is Skipness House, built for the Graham family at the end of the 19th century, although it incorporates some of a much older house. This house is still occupied.

Skipness is said to have a gruagach, a 'Green Lady', described as being as small as a child but dressed in green and with golden hair. The spirit would clean and tidy, and feed hens; but it is also accused of nearly killing a man it believed was sleeping in the wrong bed. The power to befuddle opponents was also attributed to the 'Green Lady', as the story goes that several times she managed to cause confusion among those attempting to attack the castle, leading to them withdraw.

The 'Green Lady' is reported as being witnessed in recent times.

Map 3, 4M (Skipness). Off B8001, 7 miles S of Tarbert, Skipness, Argyll.
His Scot: Castle (and chapel on shore) access at all reasonable times (tower, open Apr-Sep): short walk to castle, then walk to chapel (which may be muddy). (www.historic-scotland.gov.uk)

SLAINS CASTLE
ILLUS PAGE 267

Perched on precipitous cliffs above the sea, the substantial ruins of Slains Castle are very atmospheric and impressive. Most of what remains is from a later mansion, but the ruins incorporate part of an ancient stronghold. There were extensive gardens and pleasure grounds, but these have all but gone.

Slains was built by Francis Hay, 9th Earl of Errol, after James VI had destroyed his castle at Old Slains, following a rebellion of 1594. Dr Johnson and Boswell visited in 1773, and Bram Stoker had the inspiration for writing *Dracula* here (although Slains was not a ruin at the time as some have suggested). The house was sold by the Hays in 1916, and was unroofed and stripped within a few years.

Recent reports in the press suggest that there are plans to turn the evocative ruins into a holiday complex.

Some accounts have the castle haunted by the ghost of Victor Hay, 21st Earl of Errol, who died in the first quarter of the 20th century.

Other eerie stories include a phantom horse and carriage, and the apparitions of two soldiers dressed in uniforms from World War II.

Map 2, 12F (Slains). Off A975, 1 mile E of Cruden Bay, Slains, Aberdeenshire.

SMUGGLERS INN, ANSTRUTHER

Overlooking the harbour, the Smugglers Inn stands in the pretty East Neuk village of Anstruther and is believed to date from the late 16th century, although there may have been an establishment on the site for 300 years before then. This was a coaching inn and was also used by smugglers as a convenient base.

The building is said to be haunted, but reports of the bogle are vague.

Map 4, 10K (Anstruther). Off A917, High Street East, Anstruther, Fife.
Hotel. (01333 310506 / /www.abbotsfordarms.com/hotels/smugglers/)

SPA HOTEL, STRATHPEFFER

The Spa Hotel was one of the first hotels to be built in Strathpeffer, and was a fine establishment in six acres of grounds with tennis courts, croquet lawns and putting greens. The hotel was used as a fever hospital during World War II, but was then accidentally burnt down to be left a ruin. The site on Kinellan Drive was eventually redeveloped and it is now occupied by housing.

A nurse is said to have been murdered in the hotel during the war, and her ghost is reported to have haunted the ruins.

Map 2, 7E (Strathpeffer). Off A834, to W of Strathpeffer, Ross and Cromarty, Highland.

SPEDLINS TOWER

Dating from the 15th century, Spedlins Tower was an impressive stronghold of the Jardine family. It was abandoned for nearby Jardine Hall, and became ruinous, but it was restored in the 1970s and is occupied again.

Spedlins was reportedly haunted by the ghost of a miller, called James or 'Dunty' Porteous, who had the misfortune to be imprisoned here around 1650, after trying to burn down his own mill (the reason why is not recorded). The laird, Sir Alexander Jardine, forgetting about his prisoner, was called away to Edinburgh and took the key to the dungeon with him. Porteous gnawed at his feet and hands before eventually dying of hunger; one account states that he was so desperate to free himself from his manacles that he had ripped his own hands off. It seems unlikely that Jardine's wife, Margaret Douglas, or his servants could not have done something to help Porteous. Some say that Margaret was a very mean and miserly woman, and left the miller to starve as she did not want the expense of feeding him.

His ghost is then said to have manifested itself with all sorts of activity, shrieking through the tower and leaving nobody in the tower in peace. Eventually his angry bogle was contained in the dungeon by a bible, held in a niche by the entrance, this only after many exorcisms had failed to lay the restless ghost. Once, in 1710, when the bible was removed for repair, the ghost is said to have followed the family to nearby Jardine Hall, and caused all sorts of commotion in the laird's bedroom, such as throwing both the laird and his wife out of their beds, until the bible was returned. It is said that the bible is preserved and in a local museum.

After the tower was ruinous, tales circulated that the apparition of a tall man with white hair had been seen in the tower basement, reportedly with no hands, and the sounds of moaning were also apparently heard. A stick poked through the lock of the prison was reported to be withdrawn all chewed up, as if the ghost had tried to eat it.

There have been no reports of the ghost since the tower was restored and reoccupied.

Map 4, 9P (Spedlins). Off A74, 3 miles NE of Lochmaben, Spedlins, Dumfries and Galloway.

SPYNIE PALACE   ILLUS PAGE 267

Reflecting the perilous position many medieval bishops found themselves in, Spynie Palace – the palace of the Bishops of Moray – consists of a massive 15th-century tower 'Davy's Tower' at one corner of a large walled courtyard. The palace was probably built by Bishop Innes, just after Elgin Cathedral and city had been burnt and plundered by Alexander Stewart, the Wolf of Badenoch. Bishop David Stewart, who died in 1475, excommunicated the Gordon Earl of Huntly, and built the great keep, Davy's Tower, to defend himself against any retribution. Famous visitors include James IV, Mary, Queen of Scots, and the Earl of Bothwell, third husband of Mary, Queen of Scots. The palace was abandoned in 1688 and became ruinous.

There were stories of the bishops being in league with the Devil, and that every Halloween witches would be seen flying to the castle. Unexplained lights and unearthly music are still said to be heard coming from the bishop's chambers.

There are several reports of ghosts.

The phantom of a piper is alleged to haunt the building, as is the ghost of a lion, said to have been a pet of one of the bishops, witnessed in Davy's Tower and the ruinous kitchen range. One witness is reputed to have observed a large paw print,

Skipness Castle (page 264)

Spynie Palace (page 266)

Slains Castle (page 265)

St Andrews Castle (page 269)

St Andrews Cathedral (page 269)

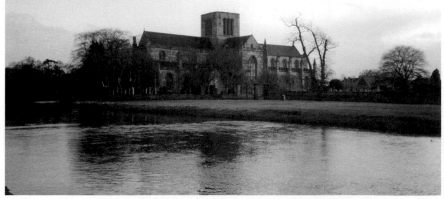

St Mary's Church, Haddington (page 271)

and another visitor reported being attacked by some large beast, although there was apparently nothing there.

There are also accounts of the spectre of a woman, seen sitting in an arched alcove by the entrance to the tower, and of a white indistinct apparition observed in the tower, along with some very uncomfortable feelings.

Map 2, 9E (Spynie). Off A941, 2.5 miles N of Elgin, Spynie, Moray.
His Scot: Open Apr-Oct, daily; Nov-Mar, wknds only; closed 25/25 Dec and 1/2 Jan.
(01343 546358 / www.historic-scotland.gov.uk)

ST ANDREWS CASTLE
ILLUS PAGE 268

Standing close to the remains of the cathedral in the historic seaside town, the castle is a ruinous stronghold of the Bishops of St Andrews. It saw action in the Wars of Independence, and this is where Cardinal David Beaton was murdered in 1546 and hung naked from the walls. His body went unburied for more than seven months, preserved in a barrel of brine, in one of the vaults of the castle. It is thought that Beaton's remains were eventually buried either at Kilrenny or in the burial ground of Blackfriars in St Andrews. The mines from the subsequent siege are accessible.

The ghost of Archbishop John Hamilton, who was hanged at Stirling after supporting Mary, Queen of Scots, is said to haunt the castle. An alternative identity has been suggested as Cardinal Beaton, who is also believed to haunt Melgund and Ethie Castle, as well as Blebo and Balfour House, while his mistress is said to haunt Claypotts (see those entries). The apparition of Beaton is also said to been seen in a phantom coach in the streets of the town (although the coach of Archbishop James Sharp, who was murdered in 1679 on Magus Muir to the west of St Andrews, is also said to have been spotted).

There are also tales of a 'White Lady', seen near the stronghold and on the nearby beach, possibly the same one seen more often at the cathedral. She has been described as being clad in white with a veil which obscures her face and carries a book (also see St Andrews Cathedral and Dean's Court).

Map 4, 10K (St Andrews). Off A91, The Pends, St Andrews, Fife.
His Scot: Open all year, daily 9.30-16.30; closed 25/26 Dec and 1/2 Jan. (01334 477196 / www.historic-scotland.gov.uk)

ST ANDREWS CATHEDRAL
ILLUS PAGE 268

Standing by the sea in the historic town of St Andrews, not much remains of what was formerly the largest and most magnificent cathedral in Scotland. The building was destroyed after the Reformation and then quarried for materials, but there is a fine museum of early Christian sculpture in what remains of the cloister.

St Rule founded a monastery here in the 8th century, and the stair of St Rule's Tower is said to be haunted by a ghostly monk, who was murdered in the building. The apparition is thought to be friendly, to appear around the full moon, and to have been witnessed in recent times, sometimes manifesting itself by pushing past people, sometimes by giving people a helping hand on the narrow stair. It is possible to climb to the top of the tower.

A 'White Lady', the apparition of a veiled woman in a flowing white dress, reputedly haunts the cathedral ruins, as well as the area within the precinct wall, near the castle, down on the beach, and in Dean's Court (see separate entry). One detail is that she is mostly seen in winter months, and on stormy evenings or nights, although evidence for this seems rather flimsy. There was a sighting in 1975 when two visitors reputedly saw the apparition coming towards them, and they were surprised to see that the face was veiled. The ghost was described as wearing a light grey dress (not white), appeared to be carrying a book (perhaps a prayer book), and the apparition then vanished as it approached closer. Other accounts also have it wearing white gloves.

There is no clear information as to who the 'White Lady' was in life. One imaginative version is that she was a nun who was so horribly disfigured that she wore the veil, and that if people should actually see her face it will drive them insane. It is not unusual, however, for ghosts to be observed wearing veils.

One of the towers defending the precinct wall is said to have been used to store the bodies of plague victims in the 17th century. Some stories have the ghost associated with this tower, indeed that she was buried here.

Map 4, 10K (St Andrews). Off A91, St Andrews, Fife.
His Scot: Open all year, daily; closed 25/26 Dec and 1/2 Jan. (01334 472563 / www.historic-scotland.gov.uk)

St Boswells

For several years around 1900 there were reports of the sighting of an apparition of a man. He was described as being clad in black, and was believed to be dressed in the manner of a minister of the Presbyterian church from around 50 years before. The bogle is reported to have been witnessed by several people, including by two sisters of the Scotts of Lessudden House, who were related to Sir Walter.

Map 4, 10N (St Boswells). On B6404, 3 miles SE of Melrose, St Boswells, Borders.

St Catherine Hotel

St Catherine Hotel was said to be haunted by a 'Green Lady', a phantom dressed in a green frock. One account had a member of staff being so terrified after she heard, and then felt, heavy breathing on the back of her neck, even although nobody else was present, that she flung a tray of drinks into the air and fled the room used as the drinks' store.

The story is that this was where a woman had hanged herself.

The hotel has been closed.

Map 3, 5K (St Catherines). On A815, St Catherines, S side of Loch Fyne, Argyll.

St John the Baptist's Church, Ayr

Only the strong tower remains of the former parish church of Ayr, which was cruciform in plan and some 140 foot long. A church here is mentioned in 1233, and was the scene of a parliament held by Robert the Bruce in 1315. In the 1650s the church and burial ground were enclosed by a fort built by Cromwell, and most of the church was demolished in the 18th century.

The tower of the church is said to be haunted by the hazy apparition of a man.

Map 3, 6N (Ayr). Off A719, Ayr, Ayrshire.
Open to the public by arrangement - tel: 01292 286385; other times view from exterior. (www.auldkirk.org)

ST JOHN'S CHURCH, GARDENSTOWN

The ruins of the old parish church, dedicated to St John the Evangelist, and its associated burial ground are located in a fine spot by the sea on Gamrie Bay. The church is believed to have been established at the beginning of the 11th century, and the building was also known as the 'Church of Skulls', from the defleshed heads of three Vikings that are said to have once been kept here. The church went out of use in the 1820s, but burials were still made here well into the 20th century.

One story is that strange eerie lights were seen around the church and burial ground on the eve of a funeral.

Map 2, 11E (Gardenstown). Off B9031, 5.5 miles E of Macduff, to W of Gardenstown, Aberdeenshire.

ST MARY'S CHURCH, HADDINGTON   ILLUS PAGE 268

In a pleasant and peaceful situation beside the River Tyne, St Mary's is a substantial cross-shaped church with an aisled nave and choir. It is the largest parish church in Scotland (although it has St Nicholas in Aberdeen to rival it). The roof is vaulted in stone, apart from the restored nave. There are interesting medieval carvings, including Green Men and scallop shells, the latter the sign of a place of pilgrimage.

The church houses an impressive marble monument to John Maitland, Lord Thirlestane and Chancellor of Scotland, who died in 1595, his wife and his son, which is now known as 'The Chapel of the Three Kings'. Beneath the monument is the Lauderdale family vault. The grim-faced ghost of John Maitland, Duke of Lauderdale, who died in 1682, is said to have been seen by the chapel, as well as at Thirlestane Castle (also see that entry). Indeed it is said that often his coffin would move about the tomb without explanation, until it was realised that the vault was often flooded by the River Tyne, which flows past the building.

Map 4, 10M (Haddington). Off A6093, Sidegate, Haddington, East Lothian.
Open Apr-Sep, daily. (01620 823109 / www.stmaryskirk.com)

ST MARY'S STREET, EDINBURGH

The street, which runs from the Canongate to the Cowgate, is said to be haunted by the apparition of a distressed young woman in begored clothes. The story goes that in 1916 a young woman was stabbed to death here by a man who sprang out of a doorway, attacked and murdered her, and then fled the scene.

Map 4, 9L (Edinburgh). Off A7, St Mary's Street, Edinburgh.

ST MICHAEL'S INN, LEUCHARS

The inn, which stands at an important crossroads, dates from 1799 and was a coaching inn. The establishment is known locally as 'St Mike's', and is an atmospheric and cosy place with low ceilings and open fires.

There are several accounts of ghostly activity in the inn, which is not believed to frightening. Manifestations are said to include the apparition of a woman seen standing at a window, as well as the window of this room appearing to have opened itself, while bedclothes have also been mysteriously disturbed. More than one guest staying at the inn has reported that someone tried to get into their room during the night, even although there were no other guests, and the sounds of a child crying have been heard when no infants were present. The lights in the function room are also said to have turned on and off by themselves, and other odd occurrences such as unnaturally cold areas, a feeling as if someone was pushing past, and a guest reporting that they had talked to a child on the stairs one morning although there was no child in the inn.

Map 4, 10K (Leuchars). Junction of A92, A919 and B945, St Michaels, 0.5 miles NW of Leuchars, Carrick Crossroads, Fife.
Inn. (01334 839220)

A paranormal investigation undertaken by Paranormal Discovery
(www.paranormaldiscovery.co.uk)

St Michael's Parish Church, Linlithgow

Standing near the extensive ruin of the royal palace, St Michael's was founded in 1242 on the site of an earlier church. The present building dates mostly from the 15th century, and was used by many of the Stewart monarchs, particularly James IV and James V. There are interesting 15th-century relief slabs in the vestry.

It was in the church that a blue-robed apparition warned James IV not to march into England – but the King ignored the warning, invaded England, and was killed at the disastrous Battle of Flodden in 1513.

A similar warning at the Mercat Cross (also see that entry) in Edinburgh was also ignored.

The phantom of a lady, clad in a blue dress, is also said to vanish near the wall of the church, after walking over from the nearby palace (see Linlithgow Palace).

Map 4, 8L (Linlithgow). Off A803, Kirkgate, Linlithgow, West Lothian.
Church open most days. (01506 842188 / www.stmichaelsparish.org.uk)

St Salvator's Chapel, St Andrews

St Salvator's Chapel is an atmospheric and serene building, founded In 1450 by James Kennedy, Bishop of St Andrews, as part of the college of which only the church survives: the college was united with St Leonard's and St Mary's into the University of St Andrews. The chapel has a tower with a distinctive 16th-century spire.

Outside the main entrance to the chapel (the spot marked in the pavement with his monogram) is the place where Patrick Hamilton was executed for heresy in 1528. Hamilton, from a noble family, was a religious reformer, but although only in his 20s he got in trouble with the authorities of the day and was denounced, tried and then burned alive. He is said to have smouldered from midday until six o'clock.

His ghost is said to haunt the area around St Salvator's Chapel and the University grounds, and there are reports of the unexplained sounds of crackling heard from near where he was executed and the stench of scorching flesh.

While standing on the monogram in the pavement, if turning towards the chapel wall there is the image of which appears to be a face in the masonry: this is said to be the face of Patrick Hamilton.

Map 4, 10K (St Andrews). Off A91, St Salvator's College, North Street, St Andrews.
Chapel (part of St Andrews University): often open – entrance is through the pend.
(www.st-andrews.ac.uk/about/UniversityChapels/ChapelofStSalvator/)

STAGHEAD HOTEL, SOUTH QUEENSFERRY

Located on the High Street above the ancient harbour, the Staghead Hotel was established in the 17th century as a coaching inn, and is now a family-run hotel.

The hotel is said to be haunted. One bogle is reported to be of Auld Mrs Wyld, a former landlady, and unexplained footsteps heard pacing about on the top floor have been attributed to the ghost; there have also apparently been sightings of her apparition. The cellar is also alleged to be haunted, this time by a ghost known as 'Jack', and manifestations are believed to include lights switching themselves on and off, and the sounds of barrels being moved about when nobody is in the cellar.

Map 4, 9L (South Queensferry). Off B924, 8 High Street, South Queensferry, Edinburgh.
Hotel. (0131 331 1039 / www.stagheadhotel.com)

STAIR ARMS HOTEL, PATHHEAD

Lord and Lady Stair had the hotel built after the construction of the bridge, designed by Thomas Telford, to cross the gorge at the village of Ford. The Stair Arms Hotel was a Temperance establishment in the early 20th century, but in 1990 was remodelled and upgraded, and is set in four acres of grounds.

The hotel is said to be haunted by the ghost of a chambermaid. The poor woman is said to have committed suicide while working here, and her apparition is claimed to have been seen in the restaurant.

Map 4, 10M (Pathhead). On A68, Ford, Pathhead, Midlothian.
Hotel. (01875 320277 / www.stairarmshotel.com)

STARZ AND DEACON BRODIE'S BARS, DUNDEE

Housed in a former Methodist church of 1867 is the Starz Bar, while Deacon Brodie's Bar is located in what was the adjacent Sunday school and dwelling.

The bars are both said to be haunted, and the buildings are reputed to have a foreboding atmosphere at times, as well as unexplained voices, and feelings as if people are being pushed or being touched by invisible hands. The apparition of man, clad in black, has reportedly been observed more than once standing by a pillar in Deacon Brodie's, and glasses are said to have fallen from a shelf behind the bar without explanation. The phantom of a wee girl has allegedly been spotted in the stair between the two bars, while the bogle of a little boy is said to have been witnessed on the balcony of the Starz Bar.

Map 4, 10K (Dundee). Off A991, 15 Ward Street, Dundee.
Bars. (01382 200246/204137)

A paranormal investigation was undertaken by Paranormal Discovery (www.paranormaldiscovery.co.uk)

STIRLING CASTLE   ILLUS PAGE 279

Stirling Castle was the most important stronghold in Scotland. It was fought over during the Wars of Independence, and was the cause of the Battle of Bannockburn in 1314. Edward II of England and his army were marching north to relieve the castle when they were defeated by Robert the Bruce.

The fortress stands on a high rock and defends what was an important route to the north, a crossing of the River Forth. The restored Great Hall which has been renovated, harled and washed – this latter event causing much controversy – and there are many interesting buildings such as the gatehouse and Prince's Tower, the King's Old Buildings, the Chapel Royal and kitchens.

The castle has a long violent history, and it saw action down the years including in the Jacobite Risings of 1745-46. Alexander I died at the castle in 1124, as did William the Lyon in 1214. Edward I of England captured Stirling in 1304, but it was recovered by the Scots in 1314 after Bannockburn. The Jacobites, led by Bonnie Prince Charlie, besieged the castle in 1746, but they soon had to withdraw, having lost several of their artillery pieces in an exchange of fire with the castle garrison.

The castle is said to have several ghosts.

One is believed to be the 'Green Lady', a harbinger of doom, often associated with fire. One tale is that she was lady-in-waiting to Mary, Queen of Scots, and saved her queen when her bedding caught fire.

Another version is that this, or another ghost, was the daughter of a governor of the castle who committed suicide. Her lover was accidentally killed by her father and she threw herself from the battlements in despair.

The ghost is claimed to have been spotted in recent times, including during when the castle was still occupied by the army and once scaring a cook so badly that the man fainted. The cook had noticed the apparition by his side, apparently interested in what he was doing. He described the figure as being misty-green, and it is said that he knew nothing about any ghosts at the castle before his spooky encounter.

There is also reputed to be a 'Pink Lady', the apparition of a pretty young woman, clad in a pink silk dress. There is more than one guess at her identity, but she has been identified as an apparition of Mary, Queen of Scots, although other stories tell that she is the spirit of a woman looking for her husband. The story goes that he was killed when the castle was besieged and captured by Edward I in 1304. Her ghost is said to have been seen in the castle, around the Church of the Holy Rude, and most commonly at Ladies' Rock, between the castle and the church.

There are also many reports of ghostly footsteps in more than one area of the castle. They are said to have been heard in an upstairs chamber of the Governor's Block. In 1946 and 1956 the footsteps are said to have been heard by soldiers occupying the room. The manifestations may be connected with the death of a sentry in the 1820s. Even more recently, footsteps were also reported by workmen who were renovating the Great Hall, in one case frightening a man so much he would not return to work. Further stories of disembodied footsteps have included those in the King's Old Building, apparently heard climbing a stair that no longer exists and going the length of a corridor that has since been divided.

Another ghost is said to be a kilted apparition, known by some as the 'Highland Ghost', one sighting being in 1952. Two sentries observed the bogle go from the Douglas Gardens, move along the wall of the King's Old Building, and then vanish at a spot at the angle created by the tower. A photo of this ghost was apparently taken in 1935 by an architect working on the building, and this purports to show a kilted figure going through the arched entrance to the upper square.

This apparition is reported to have been seen more than once in recent times, and it is claimed that the bogle has been mistaken for a costumed guide because of his dress.

Map 4, 8L (Stirling). Off B8052 or A811, Upper Castle Hill, Stirling.
His Scot: Open all year, daily; closed 25/26 Dec; open 1/2 Jan: tel for opening times.
(01786 450000 / www.historic-scotland.gov.uk)

STOBHILL HOSPITAL, GLASGOW

The hospital was founded in 1904, having some 1867 beds for patients with serious illnesses such as TB. The hospital was used during World War I to treat battle casualties, and was then expanded and developed during the rest of the 20th century. The hospital has recently undergone a £100 million refurbishment and is due to reopen in June 2009.

The hospital is said to be haunted by the apparition of a woman in a white uniform, seen by nurses as they enter wards or heard by staff as a voice calling them. One story is that the benign ghost alerts staff to patients who are very seriously ill.

Map 4, 7M (Glasgow). Off A803, 133 Balornock Road, Springburn, Glasgow.
Hospital. (0141 201 3000)

STONEHAVEN

On the High Street is a 17th-century town house of three storeys, which at one time was held by the Ogilvies of Lumgair. There is a moulded entrance and the remains of a corbelled-out stair-turret, which has been reduced in height. There are stories of a tunnel linking this house to Fetteresso and to Dunnottar Castle.

The house is said to be haunted by a 'Green Lady', perhaps the same bogle that haunts Fetteresso Castle (also see that entry).

Map 2, 11H (Stonehaven). Off A957, 51 High Street, Stonehaven, Kincardineshire.

STRATHAVEN CASTLE

Standing on a rocky mound in a prominent position, Strathaven Castle (also known as Avondale Castle) is a ruinous stronghold, dating from the 15th century. Although the ruin looks fine from the road, it was consolidated in a less than sympathetic way in 1912. The castle was once a property of the Black Douglases, but was sacked and slighted following the fall of that family in 1455. Strathaven then passed to the Stewart, Lord Avondale, and then to the Hamiltons, who occupied the castle until 1717, after which it was abandoned and fell into ruin.

The castle is said to be haunted by a 'White Lady', the bogle of the wife of one of the lairds, who is reputed to have so displeased her husband that he had her sealed up in the building. A skeleton, found hidden in one of the walls, is said to have been discovered when part of the castle was demolished.

Map 4, 7M (Strathaven). On A71, Strathaven, Lanarkshire.
Access at all reasonable times. (www.strathavencastle.t83.net)

STRATHKINNESS ROAD, ST ANDREWS

Archbishop James Sharp, the Protestant head of the church in Scotland for Charles II, was assassinated in 1679. Sharp was a controversial and self-seeking figure, and had already survived one attempt on his life. Covenanters, including David Hackston of Rathillet and John Balfour of Kinloch, came across Sharp accidentally on Magus Muir on 3 May; they had been waiting to waylay someone else. Sharp, who was with his daughter, was dragged from his coach, and then was set upon: being shot, stabbed and beaten to death. Balfour escaped punishment, although he had to flee to the Continent, while Hackston had his hands cut off before being executed.

The murder of Sharp is commemorated by a monument in trees on Magus Muir.
Strathkinness Road is said to be haunted by a spectral coach, drawn by four large
black horses, a manifestation thought to be associated with Sharp's murder.

Map 4, 10K (St Andrews). On B939, St Andrews to Cupar road (Strathkinness Road), Fife.

SUNDRUM CASTLE

Sundrum Castle, a mansion of 1793, incorporates a 14th-century keep of the Wallace family. The property passed to the Cathcarts, and then to the Hamiltons by
1750.

The old part of the building, centred in the vaulted dining room, was reputedly
haunted by a 'Green Lady', said to have been the wife of one of the Hamilton
lairds. The disturbances have apparently ceased since the building was renovated
and divided.

Map 3, 6N (Sundrum). Off A70, 4.5 miles E of Ayr, Sundrum, Ayrshire.
Can be let. (01530 244436 / www.sundrumcastle.com)

SUNIPOL

The farm here was at one time said to be haunted by poltergeist activity, and
objects were seen flying about the house, as well as many other disturbances.

Map 3, 2J (Sunipol). Off B8073, 1 mile N of Calgary, Sunipol, Mull.

TANTALLON CASTLE   ILLUS PAGE 279

One of the most impressive castles in southern Scotland, Tantallon is a large and
strong 14th-century courtyard castle, which is now ruinous. It has a thick 50-foot-
high curtain wall, blocking off a cliff-top promontory, with towers at each end and
a lofty central gatehouse. The castle was built by Douglases, later the Earls of
Angus, and has a long and violent history. A siege in 1528 was fought off, but in 1651
Tantallon fell to Cromwell's forces after being bombarded for some 12 days. The
building was slighted after being captured and remained ruinous.

Although there are apparently no ghost stories regarding Tantallon, an intriguing
photo of a supposed ghost was taken here in April 2009, which may show a ghostly
apparition, although perhaps this 'bogle' is just a visitor to the castle who had been
unusually lit (see www.scienceofhauntings.com).

Map 4, 10L (Tantallon). Off A198, 3 miles E of North Berwick, Tantallon, East Lothian.
His Scot: Open Apr-Oct, daily; Nov-Mar, Sat-Wed, closed Thu-Fri; closed 25/26 Dec
and 1/2 Jan. (01620 892727 / www.historic-scotland.gov.uk)

TARRAS

Tarras Water is a swift burn which flows down from the hills north of Langholm and
joins the River Esk at Auchenrivock. The area around the Tarras is said to be haunted
by a 'White Lady'. An account states that a local farmer murdered and robbed a
woman, then hid her body somewhere on the moors. The woman is said to have
lodged with the farmer, and it was then that he discovered that she had much gold
and other valuables – and her fate was sealed.

Her apparition has reputedly been seen by many people.

Map 4, 10O (Tarras). Off A7, 2 miles NE of Langholm, Tarras, Dumfries and Galloway.

TAY BRIDGE

The Tay Bridge, designed by Thomas Bouch for the North British Railway, was nearly two miles across when it was opened in 1878, making it the longest bridge in the world at that time; it had 86 spans and rose to 77 foot above the sea. Faults, poor design, cost cutting in its construction, and lack of maintenance, however, led to it collapsing in a violent storm on 28 December 1879 at about 19.15, taking a passenger train with it into the Firth of Tay. Seventy-five people were killed; nobody survived. The engine and carriages were recovered (the engine was repaired and saw further service), but only 60 bodies were ever found; some of the personal items of those that perished can be seen in the McManus Galleries in Dundee. Bouch was a further victim, and died soon after the disaster; a new Tay Bridge was subsequently built close to the old one.

It is said that on the anniversary of the disaster, on 28 December each year, a train can be seen hurtling across the Tay where the first bridge was located, before falling headlong and crashing into the sea.

Map 4, 10K (Dundee). Bridge across the Tay, between Wormit in Fife and Dundee.

TAYMOUTH CASTLE

Taymouth Castle, a large castellated mansion built between 1801 and 1842, incorporates part of a 16th-century castle of the Campbells. The family were made Earls of Breadalbane in 1681, then Marquises in 1831. The castle and estate were put up for sale in 1997 for offers over £5,500,000, and the castle was planned to be part of a luxury development, although the refurbishment was recently halted when the development company went into administration.

The castle is reputedly haunted, and ghostly footsteps have been reported. The ghost is said to appear as a harbinger of tragedy in the Campbell family. During Taymouth's use as a school in the 1980s, it is said that some students were so scared by unexplained events that they refused to stay in the castle.

Map 4, 8J (Taymouth). Off A827, 5 miles W of Aberfeldy, Taymouth, Perthshire.

TERALLY

A house here was said to be haunted, and many unexplained and disturbing noises were heard. The spooky activity is reputed to have been caused by the ghost of a doctor, who had lived here, and whose apparition was also seen on the beach nearby.

Map 3, 5Q (Terally). Off A716, 2 miles E of Port Logan, Rhins of Galloway, Dumfries and Galloway.

THAINSTONE HOUSE

Thainstone House is a handsome mansion, which dates from the 18th century, although it was extended in 1840, and again in 1992. An older house here was sacked by Jacobites in 1745, and was home to James Wilson, who emigrated to North America and signed the Declaration of Independence. Sir Andrew Mitchell, another owner, was ambassador to the Court of Prussia in the time of Frederick the Great. The house is now a hotel and country club, and it stands in 40 acres of lush meadow and park land.

The building is said to be haunted by a 'Green Lady', daughter of a former owner of the house. She was killed in a riding accident, and sightings of her apparition describe her as wearing a green cloak. An alternative version is that she was killed when the house was torched during the Jacobite Rising of 1745-46. Manifestations reported include objects moving by themselves, and pets being too scared to enter one of the bedrooms. A member of staff also told how he turned and walked though a misty shape about the size of a person, but there was nothing to see when he turned back.

Map 2, 11F (Thainstone). Off A96, S of Inverurie, Thainstone, Aberdeenshire.
Hotel. (01467 621643 / www.swallow-hotels.com/hotels/thainstone-house.aspx)

THE BINNS

Set in picturesque grounds by the banks of the Firth of Forth, The Binns is a fine castellated mansion, delicately washed in a fine shade of pink, dating from the 17th century, with impressive plaster ceilings. The Binns was a property of the Livingstones of Kilsyth, but was sold to the Dalziels in 1612. There is a story of a tunnel leading from The Binns along the coast to Blackness Castle (also see that entry).

General Tam Dalziel of The Binns was taken prisoner in 1651 at the Battle of Worcester, but escaped from the Tower of London. He went into exile three years later, after a Royalist rising collapsed, and he travelled to Russia, where he served with the Tsar's cossacks. During this time, he is reputed to have roasted prisoners over open fires; he is also said to have introduced thumbscrews to Scotland. Dalziel returned to Scotland after the Restoration and was made commander of forces in Scotland, leading the force that defeated the Covenanters at the Battle of Rullion Green in 1666. He died in 1685, at more than 80 years of age, and is buried in the family tomb at nearby Abercorn Church (which is open to the public). All sorts of interesting quirks were attributed to Dalziel by his Covenanter enemies, including musket balls bouncing off when shot at him at Rullion Green.

The house and grounds are reportedly haunted by Tam's ghost, which is sometimes said to be seen on a white horse riding up to the door of The Binns. One story is that Dalziel often played cards with the Devil, and once, when he won, the Devil was so angered that the Evil One threw a massive marble table, on which they had been playing, into the nearby Sergeant's Pond. The cards, goblet, spoon and table, which are said to have been used, are preserved in the house. When the water of the pond was low after a drought, this table was supposedly found, some 200 years after Dalziel's death. Tam's boots, also preserved in the house, are said to vanish whenever his ghost is out on its horse in the grounds.

Another ghost said to haunt the area is that of an old man gathering firewood, said by some to be a Pict (although how anyone could know that the apparition is so definitely that of a Pict, and not of a Briton, of an Angle or of a Scot, sadly is not recorded).

Map 4, 8L (The Binns). Off A904, 3 miles NE of Linlithgow, The Binns, West Lothian.
NTS: House open Jun-Sep, Sat-Wed , closed Thu &Fri; parkland open all year. (01506 834255 / www.nts.org.uk)

THE LODGE, EDINBANE   ILLUS PAGE 279

The Lodge, standing by the head of Loch Greshornish on the north end of the Isle of Skye, is an old hunting lodge and coaching inn, and is believed to date from the 16th century. The Lodge was built by the MacLeods of Greshornish, whose main resi-

Stirling Castle (page 273)

Tantallon Castle (page 276)

The Lodge, Edinbane (page 278)

Thirlestane Castle (page 281)

Thunderton House, Elgin (page 283)

dence at Greshornish House (also see that entry) is further north, on the west side of the loch. The Lodge is now used as a comfortable and friendly hotel.

The Lodge is said to be haunted, and activity is reputed to be centred on the ground floor of the building, although none of the bogles are reckoned to be frightening. One apparition is said to be of a gentleman clothed in black, sometimes seen at the entrance, while another is reputed to be of an old woman, also dressed in black, observed knitting by the fire, sometimes with a spaniel. A third phantom is alleged to have been seen in the passage behind the bar. This bogle is also of an elderly lady, this time dressed as if for bed.

Map 1, 2E (Edinbane). Off A850, Old Dunvegan Road, W of Edinbane, Loch Greshornish, Isle of Skye, Highland.
Hotel. (01470 582217 / www.the-lodge-at-edinbane.co.uk)

THE MITRE, EDINBURGH

The Mitre is a popular public house on the High Street, and it is said that it is haunted by a ghost, which seems to be mostly witnessed in the cellar, but is also believed to turn on the jukebox at times.

Map 4, 9L (Edinburgh). Off A1, The Mitre, High Street (Royal Mile), Edinburgh.
Public house. (0131 524 0071)

THEATRE ROYAL, EDINBURGH

The old Post Office building, constructed in the 1860s, stands on the site of the Theatre Royal, which dated from 1768.

This building was said to be haunted by the sounds of actors performing on an empty stage, but the manifestations are said to have stopped when the theatre was demolished. The Post Office building has itself been renovated to house offices, retail units and apartments.

Map 4, 9L (Edinburgh). Off A1, at corner of South Bridge and Princes Street, Edinburgh.

THEATRE ROYAL, GLASGOW

The theatre here, which dates from 1867, has a fine interior with three levels of circles and sumptuous decoration. The building was threatened with closure, but is now the home of Scottish Opera.

The theatre is said to be haunted by the ghost of a former cleaner, 'Nora'. She was an aspiring actress but was not taken seriously, and is reported to have thrown herself to her death from the top circle. Her ghost is thought to manifest itself with moaning and slamming doors. The apparition of a fireman, killed here in the 1950s, has reportedly been seen in the orchestra pit.

Map 4, 7M (Glasgow). Off M9, 282 Hope Street, Glasgow.
Theatre. (0141 332 3321 / www.ambassadortickets.com/Theatre-Royal-Glasgow)

THIRLESTANE CASTLE   ILLUS PAGE 280

Standing in picturesque countryside, Thirlestane Castle is a massive, imposing and splendid mansion with many towers and spires, and has an old castle, dating from the 16th century, at its core. Fine 17th-century plasterwork survives in the plush interior, and Bonnie Prince Charlie stayed here in 1745 on his way south.

Thirlestane was a property of the Maitlands, and John Maitland, Duke of Lauderdale, had the house remodelled in 1670. Lauderdale was Secretary of State for Scotland from 1661-80, but he was eventually replaced after the Covenanter uprising which ended in their defeat at the Battle of Bothwell Brig.

His ghost is said to haunt Thirlestane, as well as St Mary's in Haddington (also see that entry), and his apparition is described as an important-looking man with long curly hair (not a description to distinguish him from many other notable men of the time) although there is a full-length portrait of him in the house, if there is any doubt. His bogle is reputed to have been seen in more than one of the chambers, but apparently mostly in a room on the third floor (not currently accessible).

Map 4, 10M (Thirlestane). Off A68, E of Lauder, Thirlestane Castle, Borders.
Open Good Fri, Easter Sun and Mon, then mid Apr-mid Sep, Wed, Thu and Sun; Bank Hol Mons in May; Jul-Aug, Sun-Thu. (01578 722430 / www.thirlestanecastle.co.uk)

THREAVE CASTLE

Standing on an island in the River Dee, Threave Castle consists of a massive tower which was defended by a courtyard with a wall, corner towers and a ditch, as well as the river. The present castle was built by Archibald the Grim – so named because his face was terrible to look upon in battle – 3rd Earl of Douglas, and Lord of Galloway from 1369 until 1390. He died at Threave in 1400. His son, Archibald, married James I's sister and was created Duke of Tourraine in France after winning the Battle of Baugé against the English. He was, however, killed at the Battle of Verneuil in 1424. William, the young 6th Earl, and David, his brother, rode from Threave to Edinburgh Castle in 1440 for the Black Dinner, where they were taken out and summarily executed. The 8th Earl, another William, was murdered in 1452 by James II at Stirling, and three years later, following defeat at Arkinholm, James II besieged Threave with artillery. The castle became a royal fortress with the Maxwells as keepers, and was finally given to The National Trust of Scotland in 1948.

Unexplained breathing noises and disembodied voices have reportedly been heard in the castle: some have suggested a supernatural origin.

Map 4, 7P (Threave). Off A75, 6 miles W of Dalbeattie, Threave, Dumfries and Galloway.
His Scot: Open Apr-Oct, daily. Owned by NTS; administered by Historic Scotland – includes walk and short ferry trip. (07711 223101 (mobile) / www.historic-scotland.gov.uk)

THREE SISTERS, EDINBURGH

Located in the historic Cowgate part of the old town of Edinburgh, the Three Sisters is an atmospheric and a popular pub in a fine building with a cobbled courtyard. It was first built as the Tailors' Hall for the Guild of Tailors in 1621; the Tailors Hall Hotel is housed here since renovation and refurbishment in 1998. The pub is believed to be named after three sisters from a theatrical troupe, who stayed and performed here.

The building is reputedly haunted, and the apparition of a 'White Lady' has been reported in the kitchen of the first floor, while there has been a series of mysterious noises heard emanating from the fourth floor.

Map 4, 9L (Edinburgh). Off A7 or A702, 139 Cowgate, Edinburgh.

A paranormal investigation was undertaken in April 2008 by Scottish Society of Paranormal Investigation and Analysis (www.sspia.co.uk)

THUNDERTON HOUSE, ELGIN

ILLUS PAGE 280

Thunderton House may incorporate part of an ancient castle, built in the 14th century to replace the old stronghold on Ladyhill in Elgin. Thunderton was later a property of the Sutherland Lord Duffus, but passed to the Dunbars of Thunderton; the building was altered in later years, and is now a public house.

The house is said to be haunted by the bogle of Bonnie Prince Charlie, who stayed here for 11 days in the Spring of 1746, before going on to defeat at the Battle of Culloden on 16 April. An alternative identity has been given as Lady Arradoul, his host over this period (the sheets which the Prince used when staying here were used as Lady Arradoul's shroud when she was buried).

Disturbances are said to include the faint sounds of bagpipes and voices coming from the second floor when unoccupied, as well as the unexplained movement of objects.

Map 2, 9E (Elgin). Off A96, Thunderton, Elgin, Moray.
Public house and accommodation (The Backpackers). (01343 554921 / www.thundertonhouse.co.uk)

TIBBIE SHIEL'S INN, ST MARY'S LOCH

Located by the lovely and tranquil St Mary's Loch, Tibbie Shiel's Inn was opened as a drinking house in 1823 by Isabella Shiel – also known as Tibbie – after her husband died and she was left penniless. The inn grew in popularity and was visited by James Hogg, the 'Ettrick Shepherd', and many other writers and poets, including Sir Walter Scott, Robert Louis Stevenson and Thomas Carlyle. Tibbie died in 1878 at the age of 96 and was buried in Ettrick kirkyard, but the inn remained open.

The building is said to be haunted by Tibbie's ghost, which reputedly manifests itself with a cold hand on the shoulder, but keeps a watchful eye on the hotel. A report of the ghost was recorded in one of the bedrooms in 1996. The spirit of a dog has also been witnessed, apparently the ghost of an animal belonging to a previous innkeeper who died while away from the inn: the dog starved to death in his absence.

Map 4, 9N (St Mary's Loch). Off A708, 1.5 miles S of Cappercleuch, St Mary's Loch, Borders.
Hotel:. (01750 42231 / www.tibbieshielsinn.com)

TIGH NA SGIATH COUNTRY HOUSE HOTEL, DULNAIN BRIDGE

The fine Edwardian mansion, dating from 1902, stands in more than two acres of old woodlands, which are graced by red squirrels that can be seen from the house. At one time the property was owned by the Lipton family, but the house is now an excellent and esteemed hotel.

The building is reputed to be haunted by the benign bogle of one of the former owners, a Lady Hartley, who is said to have so loved the house that she did not wish to be parted from it, even in death. Unexplained footsteps heard coming from the stairs down to the cellar have been reported.

Map 2, 8F (Dulnain Bridge). Off A95 near junction with A938, 2 miles SW of Grantown-on-Spey, Dulnain Bridge, Highland.
Hotel. (01479 851345 / www.tigh-na-sgiath.co.uk)

TODSHAWHILL

There has been a farm or house, perhaps once even a tower house, here for centuries, and the property was held by the Scotts, and then by the Rennicks from the middle of the 17th century.

The farm was said to have had a brownie, known as the 'Bogle of Todshawhill'. The brownie was described as looking like a little old woman but with very short legs, meaning it waddled in a comical way when it walked.

Map 4, 9O (Todshawhill). Off B723, 10 miles E and N of Lockerbie, Todshawhill, Castle O'Er Forest, Dumfries and Galloway.

TOLBOOTH, STIRLING

The Tolbooth (or Town House) dates mostly from the beginning of the 18th century, although it incorporates an earlier tolbooth, while a courthouse and jail were added in 1806-11. Among those imprisoned and executed here were John Baird and Andrew Hardie, radical weavers who were convicted of high treason in 1820, after they tried to seize the Carron Iron Works, near Falkirk. The building was renovated in 2002 and the Tolbooth is now a venue for live music and the arts.

The building is said to be haunted by the spirit of Allan Mair, an apparition seen in what appears to be 18th-century clothing. Other manifestations are reported to be unexplained sounds in the old cells, and bottles of alcohol being mysteriously smashed.

Mair was hanged in 1843, when already 84 years old, after the old farmer had been found guilty of beating his wife to death. During the execution, Mair managed to get his hands free and tried to remove the noose from around his neck, as he swung and choked. The hangman was obliged to grab on to Mair's legs and this extra weight finished Mair off. In 2000 a skeleton was found buried by the entrance to the courtyard, and forensic examination suggested that this could well be Mair's remains. The bones were then buried at Ballengeich cemetery in an unmarked grave.

Map 4, 8L (Stirling). Off B8052 or A811, Jail Wynd, Stirling.
Theatre with cafe-bar. (01786 274000 / www.stirling.gov.uk/tolbooth.htm)

TOLQUHON CASTLE

Once a stout stronghold and a comfortable residence, Tolquhon Castle is a fine and substantial ruinous building, with the remains of ranges around a courtyard, the entrance being through a petite drum-towered gatehouse. The original castle was built by the Prestons of Craigmillar, but the property passed by marriage to the Forbes family in 1420. William, 7th Laird, built the castle as it now is; his finely carved tomb survives at nearby Tarves. The property was sold in 1716 and part was later used as a farmhouse, before becoming completely ruinous.

There are recent reports of sightings of a 'White Lady', reputedly seen unmoving at the top of a staircase. Other manifestations are said to be unexplained footsteps and a humming sound. Accounts have also been recorded of a 'Grey Lady', who was apparently seen wandering through the ruins at midnight, accompanied by the sounds of groaning.

Map 2, 11F (Tolquhon). Off A999, 8 miles NE of Inverurie, Tolquhon, Aberdeenshire.
His Scot: Open Apr-Oct, daily; open Nov-Mar, wknds only; closed 25/26 Dec and 1/2 Jan. (01651 851286 / www.historic-scotland.gov.uk)

Tomnaverie (page 287)

Tron Theatre, Glasgow (page 289)

Traquair House (page 288)

Winnock Hotel, Drymen (page 297)

TOMBUIE

Tombuie, a farmhouse, is said to be haunted by the apparition of a young girl. She had fallen in love with the son of the house, but it was not reciprocated and he was soon married to another woman. The story goes that the poor girl despaired and drowned herself in the water butt at Tombuie. Her weeping apparition then appeared to the couple in the bedroom of the house, and has reputedly been seen on other occasions.

Map 4, 8J (Tombuie). Off A827, 2 miles NE of Aberfeldy, Tombuie, Perthshire.

TOMNAVERIE STONE CIRCLE ILLUS PAGE 285

With excellent views to Lochnagar and the Cairngorms, the stone circle at Tomnaverie consists of four upright stones with the recumbent stone still in place. Within the main setting is a circle of smaller stones, the kerb of a cairn.

There is an account from 1992 that two people decided to sleep in a field by the circle, but were woken when a dark cloaked and hooded apparition passed their vehicle. The phantom apparently vanished, and a search of the area revealed nothing.

Map 2, 10G (Tomnaverie). On B9094, 3.5 miles NW of Aboyne, Tomnaverie, Aberdeenshire. **His Scot: Access at all reasonable times - short walk. (01667 460232 / www.historic-scotland.gov.uk)**

TONTINE HOTEL, PEEBLES

Housed in a fine building on the High Street, the Tontine Hotel dates from 1808, from during the Napoleonic Wars, and French POWs helped construct the building. The name comes from the idea of a tontine, where a number of people invest in an enterprise, but, as they die, each share goes back into the pot to be divided among the surviving investors until only one person is left – and they inherit the whole enterprise.

The building is said to be haunted by a bogle known as 'Dougie', which is reputed to be mostly witnessed outside the wine cellar.

Map 4, 9N (Peebles). On A72, High Street, Peebles, Borders. **Hotel. (01721 720892 / www.tontinehotel.com)**

TOR CASTLE

Tor Castle is a massive but very ruinous tower which had a walled courtyard, and there is believed to have been a castle here since the 11th century. Indeed, this is said to have been the stronghold of Banquo, of *Macbeth* fame, who in the play was murdered on the orders of Macbeth, although his son Fleance escaped the assassins. Banquo's Walk, near Tor, is a track running north through an avenue of trees, which is said to have been used by Banquo in life, and frequented by his phantom in death.

The lands were a property of the Macintoshes, who built a castle, but Tor was seized by the Camerons around 1380. The castle was used until the Jacobite Rising of 1745-46, after which the last Cameron owner went into exile.

Map 1, 5H (Tor). Off B8004, 3 miles NE of Fort William, Torcastle, Lochaber, Highland.

TRANSPORT DEPOT, ABERDEEN

The building here, dating from about 1861, was used as an army barracks until World War I, but is now a depot and bus station.

The building is said to be haunted by the ghost of a Captain Beaton of the Gordon Highlanders, who reportedly hanged himself here on the eve of being sent back to France after having already been wounded in the head. His apparition has reputedly been seen in recent times, and there are stories of a phantom being spotted in a khaki uniform with bandages on his head and his hands; and another also in uniform, but wearing a kilt and a great coat. Other manifestations are alleged to include tapping on windows, mysterious voices coming from unoccupied areas, the unexplained switching on and off of lights, areas of the premises becoming suddenly very cold, and drivers feeling as if someone is blowing on their necks.

Map 2, 12G (Aberdeen). Off A9103, King Street, Aberdeen.

TRAQUAIR ARMS HOTEL, INNERLEITHEN

The hotel, which dates from the middle of the 19th century, is said to be haunted by a 'Grey Lady', although it is not known who she is. The ghost is said to have been witnessed in the old part of the building, and is only reportedly seen from the back, so that her face is not visible. Her dress is claimed to be long and grey with a bustle, while her hair is tied up in a bun.

Map 4, 9N (Innerleithen). Off B709, Traquair Road, Innerleithen, Borders.
Hotel, restaurant and courtyard cottages. (01896 830229 / www.traquairarmshotel.co.uk)

TRAQUAIR HOUSE   ILLUS PAGE 286

One of the oldest continuously inhabited houses in Scotland, Traquair House is a magnificent castle and mansion, set in landscaped grounds. The building incorporates an altered and extended tower house, which may date from as early as the 12th century. There are many furnished rooms, along with the remains of 17th-century painted ceilings. There are also Jacobite and Stewart mementoes, including a crucifix and rosary belonging to Mary, Queen of Scots, and a fine collection of miniature portraits.

Alexander I had a hunting lodge here, and Traquair was visited by many of the kings of Scots, and some of England: Edward I and Edward II in the 14th century. Traquair passed through several families until sold to the Stewart Earls of Buchan in 1478. Mary, Queen of Scots, visited with Lord Darnley in 1566 when she was pregnant with the future James VI. She left behind a quilt, said to have been embroidered by herself and her four Marys. The 4th Laird was one those who helped her escape from Lochleven Castle in 1568, but she was soon defeated at Langside and fled to England. At Traquair is the bed, rescued from Terregles, where Mary spent some of her last nights on Scottish soil.

Bonnie Prince Charlie visited the house on his way south in 1745 to invade England. He entered Traquair through the famous Bear Gates. The story goes that the 5th Earl closed and locked them after Charlie's departure, swearing they would not be unlocked until a Stewart once more sat on the throne of the country. They are still locked, of course.

Traquair is not believed to be haunted, and this is apparently not one of the places that the spirit of Bonnie Prince Charlie frequents. The grounds, however, are believed to be. The apparition of Lady Louisa Stewart, sister of the 8th and last Earl of Traquair, is reported to have been sighted in the grounds around the house, going on her favourite walk by the Quair. An account of 1900 describes how she walked through two locked gateways.

Louisa lived to a ripe old age, dying in 1875 when she was 100 years old. Her portrait hangs in the house.

Map 4, 9N (Traquair). Off B709, 1 mile S of Innerleithen, Traquair, Borders.
House early Apr-Oct, daily; Nov, wknds only. It is advisable to contact house to confirm opening. (01896 830323 / www.traquair.co.uk)

TRON THEATRE, GLASGOW

ILLUS PAGE 285

A church, dedicated to St Mary and St Anne, was established here by 1484, and this was raised to collegiate status in 1525; after the Reformation it was used by Protestants and it became the Tron Kirk in 1592. The distinctive tower dates from around then, while the steeple was added in the 1630s. The tower survived a fire in 1793, believed to have been started by the Hellfire Club, while the rest of the church had to be rebuilt. The building was later used as a meeting hall, place of execution, store, and briefly as a police station, while now it is a theatre and conference centre, after having been given a major refurbishment in 1995. The 'tron' was the beam on which goods for market were weighed by the city authorities.

The theatre has several stories of ghosts. One ghost is said to have been witnessed in the boiler room, where a dark and threatening apparition has been spotted by staff; the phantoms of two children are also said to have been spotted here. Other bogles are reputed to have been seen in the Victorian bar, and in the box office, where the apparition of a man in horse-riding gear is alleged to have been seen. Other manifestations are reported to be uncomfortable feelings, as if being watched, and a member of staff feeling as if an icy finger was being drawn across the back of his neck.

Map 4, 7M (Glasgow). Off A8, 63 Trongate, Glasgow.
Theatre with bar/restaurant. (0141 552 4267 (box office) / www.tron.co.uk)

A paranormal investigation was undertaken in January 2007 and in February 2006 by the Ghost Club (www.ghostclub.org.uk) and in November 2003, in July 2004 and in July 2005 by Scottish Paranormal Investigations (www.scottishparanormalinvestigations.co.uk)

TRUMPAN CHURCH

Trumpan Church, the ruins of a medieval church formerly with a thatched roof, is the scene of a cruel massacre. A raiding party of MacDonalds, who were enemies of the MacLeods, came ashore here one Sunday about 1578. The congregation of MacLeods was at worship, and the MacDonalds set fire to the thatch. They then cut down anyone who tried to flee, while the rest of the congregation was burnt alive. Only one woman escaped and the alarm was raised. The MacLeods of Dunvegan, bringing with them the Fairy Flag, quickly arrived and the MacDonalds were exterminated to a man. On the anniversary of the massacre it is said that the singing of a ghostly congregation can be heard.

In the churchyard is the Trial Stone, which has a small hole near the top. The trial was carried out by blindfolding the accused, who would be proved to be telling the truth if they succeeded in putting their finger in the hole at the first attempt. Lady Grange, Rachel Chiesly, is believed to be buried here (see Dalry House).

Map 1, 1E (Trumpan). Off B886, 8 miles NE of Dunvegan, Trumpan, Isle of Skye, Highland.
Open at all reasonable times.

Tulliallan Castle

Tulliallan Castle is an impressive castellated mansion, and was built in 1817-20 for George Keith Elphinstone, Admiral Lord Keith. Elphinstone was a senior officer in Lord Nelson's forces during the Napoleonic Wars, and the house was financed by prize ships captured during the fighting, and was built by workers including by French prisoners of war. During World War II Tulliallan was used by the Free Polish Army as their headquarters in Scotland. Since 1954 the mansion has been used by the police as a training college, and there have been many extensions.

One story has one part of the mansion haunted by the sounds of children laughing and playing.

Map 4, 8L (Kincardine). Off A977, 0.5 miles N of Kincardine, Tulliallan Castle, Fife.
Police college. (01259 732000 / tulliallan.police.uk/)

Tulloch Castle

Standing on a ridge overlooking Dingwall, Tulloch Castle is an attractive mansion and castle, with work from as early as the 12th or 13th century. Tulloch was held by the Bains from 1542 until 1762, when the property was sold to the Davidsons, and they held it until 1945. The building was used as a school for some years, but has been a hotel since 1996.

There is reputed to be a tunnel from the basement of the castle, which is believed to have led across the town to Dingwall Castle. The tunnel has collapsed but part of it can be seen from the middle of the front lawn.

The castle is said to be haunted by a 'Green Lady' (and indeed the hotel bar is named after her). The story goes that a child surprised her father with another woman. The child was so startled that she fled the room and fell down a flight of stairs, killing herself. The identity of the bogle has also been suggested as Elizabeth Davidson, whose portrait hangs in the Great Hall.

The apparition of a maid is said to have been witnessed in the Pink Room, and the hall is reputed to be the location of some uncanny activity, including the sighting of a ghost, believed to be the spirit of a former owner.

A guest who was staying in Room 8 reported waking up with the room deathly cold and him being pinned into the bed and unable to breathe (although this may be a case of sleep paralysis, rather than a bogle attack).

Map 2, 7E (Tulloch). Off A862, 1 mile N of Dingwall, Tulloch Castle, Ross, Highland.
Hotel. (01349 861325 / www.tullochcastle.co.uk)

A paranormal investigation was undertaken in October 2007 by Ghost Finders (www.ghostfinders.co.uk/tullochcastle.html)

Tynron Doon

At Tynron Doon are the impressive ramparts of an ancient fort, in which was built a medieval castle. The castle was a property of the Kirkpatricks, and Robert the Bruce is said to have sheltered here, with Kirkpatrick of Closeburn, in 1306 after stabbing the Red Comyn in front of the altar at Greyfriars (also see that entry) at nearby Dumfries.

The area is said to be haunted by the apparition of a headless horseman on a black horse. The story goes that the rider, apparently one of the MacMilligans of Dalgarnock, wished to marry a daughter of the then laird, but her brothers were having none of it. They chased after the horseman but, as the poor fellow galloped away, he fell from his horse, decapitating himself.

Map 4, 70 (Tynron Doon). Off A702, 4 miles W of Thornhill, Tynron Doon, Dumfries and Galloway.

VAYNE CASTLE

Vayne Castle is a ruinous tower house, built on the Z-plan, with a main block and a rectangular tower and a round tower at opposite corners, dating from the 16th century. The lands were once a property of the Mowats, but passed to the Lindsays in 1450, then to the Carnegies, then to the Mills in 1766. The castle was replaced by the nearby mansion of Noranside, which is now used as an open prison.

The castle ruins at Vayne are said to be haunted by a monstrous guardian, which protects a great treasure hidden here. The guardian is only reputed to stir when the safety of the treasure is threatened.

Map 2, 10I (Vayne). Off B57, 7 miles W of Brechin, Vayne, Angus.

VOGRIE HOUSE

Vogrie House, which dates from 1875, is a large and unusual mansion with Elizabethan and Arts and Crafts features. The mansion was built for James Dewar, who made his fortune from the Perth whisky company, Dewars. The house was used as the Royal Edinburgh Hospital for Mental and Nervous Disorders from 1924 until 1962, was then used as a communications centre during the Cold War, and is now the centrepiece of a country park. The stables were housed in an exceptional gothic building.

It is said that Vogrie House is haunted, and that many inexplicable occurrences have happened in recent years. Activity is reputed to include unexplained footsteps and mysterious voices, as well as the phantom of a woman, who has been seen in the corridors of the building.

Map 4, 10M (Pathhead). On B6372, 2 miles E of Gorebridge, Vogrie, Midlothian. **Country park open all year, daily; cafe. (01875 821990 (ranger service) / www.midlothian.gov.uk)**

A paranormal investigation was undertaken in December 2005 by Borders Paranormal Group (www.bordersparanormal.co.uk)

WAMPHRAY TOWER

Wamphray Tower was once a strong castle, but little remains except some walls. The property was held by the Johnstones from 1476, and was home to William Johnstone, the 'Galliard'. His horse-stealing raid and death, and Willie o' Kirkhill's (another of his family) subsequent revenge, are recorded in the old ballad 'The Lads of Wamphray'. John Johnstone of Wamphray was imprisoned here for his part in the Jacobite Rising of 1745-46, and only escaped execution by changing places with a kinsman. The property was sold the following year and the tower soon became ruinous.

The story goes that for some 300 years the tower had a brownie, which did all manner of chores but also brought the family and tower good luck. A new laird came into possession of Wamphray (which was also known as Leithenhall), but when he saw the brownie was appalled to think that one of his servants was so famished, hairy and dressed in rags. The laird commanded that the brownie was to be given new clothes and to be fed. But this present of garments so angered the brownie that he up and left on the spot, taking any good luck with him, abandoning Wamphray delivering the malison:

Ca', cuttee, ca'!
A' the luck o' Leithenha'
Gangs wi' me to Bodsbeck Ha'!

Boadsbeck Tower (see that entry) and its owners were, however, also to have little luck, and other versions of the story have the brownie coming in the opposite direction and moving to Wamphray.

Map 4, 9O (Wamphray). Off M74, 5 miles SE of Moffat, Wamphray, Dumfries and Galloway.

WANLOCKHEAD

Wanlockhead and nearby Leadhills were both centres of mining, and there are many old mine workings in the area, as well as pumping engines and ore processing and smelting sites. The Museum of Lead Mining is located in Wanlockhead and has many displays on the industry and the local area: one of the exhibits is a stone with the legend 'In memoriam, Jenny Miller, January 1877'. This is believed to have come from a cairn marking the spot where Jenny Miller died in a blizzard, after setting out to attend her sister's marriage in Wanlockhead. She lost her way and fell into old mine workings.

A walker visiting the Lowther Hills in 1977 reported seeing a young woman coming towards him, looking distressed, carrying a wicker basket and dressed in old-fashioned clothes. The figure reputedly said to him 'Look in the stones' but, before he could approach closer, the figure disappeared. The walker returned to his home and was then told the story of Jenny Miller, including that she carried a teapot, a wedding gift, in the wicker basket. They returned to the spot, and found a cairn of stones. When they searched it, they found the stone with Jenny Miller's name.

This is apparently not the only time that the ghost has been seen.

Map 4, 8N (Wanlockhead). Off B797, 5 miles E and N of Sanquhar, Dumfries and Galloway. **Museum open late Mar-Oct, daily. (01659 74387 / www.leadminingmuseum.co.uk)**

WARMANBIE

Located in 45 acres of woodlands and grounds, Warmanbie is a small 19th-century mansion, which rises to two storeys, and probably stands on the site of a tower house. The property was held by the Carruthers family at the end of the 16th century, but had passed to the Spencers by 1943.

The building is said to be haunted, with activity such as apparitions being reported in the kitchen and in some of the rooms. One phantom was described as being dressed like a dairy maid.

Map 4, 9P (Warmanbie). Off B722, 2 miles N of Annan, Warmanbie, Dumfries and Galloway.

WEDDERLIE HOUSE

Wedderlie House, an atmospheric three-storey mansion of 1680 with corbiestepped gables, incorporates a 16th-century L-plan tower house. Wedderlie was a property of the Polwarth family in the 13th century, but is most associated with the Edgars, who held Wedderlie from 1327 until 1733. Sir Richard Edgar was a witness at the marriage of Robert the Bruce to Elizabeth de Burgh, and three of the family were Members of Parliament. There was a probably an even earlier castle here, part of which may be incorporated into the tower house. In 1733 Wedderlie was acquired by the Stewart Lord Blantyre. Although ruined by the later part of the 19th century, the house has since been restored and is still occupied.

The house is said to have a 'Green Lady'.

Map 4, 10M (Wedderlie). Off B6456, 1 mile N of Westruther, Wedderlie, Berwickshire, Borders.
Farm. (01578 740213 / www.wedderliefarm.co.uk)

WELLGATE CENTRE, DUNDEE

The shopping centre was built on an old street, the Wellgate (or Wellgait), and was opened in the 1970s, although nothing of the original streets was retained.

There are stories of the apparition of a woman having been witnessed, although most manifestations are said to be 'unexplained' noises, such as strange creaking sounds. This has been explained, however, as the building cooling down.

Map 4, 10K (Dundee). Off A92, Wellgate, Dundee.
Shopping centre.

WELLWOOD HOUSE

Wellwood House, a mansion of 1878, incorporated an old house or tower of the Campbells, which dated from about 1600. The later house was built by the Bairds, who bought the estate in 1863. The house was demolished in 1926.

The house was reputedly haunted by the apparition of young woman, called 'Beanie' (or 'Beenie', in one version). She appears to have been murdered by a jealous lover or by a rival for her affections, perhaps on the stairs of the house, for it was said a blood stain there could not be removed. Her ghost was allegedly seen walking from her room in the older part of the house out to the grounds, where the bogle was seen to weep. If her apparition was closely approached, it reportedly would slowly vanish.

Map 4, 7N (Wellwood). Off A70, 2 miles W of Muirkirk, Ayrshire.

WEMYSS CASTLE

Wemyss Castle is the large sprawling stronghold and mansion of the Wemyss family, who have held it from ancient times until the present day.

Sir Michael Wemyss was one of the ambassadors sent to Norway at the end of the 13th century to bring Margaret, Maid of Norway, back to Scotland. The castle was sacked by the English during the Wars of Independence. Royal visitors include Mary, Queen of Scots, who first met Lord Darnley here in 1565, and Charles II, who visited in 1650 and 1657. The Wemyss family were forfeited for their part in the Jacobite Risings, but later regained the property.

A 'Green Lady' – Green Jean – reputedly haunts the castle, and is said to have been seen in all parts of the building. A sighting of the ghost was made in the 1890s, when she was described as 'tall and slim and entirely clad in green, with her visage hidden by the hood of her mantle'. Further manifestations were recorded in 1904 during Christmas celebrations, and one of the family walked alongside the bogle for some time until the ghost finally disappeared.

Map 4, 9L (Wemyss). Off A955, 3 miles NE of Kirkcaldy, Wemyss, Fife.
Gardens can be visited by prior appt May-Jul, 12.00-17.00: write to Charlotte Wemyss, Wemyss Castle, Fife, KY1 4TE or phone or email. (01592 652181 / www.wemysscastlegardens.com)

WEST BOW, EDINBURGH

A house in the West Bow, the street between Victoria Street and the Grassmarket, was occupied by a Major Thomas Weir and his sister Grizell. On the face of it, Weir was an upstanding member of the community: he was commander of the city guard and it was he who led the Marquis of Montrose to the scaffold. In 1670, however, he confessed to many crimes, including witchcraft and meetings with the Devil, and implicated his sister. The couple were convicted and both executed: Weir was strangled then burnt at Gallowlea, beneath Calton Hill, while his sister was hanged in the Grassmarket.

Both their apparitions were then reportedly seen around the West Bow, sometimes on a dark horse. His house was also reputed to be haunted and, although empty, strange lights were seen at the windows and the sounds of partying and screaming were heard. A black coach and horses, sent by the Devil, are supposed to have arrived at the house to take Weir and his sister back to Hell after the forays into the corporeal world. In the 1850s, a couple occupied the house but only stayed one night after an apparition of a calf was seen in their bedroom. The house was finally demolished around 1830, although ghostly manifestations are still reported, including the headless ghost of Weir and the apparition of his sister, blackened by fire.

Sightings of an apparition of William Ruthven, Earl of Gowrie, have also been reported here. Gowrie led the 'Ruthven Raid' of 1582, in which the young James VI was imprisoned in Huntingtower Castle. James had him executed two years later. Gowrie had a town house here, but it has also been demolished.

Map 4, 9L (Edinburgh). Off A1, E of Edinburgh Castle, off the Royal Mile, Edinburgh.
Accessible at all times.

WEST PORT HOUSE, LINLITHGOW

West Port House is a plain three-storey town house, dating from the 16th century but much altered in later years. The house was a property of the Hamiltons of Silvertonhill, and Mary of Guise, wife of James V, is said to have stayed here.

According to an old account, the building is said to be haunted.

Map 4, 8L (Linlithgow). On A803, W end of High Street, Linlithgow, West Lothian.

WESTER ELCHIES

Wester Elchies was a fine and romantic old house dating from the 17th century, but unfortunately the whole building was demolished in the 1970s because of dry rot. The lands were a property of the Grants, but after 1947 the house was used as a prep school, part of the Gordonstoun establishment.

The old part of the building was said to be haunted by a 'Green Lady', described as being a thoroughly unpleasant ghost. The bogle is reputed to have been witnessed mostly before the house was used as a school, but it is said that the ghost was once seen by the school matron.

Map 2, 9F (Wester Elchies). Off B9102, 1 mile W of Charlestown of Aberlour, Wester Elchies, Moray.

WESTERN INFIRMARY, GLASGOW

The infirmary, dating from 1871 and first built as a massive castellated building, has been much altered and extended in later years.

The buildings are said to be haunted by the ghost of Sir William MacEwen, who was a neurologist and surgeon and died in 1924. His apparition is said to have been witnessed several times, a tall man in a white coat, before vanishing outside an operating theatre. The story goes that a sick patient complaining of a terrible headache had asked the surgeon to operate on him, but that MacEwen had, perhaps selfishly, refused. The patient had gone on to become very ill and soon died, having collapsed down stairs, and it was later discovered that MacEwen could have saved him had he operated. MacEwen is said to have been very remorseful and his ghost returned to the scene of his guilt.

Map 4, 7M (Glasgow). Off A82, Dumbarton Road, Glasgow.

WHISTLE BINKIES, EDINBURGH

The bar, which is housed in arched vaults in an old tenement in Niddry Street, is reputedly haunted.

One ghost is said to be that of a man with long hair dressed as if from the 17th century, which is known as 'The Watcher'. A misty apparition has reputed to have been spotted in the cellars, and there are also many reports of mysterious noises and doors slamming by themselves. Other strange occurrences are believed to include oranges cutting themselves in half, and a clock repeatedly stopping working at the same time, 4.15, in the morning.

Map 4, 9L (Edinburgh). Off A7, 4-6 South Bridge (off High Street/Royal Mile), Edinburgh. **Public house featuring live music. (0131 557 5114 / www.whistlebinkies.com)**

WHITE HART INN, EDINBURGH

The White Hart Inn is a popular public house in the Grassmarket (where, as mentioned elsewhere, public executions took place), and the oldest part of the building in the cellar dates from 1516. Robert Burns spent a week here while visiting Edinburgh, and William and Dorothy Wordsworth stayed the night at the inn in 1803. Burke and Hare also used the inn while luring victims to their deaths and then selling their corpses to the medical school.

The pub is said to be haunted, and manifestations appear to be centred in the cellar and to have been experienced over many years and by many different people. The sighting of a shadowy apparition has been reported at the doorway behind the bar, which is then seen going into the cellar, as well as another, or the same phantom, in the cellar itself. Subsequent investigations have shown nobody was present. Other manifestations are reported to be a door slamming by itself, casks being moved around the cellar although nobody has been present, alcohol taps being switched off by themselves, and gas cylinders being unattached without explanation, even though it takes a spanner to remove them. Loud banging has allegedly been heard, coming from the cellar when empty, and crockery is said to have mysteriously fallen from a shelf on more than one occasion.

Map 4, 9L (Edinburgh). Off A7 or A702, 34 Grassmarket, Edinburgh.
Public house. (0131 226 2806)

A paranormal investigation was undertaken in October 2004 by the Ghost Club (www.ghostclub.org.uk)

WHY NOT?, EDINBURGH

The present impressive classical edifice was built in 1844 in the style of a Graeco-Roman temple to house a branch of the Commercial Bank of Scotland (latterly the Royal Bank of Scotland), but it stands on the site of the Physicians Hall of 1775. The bank was closed in 1993 and the building now houses the Dome Bar and Grill in the upper part, and the Why Not? night club in what used to be the vaults for the bank.

The part of the building used as the Why Not? night club is reputed to be haunted, the bogle going back to the days when the Physicians Hall stood here.

Map 4, 9L (Edinburgh). Off A1, 14 George Street, Edinburgh.
Night club. (0131 624 8633)

WINDGATE HOUSE

Known locally as 'The Vaults', Windgate House is a small ruined tower house of the Baillies of Lamington.

An apparition of a couple in Victorian dress has reportedly been witnessed here, and the story goes that they only appear when something significant is going to happen in the lives of the Baillie family.

Map 4, 8N (Windgate). Off A702, 5 miles SW of Biggar, Lanarkshire.

WINDHOUSE

In a desolate and windswept location, the two-storey house dates from 1707 and was remodelled with castellated wings about 1880. It was abandoned in the 1930s and is now ruinous, and stands in a bird sanctuary. Windhouse was a property of the Swanieson family, but passed to the Nevens in the early 17th century. The house was sold in 1878, and during renovations a large human skeleton was found.

One apparition was reportedly that of a large man, dressed in a black cloak and hat. The story goes that the ghost appeared out of the ground outside the house, then walked through the wall, and may have been the spirit of a pedlar who disappeared and whose skeleton was found, as mentioned above.

Another phantom was reputedly a lady dressed in silk. The swishing of her skirts was reported at the top of the stair. She was said to be a housekeeper and mistress, whose neck was broken after she had fallen down the stairs.

A third ghost was thought to be that of a child, witnessed in the kitchen, while yet another was that of a black dog.

Ghostly footsteps were also recorded as having being heard.

Map 2, 11A (Windhouse). Off A968, Windhouse, Yell, Shetland.

WINNOCK HOTEL, DRYMEN

ILLUS PAGE 286

Standing in the peaceful village of Drymen, the Winnock Hotel dates from the 18th century and was a coaching inn and smithy. The hotel has been extended several times, and is a large and welcoming establishment.

The building is said to be haunted, and activity is reputed to be in Rooms 38 and 39 and in the corridor outside. Apparitions witnessed here are said to include a 'Grey Lady' and a young lad, thought to be a blacksmith's apprentice.

There are ghost-hunting weekends at the hotel, during which guests can carry out paranormal investigations, accompanied by professional investigators and mediums using specialised equipment.

Map 4, 7L (Drymen). The Square, Drymen, near Loch Lomond, Stirlingshire.
Hotel with restaurant and bars. (01360 660245 / www.winnockhotel.com)

A paranormal investigation was undertaken in October 2008 by the Scottish Society of Paranormal Investigations and Analysis (www.sspia.co.uk) and by Ghost Hunters Scotland (www.ghosthunters.org.uk).

WITCH'S STONE, DORNOCH

The stone, a small upright slab inscribed with the date 1722, is said to mark the place where Janet Horne was executed, reputedly the last witch to be burned in Scotland. Janet Horne was a real person and she was accused of, among other things, turning her daughter into a pony, getting her shod, and riding her to meetings with the Devil. In the documents of the time, her fate is not recorded, although the accusation appears to have been in 1727, rather than in 1722.

It is thought that poor Janet was dragged through the streets of Dornoch, and was then burned alive in a barrel of tar (although it was usual to burn witches' bodies, it was normal practice to throttle the accused before they were burnt). The stone, known as the 'Witch's Stone', is thought to stand near where this happened and, although it is now in a private garden, can be viewed.

It is said that at times Janet's ghost can be seen in the vicinity of the stone, still desperately struggling as she is consumed by phantom flames.

The Dornoch Castle Hotel, formerly the palace of the bishop, in the town is also said to be haunted (see that entry).

Map 2, 7D (Dornoch). Off A949, Littledown, Dornoch, Sutherland, Highland.
Access at all reasonable times.

WRYCHTISHOUSIS, EDINBURGH

Wrychtishousis, or Wrightshouses, was once described as 'a curious old pile', with an ancient tower and Renaissance extensions, and the building had numerous heraldic devices and inscriptions. Wrychtishousis was demolished in 1802 to build James Gillespie's School, on the site of which was the Blind Asylum – Gillespie's was moved to Bruntsfield House (also see that entry).

Wrychtishousis was long a property of the Napiers, being held by them from the 14th century or earlier until the property passed to the Clerks in 1664. By the end of the 18th century the rambling old building was occupied by a Lieutenant General James Robertson of Lawers (or Lude), a veteran of the American War of Independence.

During his occupancy, a black servant, occupying a chamber (which already had an uncanny reputation) on the ground floor of the building, reported seeing the apparition of a headless woman, with an infant in its arms, appearing – on several occasions – from the hearth in his bedroom, much to his great consternation. The servant was not believed; indeed it was thought that his distress was due to being intoxicated. The chamber, however, was not used again as a bedroom.

The building was demolished a few years later, and under the hearth in a box was found the remains of a woman and a baby, the latter wrapped in a pillowcase. The woman's head had been severed, possibly to fit the rest of her into the space under the hearth. It appeared that she had been murdered unawares: she still had a pair of scissors hanging on a ribbon and a thimble that she had been wearing was found beside her 'having fallen from her shrivelled fingers'.

The story goes that after 1664 the house was occupied by a James Clerk, his wife and child. Clerk was killed in battle, and his younger brother murdered James's wife and child so that he would inherit the property.

Map 4, 9L (Edinburgh). Off A702, Gillespie Crescent, Edinburgh.

YESTER CASTLE

Standing on a promontory at the meeting place of two rivers, Yester Castle is an ancient ruinous stronghold, which was originally triangular in plan, and was defended by a ditch on the 'landward' side. A fine vaulted underground chamber, known as the 'Goblin Hall', is reached down a flight of steps. The castle often changed hands between the Scots and the English.

The lands were a property of the Giffords in the 12th century. Sir Hugo Gifford, who was reputedly a wizard, built the Goblin (or Hobgoblin of Bo') Hall, according to tales with the help of magic, spirits or goblins, hence the name. The 'Colstoun Pear' was a magic pear (actually a plum) given by Hugo to his daughter on her marriage to a Brown of Colstoun. So long as her family held and preserved the pear they would prosper. Yester Castle passed by marriage to the Hays early in the 15th century, and nearby Yester House, dating from the 18th century, replaced the castle. The estate, comprising some 500 acres, and the house and castle were recently put up for sale for offers of £12-15 million.

The Goblin Hall is said to be haunted, presumably based on the legend of the building of the chamber.

Map 4, 10M (Yester). Off B6355, 5.5 miles SE of Haddington, 1.5 miles SE of Gifford, Yester Castle, East Lothian.

Paranormal investigations have been undertaken by Ghost Hunters Scotland (www.ghosthunters.org.uk) and by Spectre (www.freewebs.com/ukspectre/ yestercastle.htm) and by Paranormal Investigation Scotland (www.paranormalinvestigationscotland.co.uk/goblinha.htm) and in October 2005 and in 2007 by Borders Paranormal Group (www.bordersparanormal.co.uk)

SOME
ADDITIONAL
INFORMATION

Some Further Reading

Adams, Norman *Haunted Neuk*, Banchory, 1994

Adams, Norman *Haunted Scotland*, Edinburgh, 1998

Adams, Norman *Haunted Valley*, Banchory, 1994

Alexander, Marc *Haunted Castles*, London, 1974

Campbell, Margaret *Ghosts, Massacres and Horror Stories of Scotland's Castles*, Glasgow (no date of publication)

Connachan-Holmes, J. R. A. *Country Houses of Scotland*, Frome, 1995

Coventry, Martin *The Castles of Scotland* (4th edition), Birlinn, 2006

Coventry, Martin *Haunted Castles and Houses of Scotland*, Musselburgh, 2004

Coventry, Martin *Wee Guide to Scottish Ghosts and Bogles*, Musselburgh, 2000

Fleming, Maurice *Not of This World*, Edinburgh, 2002

Groome, Francis *Ordinance Gazetteer of Scotland* (5 volumes), Glasgow, c1890 (?)

Halliday, Ron *Haunted Glasgow*, Fort Publishing, 2008

Halliday, Ron *Paranormal Scotland*, Edinburgh, 2000

Love, Dane *Auld Inns of Scotland*, London, 1997

Love, Dane *Scottish Ghosts*, London, 1995

Love, Dane *Scottish Spectres*, London, 2001

MacGibbon, D & Ross, T *The Castellated and Domestic Architecture of Scotland*, Edinburgh, 1887-92

Mason, Gordon T*he Castles of Glasgow and the Clyde*, Musselburgh, 2000

McKean, Charles (series editor) *The Illustrated Architectural Guides to Scotland* (volumes by area), Edinburgh, from 1985

McLeish, Norrie *The Haunted Borders*, Jedburgh, 1997

Maxwell Wood, J *Witchcraft and Superstitious Record in Southwest Scotland*, Edinburgh, 1911

Milne, G *The Haunted North: Paranormal tales from Aberdeen and the North East*, Aberdeen, 2008

Mitchell, Robin *Adam Lyal's Witchery Tours*, Edinburgh, 1988

RCAHMS *Tolbooths and Town-houses: Civic Architecture in Scotland to 1833*, Edinburgh, 1996

Robertson, James *Scottish Ghost Stories*, London, 1996

Seafield, Lily, *Scottish Ghosts*, Edinburgh, 2001

Tales from Scottish Lairds, Norwich, 1985

Thompson, Francis *The Supernatural Highlands*, Edinburgh, 1997

Tranter, Nigel *The Fortified House in Scotland*, (5 volumes), Edinburgh, 1986

Tranter, Nigel *Tales and Traditions of Scottish Castles*, Glasgow, 1993

Underwood, Peter *Gazetteer of Scottish Ghosts*, Glasgow, 1973

Underwood, Peter *Guide to Ghosts and Haunted Places*, London, 1996

Underwood, Peter *This Haunted Isle*, London, 1984

Whitaker, Terence *Scotland's Ghosts and Apparitions*, London, 1991

Wilson, Alan J; Brogan, Des & McGrail, Frank *Ghostly Tales & Sinister Stories of Old Edinburgh*, Edinburgh, 1991

Guidebooks are also available for (virtually) all the places which are open to the public, and more information about sites (such as opening and facilities) are available on websites.

Some Websites

Paranormal Database
www.paranormaldatabase.com

Ghost Stories from Clyde Valley
www.christine.tweedly.com

Mary Kings Ghost Fest
www.marykingsghostfest.com

Ghost Events Scotland
www.ghostevents.co.uk

SOME GHOST WALKS

EDINBURGH

Auld Reekie Tours
This tour takes place in the old town and includes a visit to underground vaults (**Niddry Street**), reputed to be one of the most haunted experiences to be had. Highlights of the tour include a Pagan stone circle, the Haunted Vault and the Torture Museum.
www.auldreekietours.com / 0131 557 4700

Edinburgh Ghost Tours
Walking tours around Edinburgh's Old Town, featuring some of Scotland's most haunted locations and candle-lit underground vaults.
Tours include:
Edinburgh Ghost Hunter Night Walking Tour
Edinburgh Underground Night Walking Tour
Murder and Mystery Walking Tour of Edinburgh
Secrets Of Edinburgh's Royal Mile Afternoon Walking Tour
Edinburgh Vaults Walking Tours
www.ghostevents.co.uk / 01236 615300

The Mercat Tours
This tour includes some of the most haunted locations in Edinburgh, including underground vaults (**Blair Street**). Highlights include:
Secrets of the Royal Mile, The Vaults Tour, Haunted Underground Experience, Ghosts and Ghouls, Ghost Hunter Trail and, a new attraction, the Gilmerton Cove.
www.mercattours.com / 0131 225 5445

The Real Mary King's Close
Tour visits sixteenth- and seventeenth-century closes to see how Edinburgh dealt with the plague epidemic of 1644-1646 and retells the story of **Mary King's Close**, an old close buried under the City Chambers.
www.realmarykingsclose.com / 08702 430160

The Witchery Tours
The award-winning ghostly evening walks by 'Witchery Tours' have been an attraction in Edinburgh for over 20 years. The evening walks are the Ghost and Gore Tour and Murder and Mystery Tour.
www.witcherytours.com / 0131 225 6745

EDINBURGH & ST ANDREWS

Blackfriars Tours
The City of the Dead tour includes a visit to **Greyfriars Kirkyard in Edinburgh.** Walking tours of St Andrews include twisted tales of St Andrews, which reveals the hidden (rather unsaintly) and haunted history of the city.
www.blackhart.uk.com / 0131 225 9044

ST ANDREWS

The Original St Andrews Witches Tour
The tours, featuring a ghostly costumed guide, walk the streets of the ancient and royal burgh of St Andrews with tales of ghosts and skulduggery.
www.st-andrewswitchestour.co.uk / 01334 655057/07758428921

ABERDEEN

Aberdeen Ghost Walks
The walks explore the stories that have shaped this city's darker history, including tales of witches, trial and punishment, smuggling and famous battles – and ghost stories
www.abdnghostwalks.co.uk / 07799 610509

INVERNESS

Walking Tours Inverness
A range of walking tours around Inverness are available.
(Davey the Ghost 07730 831069)

Some Paranormal Investigators

Alba Paranormal Investigations
www.albaparanormal.com
Alba Paranormal, based in Central Scotland, works in the field of paranormal investigations and psychic rescue. They carry out paranormal investigations using electronics, psychology and spiritualism.

Borders Paranormal Group
www.bordersparanormal.co.uk
Borders Paranormal Group are paranormal investigators based in the Scottish Borders. Established in 2004, the group conducts investigations using sophisticated equipment to obtain the best possible evidence of any ghost activity.

Dunfermline Paranormal Research Fellowship
A Fellowship which seeks to prove conclusively the existence of ghosts.

Ghost Club
www.ghostclub.org.uk
Founded in 1862, the Ghost Club is the oldest organisation in the world associated with psychical research. They conduct serious research into paranormal phenomena associated with ghosts and hauntings. Members are also sent quarterly newsletters.

Ghost Finders Scotland
www.ghostfinders.co.uk
Ghost Finders Scotland is a team of experienced paranormal investigators/ researchers who investigate cases of suspected paranormal phenomena. They conduct investigations using scientific equipment as well as more traditional methods of spirit communication.

Ghost Hunters Scotland
www.ghosthunters.org.uk
Ghost Hunters Scotland is a group of professional paranormal investigators with expertise in technology, historical research, demonology, research, psychology, and psychic abilities. They have completed over 100 investigations.

East of Scotland Paranormal
esparanormal.org.uk
East of Scotland Paranormal is a paranormal investigation group interested in providing reliable information to the general public in aid of furthering

research in the field of paranormal investigation. Started in 2007, ESP investigates locations in the Grampian region.

Paranormal Discovery
www.paranormaldiscovery.co.uk
Paranormal Discovery is a team of paranormal investigators based in the city of Dundee. The team was formed in 2006 and aims to carry out investigations into alleged haunted locations.

Paranormal Encounters Group
www.p-e-g.co.uk
PEG is a self-help group, which offers support to anyone who has experienced strange or troubling events that they cannot explain. They can also provide the help of trained counsellors and psychic mediums. PEG is interested in the links between conventional paranormal activity and UFOlogy.

Paranormal Investigation Scotland
www.paranormalinvestigationscotland.co.uk
The investigation team is composed of experienced and dedicated paranormal investigators, making use of both the latest technology, as well as more traditional techniques such as mediums and clairvoyants.

Paranormal Research Scotland
www.paranormalresearchscotland.moonfruit.com
Founded in April 2007 and taking a unique approach, PRS are primarily based in Dundee although recent projects have concentrated on Angus.

Renfrewshire Ghost Hunters
www.teamrenfrewshireghosthunters.com
Team Renfrewshire Ghost Hunters are currently starting up an events night organised by Team Renfrewshire Ghost Hunters and Partnership team Ghost Town UK Paranormal.

Scottish Paranormal
www.scottish-paranormal.co.uk
Scottish Paranormal investigates claims of paranormal phenomena and alleged hauntings.

Scottish Paranormal Investigations
www.scottishparanormalinvestigations.co.uk
Scottish Paranormal Investigations are dedicated to the scientific research and investigation of any claimed paranormal phenomena and to collect evidence for the understanding of paranormal phenomena through scientific investigation, research, and documentation.

Scottish Society of Paranormal Investigation and Analysis
www.sspia.co.uk
Since 2006 SSPIA, a sceptical organisation, has been researching and investigating all areas of paranormal phenomena using purely scientific techniques in order to prove natural explanations.

Shieldhill Clairvoyance and Ghost Hunt
www.northwestspiritseekers.co.uk
This company organises events at some of the most haunted locations in the UK. Events include: Overnight and Mini Ghost Hunts, Ghost Walks, Ghost Talks Evenings of Clairvoyance and Haunted Weekends.

Spectre
www.freewebs.com/ukspectre
Spectre is an experienced organisation dedicated to the investigation and research of all areas of paranormal activity.

Spiritfinders Scotland
www.spiritfindersscotland.com
Spiritfinders Scotland use technical equipment, cameras and sound machines, and spirit mediums and psychics in their investigations.

West of Scotland Paranormal Research
www.wospr.com
A paranormal research group that carries out paranormal investigations.

Glossary of Some Terms Use in Investigation
Beam barriers: generate a high-pitched sound when set off by any unexpected movement through the trigger beams
EMF meter: is a magnetic field detector used for localising unusual magnetic disturbances
EVP: Electronic Voice Phenomena, anomalous voice recordings, presumed to have been made by spirits that were not observed at the time
Infra-red illuminators: act like spotlights and give a better coverage in a blacked-out room or hall
Ion detector: a piece of equipment which sounds an alarm when the ion count rises or falls between two preset levels
Laser thermometer: used to measure temperature and humidity fluctuations and in static areas. Also known as a hygro-thermometer.
Tri-field meter: measures magnetic and electric fields to provide a summation of them
Trigger objects: various items placed in a sealed-off room or part of a location where no-one has access to, to see if the objects move. A video camera is often left in this location to record any movement of the objects

INDEXES

INDEX BY GHOST TYPE

Traquair Arms Hotel,
Innerleithen
Winnock Hotel, Drymen

BLACK LADIES
Applebank Inn, Millheugh
Auchlochan House
Blair Street Vaults,
Edinburgh
Broomhill
Chessel's Court, Edinburgh
Johnstone Lodge, Anstruther
Logie House, Dundee
Mary King's Close,
Edinburgh

BLUE LADIES
Barcaldine Castle
Cawdor Castle
Linlithgow Palace
Lochailort Inn
Royal Lyceum, Edinburgh
St Michael's Parish Church,
Linlithgow

PINK LADIES
Ballindalloch Castle
Burnett Arms Hotel, Kemnay
Stirling Castle

BROWN LADIES
Dalzell House
Neidpath Castle

**MARY, QUEEN OF
SCOTS**
Borthwick Castle
Covenanter Hotel, Falkland
Craignethan Castle
Dalkeith House
Doune Castle
Hermitage Castle
Linlithgow Palace
Lochleven Castle
Melville Castle
Stirling Castle

**NURSEMAIDS AND
HOUSEKEEPERS**
Airth Castle
Ardbrecknish House
Broadford Hotel
Dalkeith House
Dunskey Castle
Duntulm Castle
Lundin Links Hotel

Ravenswood Hotel, Ballater
Windhouse

OTHER LADIES
Aberdeen Arts Centre
Abergeldie Castle
Achindown
Aden House
Alhambra Theatre,
Dunfermline
Allanbank House
Amatola Hotel, Aberdeen
Arbigland House
Ardachy
Ardchattan Priory
Ardgay
Ardlarach
Ardvreck Castle
Atholl Arms Hotel, Dunkeld
Auchendennan Castle
Auchentiber
Auchinvole House
Aultsigh
Balavil House
Ballachulish House
Ballindalloch Castle
Barbreck House
Barlinnie Prison, Glasgow
Bedlay Castle
Blair Street Vaults,
Edinburgh
Bonshaw Tower
Borthwick Castle
Braemar Castle
Brodie Castle
Buck's Head Hotel,
Strathaven
Bunchrew House
Busta House
Cairnsmore
Caisteal na Nighinn Ruaidhe
Calda House
Camera Obscura, Edinburgh
Canongate, Edinburgh
Cartland Bridge Hotel
Cassillis House
Castle Coeffin
Castle Fraser
Castle Grant
Castle Venlaw Hotel, Peebles
Central Hotel, Glasgow
Cessnock Castle
Charlotte Square, Edinburgh
Coffin Works, Dundee
Coroghon Castle, Canna
County Buildings, Lanark

County Hotel, Peebles
Craigard House Hotel
Craigdarroch House
Craighall
Craignethan Castle
Crawford Priory
Cross Keys Hotel, Peebles
Cross Kirk, Peebles
Culcreuch Castle
Cultoquhey
Dalpeddar
Delgatie Castle
Devanha House, Aberdeen
Doune Highland Hotel
Dreadnought Hotel,
Callander
Drumlanrig Castle
Dunbar Castle
Dunfermline Palace
Dunrobin Castle
Duntarvie Castle
Duntulm Castle
Earlshall, Leuchars
Edinburgh Festival Theatre,
Edinburgh
Edinburgh Filmhouse
Eilean Donan Castle
Fasque
Ferguslie Park, Paisley
Floors Castle
Forest Hills Hotel,
Auchtermuchty
Forfar
Fortingall
Fountainhall, Aberdeen
Frendraught Castle
Fulford Tower
Gairnshiel Lodge
Galloway Arms Hotel,
Crocketford
Garth Castle
Gartloch Hospital
George Street, Edinburgh
Georgian House, Edinburgh
Glamis Castle
Glenmallan
Globe Inn, Dumfries
Grangemuir House
Greenlaw House, Glencorse
Guthrie Castle
Hallgreen Castle
Hillhead Underground
Station, Glasgow
Hilton Hotel, Glasgow
His Majesty's Theatre,
Aberdeen

Howlet's House, Loganlea
Inchdrewer Castle
Johnstounburn House
Keavil House Hotel
Kellie Castle
Kelvingrove Art Gallery and
Museum
Kilmarnock House
King's Arms Hotel,
Lockerbie
Kinnaird Head Castle
Leith Hall
Loch of Leys
Lochhouse Tower
Lunan Lodge, Montrose
Maiden's Well, Glenquey
Mains Castle, East Kilbride
Manderston
Mansfield Castle Hotel, Tain
Mary King's Close,
Edinburgh
Maryculter House
Meggernie Castle
Mellerstain
Melville Castle
New Lanark
Newark Castle, Port Glasgow
Nivingston House Hotel
Norwood Hall, Aberdeen
Old King's Highway,
Aberdeen
Old Smugglers Inn,
Auchencairn
Ord House
Overtoun House
O'Brien's, Glasgow
Pavilion Theatre, Glasgow
Pittodrie House
Powis House, Aberdeen
Premier Lodge, Edinburgh
Prestonpans Community
Centre
Princes Street, Edinburgh
Provost Skene's House,
Aberdeen
Queen Margaret Drive,
Glasgow
Ramshorn Theatre, Glasgow
Ravenswood Hotel, Ballater
Rossdhu House
Rosshall Hospital, Glasgow
Rothiemay Castle
Skaill House
Skibo Castle
Spa Hotel, Strathpeffer
Spynie Palace

INDEX BY GHOST TYPE

INDEX BY SITE TYPE

BATTLEFIELDS
Culloden Moor
Glenlivet
Killiecrankie

BRIDGES
Ballindalloch Castle
Bonchester Bridge
Buckland Glen
Castle Huntly
Cuckoo Bridge, Castle
  Douglas
Dalmarnock Road Bridge,
  Glasgow
Evelick Castle
Kemback House
Kirkdale Bridge
Overtoun House
Tay Bridge

**CASTLES AND TOWER
  HOUSES**
Abergeldie Castle
Ackergill Tower
Airlie Castle
Airth Castle
Aldourie Castle
Alloa Tower
Ardblair Castle
Ardincaple Castle
Ardrossan Castle
Ardvreck Castle
Ashintully Castle
Auchinvole House
Balcomie Castle
Balconie
Baldoon Castle
Balgonie Castle
Balmuto Tower
Balnagown Castle
Balvenie Castle
Balwearie Castle
Barcaldine Castle
Barnbougle Castle
Bedlay Castle
Benholm Castle
Berwick Castle
Bishop's Palace, Kirkwall
Blacket House
Blackness Castle
Boadsbeck Castle

Bonshaw Tower
Borthwick Castle
Braco Castle
Braemar Castle
Brahan Castle
Bridge Castle
Brims Castle
Brodick Castle
Brodie Castle
Bruntsfield House
Buchanan Castle
Buckholm Tower
Burleigh Castle
Cairneyflappet Castle,
  Strathmiglo
Caisteal Camus
Caisteal na Nighinn Ruaidhe
Careston Castle
Carleton Castle
Cassillis House
Castle Cary
Castle Coeffin
Castle Fraser
Castle Grant
Castle Huntly
Castle Lachlan
Castle Leod
Castle Levan
Castle Loch Heylipol
Castle Menzies
Castle Spioradain
Castle Stalker
Castle Stuart
Castle Tioram
Castle of Mey
Castle of Park
Castlehill, Cambusnethan
Castlemilk
Cawdor Castle
Cessnock Castle
Cherry Island
Clackmannan Tower
Claypotts Castle
Cloncaird Castle
Closeburn Castle
Colquhonnie Castle
Comlongon Castle
Corgarff Castle
Coroghon Castle, Canna
Corstorphine Castle,
  Edinburgh

Cortachy Castle
Coull Castle
Craigcrook Castle,
  Edinburgh
Craighall
Craighlaw Castle
Craighouse, Edinburgh
Craigievar Castle
Craigmillar Castle,
  Edinburgh
Craignethan Castle
Craignish Castle
Cramond Tower, Edinburgh
Cranshaws Castle
Crathes Castle
Crichton Castle
Cromarty Castle
Culcreuch Castle
Culzean Castle
Dalhousie Castle
Dalswinton Castle
Dalzell House
Dean Castle
Dean's Court, St Andrews
Delgatie Castle
Dolphinston Tower
Donibristle Castle
Dornoch Castle Hotel
Douglas Castle
Doune Castle
Duchal Castle
Dunbar Castle
Dundonald Castle
Dunnottar Castle
Dunollie Castle
Dunphail Castle
Dunrobin Castle
Duns Castle
Dunskey Castle
Dunstaffnage Castle
Duntarvie Castle
Duntrune Castle
Duntulm Castle
Dunure Castle
Dunvegan Castle
Dunyvaig Castle
Durris House
Earlshall, Leuchars
Edinample Castle
Edinburgh Castle
Edzell Castle

Eilean Donan Castle
Ethie Castle
Evelick Castle
Fairburn Tower
Falside Castle
Fedderate Castle
Fernie Castle
Ferniehirst Castle
Fetteresso Castle
Finavon Castle
Finlarig Castle
Frendraught Castle
Fulford Tower
Fyvie Castle
Galdenoch Castle
Garleton Castle
Garth Castle
Gight Castle
Glamis Castle
Glensanda Castle
Gorrenberry Tower
Grandtully Castle
Grange House, Edinburgh
Greenknowe Tower
Greenlaw House, Glencorse
Guthrie Castle
Hailes Castle
Hallgreen Castle
Hermitage Castle
Houston House
Howlet's House, Loganlea
Huntingtower Castle
Illieston House
Inchdrewer Castle
Inverawe House
Inverey Castle
Invergarry Castle
Inverness Castle
Inverquharity Castle
Jedburgh Castle Jail and
  Museum
Kellie Castle
Kilbryde Castle
Kilmarnock House
Kilmory Castle
Kilspindie Castle
Kindrochit Castle
Kinghorn Castle
Kinnaird Head Castle
Kirkconnel Hall
Knock Castle

INDEX